Cambridge Introductions to Music
# Program Music

Program music was one of the most flexible and contentious novelties of the long nineteenth century, covering a diverse range that included the overtures of Beethoven and Mendelssohn, the literary music of Berlioz and Schumann, Liszt's symphonic poems, the tone poems of Strauss and Sibelius, and compositions by groups of composers in Russia, Bohemia, the United States, and France. In this accessible *Introduction*, Jonathan Kregor explores program music's ideas and repertoire, discussing both well-known and less familiar pieces by an array of nineteenth- and twentieth-century composers. Setting program music in the context of the intellectual debates of the period, Kregor presents the criticism of writers like A.B. Marx and Hanslick to reveal program music's growth, dissemination, and reception. This comprehensive overview features numerous illustrations and music examples and provides detailed case studies of battle music, Shakespeare settings, and Goethe's *Faust*.

JONATHAN KREGOR is Associate Professor of Musicology at the University of Cincinnati, College-Conservatory of Music. He is the author of *Liszt as Transcriber* (Cambridge, 2010), winner of the inaugural Alan Walker Book Award from the American Liszt Society, as well as articles and reviews in numerous academic journals. Since 2012 he has been editor of the *Journal of the American Liszt Society*. His research interests in musical reproduction, confluences of virtuosity and gender, and music and memory have led to critical editions of works by C.P.E. Bach and Clara Schumann.

*A complete list of books in the series is featured at the back of this book.*

Cambridge Introductions to Music

# Program Music

JONATHAN KREGOR

CAMBRIDGE
UNIVERSITY PRESS

# CAMBRIDGE
## UNIVERSITY PRESS

University Printing House, Cambridge CB2 8BS, United Kingdom

Cambridge University Press is part of the University of Cambridge.

It furthers the University's mission by disseminating knowledge in the pursuit of
education, learning and research at the highest international levels of excellence.

www.cambridge.org
Information on this title: www.cambridge.org/9781107657250

First published 2015

Printed in the United Kingdom by TJ International Ltd., Padstow, Cornwall

*A catalogue record for this publication is available from the British Library*

*Library of Congress Cataloguing in Publication data*
Kregor, Jonathan, 1978–
Program music / Jonathan Kregor.
    pages   cm. – (Cambridge introductions to music)
Includes bibliographical references and index.
ISBN 978-1-107-65725-0
1. Program music.   I. Title.
ML3300.K724   2015
781.5′6–dc23
                                              2014032237

ISBN 978-1-107-03252-1 Hardback
ISBN 978-1-107-65725-0 Paperback

# Contents

# Figures

# Music examples

# Tables

# Acknowledgments

I am grateful to the following people for their advice and expertise: Kathy Abromeit, Aaron Allen, Ben Arnold, David Cannata, Anna Celenza, Zsuzsanna Domokos, Kyle Gould, Sigrun Haude, James Johnson, Adrienne Kaczmarczyk, Helena Kopchick-Spencer, Matthew Kregor, Shay Loya, Evan MacCarthy, Mary Sue Morrow, Rena Mueller, Jordan Newman, Dolores Pesce, Jesse Rodin, Patrick Rucker, Alex Stefaniak, Mark Thomas, and Bob Zierolf.

This project got off the ground thanks to a generous Faculty Research Stipend from the University Research Council, and it concluded with the help of a sabbatical leave granted by Provost Larry Johnson and supported by Dean Peter Landgren. Along the way, the Interlibrary Loan staff at the University of Cincinnati tracked down dozens of hard-to-find sources. Vicki Cooper, Fleur Jones, Rachel Cox, and Janice Baiton made the many moves from idea to finished product painless. I thank all of these individuals for their assistance.

For their unwavering support and constant encouragement, I dedicate this book with love and gratitude to my family, especially Emily, Isaac, and Luke.

# Note on the text

- Bar numbers follow critical editions, where available. Otherwise, first editions and other editions close to the composer have been used to establish bar numbering.
- Unless otherwise noted, all translations are by the author.
- In tables and music examples, lower-case and upper-case lettering denote minor and major keys, respectively.
- Composer names are spelled according to entries in the *New Grove Dictionary of Music and Musicians*, ed. Stanley Sadie, 2nd edn. (London: Macmillan, 2001).

# Introduction

## Music and meaning

In his autobiography, published in 1936, Igor Stravinsky asserted that

> music, by its very nature, is essentially powerless to *express* anything at all,
> whether a feeling, an attitude of mind, a psychological mood, a phenomenon
> of nature, etc. . . . . *Expression* has never been an inherent property of music. That
> is by no means the purpose of its existence. If, as is nearly always the case, music
> appears to express something, this is only an illusion and not a reality. It is simply
> an additional attribute which, by tacit and inveterate agreement, we have lent it,
> thrust upon it, as a label, a convention – in short, an aspect which, unconsciously
> or by force of habit, we have often come to confuse with its essential being.[1]

This view of music – its nature, limits, and impact on the senses and intellect –
was controversial, but not new. Twenty years earlier, author Jean Cocteau, composer
Erik Satie, and impresario Sergei Diaghilev collaborated to produce the ballet
*Parade*, a conscious experiment in non-expressive, non-meaning art.[2] Sixty years
before that, critic Eduard Hanslick professed that "the content of music are forms
moving in sound." And almost a half-century earlier, the writer E.T.A. Hoffmann
voiced preference for instrumental music, "which scorns all aid, all admixture of
other arts – and gives pure expression to its own peculiar artistic nature . . . [It]
leaves behind all feelings circumscribed by intellect in order to embrace the
inexpressible."[3]

The backlash against music as an agent of expression and conveyor of fixed
meaning during the "long" nineteenth century, 1789–1914, can be partly attributed
to the rise of program music. Program music sought a dialogue with other arts,
especially literature, a pursuit that led to depictive character pieces, programmatic
symphonies, symphonic poems, and tone paintings. In the eyes of critics, however,
these generic hybrids diluted music's uniqueness and transgressed its natural, time-
honored hermeneutic boundaries. Program music remained a contentious issue for
as long as it did because, as Carl Dahlhaus notes, "The battle over program music
was waged . . . with changing arguments resting on changing premises."[4]

1

Music does not limit interpretation, programmatic or otherwise, but certain premises and types of interpretive analysis arouse more suspicion than others. Take the idea that music can be a vehicle for narration. At least in Western instrumental music from about 1700 to about 1900, the tonal system in conjunction with forms like the rondo, theme and variations, and especially the sonata (with its tripartite design of exposition, development, and recapitulation) yields a set of expectations that produce what Susan McClary has dubbed a "narrative effect."[5] This effect can intensify when a composer actively manipulates conventions of form, tonality, instrumentation, and the like, since those elements routinely participate "in the composer- and listener-activated process of measuring what one hears against what one is invited to expect."[6]

The leap from effect to fact is fraught with danger, as it often involves committing to a set of practices outside of music's purview. McClary calls this a "verbal tale," and like most tales, they are easily prone to embellishment and exaggeration, as well as a shadowy genealogy that is often difficult to trace to the composer. Probably the most famous example of such a specious program comes from Beethoven's amanuensis and early biographer, Anton Schindler, who claimed that Beethoven's Fifth Symphony opens with "Fate knock[ing] at the door."[7] Indeed, Jean-Jacques Nattiez emphasizes how "The narrative, strictly speaking, is not *in* the music, but *in the plot imagined and constructed by the listeners* from functional objects."[8] In short, music means, but whether a given meaning is intrinsic to the music is – and long has been – open for debate.

This is the point where program music considerably muddies the waters. At least as practiced by Berlioz and Schumann, Liszt and Strauss, program music is not just music. Rather, it is music plus a title, a poem, a person – that is, something extrinsic to the music itself. Thus, the decision for the analyst and listener becomes whether to accept that extrinsic element as part of the work's identity and, by extension, how then to involve it in the search for a work's meaning. Indeed, as James Hepokoski notes,

> Essential to the production of programmatic musical scenes is an assumed generic contract between composer and listener whereby musical ideas are agreed to be mappable onto aspects of specific characters or situations: let motives A, B, and C represent narrative-images X, Y, and Z. Without an initial agreement to accept this principle of musical metaphor, the tone-poem premise collapses. To suggest that it might be appropriate to listen to these works as absolute music[9] or that they are adequately comprehensible in terms of pure music alone is to blind oneself to the historically controversial and witty aesthetic game that the tone poems are playing.[10]

While technically limited to the tone poems of Richard Strauss (see Chapter 7), Hepokoski's observation is – with a few modifications – extendable to the nineteenth-century programmatic enterprise as a whole.

## Repertoire and scope

To be sure, examples of program music exist prior to the late eighteenth century. One of the most well known is Antonio Vivaldi's *Le quattro stagioni* (*The Four Seasons*), the first four violin concertos of *Il cimento dell'armonia e dell'inventione*, op. 8, published in 1725. In its traversal of the year, Vivaldi references birds of several varieties, storms, barking dogs, and sleeping lushes – events and characters concretely referenced by a complementary set of sonnets that Vivaldi may have authored. The same year that his concertos appeared in print, a French contemporary, Marin Marais, issued his fifth book of *Pièces de violes*, whose one hundred and eighth entry is entitled "Le tableau de l'opération de la taille" ("The Bladder-Stone Surgery"). Above Marais's graphic music sits a bevy of graphic prose descriptions: the poor patient trembles before the sight of the operating table; serious thoughts fly through his head as attendants strap him down; an incision is made, his voice falters, and blood flows; he descends the table and is taken off to bed.

Such examples remain extraordinarily interesting curiosities, however, as they neither characterize the output of their respective composers nor the prevailing artistic interests of their day. By contrast, a significant portion of music by composers of the post-Beethoven generation – including Felix Mendelssohn, Hector Berlioz, Robert Schumann, and Franz Liszt – is programmatic. Moreover, the programmatic experiments of this generation were developed or fiercely contested by those that followed: hence the New German School of the 1860s, Johannes Brahms's "classical," four-movement symphonies or Camille Saint-Saëns and the Société nationale de musique in the 1870s and 1880s, and Richard Strauss's tone poems toward the end of the century.

The volume of programmatic compositions and attendant theorizing in the nineteenth century suggest several trends that shape the scope of this book:

- Program music developed out of an urgent need to address issues of Beethoven's musical legacy and music's future direction, especially in the wake of his Ninth Symphony. Schumann wrote of a symphonic crisis, an assessment underscored by the emergence of the symphony-cantata (Mendelssohn), programmatic symphony (Berlioz), symphonic poem (Liszt), and music drama (Wagner). All of these new genres took Beethoven's music as a model, in that they further challenged traditional notions of form and expression.
- By extension, program music began as an Austro-German phenomenon that was subsequently adapted to local needs. French and Russian composers of program music arguably eclipsed their German colleagues in both qualitative and quantitative terms by the beginning of the twentieth century, but the roots of their respective programmatic traditions were not indigenous.

- While Bedřich Smetana's two string quartets and César Franck's *Les djinns* are clearly programmatic, the overwhelming majority of nineteenth-century program music was written either for the orchestra or solo piano. The prestige of the symphony and its community-building abilities notwithstanding, by the middle of the century composers could enlist English horns, harps, bass tubas and clarinets, a battery of percussion, and other new or long-neglected instruments to produce levels of sound and timbral variety that directly impacted a work's form, character, and programmatic message. Likewise, the piano grew into a design and size consistent with today's models, and became the domestic instrument of choice.
- In terms of source material, literature enjoys primacy of place in program music, with nature (e.g., the seasons or natural phenomena like mountains or oceans) coming in second. Visual arts, such as painting or sculpture, tend to be referenced rarely, and when they do, there is often either a concomitant literary component,[11] or the model artwork is embedded with strong processual qualities, such as Mihály Zichy's drawing *Du berceau jusqu'au cercueil* (*From the Cradle to the Grave*; Figure 0.1), which served as inspiration for Liszt's final symphonic poem. That being said, while Felix Draeseke's *Fata morgana. Ein Ghaselenkranz* and the "Pantoum" movement from Ravel's Piano Trio draw on arcane literary procedures to shape their formal profiles, they do not explicitly adopt a programmatic premise.
- Finally, program music remains intimately tied to developments in opera and the theatre, be it in the use of topics by Dittersdorf, Bartók, and Debussy, the uninterrupted composition of dramatic overtures by Beethoven, Mendelssohn, Liszt, Joachim, and others during the nineteenth century, or the more general aesthetic debates surrounding the relationship between text and music.

## Historiography and structure

Program music is both an idea and a specific repertory, yet relevant publications to date tend to focus only on one aspect or the other. Leslie Orrey's *Programme Music: A Brief Survey from the Sixteenth Century to the Present Day* (1975), for instance, pays little attention to the music itself, and instead focuses on the composition's extra-musical program. (Moreover, excerpts from primary sources are given in their original language without translation.) Lawrence Casler's two-volume *Symphonic Program Music and Its Literary Sources* (2001) is more an analytic catalogue than a stylistic and historical synthesis.

The best English-language study of program music remains one of the earliest: Frederick Niecks's 1907 *Programme Music in the Last Four Centuries: A Contribution*

**Figure 0.1** Mihály Zichy, *From the Cradle to the Grave* (*Du berceau jusq'au cercueil*)

*to the History of Musical Expression*. While Niecks adopts a very loose definition of program music that allows him to incorporate works by Monteverdi, Handel, Mozart, and even Brahms, his presentation of the material abides by a nineteenth-century philosophical model (adapted from Hegel) in which the sixteenth century witnessed "early attempts," the seventeenth and eighteenth centuries "achievements in small forms and serious strivings in larger forms," and the nineteenth century "fulfilments." Beyond this outmoded historical framework, his coverage ends around 1900, his text lacks music examples completely, and citations and bibliographies are non-existent. The majority of material on the New German School and the Strauss–Mahler generation that followed is to be found mostly in German publications, as are the remaining few monographs on the subject of program music itself.

While this book is structured in roughly chronological order through the long nineteenth century, it occasionally interrupts the timeline in order to highlight themes and practices that run across several periods and geographical boundaries. Thus Chapters 2 and 7 feature brief considerations of Shakespeare's treatment by composers of program music through stylistically diverse instrumental settings of *Hamlet* and *Macbeth*. The excursus on Goethe's *Faust* in Chapter 6 illustrates how composers lavished attention on one particularly programmatically pregnant topic across the entire period under consideration.

Even when defined conservatively, the repertoire of program music is exceedingly vast, numbering well into the thousands. Thus, given that catalogues of program music are readily available, this book does not seek to be repertorially comprehensive. Nor does it take the opposite approach by exclusively profiling "famous" pieces of program music. Instead, it draws attention to composers of program music and programmatic compositions that displayed experimental tendencies and/or were highly influential. Thus composers like Niels Gade and Joachim Raff appear for their creative approaches, as do Liszt's lesser-known orchestral pieces, which were fiercely debated in his day even though they have since fallen into relative obscurity. Similarly, other names and compositions appear in the following pages in order to put other, more famous pieces in larger contexts. It is hoped that this design will add much-needed flesh to a history and repertory that has long remained skeletal.

## Chapter 1

# Characters, topics, and the programmatic battlefield

In his massive *Musikalisches Lexikon*, the German theorist Heinrich Christoph Koch described the curious, niche genre of "Simphonies à programmes," or "programmatic symphonies," as follows:

> A category of music, which remains little explored, whereby the composer sets for himself the goal of representing or depicting by tone painting alone certain historical events without the assistance of the poetic arts. Despite apparently being a German invention – since [Carl Ditters von] Dittersdorf, [Antonio] Rosetti, and [Joseph] Haydn were undoubtedly the first to tackle it – there has yet to be agreement on an appropriately artistic German name for the genre. Moreover, with the exceptions of Dittersdorf's "Four Ages," "Phaethon," and other ["Ovid" Symphonies], Rosetti's *Telemachus*, and Haydn's *Die sieben letzten Worte unseres Erlösers am Kreuze*, no other examples of this genre are known, at least among the public.
>
> In order for this genre to be afforded due respect, however, the question must first be answered: whether it is within the limits of music to represent historical topics, or at the very least, to what extent a historical event can serve as the basis for expressing musical sentiments (aroused by the historical event) without the assistance of the poetic arts.[1]

Published in 1802, the *Lexikon* sits at a crossroads: It assesses numerous developments in music of the recent past, especially the last fifty years, in which the symphony and string quartet came into their own, serious opera underwent radical reforms, and music had abandoned affect and mimesis in favor of sentiment and rhetoric. At the same time, Koch's tome anticipates many of the issues that would occupy musicians and critics for the rest of the nineteenth century and even beyond, including the relationship between poetry and music, the aesthetic and social position of instrumental music (especially in relation to opera), and the role of folk and national music in the arts, among others.

Koch's take on programmatic symphonies is similarly bidirectional. He sees their promise, especially given that symphonic heavyweights like Dittersdorf and especially Haydn have seen fit to produce them, yet he casts doubt on whether instrumental music can adequately narrate specific events, and – more importantly – if such music could even fulfill its most important role of portraying sentiments and provoking them in listeners (Rosetti's *Telemachus* Symphony is lost). Even his reluctance to provide the phenomenon with a tentative name for the benefit of his readers speaks to a fundamental problem of establishing boundaries for program music at the turn of the nineteenth century. Nor was he alone: An anonymous report in the *Allgemeine musikalische Zeitung* from July 1800 on recent developments in French music translated "Les Simphonies à programmes" as "symphonies that paint" ("die malenden Simphonien"), although the journal's editorial team saw the need to note that "one might also call them 'historical' [symphonies], although perhaps that might be too restrictive."[2]

Koch's ambivalent report also speaks to a widespread reassessment of the musical status quo that was currently taking place. By about 1800, certain philosophers, authors, and even musicians centered primarily in Germany had come to the conclusion that instrumental music, and particularly the symphony, eclipsed vocal music in purity of expression because it, through a type of wordless rhetoric, could better approach the realm of pure thought, of the sublime. While taking aim primarily at opera, and to a lesser extent the oratorio, these apologists were also involved in a smaller civil war of words over the validity of recent "Simphonies à programmes." The article from the *Allgemeine musikalische Zeitung* mentioned above is one such document. Its author eagerly lists the genre's shortcomings and exposes the deleterious interpretive snowball effect that it has already created:

- The audience would be completely unaware of the symphony's specific narrative content were it not for the presence of a written program, regardless of how successful the work itself may be.
- Critics have gotten into the bad habit of finding specific objects or historical events apparently being represented in Haydn's symphonies, or "discovering subtleties contained within them that [he] certainly never put there." Such critical zeal does the composer a disservice, however, since Haydn is more than competent and willing when necessary to provide them with interpretive cues.
- While the reviewer's emphasis on Haydn as "one of the most celebrated German symphonic composers" stems primarily from national pride, the use of a program or supplemental media to support or complement a piece of music seems to be a cultural/national proclivity.

Without doubt, Haydn – by virtue of a symphonic catalogue that numbers over one hundred works, spans almost forty years, and reached all corners of western Europe – was chief architect of a robust musical discourse network that flourished during the second half of the century and set the stage for the aesthetic reassessment of instrumental music in the early nineteenth century. Indeed, both the critic and his adversaries could agree that Haydn incomparably used music as a vehicle for artistic communication and expression. Yet the question remains: How did his symphonies, or, for that matter, those of his contemporaries, communicate? Or put another way: How did a contemporary listener generate meaning from them? According to the reviewer, it was not the presence of supplemental programs, but rather the composer's skilled manipulation of musical referents, which could yield music that ran the expressive gamut. For him, Haydn's music was "serious, proud, military, or fiery; then cheery, comfortable, *galant*; then serious and sublime."

## Program music's building blocks: topics and character pieces

Scholars have grouped many of these various effects, gestures, and style markers under the umbrella term "topic" or "topos" (plural: "topoi"). A topic is both literal and associative, a gateway through which music expresses and creates meaning. In Leonard G. Ratner's classic definition, topics are simply "subjects for musical discourse."[3] For instance, the "French overture" topic sports a two-part structure, employing over-dotted rhythms in the first and fugue in the second, and projects a dignified and composed character. As such, it is often found in music with a strong theatrical component. The *Sturm und Drang* topic, however, has no structural dimension, as its chief characteristic is unpredictability, and is suitable in a wide variety of musical media. Cataloguing topics inevitably limits their discursive freedom and their interpretive potential – some topics, for instance, employ other topics in order to achieve their full effect. Moreover, as the anonymous reviewer suggests, the best composers, like Haydn, skillfully blend several topics within a single composition, movement, or even passage.

Take a work that the reviewer would have considered to be new, Haydn's Symphony no. 100, known colloquially as the "Military" Symphony. The military topics come primarily from the famous second movement: triangles, cymbals, and bass drum appear; duple-time march rhythms abound; and the trumpet signal at m. 152ff and the timpani's response invite the surprised listener onto the battlefield. But the symphony also offers plenty of other topics, such as the singing style of the first movement, the *Sturm und Drang*-like perversion of the dotted figure in the trio of the third movement (mm. 69–73), or the examples of learned style in the fourth (chains of suspensions: mm. 189–198; imitative counterpoint: mm. 312–318). And even though the second movement's supplemental band returns in the finale, the military component is largely absent; instead, the group plays a supporting role in something more celebratory and folksy. When the reviewer criticized audiences for allowing their interpretations to run amok, he probably had in mind their proclivity to latch onto the more superficial topics of a composition and extrapolate general meaning or truth from them. Indeed, while the enduring appeal of titles like Mozart's "Hunt" Quartet, K458, or Haydn's "Military" Symphony is understandable, their presence potentially limits interpretation as much as helps shape it by topically pigeonholing an entire composition on the basis of what usually amounts to only a memorable few measures or single theme of music.

The topic appears in its most unadulterated form in the character piece. While isolated examples of the character piece have been traced back to the earliest days of notated instrumental music, and while François Couperin's four books of *Pièces de clavecin* (1713–1730) and various keyboard works by Carl Philipp Emanuel Bach speak to the vitality of the genre in the eighteenth century,[4] it was not until the nineteenth century that the character piece truly saturated all corners of the musical marketplace. Felix Mendelssohn's eight books of *Lieder ohne Worte* (*Songs without Words*; 1829–1845), Franz Liszt's *Consolations* (late 1840s), most of Charles-Valentin Alkan's piano music, Edvard Grieg's *Lyriske stykker* (*Lyric Pieces*; 1867–1901), and most of Johannes Brahms's solo piano music from op. 10 onwards sit atop a huge mountain of nineteenth-century character pieces that overwhelmingly take as their starting point a single musical topic. This repertorial explosion paralleled the repurposing of many eighteenth-century topics,[5] as well as the creation or identification of several new ones. By the end of the nineteenth century, the topical lexicon had grown to encompass exotic dialects such as the folkloric or *style hongrois* and – in the wake of Ludwig van Beethoven and Carl Maria von Weber – the heroic and demonic styles.

For instance, Adolf von Henselt's popular *12 Études caractéristiques*, op. 2, features a mixture of the old and the new (see Table 1.1). The storm dominates nos. 1 and 5, although both titles reflect the transferal of the eighteenth-century

**Table 1.1** *Adolf von Henselt's 12 Études caractéristiques, op. 2*

1. "Orage, tu ne saurais m'abattre!" ("Storm, you cannot keep me down!")
2. "Pensez un peu à moi, qui pense toujours à vous!" ("Think a bit of me, who always thinks of you!")
3. "Exauce mes vœux!" ("Grant my wish!")
4. "Repos d'amour" – Duo ("Love's rest")
5. "Vie orageuse" ("Stormy life")
6. "Si oiseau j'étais, à toi je volerais!" ("If I were a bird, I would fly to you!")
7. "C'est la jeunesse, qui a des ailes dorées!" ("Youth has gilded wings")
8. "Tu m'attires, m'entraînes, m'engloutis!" ("You entice me, lead me, engulf me!")
9. "Jeunesse d'amour, plaisir céleste, ah tu t'enfuis! mais la mémoire nous reste" ("Young love, heavenly delight, oh! how you vanish! But the memory of us remains")
10. "Comme le ruisseau dans la mer se répand, ainsi, ma chère, mon coeur t'attend" ("Like streams in the ocean spread out, so too, my love, does my heart wait for you")
11. "Dors tu, ma vie?" ("Are you sleeping, my life?")
12. "Plein de soupirs, de souvenirs, inquiet, hélas! Le coeur me bat" ("Full of sighs, memories, anxiety, alas! My heart beats")

**Example 1.1** Henselt, "Si oiseau étais, à toi je volerais," mm. 1–4

nature storm to a more ego-centric, Romantic sense of storminess and generalized personal disruption. However, no. 11 employs almost the exact same texture as no. 1, but moderate tempo, restricted dynamic range, and a lilting left-hand accompaniment code it as a lullaby.

Indeed, Henselt's twelve studies turn out to be a complex case, for while they clearly employ various musical topics, their poetic musical titles also add another layer of characteristic meaning. The sixth and most famous of the set, "Si oiseau étais, à toi je volerais," is a case in point. From a topical perspective, there is something of a fairy-tale-like quality to the cascading double-stops, which Henselt further emphasizes with the performance instruction at the outset: "con leggierezza quasi zeffiroso" – "with a wind-like levity" (see Example 1.1). But the étude's title serves as a potent reminder that something is holding the poet back from immediately flying into the arms of his lover. Thus a tinge of melancholy pervades the piece. However, just because the topical and the characteristic elements of the piece do not always synchronize does not mean that they are irreconcilable. An English reviewer in 1838 had no problem understanding the short piano study to be a little bit of both: "A most fairy-like composition – the low, sweet, harp-like murmurings from the beating and burning heart of the captive Sylph, pining for the lost loveliness of its native home, and haunted by the images too beautiful to be endured, whilst it looks back to those blissful regions where it lived in Paradise."[6]

While topics and character pieces can often provide important interpretive cues to guide performer, listener, or analyst, their presence does not necessarily confer programmatic status on a work: A critical mass of topic, characteristic, and other contextual and extra-musical material needs to be present. Henselt's Études, despite the effusive storyline provided by the above-mentioned reviewer, do not routinely hit their programmatic benchmarks. By contrast, Liszt's three books of characteristic travel pieces, the *Années de pèlerinage*, frequently do. The second movement of the first, "Swiss" volume, "Au lac de Wallenstadt" ("At Lake Wallenstadt"), is both topically and characteristically water music, yet the specificity of its location distances it from abstract depiction of water. Moreover, the movement is preceded by an epigraph from Canto III of Byron's *Childe Harold's Pilgrimage*, which not only endows the piece with specific philosophical-poetic elements, but also endeavors to situate it within a non-musical tradition to which Henselt's pseudo-poetic titles do not aspire. Finally, the piece can also be situated within a larger musical argument that plays out across movements; indeed, the fourth movement, "Au bord d'une source" ("Beside a Spring") is also water music in A♭ major, but the structure, requisite technique, and citation of Schiller's "Der Flüchtling" can lead to an altogether different programmatic conclusion.

Still, drawing something like a plot from a topically rich composition or a collection of character pieces results, as V. Kofi Agawu argues, from "sheer indulgence: [plots] are the historically minded analyst's engagement with one aspect of a work's possible meaning . . . Topics, then, are points of departure, but never 'total identities.' In the fictional context of a work's 'total identity,' even their most explicit presentation remains on the allusive level. They are therefore suggestive, but not exhaustive."[7]

With this overview of topics and character pieces in hand, and keeping Agawu's caveat in mind, it is worth returning to Koch's dictionary entry on program music and examining some of his observations in greater detail. In particular, the remainder of this chapter will consider Carl Ditters von Dittersdorf's "Ovid" Symphonies, which represent some of the earliest compositions to employ topics in order to advance a programmatic musical agenda; and the battle piece, a subgenre of program music whose long life – it survived well into the twentieth century – can be in part explained by its ability to synthesize and dramatize topically rich character pieces.

## Dittersdorf's "Ovid" symphonies

The most ambitious group of characteristic compositions from the second half of the eighteenth century comes from the Austrian composer Carl Ditters von Dittersdorf (1739–1799), whose symphonies based on scenes from Ovid's *Metamorphoses* test instrumental music's ability to objectively represent and subjectively express. Around 1781, Dittersdorf began to compose single-movement works – what he called "fragments" – on selected scenes from Ovid's enduring narrative poem, which he premiered privately to a group of admirers in Silesia. Emboldened by their success, Dittersdorf expanded his Ovid fragments into fashionable, four-movement symphonies ("symphonies en règle selon le style d'aujourd'hui"). In a prospectus he sent to the Viennese publisher Artaria in 1781, he promised fifteen such symphonies – one for each book of the *Metamorphoses* – but seems to have only had the first twelve in hand when he descended on the Imperial City in 1786. From this dozen, only the first three appeared in print during the composer's lifetime, while the following three appeared exactly a century after his death; the remaining six are lost, although four-hand reductions of numbers seven, nine, and twelve were published in 2000. Fortunately, several supplemental documents supplied mostly by Dittersdorf himself allow for the poetic contents of all fifteen to be reconstructed, as shown in Table 1.2.

The "Ovid" Symphonies practice an artistic syncretism that would not be attempted again until Franz Liszt advanced the notion of a symphonic poem in the 1850s (see Chapter 4). Dittersdorf at one point planned to have his symphonies issued with engraved illustrations of the scene(s) from the *Metamorphoses* to which the music was responding. For the Fourth "Ovid" Symphony, he suggested the following images:

1. A landscape depicting an expansive ocean. The break of day, and the brilliant morning star.
2. The expansive ocean, peppered here and there with brilliant crags. Perseus in the air on a winged horse, with helmet, armor, lance, sword, and wings on his feet.
3. An ocean crag to which Andromeda is chained. Perseus, as above, in the air.
4. The same scene. An animal in the form of a dragon is stabbed by Perseus, at which several onlookers rejoice.[8]

Dittersdorf's descriptions are notable for what they omit: there is no reference to Perseus's heroism or Andromeda's anxiety – that is, no reference to the passions or affects. Instead, the images function more like operatic sets, in front of which Dittersdorf transforms Ovid's poetry into wordless expression through a judicious blend of theatrical and instrumental music practices.

The Fourth Symphony offers a nice compendium of his approaches in this regard. Perseus, following his slaying of the Gorgon Medusa and the metamorphosis of Atlas, spots Andromeda chained to a rock, she having been made an offering to the sea monster Cetus. None of the characters makes an appearance until the second movement, however, as the first concerns itself solely with the sun slowly rising over the ocean. While Dittersdorf frequently populates his musical tableaux by layering motives and melodies, in the first movement he differentiates two entities: the expansive ocean and the morning star. The former is the first to sound, with a gentle melody in the first violin rising through a fifth and supported by patterned figures in the lower strings. As a theme, it is more than sufficient to shape a satisfactory movement, which makes the solo oboe's appearance at m. 13 such a genuine, pleasant surprise. The two themes occupy separate space, with the "ocean" theme staying in the octave above middle C, the "morning star" theme one octave higher. A secondary theme group materializes at m. 29, and while a short development (mm. 50–67) is discernible and "resolves" with the oboe playing the "ocean" theme as part of a codetta (mm. 117ff), the movement lacks the tension associated with sonata form. Indeed, the scene is the epitome of nature, as yet unspoiled by the presence of Perseus, Andromeda, or Cetus.

**Table 1.2** *The subjects of Dittersdorf's "Ovid" Symphonies*

| Symphony | Subject Matter by Movement | Source in Ovid's Metamorphoses (Book, Line[s])* | Musical Characteristics |
|---|---|---|---|
| I. The Four Ages of the World | I. Gold | I, 89 | Larghetto, C, 2/4 |
| | II. Silver | I, 114–115 | Allegro e Vivace, C, ¢ |
| | III. Bronze | I, 125 | Minuetto con Garbo → Alternativo → Da capo → Coda, a, 3/4 |
| | IV. Iron | I, 127 | Presto, C, ¢ → Allegretto, 2/4 |
| II. The Fall of Phaethon | I. Phoebus's Palace | II, 1 | Adagio non molto, D, e → Allegro, D, 3/4 |
| | II. Conversations between Phoebus and Phaethon | II, 41 | Andante, G, 2/4 |
| | III. Phoebus's Remorse | II, 49 | Tempo di Minuetto → Alternativo → Da capo → Coda, D, 3/4 |
| | IV. Phaethon's Fall | II, 311–313 | Vivace ma non troppo presto, b, ¢ → Andantino, D, 3/4 |
| III. Actaeon's Metamorphosis into a Stag | I. Hunters on the March | III, 146–147 | Allegro, G, 6/8 |
| | II. Diana's Pool in the Woods | III, 163–164 | Adagio (più tosto Andantino), D, e |
| | III. Intrusion of Actaeon | III, 174 | Tempo di Minuetto, G, 3/4 → Alternativo, D, 3/4 → Da capo |
| | IV. Dogs Attack and Devour the Stag | III, 250 | Vivace, G, ¢ |
| IV. Andromeda Saved by Perseus | I. Awaiting the Rise of the Morning Star | [IV, 664–665] | Adagio non molto, F, e |
| | II. Perseus in Flight | IV, 667 | Presto (Vivace), F, 3/4 |
| | III. Andromeda Captive | [IV, 675] | Larghetto, f, 3/4 |
| | IV. Perseus in Combat, Victory, and Rejoicing | IV, 736 | Vivace, d, ¢ → Tempo di Minuetto, F, 3/4 → [Alternativo], C, 3/4 → Written out Da capo → Coda |

| | Reference | Tempo/Key/Meter |
|---|---|---|
| **V. The Petrification of Phineas and his Friends** | | |
| I. Wedding Feast Interrupted by Violence | [V, 4] | Andante più tosto Allegretto, D, 2/4 |
| II. Death of Lycibas | V, 70–72 | Allegro assai, b → D/d, 3/4 |
| III. Peaceful Song with Lute | V, 112 | Andante molto, A, 2/4 |
| IV. Raising of Gorgon's Head and Petrification | V, 180 | Vivace, D, ¢ → Tempo di Minuetto, D, 3/4 |
| **VI. Peasants Transformed into Frogs** | | |
| I. Gathering of the Peasants | VI, 344–345 | Allegretto non troppo presto, A, ¢ |
| II. Arguments with Latona | [VI, 348ff] | Adagio, ma non molto, D, 2/4 → |
| III. Peasants' Persistent Refusal | [VI, 361ff] | Minuetto (Moderato), A, 3/4 → Alternativo, f♯, 3/4 → Da capo |
| IV. Struggles, Transformation into Frogs | [VI, 366ff] | Adagio, a, 3/8 → Vivace, ma moderato, a, ¢ → Adagio, a, 3/8 → Vivace, ma moderato, a → A, ¢ |
| **VII. Jason, who Captured the Golden Fleece [* piano arr.]** | | |
| I. Jason Demands the Fleece, Medea's Passion | VII, 1–7 | Largo ma non troppo, C, 3/4 → Allegro, C, 4/4 |
| II. Medea's Tenderness | VII, 7 | Andante, F, 2/4 |
| III. Medea's Soliloquy on Jason and the Future of their Relationship | VII, 55–56 | Minuetto, C, 3/4 → Alternativo, C, 3/4 → Da capo |
| IV. Victorious Voyage Home | VII, 157–158 | Ciaconna, C, 3/4 |
| **VIII. The Siege of Megara** [lost] | VIII, 1–80 | |
| **IX. Hercules Becomes a God [* piano arr.]** | | |
| I. Juno's Hatred of Hercules, Deianira's Pain and Jealousy | IX, 135 | Allegro e vivace, C, ¢ |
| II. Deianira's Reflection | IX, 142–143 | Adagio non troppo, c, 3/8 |
| III. Hercules Dons Nessus's Poisoned Shirt | | Tempo di Minuetto – Allegro, C, 3/4 → Alternativo → Minuetto da capo |
| IV. Hercules's Rage and Immolation → Transformation, Placement under the Stars | IX, 158 → IX, 273 | Vivace, a, 3/8 [four-voice fugue] → Adagio, A, c |
| **X. Adventures of Orpheus** [lost] | X, 1–85 | |

**Table 1.2** (*cont.*)

| Symphony | Subject Matter by Movement | Source in Ovid's *Metamorphoses* (Book, Line[s])* | Musical Characteristics |
|---|---|---|---|
| XI. Midas at the Contest of Pan and Apollo | [lost] | XI, 146–171 | |
| XII. The Tale of Iphigenia | [lost] | XII, 1–38 | |
| XIII. Ajax and Ulysses Disputing the Weapons of Achilles [* piano arr.] | I. Ajax's Pedantry | XIII, 4–5 | Allegro moderato, c, ¢ |
| | II. Ulysses Convincingly Argues His Case | XIII, 135–138 | Recitativo Andante, F, ¢<br>Andante arioso, F, 2/4 |
| | III. Ulysses's Victory, Ajax's Discontent | XIII, 383 | Minuetto, C, 3/4 → Alternativo, a, 3/4 → Minuetto da capo |
| | IVa. Ajax's Rage, Suicide, Blood Spilling | XIII, 385, 392, 394 | Allegro molto, f, 3/4 |
| | IVb. "Purple Flower Springs Forth" | XIII, 395 | Adagio non troppo, F, 3/8 |
| XIV. Aeneas and Dido | [lost] | XIV, 75–81 | |
| XV. Julius Ceasar | [lost] | XV, 745–842 | |

*Citations without brackets for Symphonies 1–6, 7, 9, and 13 are taken from the published scores of Dittersdorf's "Ovid" Symphonies. Citations in brackets for Symphonies 1–6 do not appear in the scores, but have been drawn from Dittersdorf's prospectus for the project of 18 August 1781 that he submitted to the publisher Artaria, reprinted in John A. Rice, "New Light on Dittersdorf's Ovid Symphonies," *Studi musicali* 29, 2 (2000): 453–498, at 474–481. Remaining citations from Ovid's *Metamorphoses* are less specific and occasionally speculative.

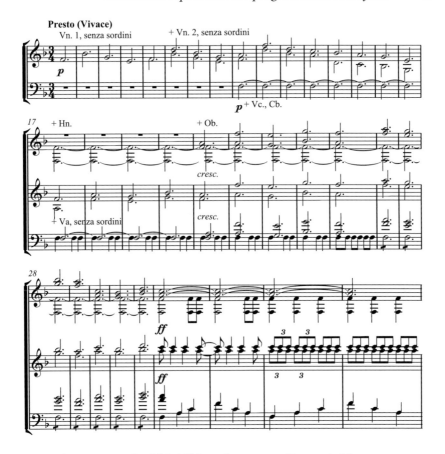

**Example 1.2** Dittersdorf, "Ovid" Symphony no. 4, II, mm. 1–36

Yet appear Perseus does, and the melodic richness of the previous movement gives way to an onslaught of scalar and wave-shaped motives presumably designed to capture Perseus in flight. Although cast in sonata form, the movement is obstinately sectional, with at least four distinct musical ideas asserting themselves in the exposition (mm. 57, 85, 98, 132). Even before presenting such bounty, however, Dittersdorf sets the scene by means of an introduction (mm. 1–56; excerpted in Example 1.2) that tricks the listener into "seeing" Perseus accelerate. The violins set the pulse with dotted half notes, under which cellos and basses introduce quarter (m. 17) and eighth (m. 25) notes; above this increased string activity join the horns and oboes. The accumulated potential energy – the orchestra also swells in volume beginning at m. 21 – explodes at m. 33, where four separate rhythmic ideas overlap. The rhythmic frenzy resolves at m. 56 with a quasi-homophonic cadence in the tonic, F major. While this procedure of faux acceler-ation is not unique to Dittersdorf or characteristic instrumental music – one famous

**Example 1.3** Dittersdorf, "Ovid" Symphony no. 4, III, mm. 1–8, annotated

example can be found in the opening of Carl Philipp Emanuel Bach's Symphony in D major, Wq 183/1, published in 1780 – it is nevertheless well suited to his symphony's overall subject matter.

The third movement, the opening of which appears in Example 1.3, betrays strong debts to a long tradition of laments in tragic opera, with sigh motives, a descending tetrachord, the distant key of F minor, and frequent off-beat emphases combining to create a picture of Andromeda as not only physically but also psychologically maligned.[9] Yet while Andromeda functions as the object of Perseus's love and as the motivation for his killing of the sea monster, her primary role is as embodiment of her people's suffering. Thus Dittersdorf's extended attention to her plight – the movement accounts for about one-quarter of the work's playing time – makes sense given the enormous scope that his symphony seeks to tackle.

While the even-numbered movements of the Fourth Symphony probably began life as single-movement "fragments," which Dittersdorf then brought into compliance with late eighteenth-century Viennese symphony practice with various levels of success, in other "Ovid" Symphonies he seems to have reversed the practice, that is, by starting with an established form such as the sonata-allegro, rondo, or minuet and trio and pruning away sections in order to better suit the programmatic context. For example, in the first movement of the Fifth "Ovid" Symphony, a wedding celebration between Andromeda and Perseus in King Cepheus's palace is interrupted by the bellicose strains of Phineas, who believes his niece – and fiancée – Andromeda to have been kidnapped. Dittersdorf presents the ceremony as a rondo (A B A C A D A), in which a stately theme in D major acts as anchor for three short developmental sections, each featuring a distinctive character. However, as Example 1.4a suggests, the well-roundedness of the form and the well-being of the wedding party and guests are threatened by the entrance of two high trumpets (clarini) at m. 96. (Prior to this passage, the clarini had only appeared at mm. 83–86, perhaps an adumbration of the carnage to come.) But while the festivities have been abruptly cut short, the persistence of theme A's walking bass line throughout the symphony – see Examples 1.4b and 1.4c – indicates the presence of a strong multi-movement narrative conception rooted in the Ovidian idea of metamorphosis.

**Example 1.4a** Dittersdorf, "Ovid" Symphony no. 5, I, mm. 94–101

**Example 1.4b** Dittersdorf, "Ovid" Symphony no. 5, II, mm. 17–20

**Example 1.4c** Dittersdorf, "Ovid" Symphony no. 5, IV, mm. 54–57

Although Dittersdorf enjoyed a sterling reputation during his lifetime as a composer of more than one hundred non-programmatic symphonies, by the beginning of the nineteenth century his music had become passé, if not forgotten. Nevertheless, his overall approach of bending and extending formal conventions and topical vocabularies in his "Ovid" Symphonies would long outlive him. A generation after Dittersdorf's death in 1799, Hector Berlioz attempted in the *Symphonie fantastique* (see Chapter 3) to coax the Beethovenian symphony into a five-movement plan that blended sonata-allegro, dance, and through-composed forms with characteristic environments like the

**Example 1.5a** Ernst Boehe, *From Odysseus's Travels*, "Odysseus" theme

**Example 1.5b** Boehe, *From Odysseus's Travels*, "Penelope" theme

pastoral, military, and supernatural, all the while chronicling the trajectory of a hero who finds a lover, loses her, and finally reunites with her in an explosive finale. Franz Liszt (Chapter 4) would draw on mythological or mythologized subjects like Orpheus, Prometheus, and Tasso in order to create single-movement symphonic poems that were both affective and depictive. Berlioz's and Liszt's younger colleague Camille Saint-Saëns (Chapter 9) took up Ovid's story of Phaethon in the early 1870s in an attempt to redefine French music during a time of crisis. And despite its post-Wagnerian musical language, Lisztian hero-worship, Straussian orchestration, and massive length – some ninety minutes – Ernst Boehe's *Aus Odysseus' Fahrten* (*From Odysseus's Travels*) from 1903 is a close aesthetic relative to Dittersdorf's "Ovid" essays, as they sport the same characteristic symphonic architecture and exegetical commentary supplied in the score by the author:

I. "Departure and Shipwreck" (*Odyssey*, Book V): Odysseus (Example 1.5a) and his companions, after ten years of war against the Trojans, set sail toward home. Odysseus's thoughts of his wife Penelope (Example 1.5b) are interrupted by a storm sent by Poseidon, which destroys the ship and leaves Odysseus stranded and alone.

II. "The Island of Circe" (*Odyssey*, Book X): An island paradise comes into view, and Odysseus is overwhelmed. He succumbs to the temptations of the beautiful

Circe, a sorceress in disguise, but takes leave of her once he recognizes his infidelity. The island recedes, dream-like, from view.

III. "The Lament of Nausicaa" (*Odyssey*, Books VI–VIII): Odysseus has left the region of Scheria for Ithaca, leaving young Nausicaa with memories of his deeds and a hope that she will one day find a husband like him. Her lament intensifies, then fades into the ocean.

IV. "Odysseus's Homecoming" (*Odyssey*, Book XIII): Odysseus's progress is again hampered. Yet with thoughts of Penelope and close proximity to Ithaca, he redoubles his efforts, imploring the gods for safe passage. His prayers are rewarded by a huge gust of wind, which urges him home.

Indeed, with the "Ovid" Symphonies, Dittersdorf deserves credit for being one of the first to offer viable solutions to a problem that would continue to challenge composers well into the early twentieth century; namely, merging literature, music, and art into a vehicle of artistic and poetic expression.

## The art of war in music (I): historical battles

Many of the "action" movements in Dittersdorf's "Ovid" Symphonies are thinly disguised battle pieces. While these movements sometimes innovate formally and programmatically, characteristically they offer little that contemporary audiences would have heard as new. Indeed, the depiction of battle in music has a history going back to at least the Renaissance, with composers like Clément Janequin (*La bataille*) and William Byrd ("The Battell," in twelve sections, from *My Ladye Nevells Booke of Virginal Music*) offering enduring examples. However, it was not until the latter portion of the eighteenth century that instrumental works of such nature grew significantly in programmatic scope and aesthetic stature. To be sure, Kuhnau's first "Biblical" Sonata recreates the showdown between David and Goliath, but it was designed, like the rest of the sonatas, as a sophisticated type of musical exegesis that draws heavily on Lutheran oratorical practices, and thus sits outside of the historical battle music tradition.[10] Nor does a characteristic title always a battle piece make: Dittersdorf's divertimento from about 1771, misleadingly entitled *Il combattimento dell'umane passioni* (*The Contest of Human Passions*), presents its subject matter in eight discrete movements, but refrains from depicting any physical combat among the passions.

Regardless, as Koch's entry on program music in his *Musikalisches Lexikon* makes clear, by the late eighteenth century, historical battles had replaced biblical or allegorical confrontations in popularity.[11] Catalysts for this change include the French Revolution and ensuing Napoleonic Wars, which significantly altered Europe politically and ideologically, and seem to have solidified this genre as commercially and even aesthetically viable. The goal of these pieces was simple: As Johann Bernhard Logier wrote in the preface to *The Battle of Trafalgar*, a "Grand Characteristic Piece" for military orchestra, "a *Battle Piece* is to represent certain *passions* and *actions*, and should, as it were, transport us to the very *scene* it describes."[12] Fortunately, composers of the period were aided by established topics like the hunt, pastoral, and funereal, as well as a common operatic narrative of positioning, combat, and victory and loss.

A model composition during the period is *The Battle of Prague* by the Czech composer František Koczwara (*c*.1750–1791). Koczwara recreates the 6 May 1757 battle between the Prussians and Habsburgs with painstaking detail (see Table 1.3). In "The Attack," for instance, individual and heavy cannon fire, "flying bullets," sword attacks, galloping horses, the advance of the "light dragoons," and "running fire" are given in the score. Koczwara's music is far from original, but its popularity was no doubt due in large part to the numerous references to fanfares, advancing and retreating forces, and the firing of cannons and other ammunition that helped to dimensionalize and personalize battle. Take cannon fire: Koczwara almost always requires the keyboardist to cross hands (see Example 1.6), a gesture which neatly

**Table 1.3** *Koczwara,* The Battle of Prague, *structure and events*

- Slow March
- Largo
  - "Word of Command"
  - "1st Signal Cannon"
  - "The Bugle Horn Call for the Cavalry"
  - "Answer to the First Signal Cannon"
- Trumpet Call
- Allegro. "The Attack, Prussians vs. Imperalists"
  - "Cannons"
  - "Flying Bullets"
  - "Trumpets"
  - "Attack with Swords" / "Horses Galloping"
  - "Light Dragoons Advancing"
  - "Heavy Cannonade"
  - "Cannon and Drums in General"
  - "Running Fire"
  - "Trumpet of Recall"
- Grave. "Cries of the Wounded"
- The Trumpet of Victory
- God Save the King
- Turkish Quick Step
- Finale. [Allegro] – Andante – Tempo primo

**Example 1.6** Koczwara, *The Battle of Prague*, "The Attack," mm. 9–12

recreates the arc of a cannon ball and its explosive landing. This simple but effective means of involving the performer in the theatrics of the composition – recall that this and similar pieces were composed for the salon, not the town or concert hall[13] – was employed by Peter Weldon in a "Military and Historical Piece" entitled *The Battle of Baylen* (Spain vs. France, 1808), Johann Wilhelm Wilms's *Die Schlacht von Waterloo* (Allies vs. Napoleon, 1815), and Theodore Moelling's *Battle of Richmond* (American Civil War, 1865), among others.

The French defeat at the Battle of Vitoria in Spain on 21 June 1813 not only marked a strategically important victory for General Wellington, but a decisive step in the Allied campaign against Napoleon. (Almost exactly two years later, Napoleon would make his last stand at Waterloo.) Beethoven, convinced by the Viennese inventor Johann Nepomuk Mälzel that a musical commemoration of the event would be an enormous popular success, produced the lavishly orchestrated and bombastic *Wellingtons Sieg; oder die Schlacht bey Vittoria* (*Wellington's Victory; or the Battle of Vitoria*) for a benefit concert he gave on 8 December 1813 and repeated four days later. The work is divided into two parts: in the first, the opposing forces take their positions on the battlefield; the English side is identified musically by "Rule Britannia," the French by "Marlbrouck s'en va-t-en guerre" ("Marlborough has gone off to war"). Each side signals its readiness by means of a trumpet fanfare, and the battle commences. Beethoven carefully notates each cannon volley in the score, itself a barrage of brass fanfares, posturing military rhythms, and cascading violin lines that move primarily through diminished seventh sonorities. As the fighting progresses, the English gain the upper hand, and the first part of *Wellingtons Sieg* ends with the French defeat by way of a mock-funereal treatment of "Marlborough" in F♯ minor – a far cry from the bright and optimistic key of C major that was identified with Napoleon's forces at the outset.

Part II is labeled a "Victory" Symphony (*Sieges-Sinfonie*) and features four movements condensed into one. The first section in D major includes only the recapitulation of a sonata-allegro form, as it remains in tonic throughout, while the following "Andante grazioso" in B♭ major introduces a dignified rendition of the nationalistic English anthem "God Save the King." However, it is interrupted by an exact repetition of the earlier sonata-allegro material. A minuet that varies "God Save the King" follows in D major, and a celebratory fughetta with extended coda on the same theme rounds out the symphony.

Beethoven was by no means the first to compose programmatic battle music, but *Wellingtons Sieg* codified characteristics of the genre that many later nineteenth-century composers interested in depicting legendary conflicts in music would draw on and develop, including:

- Identifying participants by highly differentiated melodies, rhythms, instrumentation, etc., that are often drawn from folk, religious, or other locally circumscribed practices.
- Using variation and fugue as emblems of transformation and struggle, respectively.
- Employing funeral marches or other commemorative devices to signal the loser, and military motives for the victor.
- Arranging the above-mentioned elements in a narrative fashion, either by altering established musical forms, by through-composition, or a mixture of both.

Finally, although he and his supporters put little stock in the quality of his occasional piece, Beethoven significantly elevated the artistic merit of the genre by writing a work for full orchestra instead of the more traditional drawing-room piece for soloist or small amateur ensemble. To be sure, battle pieces designed for domestic use continued to be composed for the remainder of the century and beyond, but several notable ensemble and orchestral compositions by Spohr, Liszt, Tchaikovsky, Strauss, Bartók, and Debussy challenged, through their programmatic representations, the battle piece's eighteenth- and early nineteenth-century domestic clientele and historical-commemorative role. Given the community-forming potential associated with the symphony in the nineteenth century, it is not surprising that these composers drew on the tradition of the battle symphony to advance particular ideological and nationalistic agendas – in effect, to help reshape history.

Ludwig Spohr was adamant that a proper performance of his Fourth Symphony of 1832 required audience familiarity with its poetic source, Carl Pfeiffer's "Die Weihe der Töne" ("The Consecration of Sounds"). Pfeiffer's thirteen-stanza work charts the ubiquity of "hallowed sounds" ("Heil'ge Töne") in the life of a typical individual. An initial section (ll. 1–24) explores the time-honored metaphor of music as a "language of nature," while the next (ll. 25–48) traces some of its familial (lullaby), social (dance), and romantic (serenade) uses. In the third and fourth sections (see Text Box 1.1),

**Text Box 1.1. Carl Pfeiffer, "The Consecration of Sounds," Sections 3 (ll. 49–64) and 4 (ll. 65–80).**

| | |
|---|---|
| Aber auch wild zum Getümmel der Schlachten | But you also call wildly to the tumult of battles |
| Rufet ihr mit der Begeist'rung Gewalt; | With the power of enthusiasm |
| Lehret den Jüngling, das Leben verachten, | You teach the youth to hold life in contempt, |
| Wenn die Trompete zum Kampfe erschallt. | Whenever the trumpet sounds for battle. |
| Sorgen und Furcht und Gefahren entschwinden | Worries and fears and dangers disappear |
| Hinter den siegenden Tönen zurück, | Behind the conquering sounds, |
| Blutige Lorbeern der Stirn zu umwinden, | The fiery glance turns forward, |
| Wendet sich vorwärts der feurige Blick. | To encircle the brow with bloody laurels. |
| | |
| Doch wenn ihr kühn und wild begonnen | Where you courageously and wildly began |
| Mit Kampfesruf und Schlachtgesang, | With battle call and battle song, |
| Dann winkt ihr, ist der Sieg gewonnen, | You beckon back with gentle sound of peace, |
| Zurück mit sanftem Friedensklang. | After the battle is won. |
| Dann tragt ihr auf der Andacht Schwingen | Then you carry the heart on the wings of prayers |
| Das Herz zum ew'gen Gott empor, | Upward to the eternal God, |
| Und lehrt der Sieger frohen Chor, | And instruct the conqueror's happy chorus, |
| Dem Gott der Schlachten Dank zu bringen. | To bring thanks to the God of battles. |
| | |
| Heil'ge Töne, euer Frieden | Sacred sounds, your peace |
| Folgt dem Müden noch hinab, | Follows the tired one ever downward, |
| Wenn er, von der Welt geschieden, | When he, separated from the world, |
| Einsam niedersank ins Grab. | Sank alone into the grave. |
| Seiner Lieben stummem Sehnen | To the mute desiring of his loved ones |
| Flüstert ihr Erhörung zu, | You murmur an answer, |
| Gebt den Thränenlosen Thränen, | You give tears to the tearless, |
| Dem Geschiednen ew'ge Ruh. | And to the deceased everlasting rest. |
| | |
| Heil'ge Töne, seid ihr schöne Träume | Sacred sounds, are you beautiful dreams |
| Aus dem unbekannten Vaterland? | From the unknown homeland? |
| Seid ihr Kinder jener sel'gen Räume, | Are you children of those blessed spaces, |
| Uns als Friedensboten zugesandt? – | Sent to us as messengers of peace? |
| O verlaßt mich nimmer, holde Töne! | O leave me never, gracious sounds! |
| Sagt mir viel von jener schönen Welt! | Tell me much about that beautiful world! |
| Daß ich mich in eurer Heimath wähne, | That I may imagine myself in your home, |
| Nicht der Fessel denke, die mich hält! | And not think of the chain that holds me. |

**Source:** Carl Pfeiffer, *Gedichte* (Kassel: n.p., 1831), 50–53. Translation adapted from Brown, *The Symphonic Repertoire*, III:A:84–85.

music calls men to arms, is the medium through which the victorious thank God, and accompanies the departed to their eternal rest. Pfeiffer's poetic trek is meant to remind readers that before, throughout, and after life, music is omnipresent.

Spohr had initially considered setting Pfeiffer's poem as a cantata, but found that "the text of this style of poem did not lend itself altogether well to it." Moreover, Spohr – whose Sixth, Seventh, and Ninth Symphonies would explore other

programmatic terrain – enjoyed the challenge posed by Pfeiffer's poem of constructing in an instrumental work "a harmonious whole from the sounds of nature."[14]
Indeed, for the composer of program music, Pfeiffer's poem is something of a low-
hanging fruit. As Robert Schumann wryly noted, "Spohr sought out a paean to
music, a poem that describes music's magical effects. With tones he depicted the
tones described by the poet; he praised music with music."[15] Moreover, the poem
divides handily into sections that seem to mirror the typical thematic content of the
four-movement symphony: a first movement whose initially nebulous motives
require intense development into harmonious, prehuman voices of nature; a slow,
contemplative, lyrical second movement; a martial scherzo; and a finale which
reflects on what has come before it. At the same time, Spohr was very keen to
keep the genre of the symphony at a relative distance, as suggested by the full title of
the work: "The Consecration of Sounds, Characteristic Tone Painting in the Form of
a Symphony, after a Poem by Carl Pfeiffer" ("Die Weihe der Töne,
Charakteristisches Tongemälde in Form einer Sinfonie nach einem Gedicht von
Carl Pfeiffer").

It is likely the second half of the symphony – with its focus on constructed sounds
as opposed to the natural sounds of the first two movements – that accounts for its
generic plenitude. Indeed, if Pfeiffer's poem is really meant to be read as a paean to
music, then Spohr significantly misreads it by exaggerating the battle and its aftermath. Consequently, the trajectory of *Die Weihe der Töne* surges not toward the
finale, but skews to the third movement, the longest and structurally richest of
the four. Spohr extrapolates five separate events from Pfeiffer's poem that create the
third movement's formal framework:

1. War Music
2. Battle Charge
3. Feelings of Those Left Behind
4. Return of the Victors
5. Prayer of Thanksgiving

Following a transition from D major to B♭ major, the final section of the third
movement (mm. 332–377) commences with a setting of the Ambrosian hymn "Te
Deum laudamus" ("We Praise You, O God") that offers a rich medley of instrumental colors and recalls the chorale preludes of J.S. Bach and Johann Pachelbel.
Indeed, as a hymn of thanksgiving delivered in a liturgically appropriate package,
Spohr's setting heightens the solemnity of Pfeiffer's poem. Yet as seen in Example
1.7, the appearance of the hymn's countersubject in the fourth movement as a foil
to the understated presentation of the chorale "Nun laßt uns den Leib begraben"
("Let us now Bury the Dead") – and its eventual transformation into an off-beat,
six-note principal theme at m. 46 that is supported more by dominant than tonic

**Example 1.7** Spohr, Symphony no. 4, motivic transformation in third (mm. 337–342) and fourth (mm. 1–16, 46–53) movements

harmonies – also adds a consolatory element to the symphony that undermines the optimistic crescendo of Pfeiffer's final stanza. Furthermore, by denying the dead a true funeral march, the fourth movement lacks the heroic dimension that most earlier battle pieces conveyed, as if to emphasize that war, regardless of period or participants, follows the same inevitable, tragic trajectory – what Spohr described in the program distributed to audiences as a "consolation in tears" ("Trost in Thränen").

**Example 1.7**  (*cont.*)

When the Viennese music critic Eduard Hanslick heard the work performed in 1855, he complained that the fourth movement had made Spohr a "hopeless casualty of his poetic program . . . Instead of the most magnificent climax . . . we get complete enfeeblement."[16] Hanslick's vilification of program music is to be expected, given his prominent role during the 1850s in shaping the aesthetic debates on music (see Chapter 5), yet his expectations hinge on a narrow definition of the symphony that generally excludes generic hybridity and follows an unspoken narrative of victory over struggle. Spohr did not necessarily agree with this position, stating for posterity that Beethoven's Fifth Symphony – a cornerstone of the heroic symphonic archetype – did not constitute "a classical whole," and that the finale was little more than "noise."[17] Despite adhering neither to classical nor early Romantic symphonic trends, Spohr's *Die Weihe der Töne* is far from desultory, however, as it clearly offers several fruitful points of intersection between symphonic forms and battle-piece narratives. (Spohr also participated as violinist in the premiere of *Wellingtons Sieg* under Beethoven's direction.) Yet despite numerous battle-music markers – marches, chorales, laments – Spohr's *Die Weihe der Töne* follows an anti-symphonic, chiastic narrative trajectory in which struggle does not inevitably lead to victory. Thus as an aesthetic statement and historical document, it marks a turning point in the poeticization of the occasional and the de-heroicization of the traditional.

## The art of war in music (II): fighting back

As European powers expanded their reach into northern Africa, India, China, South America, and other parts of the globe in the nineteenth century, the issue of cultural loss and gain resurfaced in art, literature, and music. Sometimes the scrutiny was subtle, perhaps even unconscious, as in Camille Saint-Saëns's popular *Suite Algérienne*, op. 60, written in 1880. The work comprises four movements, each of which includes a programmatic preface:

I. *Prelude. Approaching Algiers.* On the deck of the ship, bobbing over a great wave, the panorama of the city of Algiers emerges. Sounds of all kinds intermingle, at the center of which can be distinguished the cry, "Ali Allah! Mohamed rasoul Allah." The ship rocks one last time as it drops anchor in the port.

II. *Moorish Rhapsody.* In one of the numerous cafés in the old city, Arabs abandon themselves to their customary dances, which grow increasingly sensual and frantic to the sounds of flutes, fiddles (rebabs), and tambourines.

III. *Evening Reverie. At Blida.* Under an oasis of palm trees, in the perfumed night, a romantic song and the caressing refrain of a flute are heard in the distance.

IV. *French Military March.* Back in Algiers. In the picturesque Moorish bazars and cafes, the double-time steps of a French regiment are heard, whose martial accents contrast with the strange rhythms and languid melodies of the Orient.

There is no battle depicted in the *Suite Algérienne*, but like Saint-Saëns's earlier *Orient et Occident*, op. 25 (1869), for military band – in which the "Oriental" music is sandwiched (see m. 136ff) between sections of "Occidental" music – the outcome is clear: France has subdued, contained, and assimilated its indigenous inhabitants and their culture. Saint-Saëns clearly reveres the Moorish music, as he depicts it with sincerity – the melodies in the first three movements are derived from a trip that the composer took to the region in 1874 – and regrets its loss. (Saint-Saëns's *Havanaise* for violin and orchestra, op. 83, of 1887; the fantasy for piano and orchestra, *Africa*, of 1891; and the Fifth Piano Concerto of 1896, "Egyptian," suggest more than a passing interest in the cultural relationship between East and West.) Indeed, the implicit narrative of the *Suite Algérienne* adumbrates an observation that Saint-Saëns would make more than thirty years later, namely, that some "primitive tribes have weapons and utensils that show a remarkable feeling for style, which they lose when they come into contact with civilization."[18]

What of the "primitives"? Of those who believe they have lost some part of the cultural heritage at the hands of colonists? How might they respond? In *Wellingtons Sieg*, Beethoven had presented both sides as antagonists of equal stature warranting the same due respect. When composers tell the story of a people staving off or succumbing to invasion, the traditional battle-piece narrative à la Beethoven or

Koczwara remains, save for two important changes: (1) the indigenous, defending force is disproportionately valorized, and (2) the invading force is debased, mocked, and parodied. This approach can be seen in important battle pieces by Tchaikovsky, Bartók, and Debussy.

Take Tchaikovsky's "1812" Overture. Written in the same year as the *Suite Algérienne*, the large orchestral work reenacts the so-called "Patriotic War" of 1812, in which Napoleon was dealt a decisive blow at the battle of Borodino in early September and retreated from Moscow less than two months later. Tchaikovsky eschews historical accuracy in favor of ideology: Instead of depicting events, the overture characterizes the Russians as righteous, pious, and tireless defenders of their homeland. The French forces, represented solely by *La Marseillaise*, are outgunned musically, as Tchaikovsky gives his kinsfolk three melodies:

- The Troparion of the Cross from the Russian Orthodox Liturgy, "Oh Lord, Save Thy People" ("Спаси, Господи, люди Твоя"), by Nikolay Ivanovich Bakhmetev (1807–1891)
- The folk song "At My Grandfather's Gate" ("У ворот, ворот батюшкиных")
- The national anthem of the Russian Empire from 1833 to 1917, "God Save the Tsar!" ("Боже, царя храни!"), by Alexei Fyodorovich Lvov (1799–1870).

More important than the musical selections is their symbolic value, however, for these three pieces explain how the Russians beat their invader: through faith in God, solidarity with each other, and allegiance to their ruler. *La Marseillaise* arguably possesses this last feature, but its haphazard presentation in the overture – it never develops beyond its first phrase – suggests that Napoleon's troops followed their leader with reckless abandon but without legitimate cause. While the "1812" Overture today has become a popular occasional piece, reserved primarily for outdoor events that indulge in spectacle, and while it certainly lost some of its dramatic and ideological impact in the early decades of the twentieth century – when the Bolsheviks banned the anthem after the October Revolution and the melody of *La Marseillaise* came to be "associated with the ideas of freedom and struggle of the people for their rights" instead of the French enemy[19] – its premiere in 1883 was an unmitigated success, as it reinforced an image of the Russian people that the ambitious new tsar, Alexander III, wanted to promote in his empire.[20]

Like Tchaikovsky's overture, Béla Bartók's *Kossuth* (1903; published 1963) can be construed as a historical battle piece designed to serve a contemporary ideological agenda. But whereas victory in Tchaikovsky's piece is a foregone conclusion, in Bartók's symphonic poem it is urgency and disquiet that characterize the titular hero, who is ultimately unable to repel the invaders. With the composer's native land still under strong political sway and even stronger cultural influence from Vienna, *Kossuth* speaks to – and attempts to balance – numerous issues germane to turn-of-the-century Hungary, as well as Bartók's experience and identification as a Hungarian composer:

- The Hungarian reappraisal of Lajos Kossuth, the spiritual leader of the failed Hungarian Revolution of 1848–1849. Kossuth, a lifelong nationalist living in exile following the revolution, condemned the Austro-Hungarian Compromise (Ausgleich) of 1867 which gave Hungary substantial but not complete independence, so that when his body was returned to Budapest upon his death in 1894, opinion was sharply divided as to how his memory should be honored.
- An urgent need among Hungarian composers to write distinctly "Hungarian," large-scale vocal and instrumental works.
- Bartók's personal desire to be the composer to fill that need, especially in the wake of the successful premiere in January 1903 of Ernő Dohnányi's Symphony in D minor.[21]
- Bartók's familiarity with Liszt's "Hungarian" Rhapsodies and symphonic poem *Hungaria*, and his more recent encounter with the tone poems of Richard Strauss, especially *Ein Heldenleben* and *Also sprach Zarathustra*.

Bartók divides his single-movement orchestral work into ten sections, which introduce Kossuth (section 1), his wife (2), his recollections of better times (3–5), his appeal to the Hungarian nation to take up arms (6–7), the approach of the Austrian army and the ensuing battle (8), and the overwhelming loss that follows (9–10). Programmatically, it moves from a very small focus to a very large one, that is, on a single individual, his personal struggles, to his army, to their fight, and finally symbolically to the whole people to which he belongs. At its core, then, *Kossuth* is a battle symphony in the tradition of Kočžwara's *Battle of Prague* and Tchaikovsky's "1812" Overture. Indeed, Bartók maintains the narrative framework of the former – minus the concluding victory celebrations – while refining the characteristic nature of the latter (recall Table 1.3). Melodically, the adversaries in *Kossuth* could not be more different: Austria is represented by the Emperor's Hymn, "Gott erhalte," while Kossuth – and by extension the Hungarians that follow him – is characterized by a sweeping melody and accompaniment (Example 1.8) whose ingredients include drone fifths, short–long accents, dotted rhythms, a prominent use of the augmented fourth scale degree, improvisatory embellishments, modal instead of tonal modulations, and a gamut of almost two octaves – in short, features coded as "Hungarian" by European musicians since the early nineteenth century. Like Tchaikovsky's use of Russian melodies and treatment of *La Marseilleise*, Bartók heroicizes Kossuth's music by

**Example 1.8** Bartók, *Kossuth*, mm. 1–6

leaving it intact throughout the symphonic poem, whereas he presents the Emperor's Hymn as a parody, which robs Haydn's religious, folk-like tune of its humane elements.

These means of differentiating the opponents musically is not necessarily original, yet Bartók's deployment of the respective musical materials is. As the Austrian army approaches, he presents "Gott erhalte" as a fugue (m. 296ff); in the heat of battle, trombones and tubas belt out the tune in augmentation as if it were a cantus firmus (m. 318ff). While these two procedures successfully create a sense of musical space, they also smack of a Germanocentric musical tradition against which the young Bartók was rebelling. His alternative appears in the funeral march (section 9), where Hungarian themes from sections 1–5 return not via arcane or baroque means, but rather by a simple layering within an ABA' structure. As Example 1.9 demonstrates, the formal simplicity of the funeral march allows Bartók to showcase not only the resilience of Kossuth's theme despite the character's absence, but also wed the political and cultural via a citation from Liszt's famous second "Hungarian" Rhapsody.[22] Bartók explained that with Kossuth's defeat, "A crushing blow was inflicted upon the Hungarian Army, and the hope of an independent Hungarian kingdom was shattered – apparently forever."[23] The "apparently" is not an appeal to political militants, but rather to like-minded artists intent on breaking away from the West by embracing the music of Mihály Mosonyi, Liszt, Ferenc Erkel, and Ödön Mihalovich, among others. Indeed, if *Kossuth* advances any message of victory, it is that the rich cultural heritage of the Hungarian people will one day reverse its atrocious political fortunes.

In fact, it would take one of the most destructive and horrible wars in human history to dissolve the empire – and those of Prussia, Russia, and the Ottomans – and let Hungary enjoy a short-lived period of political independence. The First

**Example 1.9** Bartók, *Kossuth*, mm. 454–461, arr. Bartók

World War also saw composers producing propagandistic, patriotic, reflective, and commemorative music at levels even exceeding those of the Napoleonic Wars from a century earlier, with notable examples by Charles Ives, Igor Stravinsky, Arnold Schoenberg, and Maurice Ravel.

The ailing Claude Debussy participated as well, but a lifelong suspicion of compositional schools and aesthetic camps meant that his patriotic pieces were not always perceived as such, even by admirers. In 1908, for instance, he went on record about what he believed was a persistent threat to French culture:

I can never understand why all people who study music, all countries that work to establish original schools, should be built upon a German foundation. It will take France innumerable years to work out of that influence, and when we look back upon the original French writers such as Rameau, Couperin, Daquin, and men of their period, we can but regret that the foreign spirit fastened itself upon that which would have been a great school.[24]

Few steps are needed to move from this position of Germany as an abstract threat to a very real one. Indeed, during the war years, Debussy doubled down on his earlier statement by adamently seeking out "authentic" French forms and means of expression. The resulting compositions to come from his pen – the *Berceuse héroïque* and Preludes for piano, the song "Noël pour les enfants qui n'ont plus de maison," and three sonatas for intimate chamber ensembles – vacillate between the timely and timeless, the xenophobic and cosmopolitan. One such work is *En blanc et noir* for two pianos, which includes short poetic epigraphs that relate to the experience of the Great War: those of the outer movements deal with the home front, while that of the second movement transports listeners to the front lines. Dedications to Serge Koussevitzky in the first movement and Stravinsky in the third complement the chosen epigraphs. For instance, Debussy dedicates the second movement to his friend Jacques Charlot, "killed by the enemy on 3 March 1915," and prefaces it with the last strophe of François Villon's "Ballade contre les ennemis de la France" ("Ballade Against the Enemies of France"), a fifteenth-century poem that promises hell to anyone "who'd wish ill on the kingdom of France."[25]

Although Debussy patently expressed his national pride by signing his name "Claude Debussy, musicien français" in 1915, the year he composed *En blanc et noir*, he nevertheless pussyfoots around Villon's take-no-prisoners text. Like Bartók's *Kossuth*, the enemy emerges about two-thirds of the way through (at m. 79), by way of a lightly parodied version of the Lutheran chorale, "Ein' feste Burg ist unser Gott." Unlike *Kossuth*, however, Debussy provides his compatriots with nothing to repel the advancing Germans: no leader emerges, no national anthem is invoked, and no iconic folk song overwhelms the din. Debussy explained to his publisher that "toward the end [of the movement,] a modest carillon sounds a pre-Marseillaise,"[26] by which he probably meant the four-bar melody that materializes first in the second piano and then passes to the first in Example 1.10. This fleeting theme is the least developed of the movement, suggesting a potential counterpoint to the German hymn but by no means an assured one. As Marianne Wheeldon has observed, the citation breaks off musically and literally, so that the fate of "Le jour de gloire" ("The day of glory") is left in a state of flux.[27]

**Example 1.10** Debussy, *En blanc et noir*, II, mm. 161–173

Even as a battle piece, *En blanc et noir* is conflicted, with the patriotic, bellicose, and funereal elements superimposed vertically. The opening, Example 1.11, seems misplaced: While it has been connected to the French tombeau tradition, in the context of a battle narrative it would be highly unorthodox to stage a funeral before the victim's death. Following this disruptive gesture, Debussy introduces the combatants, but rather than propose a narrative of struggle and victory (or loss), he jumbles the traditional constituent elements together without much rhyme or reason. The German hymn and the French anthem arrive much later than usual, and even then incomplete. The carillon makes frequent appeals, but haphazardly. A pastoral melody (see m. 12ff and Example 1.10, mm. 170–173) suggests psychological escape similar to *Kossuth* or the merry-making of the victors in more traditional battle pieces, but it, too, seems to represent more a fugitive moment than a patent scene.

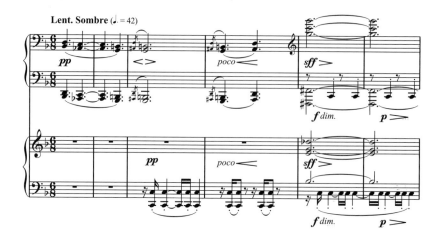

**Example 1.11** Debussy, *En blanc et noir*, II, mm. 1–6

In 1915, the French army had yet to find its voice, so to speak, which Debussy reflects in the bits and pieces of hackneyed folk song, uninspiring military music, and misplaced affective gestures. At best, he could express hope that if and when the tide of war turned in France's favor, then the reconstituted *Marseillaise* would lead its enemies to the fate that Villon believed they deserved.

Topics and characters were important means by which instrumental music created meaning for listeners in the eighteenth century, and they still continued to hold sway in the production and interpretation of music in the next century. That audiences appreciated and took topical promises seriously can be succinctly illustrated by Beethoven's Third Symphony. Beethoven introduced the massive work as a grand symphony in E♭ major to select Viennese audiences in the summer and fall of 1804. Listeners apparently left the performances scratching their heads: they had trouble with the long, drawn-out first movement, the strange funeral march of the next movement, the overly playful (and long) scherzo, and the concluding set of variations based on a theme from Beethoven's ballet *Die Geschöpfe des Prometheus*. This criticism presumably accounts for the title that the parts carried when they appeared in 1806: "Sinfonia eroica."[28]

In fact, the "Heroic" Symphony is one of many compositions – along with the "Pathétique" and "Les adieux" piano sonatas, the "Spring" Sonata for violin and piano, and "Pastoral" Symphony – in which Beethoven, who was constantly seeking new expressive means, would provide his listeners with extra-musical interpretive clues. And a vast number of his works drop musical topics into atypical environments, such as the distant strains of war in the "Agnus Dei" movement of the *Missa solemnis,* or the "Turkish" March in the finale of the Ninth Symphony. More generally, such constellations of topics and characters helped fuel experimentation in the programmatic overture, symphony, and multi-movement instrumental cycle that lasted for another century.[29]

## Chapter 2

# Expression, musical painting, and the concert overture

Given that many of the expressive devices found in instrumental music in the second half of the eighteenth century were first tested and approved on the operatic stage, it was natural that the opera overture soon became one of the main sites for significant programmatic innovation. In the famous preface to the printed score of his "reform opera," *Alceste*, from 1769, Christoph Willibald Gluck stressed how "the overture ought to apprise the spectators of the nature of the action that is to be represented and to form, so to speak, its argument."[1] Writing over seventy years later, Richard Wagner pinpointed the aesthetic difference between the sectional, mono-expressive overture before Gluck, and those that subsequently "weld[ed] the isolated sections to a single undivided whole, whose movement [was] sustained by just the contrast of those different characteristic motives." Accordingly, outstanding examples of the poly-characteristic opera overture resolved "the conflict between [opposing] musical themes in a manner analogous to the resolution of the drama in question."[2] Yet the most outstanding overtures went even further, Wagner argues, by shedding the claustrophobic mandate to analogously reenact and resolve the upcoming stage work in favor of creating self-sustaining, independent instrumental dramas. And while he singled out notable examples in the history of the opera overture's development since Gluck – including W.A. Mozart, Luigi Cherubini, and Carl Maria von Weber – for Wagner the epitome of the dramatic overture was Ludwig van Beethoven, whose concert overtures not only heavily influenced the composition of the overtures or preludes to Wagner's own operas from the period, such as *Der fliegende Holländer*, *Tannhäuser*, and *Lohengrin*, but also the single-movement dramatic or poetic overtures of Beethoven's contemporaries.

## Beethoven and the overture

Beethoven's eleven overtures – especially those to *Coriolan*, *Egmont*, and those associated with his only opera, *Fidelio* – elevated the genre significantly in the first quarter of the nineteenth century. As Table 2.1 shows, while they technically span the

**Table 2.1** *Beethoven's overtures*

| Title | Opus | Composition | Related Material | Notes |
|---|---|---|---|---|
| *Die Geschöpfe des Prometheus* | 43 | 1800–1801 | Viganò, "mythical allegorical ballet" | Overture, intro + 16 numbers |
| *Leonore* No. 2 | 72a | 1805 | Sonnleithner–Beethoven, *Fidelio*, 1805 | |
| *Leonore* No. 3 | 72b | 1806 | Sonnleithner–Breuning–Beethoven, *Fidelio*, 1806 | Revision of op. 72a |
| *Coriolan* | 62 | 1807 | Collin, *Coriolanus*, 1802 | |
| *Leonore* No. 1 | 138 | 1808 | Sonnleithner *et al.*, *Fidelio*, 1806 | For aborted Prague performance |
| *Egmont* | 84 | 1809–1810 | Goethe, *Egmont*, 1786 | + 9 i.m. |
| *König Stephan* | 117 | 1811 | Kotzebue, *König Stephan oder Ungarns erster Wohltäter* | + 9 i.m. |
| *Die Ruinen von Athen* | 113 | 1811 | Kotzebue, *Die Ruinen von Athen* | + 10 i.m. |
| *Fidelio* | 72 | 1814 | Sonnleithner–Breuning–Treitschke–Beethoven, *Fidelio*, 1814 | Not related to *Leonore* Overtures |
| "Namensfeier" | 115 | 1814 | None | 4 Oct. = Feast of St. Francis of Assisi |
| *Die Weihe des Hauses* | 124 | 1822 | Kotzebue, *Die Ruinen von Athen*, revision | Kotzebue's text rev. Carl Meisl |

i.m. = movements of incidental music

whole of his career – from the first-period overture to *The Creatures of Prometheus* to those incidental and comparably lackluster orchestral essays of the late period – Beethoven's most popular and influential concert overtures were written between 1805 and 1810, during his "heroic" period. At the same time, all but the "Namensfeier" ("Name-Day") Overture are associated with the musical theater – opera, play, or ballet – a fact that speaks to Beethoven's lifelong interest in imbuing his instrumental music with as much expressive and dramatic power as possible.

Along these lines, it is worth establishing a baseline, so to speak, and this is where the dramatically static "Namensfeier" Overture can prove useful. Beethoven had composed the work more than ten years before he published it in 1825, and while its title explained that it was "gedichtet" ("poeticized") instead of merely "komponiert" ("composed") by Beethoven, such a distinction illustrates more the composer's interest in the poetic dimension with the music of his late years than the content of this specific orchestral piece. Indeed, Beethoven envisioned it as dramatically ambivalent or open-ended, as an overture "for any purpose, or for use in concerts." The orchestral show-piece owes its name to Emperor Francis I of Austria (r. 1804–1835), formerly Emperor

**Example 2.1** Beethoven, "Namensfeier" Overture, mm. 17–21

Francis II of the Holy Roman Empire, which Napoleon and his *Grande Armée* had obliterated in 1806. Beethoven planned to premiere the piece on 4 October 1814, the Emperor's Name-Day, but missed the deadline; more than a year passed before it found a spot on the program of a Viennese charity concert.

The overture revolves around three different themes, with the primary theme (Example 2.1) supplying important material to the other two. The falling three-note line, for instance, first encountered at m. 18 in the bassoon and elaborated four measures later by the first violin, becomes the second theme (m. 71ff), while the arch-like contour serves as a basis for the lyrical material at m. 87ff. Topical inflections such as the 6/8 time signature, frequent harmonizations in thirds, and limited harmonic range code the overture as a nonchalant characteristic work – perhaps a languid hunt or energetic pastoral scene – that is appropriate for general celebrations (especially with its pseudo-baroque slow introduction) or passing entertainment.

At the same time, these themes engender next to no conflict. Themes rarely fragment, they do not ever overlap, and they appear and reappear in an orderly fashion. From a structural point of view, the "Namensfeier" Overture is unquestionably – and not surprisingly – a sonata-form movement. But the surprise comes from the limited space that Beethoven devotes to the development section. In a work of 335 measures, the development takes up about thirty-five. It begins at m. 107 with the primary theme in G major, then moves to the secondary themes, which are responsible for the piece's more distant modulations: A major (m. 129), A minor (m. 133), and F major (m. 137). A long dominant prolongation beginning at m. 141 rounds out the section until the familiar main theme appears at m. 165. The recapitulation does its job efficiently and transparently, despite Beethoven occasionally extending transitional passages. But even with the coda (m. 281ff) that draws on the secondary theme from m. 87 and concludes with a grandiose restatement of the primary theme, the "Namensfeier" Overture does not match the intensity of Beethoven's earlier dramatic overtures.

However, Beethoven's concern for the proper balance of form and content shows clearly in the two overtures he composed for the first version of his only opera, *Fidelio*, between 1805 and 1806. Despite an abundance of small changes, including compressing three acts into two for the second version, the opera's main narrative remained intact: Florestan has been jailed by a Spanish governor, Pizarro, his political rival. Florestan's wife, Leonore, mounts a one-woman rescue effort by disguising herself as Fidelio and securing a job as assistant to Florestan's jailer, Rocco. Fidelio also manages to woo Rocco's daughter, Marzelline. Pizarro resolves to kill Florestan once he learns that Don Fernando is due to arrive to confirm rumors that Pizarro is holding prisoners without legitimate cause. In the dramatic final act, Leonore, disguised as Fidelio, manages to locate Florestan, Pizarro confronts them, Don Fernando's arrival is announced, Pizarro flees but is caught, and Florestan and Leonore rejoice in their reunion and Florestan's liberation.

Much of the opera's dramatic tension hinges on Florestan's fate, and it is this same tension that surrounds the *Leonore* Overtures, all of which take as their dramatic basis a theme from Florestan's "In des Lebens Frühlingstagen" ("In the Spring Days of My Life"), the opening aria of the opera's last act. Florestan, alone in his cell, laments a situation all too common during the Reign of Terror, the period in which the libretto was fashioned: he "dared to speak the truth, / and was rewarded with chains." But despite the dire circumstances, his belief in God's righteousness and thoughts of Leonore give him comfort.

At this point in the opera, Florestan's rescue is far from assured. Beethoven intimates this uncertainty in the overtures by avoiding or significantly delaying the various building blocks of sonata form. In the second *Leonore* Overture – the first to be written – a long, harmonically unstable introduction precedes an exposition nominally in C major. However, an interruption at m. 128 begins a modulation toward E major that is fully achieved at m. 156, where Florestan's theme reasserts itself. The unusual modulation follows another work from the "heroic" period, the "Waldstein" Sonata, op. 53, from 1803/4. Unlike the piano sonata, however, the development – careening toward C minor – is interrupted by a trumpet fanfare in E♭ major at m. 392 that signals in the opera Don Fernando's approach. Florestan's theme appears at m. 426 in C major in its Adagio incarnation. But rather than serve as retransition to the recapitulation, the pentatonic primary theme explodes in a Presto tempo seventeen bars later. With the exception of mm. 478–498 (cf. m. 210ff), this coda has completely forgotten the exposition's material.

The absent recapitulation in the second *Leonore* Overture closely mirrors the trajectory of the opera: Don Fernando's appearance on the scene eventually leads to Florestan's freedom. Beethoven's revision of the second overture into the third overture uses most of the second overture's thematic material, which he organizes into a more conventional but brilliantly dramatic sonata form. The introduction (mm. 1–36) and exposition (mm. 37–180) are similar in structural design and thematic deployment. The development, however, explores the dominant with great intensity, an interest that carries into the recapitulation that begins at

m. 378. Indeed, while the primary and secondary themes appear in tonic at the expected formal junctures, surrounding events seek to undo C major, such as the move toward the subdominant at m. 390 or the assertion of D♭ major beginning at m. 411. However, once the tonic is decidedly established at m. 452, Beethoven relishes in the accomplishment for almost two hundred more measures. For Wagner, the dramatic power of the third *Leonore* Overture – "*Beethoven's* poem," as he dubbed it – overwhelmed all that followed: "far from giving us a mere musical introduction to the drama, it sets that drama more completely and movingly before us than ever happens in the broken action which ensues. This work is no longer an overture, but the mightiest of dramas in itself."[3]

(In the remaining two overtures composed for *Fidelio*, Beethoven continued the trajectory of the third *Leonore* Overture by moving even further away from the opera's drama. In the first *Leonore* Overture – only discovered in the 1870s to have been composed in 1808 for an aborted performance of the opera in Prague – Florestan's theme appears, but it is restricted to the development section. Furthermore, no trumpet call appears to herald his salvation. The *Fidelio* Overture of six years later is even more dramatically independent, as it makes no thematic reference to the forthcoming opera at all.)

Dramatic integrity is at the forefront of the *Coriolan* Overture, composed in early 1807 to serve as a prelude to a five-act tragedy of the same name by Heinrich Joseph von Collin from 1802. Collin's *Coriolan*, based, like Shakespeare's *Coriolanus*, on Plutarch's *Parallel Lives*, chronicles the downfall of Gaius Marcius Coriolanus, a celebrated Roman military leader turned to revenge. His plans to destroy Rome are halted at the last minute by the intercessions of his mother, Veturia, and wife, Volumnia. In the end, Coriolanus – proud, conflicted, and seeing no way out of his predicament – takes his own life.[4]

Beethoven's *Coriolan* Overture is as terse as Collin's play is overwrought, a result of the composer's decision to focus on Coriolan's character instead of his actions. Two scenes are especially germane: Act I, scene 6, and Act IV, scene 8. Both scenes feature lengthy dialogues between Coriolan and his wife and mother. In the former, Coriolan grapples with the loss of support from the Roman citizenry. In a confusing diatribe that hints at his psychologically fragile state, he lashes out at those trying to comfort him, chiefly the women closest to him:

> Do not wail and whine! You must see –
> How I'm holding it together – And – what has come of it?
> Here I was a citizen; now no longer.
> No longer?? – – – All of you are witnesses, you gods!
> I appeal to you. – Would I break free on my own?
> [No.] They threw me out, they hate me![5]

**Example 2.2** Beethoven, *Coriolan* Overture, mm. 46–55, strings

By Act IV, Coriolan has put a plan into motion that would mean the sacking of Rome, and it is in scene 8 that Volumnia and Veturia beg him to see the folly of his ways, both for their sakes and for the sake of their fatherland. Coriolan's mother is particularly afflicted, torn between a love for kin and country:

> Embrace me, son! Let this heart of mine
> Touch you! Do you not feel how it beats? Still
> I love you! – I should not. You are the enemy
> of the Fatherland; I should hate you.
> – But I love you – a mother's love prevails!
> Give pardon, ye gods! – oh, I am too weak!
> I still cannot hate him! Still not![6]

Beethoven distills Collin's extended back-and-forths between unstable son and faithful mother into two themes that, on the surface, show extraordinary independence from each other: the first, undoubtedly associated with Coriolan, is less a cohesive theme than it is a patchwork of related motives, including the brooding opening note that explodes with a knee-jerk leap two octaves higher (mm. 1–3), a set of restive leaps that gradually become metrically unhinged (mm. 15–20), and a relentless upper-neighbor motive in mm. 46–50 that destabilizes dominant harmonies (see Example 2.2).

Coriolan's materials are sometimes omnidirectional, sometimes wayward, but always destabilizing – as if they are trying to make sense of the character they embody.

By contrast, the one true melody in the entire overture is a beautiful appeal – arguably one of Beethoven's finest – that exhibits harmonic assuredness, lyrical persuasion, metric balance, and characteristic self-confidence (Example 2.2, mm. 52–55). Presumably, this material reflects Veturia and Volumnia, as it not only appears in the second theme area (the "feminine" theme area, as discussed below), but also sports the warm timbres of horns and strings, then clarinets, then flutes, oboes, and bassoons. Vestiges of earlier material also speak to a genetic relationship, as this melody recharacterizes Coriolan's truculent half-step motive into a more soothing whole-step upper neighbor that appears at both the beginning and the end of the phrase. Beethoven smooths the transition between son and mother and heightens the dialogic element by double-tasking the first violin's F at m. 50 with ending Coriolan's phrase and beginning Veturia's. The theatrical analogy is appropriate, for what follows the exposition of this material is not a typical sonata form, but rather a series of dialogues between the three Coriolan motives and the plea theme – that is, as a type of musical recreation of the crucial scenes between son and mother from Collin's play.

One long and busy exchange anchored in G minor covers mm. 102–118, which Beethoven develops further down the flat side until m. 151. Measure 152 returns motivically to the opening, but in the "wrong" key of F minor. In fact, none of Coriolan's material recapitulates in the home key; only with the appearance of the plea theme at m. 178 is the key of C established. The mode turns from major to minor at m. 202, a change which begins the process of affirming C minor as the overture's true home key. Surprisingly, the dialogue from mm. 102–151 reappears at m. 230 in C minor, although it is cut short by a first-inversion Neapolitan chord at m. 240.

After a dramatic pause of one empty measure, the plea theme appears for a second time – albeit without the usual lead-in – at m. 244 in C major, although it, too, succumbs to the weight of the minor mode four bars later. Now long overdue, the opening material finally appears at m. 276 in the correct key, although by this point Coriolan's fate is sealed: when he tries to offer more of his own material (Example 2.3), it either falls apart in rhythmic augmentation (cellos) or betrays his memory and its harmonic function by intervallic inversion (first violins). The *Coriolan* Overture seems to end with the words spoken by the Volscian supreme commander, Attus Tullus, in Act V, scene 8: "He is now [finally] at peace."

The *Coriolan* Overture goes beyond its mandate to introduce. With a dramatic scope far larger and more intense than, say, the "Namensfeier" or *König Stephan* Overtures, the *Coriolan* Overture distills Collin's material to such a degree that it arguably makes the ensuing play redundant, if not superfluous. To a lesser extent, the same is true of Beethoven's next original overture, on Johann Wolfgang von Goethe's *Egmont*. Beethoven composed the overture and nine pieces of incidental

**Example 2.3** Beethoven, *Coriolan* Overture, mm. 296–314

music in late 1809 and early 1810 for a production of Goethe's 1787 play at Vienna's Court Theater. The play takes place in the Netherlands during the 1560s, where the brilliant general and national hero, Count Egmont, and his people are under Spanish occupation. Tired of the local princes disobeying his commands, the Spanish king sends in a force led by Count Alba to round up and execute the native leaders. As other nobles flee, Egmont remains with his people, especially Klärchen, a peasant with whom he has fallen in love. Egmont is arrested, and Klärchen tries to round up support from the townspeople for a rescue. Her efforts are in vain, however, as her countrymen and countrywomen choose to live safely in perpetual fear. Seeing no hope, she poisons herself, and Egmont is executed.

A tragedy, to be sure, but the takeaways from Goethe's play around 1810 were messages of hope, bravery, and liberty. In a long monologue before the scaffold in Act V, scene 4, Egmont stands firm in his cause:

> Press on, brave people! The goddess of Victory leads you. And as the sea bursts through the dykes you build, so you shall burst and tumble down the mound of tyranny and, flooding all, wash it away from the dear site it has usurped. . . . I die for freedom, for which I lived and fought and for which I now passively offer up myself.[7]

Structurally, Beethoven's *Egmont* Overture is one of his most straightforward: a slow introduction of twenty-four bars precedes an exposition with two strongly differentiated themes (mm. 28, 83) in the tonic of F minor and its mediant of A♭ major, respectively. A brief development beginning at m. 116 focuses on the first

**Example 2.4** Beethoven, *Egmont* Overture, mm. 1–9, arr. Richard Metzdorff

theme and some transitional material first heard in the violas and cellos at m. 37 that recalls the first movement of Beethoven's Fifth Symphony. The recapitulation follows the exposition's course, and a transitional passage at mm. 259–276 paves the way for a rousing coda of seventy measures.

Yet important anomalies exist. Most acute is the failure of the second theme at m. 225 to recapitulate in the home key of F minor or major. To be sure, the arpeggiated first theme stresses the flattened sixth – as Beethoven often does in his minor-mode compositions – and this feature may have encouraged the second theme to explore the submediant key area. Yet, it never fully accepts F as tonic, a decision which, as James Hepokoski notes, "purposely display[s] a generically transgressive tonal path, one of nonresolution." Instead, tonal resolution occurs "*outside* of sonata-space, namely, in the [F-major] coda."[8] Programmatically, it is perfectly reasonable to interpret the coda as the true fulfillment of the second theme's latent tonal potential, given that Count Egmont's sacrifice will only pay off at a time beyond the chronological boundaries of Goethe's play. In fact, Goethe closes the play with the following stage direction: "Drumbeats. As [Egmont] walks toward the guards, toward the back exit, the curtain falls; the music strikes up and concludes in a victorious strain [Siegessymphonie]."[9] (The concluding movement of Beethoven's incidental music, a short *Siegessymphonie*, is almost a note-for-note copy of the Overture's coda.)

However, the second theme has a checkered trajectory throughout the *Egmont* Overture. As seen in Example 2.4, it first appears at m. 2 as a marker of chronological and stylistic distance from Beethoven's (and Goethe's) contemporary listener: the archaic 3/2 meter evokes a bygone era by means of an ossified grandeur, while the rhythm ♩ ♩ 𝄽 𝄾 ♪ carves out a unique geographical locale. These two features unambiguously code the theme as a sarabande, a Spanish and Latin American

**Example 2.5** Beethoven, *Egmont* Overture, mm. 82–100, amended

**Example 2.6** Beethoven, *Egmont* Overture, mm. 307–310, arr. Metzdorff

dance that first came to European attention in the mid-sixteenth century; that is, the time period of Goethe's play. Thus with one well-chosen theme, Beethoven creates the specter of the Spanish king in period-appropriate garb.

When the theme appears in the sonata-proper, it retains its regal and determined character. But the second repetition at m. 90, Example 2.5, goes harmonically haywire – for six measures, a concerted effort to modulate to A major ($\sharp\hat{1}$) takes place. And even though Beethoven softens the dissonances by enharmonic common tones, there remains a clear sense that this theme engenders a foreign, recalcitrant element that shows no interest in assimilating itself into the surrounding musical, characteristic, and structural fabric. Given that the Spanish occupation remains a constant throughout Goethe's play, it makes sense that this theme never factors into Beethoven's development. If anything, Beethoven's choice to present it in A♭ major and D♭ major – two steps on either side of F minor – is a graphic depiction of the overwhelming suffocation that Egmont's people endure.

By contrast, the plangent theme that follows the sarabande at m. 5ff in the introduction remains silent until the coda (see Example 2.6), where its affective leaps – previously designed to elicit sympathy – now work in a giddy frenzy to accelerate the harmonic rhythm toward victory. To be sure, Egmont is the protagonist of the play and sonata-proper, but it is his people who ultimately are freed by his sacrifice. It is only fitting, then, that Beethoven concludes his overture with their voice.

With the exception of the "Namensfeier" Overture, all of Beethoven's overtures owe their existence to specific performances – not abstract readings – of (musical-) theatrical works. As such, Beethoven tries to strike a balance between the requirements of the drama and the traditions of the symphony; or, put another way, between the theater and concert hall. By no means are these two venues compatible, as the *Leonore* and *Egmont* Overtures amply demonstrate. In the former, Beethoven's numerous revisions and eventual rewrite as the overture to *Fidelio* speak to his interest in capturing the spirit of his opera without being redundant or too comprehensive. Likewise, the *Egmont* Overture works fantastically as a dramatic concert piece, but many of its theatrical elements potentially lose meaning when divorced from Goethe's tragedy and the other pieces of incidental music that Beethoven composed for it. However, when the overture does precede a performance of the play, the coda becomes something of a spoiler, since it gives away the tenor of the ending before the curtain has even risen.

In short, along with his Sixth Symphony (discussed in Chapter 3), the overtures demonstrate Beethoven's important but publicly ambivalent contribution to the development of program music. As Lewis Lockwood notes, "Beethoven's reluctance to admit his strong interest in the programmatic because he might be wrongly judged by history partly conceals his true beliefs ... As a tone poet he accepted and exploited music's power to evoke nameable, identifiable externalities; as a pure musician, he rejoiced in composing music whose structural and expressive power reinforced its claim to autonomy."[10]

## Excursette: Shakespeare's *Hamlet*

It is not surprising that the famous author, composer, and critic E.T.A. Hoffmann, and later Wagner, aligned the *Coriolan* Overture with Shakespeare's tragedy. For even if Beethoven did not explicitly draw on Shakespeare,[11] the models of his dramatic overtures and the growing cult of Shakespeare throughout Europe ensured a healthy stream of Shakespearean musical products by subsequent generations. Indeed, Shakespeare enjoyed a phenomenal renaissance in the second half of the eighteenth century that only snowballed as the nineteenth century wore on. As the story goes, ground zero was Germany, where, impelled by recommendations from Gotthold Ephraim Lessing and Johann Gottfried Herder, *Sturm und Drang* writers embraced the English playwright as a means to liberate German theater from the hegemony of French style. Prose translations of large chunks of Shakespeare's output were undertaken by Christoph Martin Wieland in the first half of the 1760s and were revised and supplemented by Johann Joachim Eschenburg a decade later, a collection against which poets such as Gottfried August Bürger (*Hamlet*), Schiller (*Macbeth*), and Goethe (*Romeo and Juliet*) produced their own renditions for personal and theatrical use. A watershed moment occurred in 1833, one year after Goethe's death, when the final volume of the definitive "classic" translation of Shakespeare's oeuvre by August Wilhelm Schlegel, Ludwig Tieck, and Count Wolf von Baudissin appeared. Thus, the chronological coincidence of Germany's canonization of Shakespeare and the mythologization of Beethoven helped along "the process of inventing a Shake-toven during the composer's lifetime."[12]

Yet the allure of Shakespeare was equally strong, albeit with less fanfare, in France. Twenty volumes of Pierre Le Tourneur's translations had appeared between 1776 and 1783, which the historian and politician François Guizot revised in 1821. In his famous preface to *Cromwell* (1827), whose text is often credited as ushering in the Romantic school of French literature, Victor Hugo anachronistically deemed Shakespeare "the poetic culmination of modern times. Shakespeare is the drama; and the drama, which with the same breath moulds the grotesque and the sublime, the terrible and the absurd, tragedy and comedy – the drama is the distinguishing characteristic of the third epoch of poetry, of the literature of the present day."[13] Six years later, in the preface to another drama, *Mary Tudor*, he further elaborated this position by bringing particular attention to Shakespeare's most preeminent Romantic character:

> At the centre of all his creations we find the point of intersection between grandeur and truth: and where things that are great and things that are true come together, art has done its perfect work. Shakespeare, like Michael Angelo, seems to have been created to solve the interesting problem, the simple enunciation of which has an absurd sound: – how to remain always true to Nature, while overstepping her bounds at times. Shakespeare exaggerates proportions, but exhibits things in their proper relations. Marvelous omnipotence of the poet! he conceived characters greater than we, who live as we do. Hamlet, for example, is as true to life as anyone of us, and far greater. Hamlet is colossal, and still true to life. The fact is that Hamlet is not you, nor I, but all of us together. Hamlet is not a man, but man.[14]

Hugo's position was not groundbreaking, as the "truth" of Hamlet had been summed up almost forty years earlier by Goethe in Book IV, chapter 14 of the bildungsroman *Wilhelm Meisters Lehrjahre* (*Wilhelm Meister's Apprenticeship*), where Wilhelm asserts that "Shakespeare set out to portray . . . a heavy deed placed on a soul which is not adequate to cope with it . . . The impossible is demanded of him – not the impossible in any absolute sense, but what is impossible for him."[15]

Rather, Hugo's position was common to his generation. Romantic composers like Hector Berlioz and Robert Schumann could empathize with Hamlet's melancholy, brooding, and inaction, not because they too had been instructed to exact revenge, but because – ironically – they could not discern how to innovate artistically in the wakes of Shakespeare and especially Beethoven. That Schumann, for instance, began but quickly abandoned an opera based on *Hamlet* in the early 1830s is telling, as is his reluctance to return to Shakespeare until 1851, when he composed the concert overture to *Julius Caesar*, op. 128. Berlioz dedicated several large-scale compositions to Shakespeare's plays, including his *King Lear* Overture and especially his *Romeo and Juliet* Symphony (see Chapter 3). His close connection to *Hamlet*, however, meant that he could only approach the play in a circumscribed way. Thus, in 1844 he composed a *Marche funèbre pour la dernière scène d'Hamlet* (*Funeral March for the Final Scene of Hamlet*) that carries as epigraph Fortinbras's famous Act V farewell to Hamlet ("Let four captains / Bear Hamlet, like a soldier, to the stage") and that draws on Mozart's Requiem, the slow movements of Beethoven's Third and Seventh Symphonies, and Carl Maria von Weber's *Der Freischütz* in order to give the departed Hamlet an appropriately heroic final send-off.[16]

At over four thousand lines, *Hamlet* is Shakespeare's longest theatrical venture, and its title character is arguably the playwright's most complex. Thus, composers looking to paint a more comprehensive portrait of Hamlet or *Hamlet* in music had to make tough choices. Would Hamlet be the existentialist, with emphasis on the famous soliloquies, or a schemer who manipulates those around him, while he himself comes undone psychologically? And of those around him, whom to include: Ophelia, his wife-to-be; Horatio, his confidant; Rosencrantz and Guildenstern, the comic relief? How can inaction be conveyed in a medium that is uncompromisingly linear? Should Ophelia's mad scene or Hamlet's conversation with the ghost of his father be highlights, given significant precedent in opera, or would their inclusion demote the independent expressive status of instrumental music? However, if formal clarity was a concern, could the Mousetrap scene (III.2), the famous play-within-a-play, be referenced without coming off as structurally inchoate? Finally, given the renown of the source material, was it wise, per Wagner, even to attempt to set Shakespeare's drama "more complete and movingly" than the Bard? Would it not be safer to focus on a smaller portion of the tragedy, as Berlioz had?

These questions inform three large-scale orchestral works produced in the 1850s and early 1860s by composers who sought both to develop and to escape from the dramatic and formal dimensions of the overture post-Beethoven. The first appears to have come from Joseph Joachim, a member of Liszt's entourage in Weimar during the early 1850s who later turned into one of his former teacher's most outspoken critics (see Chapter 5). Joachim's *Hamlet* Overture, op. 4, hails from 1853, the year that the twenty-two-year-old violinist began a lifelong friendship with Johannes

**Example 2.7** Joachim, *Hamlet*, mm. 205–208

Brahms, and bears the imprint of his other famous teacher, Felix Mendelssohn, on account of its pointed musical characterizations. Nevertheless, the Liszt connection is palpable, primarily in the intimations of, but never strict adherence to, traditional symphonic forms.

The ambition of Joachim's setting is evident in the introduction (mm. 1–36), whose expansive 3/2 meter accumulates dramatic weight through the gradual accretion and transformation of two three-note motives – one ascending diatonically to the minor third, the other falling back down with modal embellishment. The former motive provides the start for the primary theme of the Allegro agitato at m. 37. Although clearly in D minor, this theme's Neapolitan leanings seem to respond to King Claudius's suspicions "Of Hamlet's transformation – so call it, / Sith nor th' exterior nor the inward man / Resembles that it was" (II.2.5–7). The single-mindedness of this theme is evident in its persistence, as Joachim in effect is forced to cut the theme off with a dramatic grand pause at m. 79 and again at mm. 83–84. By this point the theme has moved toward G minor, but the Neapolitan, having inveigled its way into the harmonic fabric of the exposition, asserts itself with a transitional passage moving from A♭ major to F minor before yielding to a second theme at m. 114 in F major.

The exposition decays, and the development dutifully develops the primary theme through a series of unstable sonorities that settle on F minor at m. 184. But in the second half of the development, it becomes clear that Joachim is more interested in developing the introduction's material over that of the exposition. Indeed, he saves his best compositional ideas for this and later similar portions, such as Example 2.7, whose metric manipulations rival Brahms's later orchestral music and may have provided Liszt with a model for the tolling of the Elsinore bells in his same-named symphonic poem that still lay five years in the future.

The remainder of Joachim's overture bears witness to the encroachment of the introduction's material. The recapitulation is heavily truncated, weighing in at about eighty measures, whereas a four-part coda – complete with a new theme in the brass at m. 339 – runs to twice that.[17] The relative weight that Joachim gives to the sections of his overture rivals the extended first movement of Beethoven's "Eroica" Symphony. But unlike his predecessor, Joachim never meets formal expectations. Instead, the overture's design points to a new stylistic path that results from Joachim's composition crisis vis-à-vis Liszt and Brahms and Shakespeare's unique subject matter.[18]

If Joachim sought to fit a traditional musical structure to Shakespeare's play, then Liszt attempted to capture a specific approach to its performance on stage. The composition of *Hamlet* overlapped with his friendship to Bogumil Dawison, a Polish-born actor who had made a career in German lands performing leading Shakespeare roles in a melodramatic style. This approach, which actively used hyperbole to heighten dramatic expression, had sprung up in the early part of the century as an alternative to the school favored by Goethe, Schiller, and many early German Romantics, and continued to be the dominant style on the stages of Liszt's Weimar, the epicenter of German theater. While Dawison's critics complained of over-the-top renditions that diminished a character's emotional range, Liszt was impressed. Indeed, melodramatic performances by Dawison and the actress Marie Seebach may have inspired him to compose four melodramas for reciter and piano between 1857 and 1860 – including one on Bürger's *Lenore*, the same ballade that would later spawn orchestral pieces by Joachim Raff and Henri Duparc – as well as capture Dawison's melodramatic take on *Hamlet* in wholly instrumental music.

Following a private meeting with Dawison in early 1856, Liszt came away with a picture of Hamlet that went against generations of German theatrical tradition: "[Dawison] does not take [Hamlet] for an idle dreamer collapsing under the weight of his task [as described in Goethe's *Wilhelm Meister*] ... but rather for an intelligent, enterprising prince, with high political aims, who *waits* for the propitious moment to avenge himself and to reach at the same time the goal of his ambition." In fact, Dawison's portrait of Hamlet struck Liszt in an even more fundamental way: "He is a *great artist* and there is an affinity between his virtuosity and mine. He creates while reproducing."[19]

Initially envisioned as a "Prelude to Shakespeare's Drama," Liszt's *Hamlet* is his most theatrical symphonic poem. The alternating chords that begin at m. 26 function as a type of off-stage music by likely referring to the strokes of Elsinore's clock prior to the appearance of the ghost. When the specter finally materializes at m. 50ff, Liszt draws on melodramatic tradition by way of the supernatural topic, directing the cellos and basses to play a chromatic wave of tremolos "very thick and eerily" ("sehr dicht und schaurig"). The strings respond to Ophelia's first appearance "ironically" (m. 176), and the orchestra's percussive, homorhythmic attacks beginning at m. 295 point to the graphic murders that stain Acts III and V.

**Example 2.8** Liszt, *Hamlet*, martial transformation of "To be or not to be" theme, mm. 105–108, arr. August Stradal

**Example 2.9** Gade, *Hamlet* Overture, mm. 20–21, arr. unidentified

Following Dawison's lead, Liszt's Hamlet follows a decisive course of action: "to take arms against a sea of troubles / And by opposing end them" (III.1.59–60). The meandering "To be or not to be" theme of mm. 1–3 – which scans quite well with Schlegel's German translation, "Sein oder Nichtsein" – is given narrative direction and transformational potential by the Ghost. Hamlet's resolution firms up beginning with the Allegro appassionato ed agitato assai and decisive turn to B minor at m. 75, and reaches a characteristic form at m. 105 as a truculent, perseverant march (Example 2.8). Two exchanges with Ophelia between mm. 160 and 218 serve simultaneously to strengthen Hamlet's determination and diminish her character's stature. He exacts revenge over his real and imagined enemies in a series of short encounters that follow, which stabilize harmonically and thematically only with his death and funeral beginning at m. 339. The truncated return of the opening's "To be or not to be" theme continues the soliloquy and closes the door on Hamlet: "To die, to sleep / No more, and by a sleep to say we end / The heartache, and the thousand natural shocks / That flesh is heir to" (III.1.60–63).

A funeral march both opens and closes Niels Gade's 1861 Overture to *Hamlet*, op. 37. The structural and programmatic implications of this decision are far-reaching, as Gade seems, like Beethoven in his *Egmont* Overture, to refer to events that take place outside of the play proper. The introduction is divided into two large sections: the first, mm. 1–16, is a strings-dominated funeral march that firmly establishes C minor, while the second, mm. 16–43, features a regal theme in the brass and lower winds over divided, tremolo strings accompaniment in D♭ major (Example 2.9). Gade's topical references in

**Example 2.10**  Gade, *Hamlet* Overture, mm. 211–232, arr. unidentified

the introduction suggest two events from the play, one mentioned, the other witnessed: the death of Hamlet's father, and the appearance of his ghost to Horatio and the soldiers in I.1 or, more likely, to Hamlet in I.4–5. Indeed, the Ghost instructs Hamlet to "revenge his foul and most unnatural murder" (I.5.25), a charge which motivates most of Hamlet's following decisions and actions. That the Ghost both impels and relates to Hamlet is suggested by shared motivic connections between the Ghost's melody in the introduction and first themes in the exposition (mm. 48, 58), although Hamlet's theme in the sonata-proper has notably returned to the funereal key of C minor.

Structurally, the sonata-proper is straightforward, but the key scheme of the secondary theme indicates a harmonic mismatch: in the exposition, it appears in A♭ major, while Gade chooses E♭ major for its presentation in the recapitulation. Thus in order to meet the harmonic demands of sonata form, Gade produces a coda that initially hammers home C minor. But in much the same way that the retransition to C minor was thwarted by a sudden episode in B major (Example 2.10), this C minor assault is beaten back by the Ghost music in D♭ major. C minor tries to make one last comeback at mm. 381–392, but its irresolution on the dominant means that the coda can only claim partial success in recovering its home key. Hamlet's inaction remains to the bitter end, leaving the funeral march – as a type of second coda – to deliver the requisite narrative and structural resolution. In other words, Gade's *Hamlet* is thus formally innovative in order to reinforce a view of Hamlet that is wholly traditional.

## A.B. Marx, Felix Mendelssohn, and musical painting

*Hamlet* would remain a challenge for composers, with notable overtures or related genres produced by Edward MacDowell (1884), Pyotr Ilyich Tchaikovsky (1888), and Aleksandr Taneyev (1906). Shakespeare's comedies, however, generated an enduring corpus of instrumental music, none being more famous than Felix Mendelssohn's *A Midsummer Night's Dream* Overture. Completed on 6 August 1826, when the composer was only seventeen years old and while Beethoven was still alive, the overture marks a seminal moment in the transition from opera or theatrical overture to stand-alone programmatic concert piece. Indeed, even before he had completed the composition, Mendelssohn recognized the "immense boldness" of his plan. As Thomas Grey explains,

> in composing an overture "to" a play that was nonetheless not necessarily, or even primarily, intended to accompany a performance of that play, Mendelssohn was making more pointed claims for the power of the music to convey something essential about the drama, to embody it or characterize it in musical terms. If one were going to listen to an overture "to" a play without subsequently watching the play itself, that overture was evidently assuming a kind of surrogate position with respect to the play, a responsibility not only to "speak of" or preface the play but even to speak *for* it, in a sense.[20]

The overture owes part of its success in speaking for Shakespeare's comedy to its ability not only to manage but also to develop numerous changing relationships among a huge cast. Thus the exposition presents five unique themes, each of which is associated with a particular character or group of characters:[21]

1. Fairies, including King Oberon and Queen Titania (m. 8).
2. Athenian court, including Theseus, Duke of Athens, and Hippolyta, Queen of the Amazons (m. 62).
3. Two pairs of lovers: Demetrius and Helena, Lysander and Hermia (m. 138).
4. Nick Bottom, a foolish weaver whom Puck has duped into wearing the head of an ass (m. 198).
5. Hunting party of the royal couple (m. 238).

In order to endow these characters with as much individuality as possible, Mendelssohn extends the timbral palette of the orchestra. The fairy music, for instance, though rhythmically square and melodically restricted to one octave, gleams and flitters about, with divided violins playing scurrying passages staccato, *pianissimo*, and with breathless speed. By contrast, the Athenian court brings together for the first time the whole orchestra, its grandeur made known thanks to a battery of brass and timpani. Likewise, Mendelssohn produces a similar

**Example 2.11**  Mendelssohn, *A Midsummer Night's Dream* Overture, mm. 198–201

**Example 2.12**  Mendelssohn, *A Midsummer Night's Dream* Overture, mm. 663–682

orchestration to represent the royal hunting party. Bottom's absurd theme is onomatopoetic, the braying of the donkey perfectly captured by a precipitous leap of a major ninth – the interval is even larger in the recapitulation – that mixes slur, staccato, and accent in the violins (Example 2.11).

However, amid this melodic and timbral variety lies a single motive that binds the entire overture: a descending line of E–D♮/♯–C♮/♯–B that incubates inside the overture's famous first four chords. From a programmatic point of view, the overture's dependence on this motive for thematic sustenance represents the theatrical boundaries of Shakespeare's play; from a technical perspective, Mendelssohn's process betrays a strong debt to Beethoven.

For instance, the final presentation of the Athenian court theme, shown in Example 2.12, follows the same technique of thematic liquidation found in Beethoven's *Coriolan* Overture (recall Example 2.3). The effect, however, is much different: With Oberon, Titania, and their train now departed, Mendelssohn follows Puck's reminder that "you have but slumber'd here / While these visions did appear. / And this weak and idle theme, / No more yielding but a dream" (V.ii.58–61). In response, the overture concludes with a slightly re-orchestrated version of the same four chords that opened the work. The dream has passed.

*A Midsummer Night's Dream* Overture was the first of about a dozen overtures composed by Mendelssohn before his untimely death in 1847. Of these, the most important programmatic essays were conceived or drafted by about 1833, when he left Berlin, his home since 1811, to take the job of Director of Music at Düsseldorf. Along with the perennial specter of Beethoven, the overtures from this period also benefitted from new ideas about program music that his Berlin colleague, Adolf Bernhard Marx, had recently put into circulation.

Marx was one of Felix's most important musical confidants in the late 1820s, arguably second only to Felix's sister, Fanny Mendelssohn. Passionately outspoken about the state of serious German music, Marx edited the *Berliner allgemeine musikalische Zeitung* from 1824 – the year of Beethoven's Ninth Symphony – until 1830. As editor, he took it upon himself to promote Beethoven and castigate Rossini, whose operas were, in Marx's opinion, strangling German music, both old and new. In this respect he found a staunch ally in Felix Mendelssohn, whose instrumental works bore strong affinities to Beethoven,[22] showed true reverence for Johann Sebastian Bach, and avoided the brilliant and ostensibly superficial stylings of his German contemporaries like Louis Spohr or Johann Nepomuk Hummel.

Although Mendelssohn and Marx had a falling out over the latter's oratorio *Moses* in 1839, Marx was instrumental in shaping Mendelssohn's programmatic music. While he later claimed credit for suggesting to Mendelssohn noteworthy details like Bottom's famous braying in *A Midsummer Night's Dream* Overture (recall Example 2.11), surely his most important contribution was the book *Ueber Malerei in der Tonkunst* (*On Painting in Music*), published in May 1828. Positioning himself as a modern, critical artist ("Künstler") against out-of-touch art critics ("Kunstdenker"), Marx argues that all composers of renown from every period have painted: "Joseph Haydn, Beethoven, the cerebral [Johann Friedrich] Reichardt, Carl Maria von Weber. All of them in their best times, in their choicest and also their most serious works."[23] Nowhere in his text does Marx use the word "program" to describe the approaches these composers took; rather, he emphasizes their use of a main idea or thought that reflects changing psychological states bounded by musico-poetic processes. According to Marx, the continual refinement of instrumental music by Haydn, Mozart, and particularly Beethoven led toward a gradual "rehumanization" that has brought about the newest epoch of poetic music without words – an epoch represented by the nineteen-year-old Felix Mendelssohn:

> Haydn poured into [instrumental music] the joys of the human breast, Mozart [gave it] its sensitivity. Beethoven completely left human society, in order to live alone with nature . . . But even he was not bold enough to fully let go of the poet [and his text] in his song of the waves. However, one of his followers, Felix Mendelssohn Bartholdy, has brought this idea to perfection, expressing *Calm Sea and Prosperous Voyage* without using Goethe's words.[24]

To be sure, Mendelssohn had provided a phenomenal model for Marx's programmatic framework with *A Midsummer Night's Dream* Overture of 1826.

Yet the critic nevertheless was going out on a limb when he prophesied the position of Mendelssohn's *Meeresstille und glückliche Fahrt* (*Calm Sea and Prosperous Voyage*),[25] which in May 1828 had just entered draft form. Whether the publication of Marx's treatise spurred Felix to complete the work is unclear, but one month later Fanny reported in a letter that Felix was at work on a composition whose structure respected the separate but related nature of Goethe's two poems, which Schiller had published in 1795. (Since then they have routinely appeared together, although Franz Schubert's hypnotic setting of "Meeresstille" for solo voice and piano, D216, from 1815 is a notable exception.) Despite positive reviews of the work when it was performed publicly in Berlin on 1 December 1832, Felix continued to tinker with the score until he released it with Breitkopf & Härtel in 1834.

Goethe's first poem depicts the dreaded isolation experienced by a sailor stranded by the deathly still water – a familiar occurrence in an age before the steam engine; in the second poem, the winds pick up and guide him toward shore:

| *Meeresstille* | *Calm Sea* |
|---|---|
| Tiefe Stille herrscht im Wasser, | Deep stillness reigns over the water, |
| Ohne Regung ruht das Meer, | Without impulse rests the sea, |
| Und bekümmert sieht der Schiffer | And the concerned mariner sees |
| Glatte Fläche ringsumher. | Fair expanse all around him. |
| Keine Luft von keiner Seite! | No air from any direction! |
| Todesstille fürchterlich! | What awful, deadly silence! |
| In der ungeheuern Weite | In the monstrous distance |
| Reget keine Welle sich. | Not a wave stirs. |

| *Glückliche Fahrt* | *Prosperous Voyage* |
|---|---|
| Die Nebel zerreißen, | The fog lifts, |
| Der Himmel ist helle, | The sky brightens, |
| Und Äolus löset | And Aeolus releases |
| Das ängstliche Band. | The fearful bonds. |
| Es säuseln die Winde, | The winds whisper, |
| Es rührt sich der Schiffer. | The mariner starts to move. |
| Geschwinde! Geschwinde! | Quickly! Quickly! |
| Es teilt sich die Welle, | The waves part, |
| Es naht sich die Ferne; | What's distant, nears; |
| Schon seh' ich das Land! | It is land that I see! |

Thus while each poem explores one extreme psychological state of the sailor, reading both poems together creates a narrative that is consistent with the typical "mythic-heroic"[26] voyage undertaken by countless instrumental works of the early nineteenth century, of which Beethoven's middle- or heroic-period symphonies

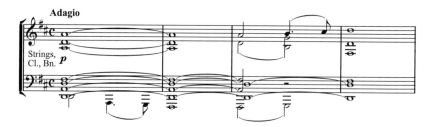

**Example 2.13a** Mendelssohn, *Meeresstille und glückliche Fahrt* (*Calm Sea and Prosperous Voyage*), mm. 1–4

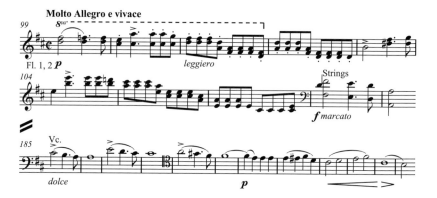

**Example 2.13b** Mendelssohn, *Meeresstille und glückliche Fahrt*, mm. 99–108, 185–196

(Third and Fifth) and sonatas ("Waldstein" and "Appassionata") are paradigmatic. Marx had actually singled out the famous "fate" motive of Beethoven's Fifth Symphony as a prime example of how a composer can articulate a dynamic musical "idea" throughout a large-scale instrumental work. In his overture, Mendelssohn proposes a similarly memorable rhythmic and melodic motive in mm. 1–2 (Example 2.13a) of *Meeresstille* that also provides much of the material for the ensuing *Glückliche Fahrt* (Example 2.13b). Like Beethoven, Mendelssohn's motive is suggestive of a key (D major) without committing to it, due in large part to its landing on the third instead of first scale degree. Unlike Beethoven, however, Mendelssohn uses tonal ambiguity of his main motive to suggest metaphorical anchor points that create most of the tension in *Meeresstille*. If the main challenge that Mendelssohn set before himself is the depiction of stillness through a medium that has to move through time, then one solution is to suggest movement without specific direction, a type of musical drift. The pervasiveness of the main motive in *Meeresstille* suggests the sailor's dire situation – the motive tries numerous reharmonizations, diminutions and augmentations, and inversions to no avail – but it

**Example 2.14** Mendelssohn, *Meeresstille und glückliche Fahrt*, mm. 29–40

also frames his environment. As Example 2.14 illustrates, he is at nature's mercy: Mendelssohn throws a barrage of non-diatonic chords at the static Ds in the violins, yet they effect no significant harmonic development; in general, the lower strings attempt to ascend, only to fall back down in defeat; and after these vain efforts, the main motive cascades down through the orchestra – violin I, violin II, clarinet I, cello, bass – so that *Meeresstille* ends in the same state in which it began. Goethe's sublime ocean has won not by force, but by apathy.

The continued presence of *Meeresstille*'s main motive in *Glückliche Fahrt* begs the question of its meaning. One legitimate answer could be as representative of the sailor, since he is named as a character in both poems. However, the sailor lacks the narrator's omniscient perspective. Yet the narrator also seems to be on board the ship, since he rejoices in the last line of *Glückliche Fahrt* that "it is land that *I* see." If

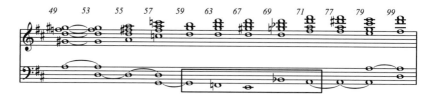

**Example 2.15** Mendelssohn, *Meeresstille und glückliche Fahrt*, harmonic reduction of mm. 49–99

the sailor is concerned in *Meeresstille*, it is the poet who shows patent relief in the next poem. Such subjective distinctions might also suggest a different way to read Example 2.14: not as confinement, but confidence. After all, the harmonic stability of *Meeresstille* and motivic preservation could well reflect the passenger's faith, which *Glückliche Fahrt* rewards not just by sighting land, but by elaborating on its motives rather than having to create new ones. In fact, the opening of *Glückliche Fahrt* imbues this passage with heretofore unknown propulsion. Provoked by the appearance of both the wind and the wind instruments – a programmatically astute choice – Mendelssohn recomposes the descending bass line of mm. 14–20 and mm. 33–38 to introduce the second poem (see Example 2.15). Thus the transition is as much psychological as it is physical.

Such are the concerns that Mendelssohn hoped to convey in his concert overtures, as he indicated in a letter of July 1831, that is, when *Meeresstille und glückliche Fahrt* was still being composed:

> I take music in a very serious light, and I consider it quite inadmissible to compose anything that I do not thoroughly feel. It is just as if I were to utter a falsehood; for notes have as distinct a meaning as words, perhaps even a more definite sense. Now it appears to me almost impossible to compose for a descriptive poem. The mass of compositions of this nature do not militate against this opinion, but rather prove its truth; for I am not acquainted with one single work of the kind that has been successful. You are placed between a dramatic conception or a mere narrative.[27]

To be sure, *Meeresstille und glückliche Fahrt* contains elements of both drama and narrative that draw on traditional or characteristic forms of musical discourse, yielding results that are often quite definite. A reviewer present at a performance of the overture conducted by Mendelssohn in January 1847 could confidently identify when "the waves begin to dance in a merry tempo" or follow "the busy hands of the sailors mak[ing] haste," and rejoiced with the crew when "A threefold cry of jubilation greets the land; thundering shots of salutation answer from the shore. Now just a few strong stretches, and the ship is in port, and with a joyful, thankful glimpse of heaven those safe from danger disembark."[28] However, Mendelssohn routinely challenges the universality of such interpretations by introducing elements that are foreign to the source material. The conclusion to the overture is a case in point. Goethe's *Glückliche Fahrt* concludes with land being sighted, but Mendelssohn (as the reviewer noted) goes further. An "Allegro maestoso" at m. 482 inaugurates a codetta that cadences at m. 495 on the diminished fifth G♯–D, at which point trumpet fanfares celebrate with a diatonic version of the first theme of *Glückliche Fahrt* (cf. Example 2.13b). The pomp is undercut by the final three measures, however, where the violas play an ascending version of the overture's main motive at mm. 3–4 (cf. Example 2.13a) over a I–V–vii$^{4/3}$–I progression. This enigmatic recollection, not present in Goethe's poems and nowhere motivated by the musical context, has prompted a number of recent interpretations: For R. Larry Todd, it represents "a circular, self-renewing act of discovery," while for Thomas Grey and Lawrence Kramer the tranquility of the sea is recalled through the eye of the grateful mariner. As Douglass Seaton hears it, however, the reminiscence could be far more bleak, on par with Ambrose Bierce's famous short story, "An Occurrence at Owl Creek Bridge": "the entire happy voyage is framed as only the hallucination of the dying mariner, and the conclusion, yielding to the reality of the calm sea, represents death."[29]

Mendelssohn left few clues as to his motivation for concluding *Meeresstille und glückliche Fahrt* in such an inconclusive manner. Yet this process of motivic recall is quite prominent in his programmatic music from the period. In the "Hebrides" Overture, for instance, the first theme returns unexpectedly at the end of the work (mm. 264–267) via a tentative first clarinet, only to be beaten back by a *fortissimo* orchestra. In *A Midsummer Night's Dream* Overture, the famous opening chords not only conclude the work, but appear at other important moments, so that their function is as much structural as it might be poetic. Notably, a fair number of non-programmatic works from Mendelssohn's youth also employ similar cyclic procedures, including his first two string quartets, opp. 12 and 13, first piano sonata, op. 6, and Octet, op. 20, suggesting either its programmatic ambivalence or latent programmatic meaning in the ostensibly abstract genres of quartet and sonata.

Indeed, the problems of linking the poetic and the procedural are clearly spelled out in Mendelssohn's "Reformation" Symphony. Second of his symphonies to be written (in 1830) but last to be published (in 1868), Mendelssohn probably envisioned it for festivities surrounding the three hundredth anniversary of the Augsburg Confession on 25 June. And while he never christened the symphony with the subtitle "Reformation" – although he did refer to it as a "church symphony" ("Kirchensinfonie") – Mendelssohn's treatment of Martin Luther's chorale "Ein' feste Burg ist unser Gott" in the last movement clearly depicts the triumph of the Protestant faith over Catholic (Mendelssohn would devise a similar liturgical narrative in his "Lobgesang" Symphony, op. 52, of 1840, commissioned by the city of Leipzig to celebrate the four hundredth anniversary of Johannes Gutenberg's invention of the printing press, an event in which religious faith, civic pride, and German values merged). The single performance of the work during Mendelssohn's lifetime (1832) seems to validate his misgivings about program music that relies on narrative. As Benedict Taylor has noted, "The problem with the 'Reformation' Symphony is that the work, with its quotations of earlier themes and preexistent liturgical melodies, is not sufficiently comprehensible without some kind of (verbal) hermeneutic key to explain these unconventional procedures."[30]

Indeed, in the last concert overture he composed during the fertile period of *c*.1825–*c*.1835, on the subject of the water nymph Melusine, Mendelssohn restricted his material both programmatically and musically. The overture avoids the large, colorful cast of characters of *A Midsummer Night's Dream* Overture, the well-known poems that inspired *Meeresstille und glückliche Fahrt*, and the specific, exotic, historical locale of the "Hebrides" Overture. The subject of Melusine had recently been treated in an opera by the composer Conradin Kreutzer, whose successful performance at Berlin on 27 February 1833 irked Mendelssohn. In particular, he could not understand the appeal of the opera's overture, which the audience encored. As he explained to his sister two months later: "[Kreutzer's success] inspired me with the wish to write an overture which the people would not *encore*, but which would cause them more solid pleasure; so I selected the portion of the subject that pleased me (exactly corresponding with the legend), and, in short, the overture came into the world."[31]

Felix outlined the overture's genesis to his sister in part as a response to her question of its literary source. The Melusine legend was old, dating back more than five hundred years, and in the intervening centuries had been given poetic treatment by the trouvère Jean d'Arras, Swiss author Thüring von Ringoltingen, and – more recently – Ludwig Tieck, Goethe, and Franz Grillparzer, who had furnished the libretto to Kreutzer's opera. Models for or derivatives of Melusine include naiads, sirens, undines, mermaids, loreleis, Rhinemaidens, and rusalki, whose cross-cultural intelligibility made it one of the most popular literary, artistic, and musical subjects of the nineteenth century. Perhaps as a way of playing into the universal appeal of the story without divulging regional particulars, Mendelssohn does not reveal a specific source; instead, as the Overture to *The Fairy Tale of the Beautiful Melusine* (*Ouverture zum Mährchen von der schönen Melusine*), the work commits only to the most enduring elements of the story: Melusine and her watery environment, to which she must routinely return; her militant lover Reymund; and their confrontation.

To Melusine, Mendelssohn gives a lilting melody whose contour and pulse paint an environment of serenity and tranquility in F major, features magnified through

**Example 2.16** Mendelssohn, Overture to *The Tale of the Beautiful Melusine*, mm. 343–360, arr. unidentified

juxtaposition with the appearance of Reymund's truculent, propulsive, melodically uninspired music in F minor at m. 48ff. (Incidentally, its more interesting counter-subject resembles the main theme of Beethoven's *Egmont* Overture.) A complete sonata-form exposition ensues, with a pair of ardent chromatic melodies at mm. 107 and 115 characterizing the second theme group in the expected key of A♭ major. Surprisingly, the development that follows (mm. 161–263) treats Melusine's and Reymund's materials separately, although Reymund's characteristic rhythm, ♩♫♫♩♩♫♫, attempts unsuccessfully to enter Melusine's domain at mm. 260–262 and – more importantly – m. 264, an event which could arguably push the recapitulation back to m. 272, where Melusine's motive is supported by a root-position tonic chord.

To call this moment a recapitulation, however, obscures the significant amount of development that follows. Indeed, the Melusine of fable can change form, and by the end of the heavily compressed recapitulation Reymund has adapted as much to Melusine's world as she has to his. His last "appearance" at m. 343 (see Example 2.16) features her trochees more than his dactyls, and the A♭ that

**Example 2.17** Mendelssohn, Overture to *The Tale of the Beautiful Melusine*, mm. 1–8, arr. unidentified

**Example 2.18** Mendelssohn, Overture to *The Tale of the Beautiful Melusine*, mm. 394–396, arr. unidentified

distinguished his mode from hers loses its harmonic moorings beginning at m. 354. In retrospect, that pitch and its attendant harmonic and formal consequences were dictated by Melusine at the overture's outset, Example 2.17, in the form of a vii$^{o4/3}$/V at m. 3 – the same chord that characterizes Reymund's last utterance at m. 355. When this chord returns at m. 395 in the coda (mm. 368–406; see Example 2.18), Mendelssohn spells it G♯–B♮–D–F instead of B♮–D–F–A♭. While enharmonically equivalent, the programmatic implication of this notational substitution is that Melusine has permanently expelled Reymund from her realm. In an excellent analysis of Mendelssohn's *Melusine* Overture, Thomas Grey suggests that it "presupposes a familiarity with certain poetic motifs or images that listeners bring to the music and that inform their 'reading' of, or listening to, it. Musical and poetic materials will interact, in the listener's mind, to construct a kind of 'poetry' that is freed from the medial restrains of either story or music as 'absolute' genres . . . while partaking of certain capacities of both."[32]

The preceding discussion of Mendelssohn's *Melusine* Overture assumes a sonata-form structure. Yet large portions of the overture do not conform easily to the traditional model. In particular, Melusine's aquatically inspired music both frames the overture and participates in its development and recapitulation, problematizing sections of "introduction," "coda," and the like. Perhaps the most unusual feature of Mendelssohn's structure, however, is the deployment of the overture's central themes. It was none other than A.B. Marx who, after exhaustive study of the Viennese Classicists, especially Beethoven, determined in 1848 that the two major themes of the exposition (and recapitulation) are related as follows:

> the main theme [*Satz*] is the first to be determined, thus partaking of an initial freshness and energy, and as such . . . leads and determines. The subsidiary *Satz*, on the other hand, is created after the first energetic confirmation and, by contrast, is that which serves. It is conditioned and determined by the preceding theme, and as such its essence is necessarily milder, its formation one of pliancy rather than pith – a feminine counterpart, as it were, to its masculine precedent. In just such a sense, each theme is a thing apart until both together form a higher, more perfected entity.[33]

Mendelssohn's second theme group (m. 107ff) is neither derivative of the first (m. 48ff) nor characteristically "feminine." In fact, in the recapitulation, it is Reymund's music that appears in the slot normally reserved for the second theme group (m. 319ff), and it becomes severely weakened following a confrontation with Melusine's music beginning at m. 327. According to Schumann, Mendelssohn summed up his overture as a "misalliance" ("mésalliance"), in which the couple's themes never achieve Marx's hoped-for "higher, more perfected entity." Mendelssohn's positioning of Reymund's material in the *Melusine* Overture may also owe something to Grillparzer's characterization of him as androgynous, whereby Reymund is torn between meeting the expectations of his society by being a man of action in the real world (as a man) and his personal gravitation toward art, poetry, and fantasy.

The function of the overture became increasingly bifurcated as the nineteenth century progressed. On the one hand, overtures continued to play their traditional role of deepening musical themes, heightening affective states, and even illustrating choice narrative moments of a forthcoming staged drama. Thus in the introduction to his Overture to *Der Freischütz* (1821), Carl Maria von Weber juxtaposes horns in sonorous, folk-like thirds in C major with dark, low-register clarinets that move toward the parallel minor via diminished seventh and Neapolitan chords. The showdown is given distinct personalities in the sonata-proper, where a theme associated with the evil Samiel (m. 37) is weighed against one (m. 123) that the virtuous Agathe sings in Act II. A coda intimates the opera's first chorus, "Victoria, der Meister soll leben," and the overture concludes with a cautious promise of salvation. Just as dramatic is the way in which Louis Spohr shapes his Overture to *Faust* of 1808 (not based on Goethe's play): beginning in a cheerful mode, it gradually succumbs to an evil such that it ends, unusually for the period, in the parallel minor.

On the other hand, the overture could also function as a fully independent site for theatrical or poetic expression. It was largely under the influence of Beethoven, whose overtures tested boundaries of both drama and form, that composers such as Mendelssohn, Berlioz, and, later, Schumann and Liszt extended the programmatic range of the overture in ways that reflected bold ideas about relationships between music, literature, and drama: ideas which the next three chapters explore in theory and practice.

## Chapter 3

# Berlioz and Schumann on music and literature

In a review from December 1899 of Hector Berlioz's recently published "private letters" ("lettres intimes"), Camille Saint-Saëns tried to put his finger on what made Berlioz, who had been dead thirty years yet whose position in French music was still being fiercely debated, tick:

> Like the mystics who reached the point of experiencing the pains of the Passion in their own bodies, Berlioz experienced the torments of Faust, Hamlet and Manfred. He incarnated in himself these poetic creations, whose imaginary sufferings were metamorphosed in him into real ones. Was it Camille and Henriette he loved, or rather Ophelia and Ariel? At some moments it is no longer he who lives, but Shakespeare who lives in him. We are observers of a curious phenomenon of poetic mysticism, leading, like the religious kind, to serious disorders of the nervous system and to a cruel and interminable torture that slowly eats into one's existence and ceases only in death.[1]

Saint-Saëns admits that Berlioz was perhaps too Romantic for his own good, having let himself get immersed in the fictional worlds of Johann Wolfgang von Goethe, William Shakespeare, and Lord Byron to the detriment of his reputation and personal life. The criticism, of course, says as much about Saint-Saëns's musical aesthetics as it does Berlioz's (see Chapter 9); but the reviewer nevertheless hits the nail on the head when, in a more extended consideration from the same year, he characterizes Berlioz as "a paradox made flesh."[2]

It would take only a few minor emendations to extend Saint-Saëns's characterization of Berlioz to Robert Schumann. Although the two composers would not meet until 1843, their independent pursuits in the 1830s exhibit significant overlap:

- As voracious readers, the two shared an interest in translating their encounters with literature into comparable musical documents.
- Both brought events of their personal lives – especially the upheavals associated with their (sometimes imagined) romantic liaisons – to bear on the profile of their compositions.
- Both left a substantial body of music criticism, in which they share a similarly high regard for tradition and disdain for convention, and which has

come to be regarded as some of the best documentation on the development of the Romantic artist.

- Finally, both produced the most innovative program music of their careers – Berlioz for the orchestra, Schumann for the piano.


## Berlioz and the programmatic symphony

Next to Beethoven's "Pastoral" Symphony, Berlioz's *Symphonie fantastique* counts as one of the handful of programmatic symphonies from the first half of the nineteenth century that have remained in the modern repertory. The two orchestral works share much in common: They are in five movements; they draw heavily on classical topics like the pastoral and *Sturm und Drang*; they feature quasi-operatic storms, dances, and marches; and they sport a multi-movement expressive arc that borders on the literary. Berlioz would have frequent recourse to Beethoven's major orchestral works from March 1828 onwards, when the conductor François-Antoine Habeneck inaugurated his Société des Concerts du Conservatoire, or Concert Society of the Conservatory, in Paris. In the first two seasons, Habeneck and his group presented Beethoven's Third, Fifth, and Seventh Symphonies, the Violin Concerto and Third Piano Concerto, and *Coriolan*, *Egmont*, and *Fidelio* Overtures. The "Pastoral" was given for the first time on 15 March 1829 and remained a fixture on the programs of the Société until its dissolution almost one hundred and forty years later. Berlioz's zeal for Beethoven, only recently deceased, leaps off the pages of some of his earliest criticism, a biography of the German composer with analysis of selected music, from the summer and early fall of 1829.

Despite these important correspondences and Beethoven's undeniable influence on Berlioz the symphonist, the *Symphonie fantastique* constantly goes out of the way to assert its individuality and independence. From the start, Berlioz envisioned it as a programmatic symphony, but as he became more immersed in Romantic literature, more critical of the Parisian establishment, and more personally and artistically self-aware, the symphony's subject matter changed. Berlioz may have been inspired by Goethe's *Faust*, a French translation of which by Gérard de Nerval appeared in 1828, the same year that Habeneck began his Beethoven campaign. One year earlier, Berlioz had attended a performance of Shakespeare's *Hamlet* given by a visiting English troupe that included the actress Harriet Smithson as Ophelia. When Berlioz recalled this "supreme drama of my life," he made no real distinction between playwright and performer: "The impression made on my heart and mind by her extraordinary talent, nay her dramatic genius, was equaled only by the havoc wrought in me by the poet she so nobly interpreted. That is all I can say."[3]

From this environment, Berlioz the artist, the poet–composer, emerged. His letters over the next three years document a search for the appropriate medium through which "the development of my infernal passion is to be painted."[4] Indeed, to Goethe and Shakespeare were added François-René de Chateaubriand, E.T.A. Hoffmann, Thomas Moore, Walter Scott, as well as less seminal figures like Thomas De Quincey. By April 1830 he was referring to his new work as "my novel, or, more accurately, my history,"[5] a sentiment which he would celebrate in what would become the symphony's autobiographical subtitle, "Episode in the Life of an Artist."

By this point, Berlioz's infatuation with Smithson had become debilitating. But as a good Romantic, he managed to funnel his personal turmoil into a unique musico-literary vessel: an "idée fixe," a "fixed idea." The concept was familiar to Parisians as a medical condition that had occasionally been pressed into the service of fiction writers, but its application in music as a nominal representation of the ways in which a protagonist perceives his environment and its inhabitants was novel.[6]

In the first movement, the "idée fixe" appears in its complete form (see Table 3.1): a two-part melody in which a balanced first half (mm. 72–86) of two eight-bar segments contrasts with a four-bar phrase (mm. 86–90) that attempts three chromatic ascents before returning in equally dramatic chromatic fashion back to tonic. Berlioz makes further distinctions within the melody – which he describes as a "canto" ("song") – by emphasizing the expressive and dynamic nuances at the opening and temporal fits and starts toward the closing. In the next movement, the theme easily adapts to the bubbly waltz. In the third movement, however, the character of the "idée fixe" changes considerably: there is increased distance between presentations of its segments, which eventually results in an incomplete

**Table 3.1** *Berlioz's* Symphonie fantastique: *program\* and permutations of the "idée fixe"*

I. **Reveries – Passions**. The author imagines that a young musician, afflicted with that moral disease that a well-known writer calls the *vague des passions*, sees for the first time a woman who embodies all the charms of the ideal being he has imagined in his dreams, and he falls desperately in love with her. Through an odd whim, whenever the beloved image appears before the mind's eye of the artist, it is linked with a musical thought whose character, passionate but at the same time noble and shy, he finds similar to the one he attributes to his beloved. This melodic image and the model it reflects pursue him incessantly like a double *idée fixe*. That is the reason for the constant appearance, in every moment of the symphony, of the melody that begins the first Allegro. The passage from this state of melancholy reverie, interrupted by a few fits of groundless joy, to one of frenzied passion, with its movements of fury, of jealousy, its return of tenderness, its tears, its religious consolations – this is the subject of the first movement.

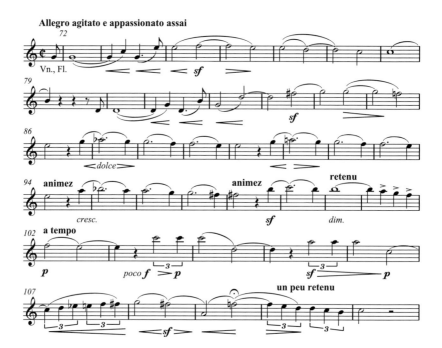

II. **A Ball**. The artist finds himself in the most varied situations – in the midst of *the tumult of a party*, in the peaceful contemplation of the beauties of nature; but everywhere, in town, in the country, the beloved image appears before him and disturbs his peace of mind.

III. **Scene in the Country**. Finding himself one evening in the country, he hears in the distance two shepherds piping a *ranz des vaches* in dialogue. This pastoral duet, the scenery, the quiet rustling of the trees gently brushed by the wind, the hopes he has recently found some reason to entertain – all concur in affording his heart an unaccustomed calm, and in giving a more cheerful color to his ideas. He reflects upon his isolation; he hopes that his loneliness will soon be over . . . But what if she were deceiving him! . . . This mingling of hope and fear, these ideas of happiness disturbed by black presentiments, form the subject of the Adagio. At the end one of the shepherds again takes up the *ranz des vaches*; the other no longer replies . . . Distant sound of thunder . . . loneliness . . . silence . . .

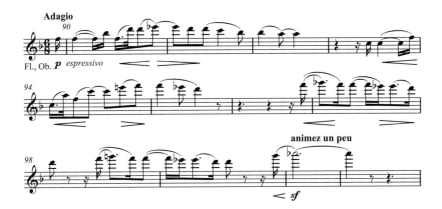

IV. **March to the Scaffold**. Convinced that his love is unappreciated, the artist poisons himself with opium. The dose of the narcotic, too weak to kill him, plunges him into a sleep accompanied by the most horrible visions. He dreams that he has killed his beloved, that he is condemned and led to the scaffold, and that he is witnessing *his own execution*. The procession moves forward to the sounds of a march that is now somber and fierce, now brilliant and solemn, in which the muffled noise of heavy steps gives way without transition to the noisiest clamor. At the end of the march the first four measures of the *idée fixe* reappear, like a last thought of love interrupted by the fatal blow.

V. **Dream of a Witches' Sabbath**. He sees himself at the Sabbath, in the midst of a frightful troop of ghosts, sorcerers, monsters of every kind, come together for his funeral. Strange noises, groans, bursts of laughter, distant cries which other cries seem to answer. The beloved melody appears again, but it has lost its character of nobility and shyness; it is no more than a dance tune, mean, trivial, and grotesque: it is she, coming to join the Sabbath . . . A roar of joy at her arrival . . . She takes part in the devilish orgy . . . Funeral knell, burlesque parody of the *Dies irae* [the hymn sung in the funeral rites of the Catholic Church], *Sabbath round-dance*. The Sabbath round and the *Dies irae* combined.

---

*Quoted in Hector Berlioz, *Fantastic Symphony*, ed. Edward T. Cone (New York: W.W. Norton, 1971), 23–25.

**Example 3.1** Berlioz, *Symphonie fantastique*, V, mm. 241–248 ("Ronde du Sabbat"), arr. Franz Liszt

presentation. And despite valiant efforts (mm. 100–112), the orchestra fails to reconstruct the missing material. The theme fares even worse in the March, where the artist can barely bring to mind a memory of his beloved before he is relieved of his head.

Berlioz divided the *Symphonie fantastique* into two parts: movements I–III, which occur in the artist's "real" world; and IV–V, which unfold in a mind addled by drugs and exhaustion. Yet the finale is so different than the previous four movements that the reality–dream division potentially hampers other programmatic approaches to Berlioz's first symphony. The "Songe d'une nuit du sabbat" is in essence a through-composed concert fantasy, complete with a slow introduction that brilliantly extends the ombra and supernatural operatic traditions of Mozart and Weber. (In this respect, at least, the *Symphonie fantastique* bears resemblance to its bizarre sequel, *Le retour à la vie* [*The Return to Life*], which concludes with a fantasy on Shakespeare's *The Tempest*.) Even the "idée fixe" is made operatic: at first it is faint, with a single C clarinet playing *ppp* as if far off in the distance ("lointain" is how Berlioz describes it in the score). Following a disruption by the orchestra that limits its presentation to the first two segments, an E♭ clarinet not only successfully carries the tune, but also spreads it to the neighboring piccolos and flutes and finally (m. 60) the entire winds and upper strings. The appearance of the "Dies irae" plainchant at m. 127 provides the motivation for the "idée fixe" – up to this point still affiliated with the beloved – to organize itself into a worthy antagonist, a witches' round dance (Example 3.1). As the beloved is replaced by her supernatural minions, a battle between the sacrilegious and religious ensues. The confrontation reaches a climax in a fugue, to which Berlioz proudly calls attention (m. 414ff), after which the movement ends in a blur of spectacular orchestral effects.

Yet while the characteristic inner movements – dance, pastorale, march – and dramatic finale substantially draw on programmatic tradition, it is in the first movement that Berlioz's most sophisticated and unique programmatic techniques appear. The "idée fixe" appears five times, never once repeated exactly. Its ubiquity is a projection of the artist's obsession. It encounters a myriad of obstacles, which highlight the extreme instability of his emotional outbursts. These encounters, in turn, reflect back on the increasingly deluded artist, who builds for himself a highly misrepresented image of his beloved. Every event in the first movement becomes relativized. The "idée fixe" serves as formal anchor, but only because it is slightly better grounded than the mind of the artist. As Stephen Rodgers points out, even the famous chromatic six-chords at mm. 198, 369, 439, and 461 clearly relate: "The madness induced by the image of the beloved contains something of that image, and the image, however pure it may seem at first, already contains the madness it spawns. The two are inextricably linked before the drama even begins – as they ought to be."[7] Similarly, the traditional first-movement, sonata-form trajectory collapses in on itself, with Berlioz's "Vagues de passions" coming dangerously close to spiraling out of control in a type of psychotic accelerando of form. Given the depths of the artist's compulsions plumbed by the first movement, the concluding "religious consolations" (mm. 513–527) begin a protracted program of catharsis that runs the remaining course of the symphony.

The *Symphonie fantastique* was not to everyone's taste. The powerful music critic François-Joseph Fétis decried the assertions of the symphony's program before the composition was even premiered on 5 December 1830, and he produced a more thorough recollection of that event once he got his hands on Franz Liszt's solo piano transcription of the score, which was published about four years later:

> I saw that [Berlioz] had no taste for melody and but a feeble notion of rhythm; that his harmony, composed by piling up tones into heaps that were often monstrous, was nevertheless flat and monotonous. In a word, I saw that he lacked melodic and harmonic ideas, and I came to the conclusion that he would always write in a barbarous manner.[8]

Felix Mendelssohn, to whom Berlioz showed his symphony in March 1831, was even harsher than Fétis, who at least acknowledged Berlioz's gift for colorful orchestral writing. Mendelssohn, however, was uniformly disgusted and thoroughly debilitated, writing privately to his family of how the finale bordered on the masochistic:

> cold passion represented by all possible means: four timpani, two pianos for four hands, which are supposed to imitate bells, two harps, many large drums, violins divided into eight different parts, two different parts for the double basses which play solo passages, and all these means (which would be fine if they were properly

used) express nothing but complete sterility and indifference, mere grunting, screaming, screeching here and there.[9]

Some portion of these criticisms surely accounts for the substantial revisions that Berlioz made to the work around 1832 – revisions which would taper but continue until the full score was published in 1845, that is, fifteen years after the symphony's first audition. But even while reworking the *Symphonie fantastique*, Berlioz was planning a new symphony of a much different character and design. As he recalled in his *Memoirs*:

> My idea was to write a series of orchestral scenes, in which the solo viola would be involved, to a greater or lesser extent, like an actual person, retaining the same character throughout. I decided to give it as a setting the poetic impressions recollected from my wanderings in the Abruzzi and to make it a kind of melancholy dreamer in the style of Byron's Childe Harold. Hence the title of the symphony, *Harold in Italy*. As in the Fantastic Symphony, a motto (the viola's first theme) recurs throughout the work, but with the difference that where as the theme of the Fantastic Symphony, the *idée fixe*, keeps obtruding like an obsessive idea on scenes that are alien to it and deflects the current of the music, the Harold theme is superimposed on the other orchestral voices so as to contrast with them in character and tempo without interrupting their development.[10]

As Berlioz notes, each symphony employs a recurring theme throughout in order to create musical unity, dramatic thrust, and autobiographical parallels. But unlike the *Symphonie fantastique*, *Harold en Italie* lacks a prose program. Instead, the symphony's overall title and the titles of its four movements situate the composition within a very specific poetic frame, Lord Byron's *Childe Harold's Pilgrimage*.

Published in four "cantos" ("songs") between 1812 and 1818, Byron's more than 3,500 lines chronicle the peripatetic Childe Harold, who seeks out the ruins of a glorious past in the vain hope of finding personal fulfillment during (Cantos I–II) and in the aftermath (Cantos III–IV) of the Napoleonic Wars. Byron later referred to *Childe Harold's Pilgrimage* as "a fine piece of poetical desolation," and recalled that "I was half mad during the time of its composition, between metaphysics, mountains, lakes, love unextinguishable, thoughts unutterable, and the nightmare of my own delinquencies."[11]

Indeed, the poem is intensely autobiographical, even confessional, such that Byron dropped his alter ego altogether in the Fourth Canto, which primarily focuses on Italy and its cultural heritage. Indeed, it would have been nothing short of incredible had Berlioz not identified himself with Byron / Childe Harold. (Liszt was similarly intoxicated by the same material around the same period; see Chapter 4.) After all, he had loved to the point of madness, plunged himself into the literature of the past, and traveled both to find solitude and to escape his personal demons. Within a month of the premiere of the *Symphonie fantastique* on 5 December 1830 (with Habeneck at the helm), Berlioz was on his way to Italy as a

**Figure 3.1** J.M.W. Turner, *Childe Harold's Pilgrimage, Italy* (1832)

**Example 3.2** Berlioz, *Harold en Italie*, "Harold aux montagnes," mm. 38–45, solo viola (Harold's theme)

recipient of the Institut de France's coveted *Prix de Rome* (Rome Prize) scholarship. In many respects, it would turn out to be a miserable two years, no doubt cementing a personal view of himself as a cultural outsider akin to Childe Harold, whom J.M. W. Turner memorably exhibited in 1832 (see Figure 3.1) with an excerpt from Canto IV, stanza 26: "and now, fair Italy! / Thou art the garden of the world . . . / Thy wreck a glory, and thy ruin graced / With an immaculate charm which can not be defaced" (ll. 227–228, 233–234). Indeed, Berlioz seems to have chosen some of the more "charming" aspects of Italian life as basis for the four scenes of his symphony:

    I. Harold in the Mountains. Scenes of Melancholy, Happiness, and Joy
    II. March of the Pilgrims Singing the Evening Prayer
    III. Serenade of an Abruzzi Mountaineer to his Mistress
    IV. Orgy of the Brigands. Recollections of the Previous Scenes

Harold's theme, Example 3.2, is even simpler than the *Symphonie fantastique*'s "idée fixe." But while that theme served as the principal subject of the

**Example 3.3** Berlioz, *Harold en Italie*, "Marche de Pèlerins," mm. 56–76, arr. Liszt

first movement and the object of the ensuing four, Harold's theme never fully functions as either subject or object in Berlioz's Second Symphony. In the first movement, it resides primarily in the introduction, while in the second it functions as a physical reference point vis-à-vis the approach and departure of the pilgrims. In the third movement it is voyeuristic, with Harold discreetly watching from a safe distance; and in the fourth it dissolves. Even when Harold participates, his theme and those that he imitates from the orchestra are usually presented tentatively, as in the second movement (Example 3.3), where the viola enters with a directionless, off-beat ramble around the pitch F♯; and once it finds the beginning of the next phrase, it offers not the Pilgrims' chant, but rather

**Table 3.2** *Berlioz,* Harold en Italie, *"Orgie de brigands," structure of introduction, mm. 1–117*

Mm. 1–11: Brigands' music, g

12–17: Recollection of mvt. I, mm. 1–6, solo viola doubles bassoons, g

18–33: Repetition and development of brigands' music, g → F♯

34–41: Viola presents *canto* of mvt. II, with usual orchestral accompaniment, F♯

41–46: Development of brigands' music, f♯ → G

46–54: Recollection of mvt. III (m. 33ff), viola solo with sustained accompanimental chords in orchestra, G

54–59: Development of brigands' music, G / e

59–70: Solo viola recollection of mvt. I (m. 125ff), C

71–80: Development of brigands' music, C → G

81–117: Viola attempts to resuscitate "Harold" theme from mvt. I in G, but it breaks apart decisively at m. 97ff as the orchestra modulates back to the brigands' music in g

superimposes (as Berlioz says) its Harold theme with limited success. Indeed, the degree to which Harold – as both theme and character – adapts to his surroundings is one of Berlioz's chief interests in his symphony.

Ironically, Harold is at his most comfortable in the introduction to the finale, which, as Table 3.2 demonstrates, is a tug-of-war between the hedonistic music of the brigands and reminiscences of tamer music from earlier movements. In each of the musical recollections, the viola shows itself – arguably for the first time in the entire composition – to be a true member of the group. In fact, its presentation of a stanza from the Pilgrims' Song at m. 34ff reveals an awareness of his surroundings by means of a kind of musical muscle memory that Harold had not shown in the second movement, where he remained continuously disengaged from the passersby. But this new connection perhaps has consequences for Harold's identity, as the introduction ends with him unable to recall his own theme. Indeed, as Mark Evan Bonds notes, "In spite of its prominence, the brigands' music is not the main event of the finale; Harold's failure to reassert himself is."[12] To be sure, Berlioz's music speaks volumes about Byron's anti-hero, who remains silent for more than three-quarters of the symphony's run-time. But the alienation effect of Harold's spotty appearances throughout the symphony and especially in the finale are even more keenly experienced in live performance: a solo violist – whom Berlioz requires to "stand in the foreground, near the public and isolated from the orchestra" – is exhibited before an audience that grows increasingly uncomfortable with his strangeness.

## *Roméo et Juliette* and the semi-symphony

It was Niccolò Paganini who commissioned Berlioz to write his Second Symphony. The famed violinist was searching for a concerto that would allow him to show off his recently acquired Stradivarius viola, but when he saw what Berlioz had in mind for the soloist, the two musicians parted ways. But two days after hearing *Harold en Italie* performed at a concert given by Berlioz on 16 December 1838, Paganini sent a gift of 20,000 francs, a godsend that allowed Berlioz to discharge his debts and focus on the composition of a symphony on Shakespeare's *Romeo and Juliet*, whose premiere he conducted to great acclaim eleven months later.

As Berlioz explained in the preface, "The genre of this work will surely not be misunderstood. Although voices are frequently used, it is neither a concert opera nor a cantata, but a choral symphony [*Symphonie avec choeurs*]."[13] Given the genre-bending designs of his first two symphonies, Berlioz's assertions about the generic identify of his Shakespeare piece, what he dubbed a "symphonie dramatique," is not surprising. Still, non-traditional symphonic elements are in such abundance that the work has recently been characterized, along with Berlioz's later *La damnation de Faust*, as a "semi-opera . . . a symphony that has swallowed an opera."[14] But if it is a question of who-eats-whom, then perhaps a slightly more appropriate term for *Roméo et Juliette* might be "semi-symphony," since the three main symphonic movements (out of seven in total) sit in the middle of the work:

II. Romeo alone – Sadness – Distant noises of the party and concert – Grand party at the Capulets'
III. Peaceful night – The Capulets' garden, silent and deserted – Young Capulets, coming from the party, pass by and sing music from the party – Love scene
IV. Queen Mab, or the Fairy of Dreams (Scherzo)

These scenes, as well as the cemetery scene from movement VI, form the dramatic core of Berlioz's symphony, and it is notable that they share much in common with the *Symphonie fantastique* and *Harold en Italie*. The second movement, for instance, recalls the social setting of the *Symphonie fantastique*'s second movement, *Harold en Italie*'s treatment of Harold's character in relation to his environment, and – as in the "Marche du supplice" – the brief interjection of an earlier, pensive theme (mm. 385–394) that momentarily arrests the momentum of the festivities. Similarly, the famous "Queen Mab" Scherzo acts as a fairy-tale counterpart to the macabre introduction to the finale of the *Symphonie fantastique* (mm. 1–20), with light, hushed strings and playful winds now fluttering throughout an orchestra that in 1830 had been saturated by static diminished seventh chords, perseverating divided strings, and flatulent winds. However, the third movement's extended Love Scene revealed a recipe to Wagner, who attended *Roméo et Juliette*'s premiere, that he would cook up over and over almost two decades later in portions of *Der Ring des Nibelungen* and especially *Tristan und Isolde*: "generate the main theme of a movement not by combining discrete elements of other themes but by allowing each theme to metamorphose imperceptibly into the next. Do not display the main theme suddenly; reveal it gradually, so that its true identity is only recognizable in retrospect. And then, once the theme has emerged, repeat it until it can be repeated no longer."[15]

Berlioz elaborates further in his preface that the content – particularly the "sublimity of this love" between Romeo and Juliet – forced him to refrain from setting the text of the drama in these instrumental movements. Such depiction, argues Berlioz, "is fraught with peril; [the composer's] invention should be allowed the scope which the exact sense of sung words restrains, but which is possible in such circumstances with instrumental music, richer, more varied, less restricted, and thanks to its very indefiniteness, incomparably more powerful."[16] Had Mendelssohn read these lines, which Berlioz published in 1847 with a revised full score, he may have well commended the French composer for coming so far in so short a time since encountering the banal finale of the *Symphonie fantastique* in 1831. Indeed, Mendelssohn had arrived at a similar conclusion by way of a different route, as he famously wrote to his distant relative Marc André Souchay, who had asked about the addition of texts to the composer's popular *Lieder ohne Worte*: "A piece of music that I love," replies Mendelssohn, "expresses thoughts to me that are not too *imprecise* to be framed in words, but too *precise*. So I find that attempts to express such thoughts in words may have some point to them, but they are also unsatisfying . . . [Words] just cannot manage any better."[17]

As a "semi-symphony," *Roméo et Juliette* must also remain "semi-programmatic." In fact, Berlioz's Third Symphony would mark the end of his experiments in stand-alone program music. His remaining dramatic compositions – *La damnation de Faust*, *L'enfance du Christ*, and *Les Troyens* – all feature programmatic moments, but they cannot be divorced from the surrounding sung and/or spoken texts. Still, their generic and source variety – a "dramatic legend" based nominally on Goethe, a "sacred trilogy" based on the Gospels, a grand opera based on a Shakespeareanized Virgil – speaks to Berlioz's endless pursuit of the new. Indeed, if the epithet "programmatic" is applied to his music in the sense that Liszt would later give it (see Chapter 4), whereby (poetic) content determines form and not vice versa, then Berlioz must rank as one of the most programmatically provocative composers of the entire century.

## Programmatic modes of music criticism

Contemporaneous with the production of his symphonies came a large body of music criticism. Unlike Schumann, Wagner, or Liszt, who took to the feuilletons to advance their respective artistic causes, Berlioz wrote primarily to pay the bills. Most of his always readable reviews cover Parisian opera, which he generally dismisses with a characteristically caustic wit, but his ruminations on instrumental music, especially that of Beethoven, are useful in uncovering how Berlioz understood the relationship of music and literature from the listener's point of audition, and, by extension, how he hoped listeners might hear his own music.

Between 9 April 1837 and 4 March 1838, he released a series of articles on Beethoven's symphonies in France's leading music journal, the *Revue et Gazette musicale de Paris*. Berlioz is clearly interested in identifying the nuts and bolts of these compositions, as he devotes significant space to matters of form, melody, harmony, and orchestration. Once those elements are established, he explains how they work together in an expressive capacity. It quickly becomes clear that Berlioz's favorite movements in Beethoven's music are those that boast equal parts technical craft and poetic spirit. Thus, the First Symphony is "not yet true Beethoven," as it leans too heavily on tradition.[18] The Second Symphony, "all nobility, energy, and pride," represents a huge step toward compositional independence, particularly the last two movements, which Berlioz likens to "Oberon's [from Shakespeare's *A Midsummer Night's Dream*] graceful spirits at play." The Third Symphony, with its leading subtitle, opens up the heroic world of Virgil and Homer. The funeral march "is like a translation into music" of the former, while the scherzo is akin to "games such as those with which the warriors of the *Iliad* celebrated their leaders at the graveside." Like the opening movement of the "Eroica" Symphony, the Adagio of the Fourth Symphony "defies analysis," yet Berlioz confidently offers the episode of Paolo and Francesca from Dante's *Divine Comedy* as a legitimate interpretive stand-in.

The Fifth Symphony, argues Berlioz, is Beethoven's most personal creation, and as such calls to mind scenes and citations from the works of his favorite authors: the first movement "depicts the chaotic feelings that overwhelm a great soul when prey to despair . . . [Not] Romeo's dark and mute grief on learning of Juliet's death, but Othello's terrible rage on hearing of Desdemona's guilt from Iago's poisonous lies." Images of Goethe's *Faust* emerge from the movement, and between these literary titans sits the Adagio, whose impression is "impossible to describe, and surely the most intense of its kind I have ever felt." While Berlioz frequently mentions the legitimate popularity of the Seventh Symphony's Allegretto, he lowers his poetic antennae, making curt references to Shakespeare (*Twelfth Night*, *Hamlet*) and Thomas Moore. As the Eighth is for him a curiosity, he offers no extra-musical cues. Understandably, his reading of the Ninth is guided by Schiller's text.

The shiniest gem of Beethoven's symphonic output is the Sixth. Berlioz, gushing with praise for the work's programmatic successes, realizes that he has gotten ahead of himself – but regret it, he does not:

> After all of this, is it absolutely necessary to discuss the stylistic oddities that are found in this tremendous work? . . . I cannot do it. For such a task, you must be able to reason coldly, and how can you steel yourself against intoxication, when your mind is full of such a work? One would far rather sleep, sleep for months, and in one's dreams keep living in the unknown realm that a genius has allowed us to glimpse.

As a kind of super-poetry, the "Pastoral" Symphony is "nature as she really is." Such a bold assertion coming from Berlioz in early 1838 warrants greater scrutiny, given that he had recently wrapped up *Harold en Italie* and would begin concentrated work on *Roméo et Juliette* within a year. In fact, Berlioz had considered the question of musical representation less than a year earlier in an article entitled "On Imitation in Music," in which the "Pastoral" provides him with the best ammunition.

Berlioz takes aim at Giuseppe Carpani, who had considered music's capacity to imitate through the lens of Joseph Haydn's oratorio *The Creation*, which since its first performance in 1798 had been celebrated for its musical pictorialism and expressive range. Carpani had discerned two main forms of imitation in the work: direct or physical ("physique"), and indirect or sentimental. He further breaks down the first in hackneyed ("servile") and dressed-up ("déguisée") modes, the second into those painterly and expressive.

Berlioz tires quickly of Carpani's taxonomies, and does not even see fit to explain them completely before he offers his own approach. Dismissing the long-standing notion – just like Beethoven had in the Sixth Symphony – that music is capable of painting, Berlioz argues instead that music "is sufficient unto itself, and possesses the power to charm without having recourse to any kind of imitation . . . [Music] can by its own means act upon the imagination in such a way as to engender sensations analogous to those produced by graphic art."[19] Berlioz admits Carpani's category of direct imitation of natural sounds, but only as long as it:

- Is a means to heighten "music's independent power," not an end unto itself;
- Is worth one's attention;
- Cannot be misinterpreted by the listener;
- Never substitutes for emotional imitation.

Berlioz demonstrates his points through Beethoven's "Pastoral" Symphony. He holds it in such high esteem because it not only occasionally imitates directly but also consistently practices "the most powerful of all forms of imitation – the one that reproduces the emotions and the passions: *expressiveness*."[20] This is the crux of Berlioz's argument, and at this juncture he takes leave of Carpani and his predominantly eighteenth-century models in order to explain how – because music does have imitative limits – multiple types of imitation coordinate in order to heighten expression. In these moments of extreme expression, an external text can aid comprehension:

I shall be told, perhaps, that there exist admirable examples of [direct] musical depiction … But on looking closer it becomes clear that these poetical beauties in no way overstep the vast circle, within which our art is circumscribed by its very nature. For these imitations are not in fact offered us as pictures of objects but only as images or analogues. They help to reawaken comparable sensations by means which music undoubtedly possesses. Yet even so, before the original of these images can be recognized, it is strictly required that the hearer be notified of the composer's intent by some indirect means, and the point of the comparison be patent.[21]

The takeaways from Berlioz's article are many, and they resonate strongly with the spirit of the first two symphonies he had produced thus far and dovetail into the assertion of *Roméo et Juliette*'s preface: Imitation of natural phenomena in music is possible, but its use should be limited. Music works best as metaphor. The composer should primarily focus on expression, which music can call forth far better than its sister arts. Depending on the type of imitation attempted, the listener might benefit from extra-musical elucidation. Finally, no better model of these precepts exists than Beethoven's "Pastoral" Symphony.

Like Berlioz, Schumann diagnosed the current state of music as artistically deplorable, with virtuoso opera singers and instrumentalists having commandeered the stages and in doing so arrested the development of serious music after Beethoven. Thus, and again like Berlioz, it was primarily to Beethoven that Schumann turned in order to help him and his fellow composers christen a "new, poetic age" for music. Schumann made this announcement at the start of 1835, in the New Year's issue of the *Neue Zeitschrift für Musik*, the music journal he had founded less than one year before and which he had just taken over as editor. Over the next eleven years, as owner, editor, and chief contributor, he would develop a brand of "poetic criticism" that would seek to combat the antiquarian tastes and soporific compositions of the day, but more importantly to solve, as John Daverio explains, the "obvious problem posed by the concept of music criticism itself, namely, its employment of a verbal medium to describe and evaluate tonal events."[22]

Long before founding his own journal, however, Schumann had already demonstrated the haziness of the boundaries between literature and music, reality and fiction, in his review of Frédéric Chopin's Variations on Mozart's "Là ci darem la mano," op. 2, in 1831, in which a group's first encounter with Chopin unfolds inside the frame of a short story. Present are a narrator named Julius, as well as characters named Florestan, Eusebius, and Master Raro, each of whom offers strikingly different impressions of the composition. Raro dismisses it. The homeless Florestan is obsessed by it, the confrontations between Don Giovanni, Zerlina, Leporello, and Masetto running through his head as he races through the street at night. So overcome is he by this new, highly evocative piece of music that he can only describe its impact by means of a telling analogy. Julius explains:

> In Switzerland, [Florestan] had experienced something similar. At the end of a
> beautiful day, when the evening sun colors the glacial peaks with red and pink
> hues before disintegrating and scattering, all of the mountains and valleys are
> filled with a calm fragrance. But the glacier stands quiet, cold, and firm, like a
> giant that has just awoken from his dreams.[23]

The scene that Julius describes is normally the type that inspires music composition, not fulfills it. For Schumann, though, it can also be the image that results from
hearing a musical work of genius. Indeed, Schumann neither explains most of his
references – When did this happen to Florestan? Why Switzerland instead of, say,
Italy? Are all giants nocturnal? – nor justifies them, and while there is a fair amount
of musical analysis embedded within the review, Schumann primarily forces his
reader to read poetically instead of technically, and in the process advance the
notion that music and literature need not remain distinct.

Not all of Schumann's criticism seeks such literary aspirations or musico-poetic
connections, nor does it unilaterally endorse program music. One of his earliest
reviews for the re-vamped *Neue Zeitschrift* was of Berlioz's *Symphonie fantastique*.
Initially undertaken as a rebuff to Fétis's harsh review (see above), Schumann
expanded his review into a celebrated analysis of the symphony's form, compositional techniques, and orchestral effects. While Schumann had much to praise about
these elements, for the program he had no sympathy:

> [Berlioz] can keep it, so far as we Germans are concerned! Such handy guides
> always have something of the charlatan about them, something degrading. At
> any rate, the titles standing at the head of the five movements would have
> sufficed on their own ... In short, the Germans, with their sensitive feelings
> and their aversion to the invasion of privacy, prefer not to have their thoughts
> led by the nose in this crude way ... Nature does something similar, in
> fastidiously covering her roots with earth. So let the artist keep his travails to
> himself.

Schumann adamantly asserts that Berlioz wrote his program for an immodest
French audience, but he also reluctantly admits that he "could see it all present in the
music."[24] (Elsewhere Schumann complained that he would have enjoyed Beethoven's
"Eroica" Symphony more without the composer's programmatic title.) He uses
Berlioz's program to launch into a discussion about the "idea," the source of poetic
inspiration and kernel of musical composition. Indeed, the composer feeds on both
simultaneously: "The more that elements related to music embody ideas or images
manifested in the notes, the more poetic or graphic [*plastisch*] will the composition
be; – and the more imaginatively and acutely the composer can observe all that goes on
around him, the more sublime and exalted will his work be." Music written along these
lines can, in fact, evoke images with a "sharpness of character."[25]

Schumann had other opportunities as a critic to address music's representative power. In a lengthy overview from 1838 of recently published études, Schumann singled out Ignaz Moscheles's twelve "Characteristic" Studies, op. 95. He likened the revered Moscheles to a poet who successfully encapsulates with utmost precision the prevailing mood of a piece by means of a choice title, "from which the composer's background [*Bildung*] becomes immediately apparent."[26] Still, not all characters are created equal, and Schumann divides Moscheles's studies into four categories: "mythological," "scenes from life and nature," "mental states," and "children's studies and dreams." Schumann believes the music of the first category to be cold, statuesque, yet formally impeccable; those studies in the second category are "romantic." For the third category, Schumann praises the music as ingenious (*geistreich*). Schumann reserves his highest praise for the music in the final category, which he contends is "the most tender and poetic in the whole collection. Here, verging on the extrasensory, on the spiritual realm [*Geisterreich*], is the music at its full force."[27] Indeed, the poetry in Moscheles's music turns Schumann into a poet. Thus his description of Étude no. 11, entitled "Dream" ("Traum"): "we know how music can dream, how we can dream in it. Only in the middle section does a more determinate thought ring out. Then everything disappears again in the quiet darkness of the opening."[28] This description is just as precise as the mountain scene that Florestan contrived after hearing Chopin's Variations, although more poetic. Yet Moscheles's music validates what Schumann poetically describes: a three-part (ABA') form, in which the music of the outer sections is driven by a musical line that moves without direction. In the second section, which begins at m. 60, the right hand announces an emphatic, fanfare-like theme, under which the opening section's line is transformed into decisive arpeggios. The largely diatonic melody is interrupted by short outbursts of eerie, ethereal oscillating diminished seventh chords. Eventually, the fanfare disintegrates, and the hazy opening section returns. Yet, vestiges of the dream remain (see Example 3.4), such as the fluttery effects at m. 121, marked *misterioso*, or the recollection of the middle section's theme at m. 127 in a key foreign to its surroundings. Moscheles also negotiates with register, rhythm, and timbre in order to foster an environment of discovery. The fluttery material ascends the keyboard with each iteration; and each time the meter slows. By contrast, the middle section's theme emerges from the opposite end of the keyboard, although it is to be played *sotto voce*. The whole passage points to the momentary collision of the conscious and unconscious.

These are the kinds of details that fired Schumann's poetic imagination. He preferred programmatic music that would allow the critic in him to wax poetic when warranted, as when he writes of Louis Spohr's Fourth Symphony, "Die Weihe der Töne," that "In order to describe this symphony well to one who has not heard it, one should give the subject a poetical form for the third time; for the poet owes his

**Example 3.4** Moscheles, 12 "Characteristic" Études, op. 95, no. 11 ("Dream"), mm. 119–129

inspired thanks once more for the art with which Spohr has translated his words into music."[29] However, if a composition promised poetic fulfillment but failed to deliver it, Schumann had no problem complaining. In a review of Julius Schaeffer's three *Songs without Words*, op. 4, Schumann explained that "There are secret states of the soul for which a written indication from the composer can lead to faster comprehension. [For this he] should be gratefully acknowledged." However, he believed that it would have been better for Schaeffer to omit his titles of "Ocean Calm," "Am I Dreaming? No, I Wake," and "Melancholy" altogether, as they were too affected and, in the case of the second, tasteless.[30]

Piecing together a composite picture of Schumann's programmatic aesthetics proves difficult, in large part because he judged each work he reviewed on its own merits. He wrote nothing comparable in scope to, say, Berlioz's "On Imitation in Music." Nevertheless, patterns do appear, and it seems that the criteria Schumann used to review the work of other composers were the same that he used to guide his own overall compositional approach. These include:

- An avoidance of a prose program;
- The allowance of specific extra-musical references;

- The use of good poetry and literature;
- A characteristic basis;
- The intersection of musical and poetic content;
- Respect for the imagination of the listener.

## Schumann and the programmatic piano cycle

In the late 1820s, Schumann sketched out material for at least three string quartets and wrote more than a dozen songs, and early in the next decade he began the Symphony in G minor (of which he completed two movements) and the first movement of a piano concerto. But he published none of this material. Instead, during the 1830s he released compositions exclusively for solo piano. That focus would change in 1840, however, when he married the pianist Clara Wieck. That year he composed over one hundred Lieder (German art songs); in 1841 came a slew of symphonic works; the next year was devoted to chamber music; 1843 saw the completion of his secular oratorio, *Das Paradies und die Peri* (*Paradise and the Peri*). Beginning about 1844, when he moved from Leipzig to Dresden, until his death in 1856, he would produce piano music, songs, choral and symphonic works, and chamber music in roughly equal measure.

The 1830s also marked his most intense period of programmatic composition. As Table 3.3 shows, the vast majority of his piano music from the period bears at least some type of programmatic trace. *Papillons* (*Butterflies*), the *Davidsbündlertänze* (*Dances of the League of David*), *Carnaval*, *Kinderscenen* (*Scenes from Childhood*), and *Kreisleriana* sport titles that go beyond the characteristic. Yet Schumann employed these as well, particularly in publications from later in the decade, such as the *Arabeske*, *Blumenstück* (*Flower Piece*), *Humoreske*, and the *Nachtstücke* (*Night Pieces*). The two books of "Paganini" Études, the *Études symphoniques* (originally bearing the more explicit title, *Études of a Symphonic Character*), and the *Concert sans orchestre* can also be viewed as characteristic, given their claims of extreme virtuosity and symphonic grandeur and the generic mismatch spelled out in their titles. Even the Piano Sonata in F♯ minor features a slow movement titled "Aria," a characteristic feature that may also reflect the influence of Beethoven's Piano Sonata in A♭ major, op. 110. The *Fantasiestücke* pull double-duty: the title is characteristic enough (*Fantasy Pieces*), but Schumann probably employed the title as an homage to E.T.A. Hoffmann, whose *Fantasiestücke in Callot's Manier* included *Kreisleriana*, but also featured a preface by none other than Jean Paul (see below).

Schumann's piano music from the 1830s also shies away from the kind of explicit links between literary narrative and musical event that Berlioz used in the *Symphonie*

**Table 3.3** *The referential spectrum of Schumann's piano compositions, opp. 1–23*

| Opus | Title | Characteristic(s) |
|------|-------|-------------------|
| 1 | "Abegg" Variations | D, G |
| 2 | *Papillons* | A, E, G |
| 3 | "Paganini" Études | B, G |
| 4 | Intermezzi | A, E, F |
| 5 | *Impromptus sur une romance de Clara Wieck* | F, G |
| 6 | *Davidsbündlertänze* | A, C, D, E, F, G |
| 7 | Toccata | [B] |
| 8 | Allegro | |
| 9 | *Carnaval* | A, B, C, D, E, F |
| 10 | "Paganini" Études | B, G |
| 11 | Sonata in F♯ minor | B, D |
| 12 | *Fantasiestücke* | [A,] B, C |
| 13 | *Études symphoniques* | B |
| 14 | *Concert sans orchestre* | [B,] G |
| 15 | *Kinderscenen* | B, C |
| 16 | *Kreisleriana* | A, E |
| 17 | Fantasy | A, G |
| 18 | *Arabeske* | B, E |
| 19 | *Blumenstück* | B, E |
| 20 | *Humoreske* | B, E |
| 21 | *Noveletten* | [A,] C, E, F |
| 22 | Sonata in G minor | |
| 23 | *Nachtstücke* | B |

Key
A. Literary reference(s)
B. Characteristic title
C. Programmatic title or event
D. (Auto)biographical reference(s)
E. Inter-work reference (i.e., cycle)
F. Extra-work reference, Schumann
G. Extra-work reference, not Schumann

*fantastique* and *Harold en Italie*. More often, Schumann uses explicit titles, narrative patterns, and other depictive techniques derived from his favorite authors without realizing specific episodes in any concrete way. *Kreisleriana*, for instance, evokes Hoffmann's literary style through wild mood swings and non-sequiturs, but it makes no attempt to recreate a blow-by-blow narrative of a specific novel, character, or situation by Hoffmann. Paradoxically, it is the "strangeness" of Schumann's musical narrative – his frequent recourse to ideas like "Witz" and the fragment, or his extensive

Jean-Paulian digressions – that often challenges the narrative of the literary model.[31] And to muddy the waters even further, much of his non-programmatic music, such as the piano sonatas, develop along the same "dysfunctional" lines.

Furthermore, behind many of the titles lurk more personal stories, literary allusions, or both. Opus 1 is a case in point. The theme comprises the notes A–B♭ (i.e., the letter "B" in German)–E–G–G. Schumann was acquainted with the pianist Meta Abegg, whom he met in Heidelberg in 1830, so the work has autobiographical meaning. Yet he dedicated it to a fictitious "Comtesse Pauline d'Abegg," perhaps as a type of literary fantasy, or like Goethe's Werther, to hide what might have been an infatuation for the real Madame Abegg. While Abegg was a passing figure for Schumann, his love for Clara leaves a stamp on several compositions: Schumann credited her as composer of the theme of his op. 5, even though he apparently composed it; and elements of her "Scène fantastique: Le Ballet des revenants," the fourth piece from her *Quatre pièces caractéristiques*, op. 5, feature in the fifth movement of his Sonata in F♯ minor. Similarly, the second movement of the *Concert sans orchestre* varies a theme by her that is no longer extant. The *Novelletten* also have strong ties to Clara, with the final piece featuring a "Stimme aus der Ferne" ("Distant Voice"), which in turn was based on Clara's "Notturno," op. 6, no. 2 – material which had also been featured in the first movement of the Fantasy. At the same time, there is a streak of irony embedded in the title of the *Novelletten* that contradicts this set as an offering to his secret fiancée: a Schumannian neologism which might be translated as "short short-stories," they are the longest of his piano cycles and mask any literary associations.[32]

What are some important sources for Schumann's extreme intertextuality, frequent red herrings, and relentless vacillation? It is not that his approach to program music is necessarily much different than that of his contemporaries Berlioz and, slightly later, Liszt, but rather that his source material is different: aphoristic, allusive, and deconstructive. For while Schumann would confront Goethe (*Hermann und Dorothea*), Schiller (*Die Braut von Messina*), and Shakespeare (*Julius Caesar*) in an impressive string of symphonic overtures from 1851, in the 1830s he was far more influenced by authors such as E.T.A. Hoffmann and especially Jean Paul Friedrich Richter.[33] Like Schumann, Hoffmann had been both author and composer, and Schumann was particularly drawn to Hoffmann's character, Johannes Kreisler, a musical genius who suffers from an "over-excitable spirit" and a "fatally inflammable imagination," and who is "tossed back and forth by his inner visions and dreams as though on an eternally stormy sea."[34] (In his Variations, op. 9, from 1854, Johannes Brahms would show a similar commitment to Hoffmann and Schumann by labeling each variation either "Kr[eisler]" or "B[rahms]" in the manner of Schumann's *Davidsbündlertänze*, although these ascriptions did not appear in print.)

The oeuvre of Jean Paul (as he is commonly known) was even more foundational, as it nourished Schumann's compositional, critical, and aesthetic profiles. One straightforward adoption Schumann made from his literary mentor is the splitting of the self into multiple, though still related, personalities: Schumann seems to have modeled Florestan and Eusebius after Vult and Walt, twin brothers who appear in Jean Paul's four-volume novel *Flegeljahre*, published in 1804 and 1805. (Other linked characters from this and Jean Paul's other hefty novels include Albano–Schoppe, Siebenkäs–Leibgeber, Gustav–Fenk, and Flamin–Viktor – all documented by Schumann in his diary as early as 1828.)[35] Schumann also latched on to certain structural cues. As Erika Reiman has noted in an exemplary study on the correspondences between writer and composer, both artists share a love of digressions that are "definitive and deconstructive – as well as surprisingly frequent."[36] This unusual literary approach helps to explain Schumann's attraction to the fragmentary and the anomalous, as well as his tendency to defamiliarize the ordinary and employ ciphers in his compositions.

A clear example of how this process works in a relatively stable environment is the "Florestan" movement from *Carnaval*. As seen in Example 3.5, Florestan's music is unpredictable, exploding with a violent turning figure in one measure and cooling off in the next. The dance, probably a waltz, is metrically undone, and the harmony luxuriates in dissonant ninth / diminished seventh chords, unstable dominant sevenths, and second inversion tonics. At m. 9, however, a scalar figure materializes out of thin air, but is swatted back by the turning figure, which responds even more emphatically than before, jumping up two octaves before descending down to its usual register. The scalar figure then makes a second attempt at m. 19. Here it is more successful, at which point Schumann / Florestan seems to recognize it, for "(Papillon?)" appears in the score. The reference could mean many things: a connection between the dances of the two piano cycles; the composer's acknowledgment of how far he has come aesthetically in only three years; that Florestan, butterfly-like, is in the midst of transformation – in fact, his turning figure is a transformation of Eusebius's main theme from the previous movement; or perhaps Schumann is simply attempting to illustrate in music how dreams work in the real world – as momentary flashes of insight that always leave room for further reflection, analysis, and skepticism. Indeed, as a musical recollection, Florestan's is far more sophisticated and realistic than Moscheles's attempt in his eleventh "Characteristic" Study.

Florestan's dream is a relatively straightforward case because it is explicitly referenced by the composer, albeit tentatively. This happens rarely in Schumann's piano music from the period. The "Abegg" theme materializes suddenly in the sixth intermezzo of op. 4, adding to an already thick web of inter- and extra-work references, yet Schumann offers no help in discerning its appearance. A melody from Beethoven's *An die ferne Geliebte* interrupts the coda of the Fantasy's first

**Example 3.5** Schumann, *Carnaval*, "Florestan," mm. 7–24

movement, but the only clue Schumann gives to its potential meaning comes in the form of an epigraph by Friedrich Schlegel.

The intertextual, characteristic, and programmatic richness of Schumann's piano music explains the challenges he faced in getting his work accepted critically and publicly in the 1830s. When the powerful music critic Ludwig Rellstab had trouble navigating Schumann's "Abegg" Variations in a review published in 1832, the composer preemptively wrote to the reviewer to guide him through *Papillons*, op. 2, which had just appeared in print. Schumann admits that the thread binding Jean Paul and his op. 2 "is barely visible to the naked eye," but offers a simple solution:

> [You] will recall that the final scene in *Flegeljahre* with its masquerade – Walt – Vult – masks – Wina [the love interest of both brothers, but who loves Walt] – Vult dancing – exchange of masks – confessions – anger – revelations – hurrying away – final scene, and then the brother leaving. I have often turned over the final page, for the ending seemed to me merely a new beginning – I was barely aware of being at the piano, and in this way one butterfly after another came into being.[37]

Manuscript evidence confirms that Schumann did in fact fashion *Papillons* according to events of the ball scene from Jean Paul's novel.[38] Why, then, did he not disseminate this information – cryptic as it remains – beyond a small circle of acquaintances? Such a bald program was off-putting to him, as it robbed the listener's own propensity for poetic invention. Moreover, that same listener should be well versed enough in Schumann's musico-literary world to make such connections. Finally, to have given such detail would likely have overshadowed other aspects of the work, such as the generic subterfuge of the ubiquitous waltz or the complex transformations of melody across the work's twelve movements – after all, he presented the composition as *Butterflies*, not *Walt, Vult, and Winna*.

Alongside *Carnaval*, the *Davidsbündlertänze* best illustrate the complexities of Schumann's poetic piano music. (The opus numbers are misleading, as the *Davidsbündlertänze* come from 1837, after *Carnaval*, the *Fantasiestücke*, and the Fantasy.) The title refers to Schumann's *League of David*, which the composer brought before the attention of the reading public in late 1833. Named in honor of King David, the biblical musician and author of the Book of Psalms and modeled after similar quasi-fictional, semi-secretive groups by Friedrich Schlegel and E.T.A. Hoffmann, Schumann's league acted as a bulwark against musical Philistanism. Florestan, Eusebius, and Master Raro were members, as were select confidants including Clara, Stephen Heller, and Mendelssohn.

According to the title of the first edition, the *Davidsbündlertänze* were composed by Florestan and Eusebius – Schumann's name appeared nowhere. Instead, an "Old Saying" ("Alter Spruch") graced the cover: "In every age / Is pleasure bound up with pain: / Remain devoted to pleasure and be / Courageous in pain." There was nothing old about this epigraph – Schumann wrote it. But even before a reader turned to the first page of the music, the composer had engineered two significant riddles.

It turns out that only four of the eighteen movements are composed by Florestan and Eusebius (see Table 3.4); each of the remaining fourteen bears either the signature "F." or "E." But Schumann does not stop there, for the first dance begins with a "motto by C[lara] W[ieck]" taken from the mazurka of her *Soirées musicales*, op. 6. Yet this motto functions more as compositional motivator than theme, since after the proclamation it makes only the briefest of appearances in the third movement of Book 1 and seventh of Book 2.

Indeed, the real drama of the *Davidsbündlertänze* follows the interplay of the two brothers. Florestan generally lives up to his reputation as a firebrand, whom Eusebius contrasts with meditative and – initially, at least – subversive contributions. His first solo number, for instance, immediately challenges the priority of dance (see Example 3.6) by its metric counterpoint. The left hand continues to prioritize the preceding movement's 3/4 pulse, although the long-short rhythm diminishes its waltz character. The right hand, however, unfolds in the compound duple meter of 6/8. The result is not only a suppression of dance music altogether, but that Eusebius is out of sync, or at odds, with himself. In fact, his notation suggests a separate inner voice that is two eighth notes behind the downbeat. This rhythmic and metric complexity – discernible across the whole of Schumann's, and,

**Table 3.4** *Schumann,* Davidsbündlertänze, *op. 6, structure*

| Book, Mvt. | "Composer" | Direction | Key |
|---|---|---|---|
| I, 1 | F. & E. | Lively | G |
| I, 2 | E. | Heartfelt | b |
| I, 3 | F. | With humor. Somewhat outrageously | G |
| I, 4 | F. | Impatiently | b |
| I, 5 | E. | Simple | D |
| I, 6 | F. | Very brisk and insular | d → D → d |
| I, 7 | E. | Not fast. With extremely strong feeling | g → A♭ → g |
| I, 8 | F. | Crisp | C |
| I, 9 | [F.] | Lively | → C |
| II, 1 | F. | Ballad-like. Very brisk | d → D |
| II, 2 | E. | Simple | b → D |
| II, 3 | F. | With humor | b → G → e → E |
| II, 4 | F. & E. | Wild and jolly | b → B → b → B |
| II, 5 | E. | Tender and singing | E♭ |
| II, 6 | F. & E. | Crisp | B♭ → E♭ → B♭ |
| II, 7 | [F. & E.] | With good humor | G → D → b |
| II, 8 | F. & E. | As from a distance | B → F? → B → b → |
| II, 9 | [E.] | Not fast | → C |

**Example 3.6** Schumann, *Davidsbündlertänze*, Book I, no. 2, mm. 1–8

later, Brahms's, output – also accounts for the ambiguous segmentation of the first phrase, which might be parsed (2+2)+(2+1+1), (2+2)+(1+2+1), or (2+2)+(1+3). At this point it might be safe to assume that this procedure is unique to Eusebius, but the next time it appears, in the first movement of Book II, Florestan is the instigator. In the first book, Eusebius is also more harmonically adventurous, as in the unprepared A♭-major first inversion chord at m. 12 and elsewhere in the fifth

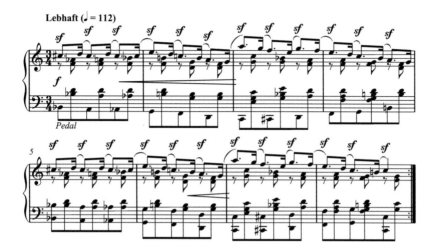

**Example 3.7** Schumann, *Davidsbündlertänze*, Book I, no. 9, mm. 1–8

movement, and the wedge-like chromatic expansion of the left hand in the outer sections of movement seven.

Indeed, Florestan remains composed harmonically for almost the whole of Book I. However, Schumann prefaces movement nine with the observation: "At this point Florestan stopped and his lips quivered with sadness." There is no explanation for this event, but the effect is palpable: As Example 3.7 shows, Florestan presents a manneristic movement that is as obsessive – note, for instance, the overdone *sforzando* markings – as it is strange. The first section, mm. 1–8, forces a surprise cadence in C major, while the middle section, mm. 9–16, becomes completely unmoored harmonically before the opening section returns without alteration (mm. 17–24). A nine-bar coda[39] explores even stranger harmonic territory before giving up and settling on the "home" key of C major.

This is a surprising conclusion to the first book, since C major was neither the original key of the work nor a significant way station for any of the intervening seven movements. And while the second book features more collaboration between Florestan and Eusebius, C major is referenced only in the final movement. This, too, is preceded by a remark from the omniscient Schumann: "Eusebius considered the following [movement] to be completely superfluous; at the same time, though, his bliss shone [*sprach*] through his eyes." The movement begins with a dominant chord in the right hand over a tonic pedal in the left, and proceeds to re-establish the now long-forgotten waltz, subsume the "distant voice" of the previous movement, and unambiguously cement the work's final home key as C major (see Example 3.8).

C major thus ends both books, which began in G major and D minor, respectively. The final destination of Book I is forced; in fact, Florestan begins its last movement

**Example 3.8** Schumann, *Davidsbündlertänze*, Book II, no. 9, mm. 41–59

**Example 3.9** Schumann, *Davidsbündlertänze*, Book II, no. 7, mm. 1–8

with E♭ major in his sights (recall Example 3.7) before correcting to C major via its dominant seventh at m. 2. The lead-up to C major at the end of Book II is more gradual and collaborative. It is first referenced in the third section (mm. 25–56; a trio?) of movement six, although it parries poorly with E♭ major, the key that closes the section. The awkwardness continues into the next movement (Example 3.9), where a dominant seventh in third inversion arrests the motion of an already metrically challenged passage, which only really regains its footing when the "Clara Wieck" motive (mm. 7–8) is invoked. A C major harmony makes a brief appearance as Neapolitan in the closing drama of the eighth movement (mm. 90–97) – a movement that features recollections from the first two movements from Book I. The ninth movement, although deemed superfluous by Eusebius (an unusual judgment coming from him), handily accounts for the unfinished harmonic business of the earlier movements. The progressive tonality toward C major of the *Davidsbündlertänze* is not surprising, however, given that it is a paean to Clara Wieck, whom Schumann perennially associated with that purest of keys.

Wieck, Schumann's most important critic, confessed several times that she did not understand the *Davidsbündlertänze*. Yet he held out hope, for he believed that programmatic meaning could be discerned by or revealed to the executant long after the process of composing the music had finished. "In der Nacht," the fifth piece from the *Fantasiestücke*, op. 12, is the best-documented case: "I found, to my delight," wrote Schumann to Clara,

> that it contained the story of "Hero and Leander" in it. You probably know it. Leander swims through the sea to his beloved every night, and she waits in the lighthouse with a burning torch to show him the way. It's a beautiful, old, romantic legend. When I play [*In der Nacht*] I always think of this image – first, he plunges into the sea – she calls – he answers – he swims through the waves and reaches land successfully – now the cantilena when they are in each other's arms – then, when he has to leave again, and they can't part – until night enshrouds everything in darkness . . . Do tell me whether you think this image suits the music.[40]

Once Schumann recognizes the literary association, he cannot let it go. Notably, the music did not create the story, but called it out of him during performance. But the specificity of this recollection explains the reason why Schumann kept it between him and Clara. His version was of two lovers separated, "a beautiful, romantic story." But had he called the movement "Hero and Leander," it not only would have disrupted the programmatic / characteristic balance of the eight *Fantasiestücke*, but listeners might have attempted to map more contemporary versions of the story onto the music. In Franz Grillparzer's tragedy *Des Meeres und der Liebe Wellen* (*Waves of the Ocean and of Love*) from 1831, Leander dies trying to reach Hero, who in turn dies of grief. Their fate is the same in Schiller's ballad of 1801, although here Hero drowns herself in the same sea that claimed her lover.

In fact, Schumann found himself confused by Julius Rietz's Overture to "Hero und Leander," op. 11, which Mendelssohn premiered at Leipzig's Gewandhaus in April 1841. The orchestral work begins with a long introduction (*Adagio sostenuto*) in D minor that features a prominent solo clarinet part, moves into a stormy *Allegro molto e vivace* in the same key, and concludes triumphantly in the relative major. Schumann wrote in a review of the published four-hand piano arrangement that while everyone knew Musaeus Grammaticus's fable, Schumann himself was embarrassed to say that he could not map the conclusion of Rietz's portrayal onto the end of the story. No matter, he concludes, for "such elated sublimity sounds from the coda that we need not grumble further, but rather convey our highest respects to the artist [Rietz]."[41]

Schumann could pass such a judgment with a clean conscience because he believed that Rietz's composition was musically sound.[42] And while, in his opinion, music and literature operated dialectically, with each informing and deepening the artistic quality of the other, programmatic elements could never substitute for musical craftsmanship. In 1835 he had cautioned about the over-investment of the artist in his work: "So let the artist keep his travails to himself. If we could see the process whereby every work comes into being, and trace it to its very origin, we would meet with some appalling things."[43] The irony here is that Schumann invested so much of himself – personality, experience, memory, influence – in his music from the same period that it practically begs to be unpacked along the lines which he himself took such pains to conceal.

   About the same time that Schumann started to move toward other, potentially more accessible genres – such as song, symphony, and chamber music – Berlioz quit composing independent programmatic instrumental music altogether. Instead, he subsumed the experiments of his early symphonies into the fabric of opera and oratorio. To be sure, each new composition continued to be shaped by its poetic frame, but it no longer exclusively relied on programmatic effects. Yet while the heyday of their interest in program music was behind them by about 1840, and while they differed significantly in their approach to handling issues of form, expression, and tradition, both Berlioz and Schumann would become important figures around which the controversies of the 1850s would rage.

## Chapter 4

# Liszt and the symphonic poem

In February 1848, the celebrated pianist Franz Liszt assumed his duties full time as Kapellmeister at Weimar, the capital of the Grand Duchy of Saxe-Weimar. Over the previous decade, Liszt had enjoyed some of his most important artistic successes in Paris, Vienna, Berlin, London, Pest, St. Petersburg, and even Constantinople; thus his decision to move to a small town of around twelve thousand citizens must have struck many of his contemporaries as a demotion. But Weimar's physical size was in inverse proportion to its reputation, as the city could boast of an illustrious group of philosophers, writers, and musicians – including Johann Gottfried Herder, Friedrich Schiller, Johann Wolfgang von Goethe, Johann Sebastian Bach, and Johann Nepomuk Hummel – who had transformed the cultural landscape of Europe in the eighteenth and early nineteenth centuries.

In the course of giving well over one thousand concerts since the late 1830s, Liszt had established himself as an unparalleled virtuoso pianist. By retiring from the hectic life of the concert performer and settling into a routine of composing, conducting, and teaching at Weimar, however, he inaugurated a self-described period of "collection and creation" that he hoped would not only turn Weimar into a "New Athens," but also put him on par with the cultural elite of the city's illustrious past. Indeed, by the time he left Weimar for Rome in late 1861 to begin yet another phase in his professional life, Liszt had produced most of his best-known works: the definitive versions of the "Paganini" and "Transcendental" Études, the *Harmonies poétiques et religieuses*, the first two books of the *Années de pèlerinage*, the Piano Sonata in B minor, the *Faust* and "Dante" Symphonies, and a dozen symphonic poems. Yet no less important is how many of these compositions also document his wide-ranging exploration of how to effect an ideal unification of poetry and music – in other words, how to compose programmatically. His output, and to a lesser extent that of Richard Wagner and select students, comprise the core repertory of German program music at mid-century.

## From overture to symphonic poem

During the late 1820s and the first half of the 1830s, Liszt was based in Paris, where he got to know Hector Berlioz, Frédéric Chopin, Heinrich Heine, Victor Hugo, Felix Mendelssohn, and other important artistic figures. During a series of travels throughout southern Europe in the second half of the decade, Liszt came to discover ways in which the composer–pianist might profit from an investment in the poetic. One resulting experimental composition was an *Album d'un voyageur* (*Album of a Traveler*), a musical travelogue of mostly Swiss locales divided into books of "Impressions and Poetry [*poésies*]," "Melodic Flowers of the Alps," and "Paraphrases." When Liszt published these nineteen pieces in 1842, he prefaced the heterogeneous collection with a long account of his compositional motivations and methods (see Text Box 4.1). The project's proto-programmatic underpinnings are undeniable: Liszt imagines "a series of pieces which, although not restricted to any conventional form, or fitted to any special design, will nevertheless by their appropriate rhythm, movement, and melody, reveal the reveries, passions, or reflections to which they owe their inspiration."

### Text Box 4.1  Franz Liszt, Preface to *Album d'un Voyageur* (1842)

I have recently travelled through many new countries, have seen many different places, and visited many a spot hallowed by history and poetry; I have felt that the varied aspects of nature, and the different incidents associated with them, did not pass before my eyes like meaningless pictures, but that they evoked profound emotions within my soul; that a vague but direct affinity was established between them and myself, a real, though indefinable understanding, a sure but inexplicable means of communication, and I have tried to give musical utterance to some of my strongest sensations, some of my liveliest impressions.

As soon as I began to work, my recollections intensified; the various images and ideas combined naturally in order; I continued to write, and soon, although I had started without any definite plan, a considerable part of the first year was disposed of, and I had sketched out the plan and the disposition for the entire work.

It will be in two parts.

The first will contain a series of pieces which, although not restricted to any conventional form, or fitted to any special design, will nevertheless by their appropriate rhythm, movement, and melody, reveal the reveries, passions, or reflections to which they owe their inspiration ...

The intrinsic and poetic meaning of things, the inherent ideal of everything, seems to manifest itself preeminently in such artistic creations as, by their beauty of form, give rise to emotions and ideas in the soul. Although music is the least plastic of the arts, it nevertheless possesses a form of its own, and has not unreasonably been defined as an architecture of

**Text Box 4.1  (continued)**

sounds. But even as architecture, besides being in style Tuscan, Ionian, Corinthian, etc., expresses an idea which is either pagan or Christian, sensuous or mystical, war-like or commercial, so music, in perhaps even greater measure, has its hidden meaning, undivined by the majority, it is true; for where a work of art is concerned the majority does not rise beyond a comparative criticism of externals, and a facile appreciation of a certain superficial skill.

As instrumental music progresses, develops, and emerges from its early limitations, it will tend more and more to bear the imprint of this ideal, which constitutes the perfection of the plastic arts. It will cease to be a mere combination of sounds and will become a poetic language more apt than poetry itself, may be, at expressing that within our souls which transcends the common horizon, all that eludes analysis, all that moves in hidden depths of imperishable desire and infinite intuition.

Convinced of this and with this tendency in mind, I undertook the work published here. It is written for the few rather than for the many – not ambitious of success, but of the approval of that minority which conceives art as having other uses than the beguiling of idle hours, and asks more from it than the futile distraction of a passing entertainment.

**Source:** Translation adapted from *Franz Liszts Musikalische Werke*, ser. II, vol. IV, ed. José Vianna da Motta (Leipzig: Breitkopf & Härtel, 1916), 3.

Liszt's general appeal to the poetic and literary would only intensify during the 1840s, and may in fact help explain Liszt's decision to settle in Weimar, whose poetic pedigree was unparalleled. According to Detlef Altenburg, Liszt saw in his Kapellmeister position an opportunity "to achieve a synthesis of great literature and music" that had materialized only piecemeal during his hectic concert years.[1] Indeed, the search for this synthesis undoubtedly marks a continuation of his earlier efforts in this vein, as the preface to the *Album d'un voyageur* clearly attests. But the synthesis was as much for the enrichment of the community as it was for himself. As early as 1844 he had already imagined a Weimar in which poet–musicians would flourish, noting that "under [Goethe's patron] Grand Duke Karl-August, Weimar was a new Athens. Let us frankly and openly rekindle the traditions of Karl-August."[2]

A great deal of "New Athens" had been built upon the foundations of the court theater, which had been in decline since Goethe ceased to be its director in 1817. Liszt imagined its return to glory through a medium secondary to Goethe: opera. On 16 February 1849 he directed Richard Wagner's *Tannhäuser*, the second opera to be presented to his new employers since arriving less than a year earlier. Liszt probably programmed the work as much to score political points as to promote an under-valued artistic product, since the locus of Wagner's opera takes place eighty-eight kilometers from Weimar, in and around the early eleventh-century Wartburg castle, a structure which had long stood as a symbol of the Grand Duchy's historical and cultural importance: the young St. Elisabeth of Hungary had resided there in the early thirteenth century; under its protection, Martin Luther, recently excommunicated from the Catholic Church, translated the New Testament from Greek into German three hundred years later; and purportedly in 1207, Minnesänger (Minstrel Singers) congregated in its halls to compete in a renowned song contest, which Wagner fancifully recreated in Act II of his opera.

A politically savvy choice, to be sure, yet *Tannhäuser* was but one event in a very busy first season for the pianist-turned-conductor, which included performances of operas by Mozart, Gluck, and Rossini, among others. Indeed, Liszt could hardly have foreseen the extent to which Wagner would become a major force in shaping the profile of his program music and its theoretical bases over the next decade. As Liszt saw in Wagner a potentially towering artistic citizen of Weimar's New Athens, he promoted the exiled composer as conductor, transcriber, and critic during his entire tenure as Kapellmeister. *Tannhäuser* was the first to benefit from Liszt's three-pronged propagandistic assault: Within a year of Liszt conducting the opera, he programmed further performances of its overture, which he also arranged for solo piano in a brilliant fashion, and introduced it to Paris – where he and Wagner hoped to see it produced – via an analysis that appeared in the press.

After conducting the world premiere of Wagner's *Lohengrin* in 1850, Liszt expanded his *Tannhäuser* essay, wrote up a similarly lengthy treatment of *Lohengrin*, and published the two under the title *Lohengrin et Tannhaüser de Richard Wagner* in 1851. Special attention was given to *Tannhäuser*'s overture, which Liszt praised for its double function:

> This great overture forms a symphonic whole by itself, so that we may consider it as an independent composition, separate from the opera that precedes it. The two leading thoughts, which are developed in it, ere they blend in their tremendous confluence, clearly express their entire character, the one with fury, the other with an irresistible influence, absorbing all into itself. These motives are so characteristic that they contain in themselves all the striking sense demanded by the musical thoughts, entrusted purely to the instrumentation. So vividly do they depict the emotions, which they express, that one needs no explanatory text to recognize their nature; not once is it necessary to know the words that are adapted to them afterwards.[3]

As Wagner had done about a decade earlier (see Chapter 2), Liszt identifies several criteria by which an overture can emancipate itself from the subsequent opera, in turn becoming an organic, wholly independent symphonic entity. Motives must be characteristic (e.g., religious, sensual, plaintive) and they must be arranged in ways that create meaningful contrast, such as the religious theme's interruption of the bacchanal.

Choice instrumentation can also heighten motivic variety and affective contrast, as when Wagner paints solemn colors with clarinets, horns, and bassoons at the opening versus the subsequent flittering, shimmering timbres of the Venusberg's divided violins. However these motives are arranged and orchestrated, their presence serves to depict emotions or striking images, such as sensual passion or sirens, and not events. In this sense, the overture becomes a poetic product drawing on symphonic foundations. Later in the analysis, Liszt puts this new type of overture – which more accurately, he asserts, should be called a "symphonic poem" – in a historical context:

> in speaking of the overture . . . one could not desire of a symphonic poem that it should be written more consistently with the rules of classical form, or that it should have a more perfect logic in the exposition, development and solution of its premises. Its arrangement is just as precise, at the same time that it is richer, than that of the best models in this kind.[4]

The timing of Liszt's analysis of the *Tannhäuser* Overture was not coincidental, as he was beginning the process of transforming his own overtures into symphonic poems. (Liszt's only completed opera, *Don Sanche*, premiered in 1825 and was quietly forgotten.) Paralleling his compositional output, his literary output would explode over the next decade, with essays appearing on Frédéric Chopin, John Field, Robert Franz, Mozart, Clara Schumann, Pauline Viardot-Garcia, and compositions by Beethoven, Gluck, Mendelssohn, Meyerbeer, Schubert, and Wagner, to name only a handful. Liszt would frequently use these composers and their works as springboards to advance a social or artistic agenda, such as program music. Thus he depicts Robert Schumann as one of the first to break down the wall separating music and literature and to bridge a rapprochement from both sides: As writer "He belongs to those who transformed musical criticism into a literary object," and as composer he

> completely grasped the significance of the program and gave the most splendid examples of its employment. He admirably succeeded in summoning forth musically the effect that the object portrayed and realized through his title would have made on us in reality, by grasping the object with his fine poetic side and thus fulfilling the true requirements of the program.[5]

By the time this essay on Schumann appeared in 1855, Liszt had a clearer idea of program music's definitions, dimensions, and suitable applications than when he grappled with the implications of Wagner's overture a half decade earlier. Indeed, he had completed several of his own symphonic poems, but his concern for their being misunderstood by audiences and critics helps account for the appearance that same year of his most extensive treatment of the subject, *Berlioz und seine "Harold-Symphonie"* (*Berlioz and His "Harold" Symphony*).[6] Divided into four parts, the essay begins with an assessment of the controversies that have dogged Berlioz since even before Liszt befriended him in December 1830. A composer–poet who thinks independently rather than follows rules blindly, Berlioz materializes as a champion of progress against unforgiving orthodox voices; and, like Beethoven, as an artist who, in his pursuit of the beautiful, operates outside of the mainstream by not adhering to a discrete system. The fourth section concerns the *Harold* Symphony itself (see Chapter 3). Part III puts program music in a historical perspective, in which Liszt cites precedents by Beethoven, Mendelssohn, Schumann, and even J.S. Bach. Part II is the aesthetic nerve center of the essay, which, unfortunately, suffers from an abundance of abstruse and contradictory statements. Nevertheless, a few basic points can be adduced:

- Musical form is but one organizing principle among many. Ideally, musical and non-musical forms should fuse and juxtapose dialectically: "Every element, through contact with another, gains new properties. It forfeits old properties, and in exercising another influence in an altered environment adopts a new form, a new name . . . The amalgamation of originally distinct forms will create in art – just like in nature – either phenomena of new beauty or monstrosities, depending on whether a harmonious union brings to life a homogeneous whole or an awkward puzzle" (p. 35).
- "In contrast to so-called classical music . . . in program music, the return, alteration, change, and modulation of motives are caused by their relationship to a poetic idea" (p. 69). Hence the designation "symphonic poem" instead of, say, "poetic symphony," and its position between, yet independent from, the symphony and overture.
- "The rationale and goal of a poem is no longer the representation of a main character's actions, but rather of the affects which play out in his soul. It is far more important to show a hero's disposition than his behavior" (p. 54).[7]
- "Exceptional figures" should be the subject of modern musico-poetic elaboration, since the current, "romantic epoch ["Epos"] . . . depicts its figures as larger than life in both size and situation. [. . . These figures] idealize tendencies that an ordinary human feels and understands, yet less completely, clearly, and spiritually" (p. 55).
- The program is not prescriptive, but rather "a preparatory suggestion of the composer's mental states that led to the creation of his work, as well as the ideas he sought to embody in it" (p. 50).

The essays from the early to mid-1850s lay the groundwork for what Liszt hoped would be the next evolutionary step in programmatic composition – a series of symphonic poems that the Leipzig publisher Breitkopf & Härtel issued between 1856 and 1861. Hence, like Schumann, Liszt is an artist keen on heightening the aesthetic experience by clueing the listener in on a composition's "poetic foundation." He capitalizes on the affective potential of characteristic motives in the Wagnerian overture and their ability to shape formal and dramatic structures. And with Berlioz as forerunner, Liszt reveres but does not always adhere to traditional form, instead letting

**Table 4.1** *Liszt's symphonic poems*

| Title | Date(s) of Composition | Publication | Source(s) |
|---|---|---|---|
| *Ce qu'on entend sur la montagne* | 1847–1856 | 1857 | Victor Hugo |
| *Tasso, Lamento e Trionfo* | 1847–1854 | 1856 | Byron; Goethe, *Torquato Tasso* |
| *Les Préludes* | 1849–1855 | 1856 | Lamartine; Autran |
| *Orpheus* | 1853–1854 | 1856 | Etruscan vase; Gluck, *Orfeo ed Euridice*; Ballanche |
| *Prometheus* | 1850–1855 | 1856 | Herder; Ballanche? |
| *Mazeppa* | 1851–1854 | 1856 | Hugo |
| *Festklänge* | 1853–1861 | 1856; rev. 1861 | – |
| *Héroïde funèbre* | 1849–1850, 1854–1856 | 1857 | Aborted "Revolutionary" Symphony, 1830 |
| *Hungaria* | 1854 | 1857 | Liszt, *Heroischer Marsch in ungarischem Stil* (*c*.1844) |
| *Hamlet* | 1858 | 1861 | Shakespeare; Bogumil Dawison |
| *Hunnenschlacht* | 1857 | 1861 | Wilhelm von Kaulbach |
| *Die Ideale* | 1856–1857 | 1858 | Friedrich Schiller |
| *Von der Wiege bis zum Grabe* | 1881–1882 | 1883 | Mihály Zichy |

the poetic content shape his musical decisions. But as Table 4.1 indicates, Liszt went much further than his predecessors by selecting choice poetic, heroic, and graphic models that crisscrossed geographical lines, historical epochs, and aesthetic intents.

## Symphony and poetry in the symphonic poem

Liszt's *Ce qu'on entend sur la montagne* (*Heard on the Mountain*), occasionally referred to as the "Mountain" Symphony, is a fitting piece to inaugurate the publication of his symphonic oeuvre, as its poetic source, Victor Hugo's poem of the same name, attempts to translate sounds into words. Surveying the landscape from atop a silent mountain, Hugo gradually identifies two competing soundscapes: one seems to emerge from and blend back into its environment with ease, flooding the world with "a deep, ineffable harmony" (l. 19) that makes its way heavenward as a "glorious hymn, from the sea's flow" (l. 37).[8] The competing sound could not be more different. It grows in cacophonous counterpoint, "like hell's rusty hinges turning round" (l. 56), so that "Everything that condemns, blights, and destroys, / Passed in that whirling flood of human noise" (ll. 61–62). Nature has produced the former, Humanity the latter.

In typical fashion, Hugo does not offer a way to resolve this prominent nineteenth-century dialectic. Instead, he concludes (ll. 77–82) with some ontological questions that his aural experience has left him:

> Why are we here, then? I began to ask;
> What can it all mean? What is the soul's task?
> Living, or simply being – which is better?
> And why does God, who alone reads his letter,
> For ever wed in one fatal embrace
> The song of Nature and the sobbing of our race?

The translation of certain images in *Ce qu'on entend sur la montagne* into music is relatively straightforward. Although man-made, the harp allies itself with nature and the religious (ll. 30, 45); Liszt employs the instrument prominently in almost every section of his symphonic poem. The winds, particularly the oboes, play pastoral music at m. 40ff, and Liszt twice flirts with the celestial by dividing the first violins into six separate voices (mm. 527–534, 566–573). However, the trumpet – a symbol of man's bellicose nature (ll. 17–18) – introduces the militant theme at m. 157 that sets the stage for the baroque-inspired "tears and cries" (l. 59) at mm. 227–235. Moreover, the scope of Hugo's poem not only partially excuses the bloat of Liszt's *Ce qu'on entend sur la montagne* (just north of one thousand measures), but also helps to explain the characteristic nature (see Chapter 1) of Liszt's motives and their inability to coalesce into real melodies, save for the hymn discussed below. Hugo describes his environment as one "Where time and space and number fade. / Like some new atmosphere spread and unfurled, / That timeless hymn covered the flooded world" (ll. 24–26). Indeed, the most prominent figure in Liszt's symphonic poem is the rise and fall of the upper neighbor: an unpitched bass drum opens the work with it (mm. 1–2) before the strings give it pitch definition (D–E♭) at m. 3. It remains the head motive for the majestic figure at m. 97, the dissonant compression at m. 157ff, and the hymn at m. 479.

This last theme perhaps offers a reconciliation of the two soundscapes that Hugo does not entertain, a mollification of the severity of the "embrace" between nature and man. As shown in Example 4.1, its five-bar antecedent phrase is composed out of a diatonic transformation of the "wave" motive ("x" at m. 3) and a dramatic, dissonant figure that captures something of humanity's sad condition ("y" at m. 209). Moreover, the conviction of this hymn is underscored by: the tempo designation, Andante religioso; its scoring for tenor and bass trombones, instruments traditionally associated with Christian ritual (cf. the fourth movement of Schumann's Third Symphony, discussed in Chapter 7); and its sonic kinship with the "Pilgrims' Chorus" of Wagner's *Tannhäuser*, whose theme is scored in the

**Example 4.1** Liszt, *Ce qu'on entend sur la montagne*, the hymn (m. 479ff) as merger of nature (m. 3ff; "x") and man (m. 209ff; "y")

overture similarly to Liszt's hymn and whose text (Act I, scene 3) proclaims, "I journey to you, my Jesus Christ, / for you are the pilgrim's hope!" ("Zu dir wall' ich, mein Jesus Christ, / der du des Pilgers Hoffnung bist!")

Despite the symphonic poem's overall "narrative" trajectory from thematic chaos to a modicum of order, the abrupt, indefinite conclusion of Liszt's hymn seems to emphasize the ongoing journey rather than a specific or final destination. In this respect, *Ce qu'on entend sur la montagne* belongs to a handful of programmatic compositions which challenge the teleologically optimistic messages of symphonic compositions like Beethoven's Ninth Symphony or Louis Spohr's Seventh Symphony, subtitled "Irdisches und Göttliches im Menschenleben" ("The Earthly and the Divine in Human Life"), from 1841. Be it the Biedermeier disillusionment of Strauss's *Also sprach Zarathustra*, the religiosity of Guy Ropartz's Third Symphony in E major (1905–1906), with a substantial poem written by the composer, or the tentative *Symphonie liturgique* of Arthur Honegger (1946),[9] the juxtaposition of nature and man in an uncertain world would continue in many different guises long after Liszt.

While *Ce qu'on entend sur la montagne* was apparently designed from the start as a stand-alone overture that gradually morphed into a symphonic poem, much of the material of *Les Préludes* (*The Preludes*) first surfaces in a quartet of choruses with piano accompaniment that Liszt composed in 1844–1845 on texts by Joseph Autran, a poet based in Marseille. Liszt performed the first piece, *Les aquilons* (*The Boreal Winds*), on 6 August 1844 in Autran's hometown, and probably completed the remaining three – *Les flots* (*The Tides*), *La terre* (*The Earth*), and *Les astres* (*The Stars*) – within the year, although he seems never to have performed them. Upon settling in Weimar, Liszt returned to *Les quatre élémens* (*The Four Elements*) – as the choruses were collectively titled – with the goal of orchestrating the piano part. Entrusting this task to his amanuensis August Conradi, Liszt began to consider writing an orchestral composition that would either introduce major themes of the chorus or draw upon them for extended developmental treatment. Thus incipient forms of *Les Préludes* bear the title *The Four Elements* Overture or *Symphony of The Four Elements*. By early 1854, however, the work was definitely called *Les Préludes*, a reference not to poetry by Autran, but by Alphonse de Lamartine, one of the most important influences in Liszt's early professional life.

Lamartine's poem was published in 1823 as the fifteenth item in *Nouvelles méditations poétiques*. Liszt had known the collection and its author well since the early 1830s, when the young pianist was actively shopping around for new ideas on art, politics, and society. One of Liszt's earliest programmatic pieces, the audacious single-movement *Harmonies poétiques et religieuses* (1835), adopts the title of another Lamartine collection from 1830; Liszt significantly expanded this work in the late 1840s and especially early 1850s, precisely the period during which *Les quatre élémens* became *Les Préludes*. While several scholars have challenged the relevance of Lamartine's poem to Liszt's symphonic poem, it is undeniable that Lamartine's style – far more than Hugo's in *Ce qu'on entend sur la montagne* – depends heavily on musical imagery and natural sound creators: harps, bugles, lyres, winds, and birds all pepper the sonic landscape of Lamartine's *Les Préludes*. Moreover, as Anatole Leikin has observed, "A much more substantial issue is the poem's heightened emotional pitch and the intensity of its expressive states: love, fear, passion, despair, futility, misery, joy, desolation, grief, exultation, melancholy."[10] Liszt's preface to his score, while admittedly flabby and obtuse, nevertheless emphasizes the distinct affects pursued by Lamartine in *Les Préludes* while simultaneously arguing for their necessary unity:

> What else is our life but a series of preludes to that unknown Hymn, the first and solemn note of which is intoned by Death? – Love is the flowing dawn of all existence; but what is the fate where the first delights of happiness are not interrupted by some storm, the mortal blast of which dissipates its fine illusions; the fatal lightning of

**Example 4.2** Elaboration of the head motive in Liszt, *Les Préludes*

which consumes its altar, and where in the cruelly wounded soul which, on issuing from one of these tempests, does not endeavor to rest his recollection in the calm serenity of life in the fields? Nevertheless man hardly gives himself up for long to the enjoyment of the beneficent stillness which at first he has shared in Nature's bosom, and when "the trumpet sounds the alarm," he hastens to the dangerous post, whatever the war may be, which calls him to its ranks, in order at last to recover in the combat full consciousness of himself and entire possession of his energy.[11]

This idea of unity in variety accounts for Example 4.2, a three-note head motive that generates all primary and several secondary themes in Liszt's *Les Préludes*. In fact, the transparency of this motive's transformation has made the work a favorite to demonstrate Liszt's technique of thematic transformation ("thematische Arbeit").[12] But while this procedure impresses at the local, melodic level, questions of form often arise when a thematically transformed piece is considered as a whole. Eduard Hanslick, whose aesthetic leanings are dealt with in the next chapter, was convinced that *Les Préludes* was nothing more than a potpourri of superficial variations on a vacuous musical idea

**Table 4.2** *Some forms of Liszt's* Les Préludes

| Location (m.) | Single-movement symphony | Characteristic variations, after Lamartine's poem | Double-exposition sonata without development. Separate thematic and tonal recapitulations | Sonata with parenthetical scherzo. "Love" themes in exposition become bellicose variants in recapitulation |
|---|---|---|---|---|
| 1 | Ia. Introduction | "Birth" | Introduction | Introduction |
| 35 | Ib. Song | "Consciousness" | Exposition I, P1 | |
| 47 | | | | Exposition, P1, "Love" |
| 67 | | "Innocent Love" | | |
| 70 | | | Exposition I, P2 | Exposition, P2, "Love" |
| 109 | II. Tempest | | | Development |
| 160 | | | Exposition II, P1 | |
| 182 | III. Pastorale | | | |
| 200 | | "Hardship, Struggle, Consolation" | Exposition II, P2 | "Inserted Scherzo" |
| 260 | | | Recapitulation, Thematic | |
| 296 | | | Recapitulation, Tonal | |
| 344 | | | | Recapitulation, P1, Variation |
| 370 | | | | Recapitulation, P2, Variation |
| 405 | IV. Coda, quoting mvt. I intro | | | Coda |

guided by a fundamentally flawed, egotistical music aesthetic: "That overambitious urge to infuse each moment with something new, unheard-of, and brilliant in fact disquiets the whole, and comes off as downright dilettantish."[13]

Liszt does tend to create rather than reuse, but Hanslick is on shaky ground in asserting that Liszt is ignorant of the German heritage crystallized by "Haydn, Mozart, Beethoven, and Mendelssohn," especially as regards to form. With a nod to the formally ambiguous finale of Beethoven's Ninth Symphony, *Les Préludes* operates as both symphony and sonata-allegro by utilizing a double-function procedure (see Table 4.2). The former is seen in the symphonic poem's four large sections, in which swapping the traditional character of the first and second movements results in song dominating the first movement and a tempest battering the second. However, these sections can also be read as something closer to Liszt's earlier opera fantasies or as prototype for Strauss's *Don Quixote*, that is, as characteristic, teleological variations that respond to Lamartine's poem.[14]

From the perspective of *Les Préludes* as a single movement, these same delineations can also suggest sonata form. Yet given the relationship among the many melodies of *Les Préludes*, identifying a truly "new" theme proves difficult. One analysis, outlined in the penultimate column of Table 4.2, hears a sonata form taking shape in the first two hundred measures, but using two expositions at the expense of the development. The recapitulation is equally thorny, as its thematic and tonal constituents return at different points. From this perspective, Liszt seems to challenge the idea of the sonata's single-tonic framework.[15] However (see Table 4.2, last column), if the storm scene is heard as the composition's development section, then it might explain why the exposition's two "love" themes return in the recapitulation – following the pastoral excursus of mm. 200–343 – as bellicose transformations. In other words, such a schema profiles its themes as variations conditioned by sonata-form narrative.[16]

In 1852, Liszt had written to the composer, critic, and piano pedagogue Louis Köhler, "all I ask is for permission to let forms be determined by the content . . . It essentially depends on the *What* of the ideas and the *How* of its execution and arrangement – and that always leads us back to the *feeling* and *invention*."[17] Perhaps Liszt ultimately decided on attaching Lamartine's *Les Préludes* to his symphonic work because it opened up the auditor's ability to privilege not a single form, not advance a wholly independent prelude, but rather intercalated affective states and structural events, preludes in the Lamartinian sense: "a sonata of poetry" ("une sonate de poésie").[18] Such was Liszt's aim in all of his mature programmatic music.

## Between mythology and history: Liszt's character studies

Along with the three movements of the *Faust* Symphony, five of Liszt's symphonic poems are, to various degrees, character studies: *Tasso*, *Orpheus*, *Prometheus*, *Mazeppa*, and *Hamlet*. *Orpheus* and *Prometheus* originally hail from Greek mythology, although Liszt's perception of their deeds and value to modern society were decisively colored by contemporary interpretations: in the case of the former, Liszt explains in his preface that his chief motivation was a depiction of Orpheus on an Etruscan vase housed in the Louvre. Yet the composer also admits that Gluck's opera *Orfeo ed Euridice* (1762), which Liszt conducted at Weimar on 16 February 1854, prompted him to compose an overture that would replace Gluck's plain-vanilla original. The ostensibly independent symphonic poem that followed about a year later nevertheless shows vestiges of its earlier function, such as the plaintive violin solo at mm. 84–86, which shows a strong affinity to Gluck's opening scene of personal and group lament at the loss of Euridice.[19] At the same time, Gluck's subject matter – Orpheus's attempt to retrieve his dead bride, Euridice, from the underworld – has little in common with Liszt's focus. Rather, Liszt emphasizes Orpheus's "divine words and songs, and his lyre resounding under the touch of his long and graceful fingers . . . which reveal to humanity the beneficent power of Art, its glorious light and civilizing harmony."[20]

This characterization of Orpheus as an agent of social change bears a strong debt to the social philosopher Pierre-Simon Ballanche, whose ambitious treatise *Essais de palingénésie sociale* sought to

> be the record of the series of births, deaths, and rebirths of social orders through all the centuries of human history . . . The social order is the arena in which humanity progressively overcomes the effects of the Fall. Each age possesses the social institutions commensurate with the stage it marks in the rehabilitation of humanity; social palingenesis is nothing other than the unfolding of the sequence of these ages.[21]

Although Ballanche did not complete the *Essais*, he did publish *Prolégomènes* in 1827 and *Orphée* in 1829, the latter of which Liszt read around 1834. As the most important figure in humanity's prehistory, Orpheus enables the civilized world (i.e., classical Rome). Liszt was clearly drawn to this figure, his admiration evidenced by the numerous citations from Ballanche's *Orphée* that he provided to his mistress, Marie d'Agoult, in a letter of 15 September 1834, including a forerunner to programmatic positions he explicated publicly in the 1850s: like Orpheus, "The poet is the living embodiment of God, of nature, and of humanity!"[22] Indeed, Liszt's famous conclusion to *Orpheus*, Example 4.3, serves multiple functions: as depiction of Orpheus's final ascension into the heavens; as symbol of his demigod-like station; as example of the cultural progress that Orpheus's intervention has inspired in Liszt, a contemporary human artist; and as model for those who would follow him. As Liszt eloquently put it in a letter to Alexander Ritter, *Orpheus* "hovers quite simply between bliss and woe, once again breathing out art's reconciliation."[23]

Ballanche conceived of history as a series of ages in which suffering ("épreuve") and atonement ("expiation") lead to rehabilitation, revolution, and rebirth. In the *Essais de palingénésie sociale*, Prometheus and Orpheus – "those two emblems of emancipation," as Ballanche describes them – bookend the so-called "primordial age," that is, the age before man. In fact, "Prometheus is the necessary forerunner of Orpheus; just as [personal] responsibility is the necessary prerequisite of social evolution, so Orpheus' civilizing mission presupposes the acquisition of responsibility."[24] Prometheus had betrayed Heaven by secretly gifting to humanity stolen fire (and partial prophecy), and for this insubordinate act of generosity, Zeus condemned him to a gruesome, endless punishment: with the immortal Prometheus

**Example 4.3** Liszt, *Orpheus*, mm. 204–215, arr. August Stradal

chained to a rock, an eagle or vulture would greedily feast upon his liver. The next day, with the liver regenerated, the bird would return for another helping. The story had shaped the Western imagination ever since Hesiod recorded it in his *Theogony* in the late eighth century BCE.

Prometheus's defiance against authority, his suffering for his ideals, civilizing contributions to – indeed, arguably the founder of – humanity, and tragic fate made him a popular figure among artists in the late eighteenth and nineteenth centuries: Goethe's ode of 1774 idealized him as a model transgressor; Mary Shelley's *Frankenstein; or, The Modern Prometheus* (1818) involves a scientist who thwarts the laws of nature to create what turns out be a monster; Byron had concluded two years earlier that "Thou art a symbol and a sign / To Mortals of their fate and force" (*Prometheus*, ll. 45–46); and during a lengthy consideration of the symphony and its prospects for modern dramatic music in his polemical *The Artwork of the Future*, Wagner offered a compelling connection between two titans of Western culture: "Like a second Prometheus who fashioned men of clay ('Thon') Beethoven had sought to fashion them of tone. Yet not from 'Thon' or Tone, but from both substances together, must Man, the image of life-giving Zeus, be made."[25]

In short, Prometheus handily straddled both social and artistic spheres, a feature which appealed both to Liszt and to another prominent star in Weimar's cultural constellation, Johann Gottfried Herder (1744–1803). In recasting the story of Prometheus as handed down by Hesiod and especially Aeschylus, Herder sought in *Der entfesselte Prometheus* (*Prometheus Unbound*) to advance his doctrine of *Humanität*, in which the march toward universal reason would eliminate national divisions. Liszt would have found much to his liking in the play, particularly the forms of universalism (as opposed to nationalism), historical struggle, and personal artistic

perseverance that Herder's Prometheus engendered. These elements feature prominently in a set of choruses derived from Herder's thirteen "mythological scenes" that
the composer premiered on 25 August 1850 to a commission by the Weimar court.
These choruses in turn furnished him with material for his symphonic poem
*Prometheus*, completed by 1856, in which Herder's concerns are realized by the transformation of misfortune ("malheur") into glory ("gloire"). In this sense, the arc of the
symphonic poem is similar to *Tasso*, discussed below, but in *Prometheus* the transformation is effected by a fugue – an abstract, archaic technique that Liszt often uses to
depict extreme physical and mental struggle. Indeed, many of Liszt's compositions
from the 1850s – including *Hunnenschlacht*, the "Dante" and *Faust* Symphonies, and
the Sonata in B minor – are bound technically and expressively by fugue, and its
function as a particularly useful programmatic device also, ironically, accounts for its
absence in the majority of his texted religious music from the later decades.

Connections abound in the symphonic poems. Like *Orpheus* and *Prometheus*,
*Mazeppa* and *Tasso* can also be treated as a pair. Both are historical figures of the
early modern period whose lives had been poetically exalted by some of Liszt's favorite
writers. But even without such literary glosses, both figures were compelling as model
artists to a pianist–composer who during the 1850s was fighting for the future direction
of his own art: misunderstood, struggling, ostracized and even persecuted during their
lives, posthumously Tasso and Mazeppa had been rewarded with immortal fame.

The Russian nobleman Ivan Mazepa (1639–1709) enjoyed a meteoric rise during
the latter reign of Tsar Peter the Great, only to be made an enemy of the state – even
today he remains a controversial figure in Russian-Ukrainian history – after forging
an alliance with the empire's enemy, Charles XII of Sweden, in 1708. Voltaire
incorporated Mazepa's defection and subsequent military campaigns into his
*Histoire de Charles XII, Roi de Suède* (*History of Charles XII, King of Sweden*), but
he also filled out Mazepa's prehistory with the following anecdote:

> A Polish gentleman named Mazeppa, born in the palatinate of Podolia . . . had an
> intrigue in his youth with the lady of a Polish gentleman. Having been discov-
> ered, the husband caused him to be bound stark naked upon a wild horse and let
> loose in that condition. The horse, which had been brought out of the Ukraine,
> returned to his own country and carried Mazeppa along with him, half-dead with
> hunger and fatigue. Some of the country people gave him assistance and he lived
> among them for a long time, and distinguished himself in several expeditions
> against the Tartars. The superiority of his knowledge gained him great respect
> among the Cossacks; and with his reputation daily increasing, the Czar found it
> necessary to make him Prince of the Ukraine.[26]

Byron introduces his English poem *Mazeppa*, published in May 1819, with the
preceding description by Voltaire, as well as two other citations from the *Histoire*, in

the original French. While Charles and Mazeppa make camp following their retreat from the disastrous Battle of Poltova, the beaten king requests a story of the Cossack (ll. 1–124). The seventy-year-old Mazeppa obliges, and recounts his affair of fifty years earlier with the seductive Theresa (ll. 125–317), their discovery by her husband's spies (ll. 318–357), Mazeppa's punishment (ll. 358–795), and his rescue by a group of itinerant Cossacks (ll. 796–846), whom Mazeppa would one day rule (ll. 847–859). Byron transforms Mazeppa into a figure that overcomes seemingly insurmountable odds, a man whose superhuman resolve – "No matter," contends Mazeppa, "I have bared my brow / Full in Death's face – before – and now" (ll. 567–568) – makes him worthy to take his place as leader. Suffering is a necessary rite of passage that leads to glory: Theresa's husband, "the vain fool who strove to glut / His rage, refining on my pain, / Sent me forth to the wilderness, / Bound, naked, bleeding, and alone, / To pass the desert to a throne" (ll. 848–852).

The most memorable event (see Figure 4.1) depicted in Byron's poem is Mazeppa's wild ride, which Carl Loewe used to shape his solo-piano tone poem ("Tondichtung"), *Mazeppa*, op. 27, from 1830. In the tradition of the perpetuum mobile, this rondo takes the pianist and listener through a wide range of running and tremolo figures in and around the key of B minor. When the horse dies from

**Figure 4.1**  Eugène Delacroix, *Mazeppa* (1824)

**Example 4.4** Loewe, *Mazeppa*, mm. 271–314, annotated

exhaustion, the coda (mm. 228–314) turns to the agony of the stranded Mazeppa and his last-minute rescue by a group of unnamed people – at least according to the "Explanation for those who are not acquainted with Byron's 'Mazeppa'" on the score's last page. In the coda, the main theme, a written out six-note turn, gradually breaks down (see Example 4.4), supplanted by a figure in the relative major that ascends through the registers of the keyboard. While passing references to the preceding ride remain until the end (see permutations of the "x" theme), there is little doubt that Mazeppa has come out of his ordeal a stronger man.

**Table 4.3** *Compositional chronology of Liszt's* Mazeppa

---

1827: Publication of twelve études, composed a year earlier. The fourth étude in D minor employs a diatonic, three-note motive whose deployment aims to improve a pianist's ability to create a single, unbroken line between the hands. Conventional melody is absent, and the most dissonant harmony is a handful of passing diminished seventh chords that function as altered secondary dominants. Binary form. No programmatic associations.

1839: Publication of twelve *Grandes études*, composed 1837–1839. The three-note motive of the 1827 version functions in no. 4 as accompaniment to a new melody:

The length has more than doubled (77 vs. 170 mm.), and the form has been greatly expanded to a series of variations which are occasionally bridged by cadenzas. No programmatic associations.

1847: Stand-alone piano piece entitled *Mazeppa* published, but composed in 1840. Its structure and set of variations are very similar to the 1839 Etude, but Liszt adds a five-bar introduction and a triumphant, albeit abbreviated, conclusion in D major, over which appears the last line of Hugo's poem, "Et se relève roi!" ("And rises a king!").

1852: Revised versions of the 1839 *Grandes études*, nos. 1–3, 5–12, and 1847 *Mazeppa* published as twelve *Études d'exécution transcendante*. *Mazeppa* now sports a sweeping cadenza in the introduction and transition to the significantly expanded B♭ major variation (mm. 62–113), as well as a longer conclusion (mm. 177–201). The structure and set of variations are similar to the 1847 version, but Liszt has rewritten many of the figurations for the sake of visual clarity and easier execution.

1856: Symphonic poem *Mazeppa* published, which includes as preface Hugo's complete poem. Similar to the 1839, 1847, and 1852 piano versions, mm. 36–402 feature a set of variations / thematic transformations on the "Mazeppa" theme, followed by an expanded "Andante" (mm. 403–435) that transitions to a newly composed march (m. 436ff).

1857: Two-piano arrangement of the symphonic poem published.

1875: Four-hand piano arrangement of the symphonic poem published.

---

But he is not yet a king. That transformation happens in Victor Hugo's treatment of the story found in his famous collection *Les Orientales* (1829), a treatment which informed the complex, decades-long development of Liszt's same-named symphonic poem. As Table 4.3 shows, the basic musical material for the symphonic poem goes back to 1827, when the teenage Liszt published twelve études in the style of his former teacher, Carl Czerny. Liszt carried out an extraordinary transformation of these youthful études in the second half of the 1830s, but he did not associate the character of Mazeppa with the fourth étude until he published a stand-alone work in 1847, entitled *Mazeppa*, that bore a dedication to Hugo. In this version, its ultimate revision for piano as the fourth item in the *Études d'exécution transcendante* of 1852, and the subsequent symphonic poem, Liszt's changes reflect a continuous interpretive refinement of Hugo's poem. For instance, Jim Samson has observed how Liszt's variations stretch and contract according to the length of Hugo's stanzas: "If the basic configuration of the etude captures the central poetic

**Example 4.5** Liszt, *Mazeppa*, mm. 122–129

image [of the horse ride] to perfection, then its subsequent unfolding as a structural *accelerando*, propelled by the ever more feverish accompaniment patterns of the outer sections, seems to convey its narrative with no less authenticity."[27]

The symphonic poem, begun while Liszt was putting the finishing touches on his "Transcendental" Études, sacrifices the structural elasticity of the piano versions in order to better approximate the thematic elements of Hugo's poem. While the bulk of the symphonic poem still prioritizes Mazeppa's propulsive theme, Liszt's added transitional material shapes those appearances into something closer to a mono-thematic sonata form, so that the overall compositional approach stresses developmental transformation and reminiscence over through-composed, sectional variation. For instance, a recapitulation of Mazeppa's first appearance (m. 36) occurs at m. 263, and a newly composed passage of ascending chromatic lines at m. 108 signals the beginning of the development. Here Liszt explores the remote keys of B♭ minor (Example 4.5) and B minor (m. 184ff) while illustrating the passing landscape with some of his most inventive orchestral writing.

**Example 4.5** (*cont.*)

This classical structure is but the first component of *Mazeppa*, however, as it responds to the first part of Hugo's poem (ll. 1–102) that details Mazeppa's ride. The two sections that follow allegorize the journey. In a short Andante (mm. 403–435) that takes place between lines 102 and 103 of Hugo's *Mazeppa*, Mazeppa's broken body is reflected in the physical fragmentation of his once proud melody, which Liszt bookends with anguished instrumental recitatives that outline various intervals of the diminished seventh chord. Mazeppa's salvation and triumph arrive in the form of a march, whose Cossack color is on full display beginning at m. 500. The sublimation of Mazeppa's theme into the fold at m. 578 nicely summarizes the symphonic poem's thematic highlights – including a passing reference to the Andante at mm. 590–592 – while also bringing it to a rousing conclusion.

*Mazeppa*'s virtuosity makes for a thrilling presentation in its various orchestral and piano incarnations, but it comes up short as a musical response to the philosophical implications of Hugo's poem, in which Mazeppa's ordeal serves as a prerequisite for his status as a preeminent modern artist. In *Tasso. Lamento e trionfo*, Liszt addresses this concern in one of the longest prefaces he ever attached to a composition. *Tasso*, Liszt explains, unfolds in three large sections, roughly corresponding to the poet's experiences and posthumous reputation in the Italian cities of Venice (mm. 27–144), Ferrara (mm. 165–347), and Rome (mm. 348–584). Typical of his programmatic approach, Liszt does not identify any events in Tasso's life that are to be depicted, but instead creates a spiritual pilgrimage of sorts, in which the ubiquitous melange of striving, misunderstanding, and suffering that artists endure in life leads to their immortality after death – what Liszt characterizes as "the great antithesis of genius" ("cette grande antithèse du génie"), not unlike Prometheus's "too-truthful tale [. . . of] suffering and apotheosis."

In this sense, *Tasso* is kindred to *Les Préludes*; but even more than *Les Préludes*, *Tasso* gains meaning through a web of intertextual references. Liszt's composition began life as an overture to Goethe's five-act play *Torquato Tasso* (1790), and it was premiered as such for a performance of the play at Weimar that took place on the centennial of Goethe's birth, 28 August 1849. (One year later, Liszt would celebrate Goethe's birthday by conducting the world premiere of Wagner's *Lohengrin*.) Liszt revised the work a year later and again in 1854, at which point he added the central section and made other substantive changes. Yet despite the original motivation for composing *Tasso*, Liszt admits in his preface that it was primarily Byron, not Goethe, who decisively shaped his characterization of Tasso.

Byron's *Lament of Tasso* details the poet's institutionalization in the hospital of St. Anna at Ferrara. To be sure, Tasso laments his fate as the author of the famed epic poem *Gerusalemme liberata* (*The Liberation of Jerusalem*; 1575) who has fallen out of social favor, but he also pines for his influential supporter and possible lover, Princess Leonora d'Este of Ferrara. Tasso's friend Giovan Battista Manso had suggested an amorous relationship among poet and patron in his popular *Vita di Torquato Tasso* (*Life of Torquato Tasso*), published in 1617, and by the time Byron penned his *Lament* two hundred years later, rumor had become unimpeachable fact – and, more importantly, fodder for the Romantic literary mind. Indeed, Byron's *Lament* concludes with Tasso, wasting away in his cell at the hospital of St. Anna, sharing posthumous glory with his muse: "No power in death can tear our names apart, / As none in life could rend thee from my heart. / Yes, Leonora! It shall be our fate / To be entwined for ever – but too late!" (ll. 244–247).

In Liszt's *Tasso*, Leonora is a non-entity, but Tasso is ever-present, marked by a descending triplet figure (Example 4.6). Yet despite his motive's thematic potential, Tasso never takes control of himself or his fate: His motive habitually forms a portion – but never the principal material – of the symphonic poem's numerous themes. In other words, Liszt treats Tasso as object, not subject, allowing Tasso's environment and emotional condition to determine the scope of his musical involvement. (Indeed, in the third part of the work, "Trionfo," Tasso has died; even the funereal atmosphere of the first part suggests the protagonist's immobility.)

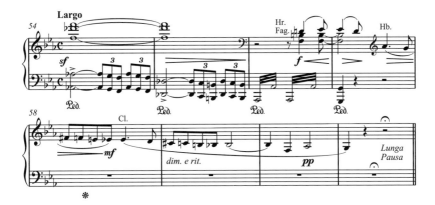

**Example 4.6** Liszt, *Tasso*, mm. 54–61, arr. Th. Forchhammer

In fact, Liszt did not even create Tasso's motive (mm. 1–26) or a principal theme associated with his lament (mm. 62–144), but rather transcribed them from a nameless Venetian gondolier whom he heard around 1840 and had already incorporated into the first version of his piano set, *Venezia e Napoli*.[28] Liszt's choice to reuse this material in *Tasso* was not random, but likely motivated by the text wedded to the gondolier's melody: "Canto l'armi pietose e'l Capitano / Che'l gran Sepolcro liberò di Cristo" ("I sing of holy war and the captain / who freed the Sepulchre of Christ") – the opening lines to *The Liberation of Jerusalem*. Thus in one pithy musical citation, Liszt masterfully encapsulates Tasso's essential characteristics and *Tasso*'s thematic foci: folk hero, historical figure, and eternal artist.

In the outer sections of his symphonic poem, Liszt generally treats Tasso with a psychological and characteristic interest not unlike his other folk (Mazeppa, St. Francis), mythic (Orpheus, Prometheus), and literary (Hamlet, Faust) subjects. The central section, however, is unique among Liszt's output, as it attempts to historically recreate Tasso's cultural milieu by way of an archaic genre. Liszt's choice of a minuet is a masterstroke, since it is an appropriately old – that is, antique – courtly dance that, more importantly, had long ago become outdated, replaced in Liszt's day by the mazurka, polka, and waltz, among other less formal social dances. Here Liszt seems to respond to Byron's Tasso, who foresees a day when "banquet, dance, and revel, are forgot, / Or left untended in a dull repose," and Tasso's humble cell, not the haughty, Ferrarese court, "shall be a consecrated spot!" (ll. 238–240). Indeed, the minuet did not come into any aristocratic prominence until more than seventy years after Tasso's death, when it appeared at – and perhaps was even invented for – the court of Louis XIV. Cosima Wagner, Liszt's daughter, noted in her diary more than twenty years after the composition of *Tasso* that her father spoke of the minuet as representing "What is proper."[29] In other words, the minuet serves to underscore

**Example 4.7** Liszt, *Tasso*, mm. 165–174

the superficial interests of the Ferrarese court, where dogmatic allegiance to social norms leads to both historical ephemerality and artistic sterility.

To be sure, the minuet begins properly enough (Example 4.7), with an orderly diatonic descent that outlines tonic in the antecedent phrase and progresses to a half cadence in the consequent. At this point, however, the orchestra appends a single bar of filigree (m. 173) that upends the typical phraseology of the dance. The two solo cellos try to make a case for their melody three more times; at each point they are rebuffed by the same obdurate winds. A solo clarinet tries later (m. 216ff), but the results are the same. The confrontation encapsulated by the minuet theme opens up once Tasso, by way of his lament theme, enters the room through divided strings at m. 270. Liszt explains in a footnote to the score that "Here the orchestra assumes a dual character: the wind instruments light and flighty; the cantabile string instruments sentimental and graceful." The wind instruments that Liszt identifies are the same ones that flustered the minuet's earliest appearance, and for the remainder of the scene, each group chooses to remain segregated from the other: It takes a dramatic recapitulation (m. 348) to force an artificial reconciliation among the partisan members of the full orchestra.

The centrality of the minuet section in Liszt's symphonic poem is out of proportion to Byron's passing references to Ferrara and the court in his *Lament*. Here Goethe's *Torquato Tasso*, despite Liszt's assurances to the contrary, must certainly have played an important role in establishing the parameters of the numerous confrontations between Tasso and his Ferrarese patrons. In Act I, Princess Leonora d'Este, her brother, Duke Alfonso II, her friend Leonore Sanvitale, and secretary of state Antonio pay homage to Virgil and Ferrara's recent poet laureate,

Ludovico Ariosto. The princess removes the laurel wreath from the bust of Virgil and places it on Tasso's head. This gesture sets the stage for the next act, in whose first scene the princess and Tasso debate the Golden Age. Tasso wishes to recreate it at all costs, arguing that poets must only live by the maxim, "What pleases, is allowed" (l. 993).[30] Leonore counters that the Golden Age "no more / Existed ever than it now exists" (ll. 999–1000), but that poetry may still flourish so long as it sticks to the rule, "What's fitting, is allowed" (l. 1005).

It is Tasso's artistic instincts, his inability to do "what's fitting," that precipitates his downfall in Goethe's drama. But Tasso is not a blameless victim. In a conversation with Antonio that escalates to Tasso drawing his sword (Act II, scene 3), Goethe paints the poet as self-centered and fiercely independent, a man unwilling to even entertain the notion that he could be wrong. "What flights of fancy!" remarks Antonio at the end of the act; "What colours does / That boy splash out his worth and destiny? / Confined and inexperienced, youngsters think / Themselves unique, elect, beyond compare, / Permit themselves all action, against all" (ll. 1598–1602). Goethe wrote the bulk of *Torquato Tasso* during the lead-up to the French Revolution, and his take on the artist in society is decidedly ambivalent, as the play repeatedly avoids moralizing generalizations.[31] Unlike Byron, the Ferrarese nobles in Goethe's drama do not get their come-uppance, but Tasso, in his loneliness and grief, finds his poetic voice as a result: "When in their anguish other men fall silent / A god gave me the power to tell my pain" (ll. 3424–3425).

An irony of Liszt's tendency to musically apotheosize his characters is their loss of individuality, their sublimation into the social fold of the orchestra. This transformation is particularly acute in Tasso's "triumph" (mm. 348–584). To be sure, his major musical materials – the triplet figure, the lament motive, echoes of the minuet scene – appear with heretofore unheard confidence; but they also often relinquish harmonic, rhythmic, and timbral nuance. Consider Example 4.8a, a theme closely associated with Tasso's lament that first appears at m. 6 in the oboes. Its rhythmic and intervallic content ally it with the main theme of Liszt "Vallée d'Obermann," the sixth piece of the piano collection, *Années de pèlerinage*, Book I, which Liszt prefaces with a reflective stanza from Byron's *Childe Harold's Pilgrimage* (Canto III, ll. 905–913) that concludes: "But as it is, I live and die unheard, / With a most voiceless thought, sheathing it as a sword." Byron's insecure, inarticulate, (self-)repressed poet transfers easily to Liszt's *Tasso*. By the end of the orchestral work, the poet has won, but only by using a prosaic voice (Example 4.8b) marked by rhythmic homogeneity, metrical lethargy, and diatonicism. In this sense, Liszt shares the same ambivalence about his subject as Goethe, as if to say that Tasso's monumentalization has necessitated his poetic ossification. In other words, Tasso has swapped one cell for another.

**Example 4.8a**  Liszt, *Tasso*, mm. 6–7, arr. Forchhammer

**Example 4.8b**  Liszt, *Tasso*, mm. 501–504, arr. Forchhammer

## History and literature "in pictures and tones"

In his essay on Berlioz's *Harold en Italie*, Liszt occasionally refers to the "painter–symphonist," an artist capable of animating two-dimensional images in real time. While the majority of Liszt's program music draws on the written word, a not negligible portion turns to the visual arts. For instance, "Sposalizio," the first item in the second book of the *Années de pèlerinage*, is named after Raphael's 1504 oil painting, while the second "Legend" for piano, *St. François de Paule 'Marchant sur les Flots'* (*St. Francis of Paola Walking on the Water*), was composed after a viewing of a painting of Liszt's patron saint by Eduard Jakob von Steinle. Yet neither "Sposalizio" nor *St. François* is designed as a musical painting of the original, but rather an artistic reflection upon it. Nor was this approach limited to a single-performer medium: Liszt's long obsession with Francesco Traini's fresco, *Triumph of Death*, culminated in the *Totentanz* for piano and orchestra, and in 1882 he completed his thirteenth and final symphonic poem, *Von der Wiege bis zum Grabe* (*From the Cradle to the Grave*), after a pen and ink drawing by Mihály Zichy. That Liszt believed music to be as painterly as a brush is evidenced by the *Historische ungarische Bildnisse* (*Historical Hungarian Portraits*), seven pieces for piano from 1885 that paint in tones towering figures of Hungary's cultural and political history.

The above-cited examples reflect a modesty and austerity that increasingly infiltrated Liszt's style from about 1860 onwards. During his Weimar years, however, Liszt

**Figure 4.2** Wilhelm von Kaulbach, *The Battle of the Catalaunian Plains (Battle of Châlons)* (1837)

had entertained ambitious ideas about the fusion of poetic, graphic, and musical arts. Almost a half-century before similar efforts by Aleksandr Scriabin and Jean Sibelius (see Chapter 8), Liszt envisioned a humongous multimedia project entitled *Weltgeschichte in Bildern und Tönen* (*World History in Pictures and Tones*), in which he would provide music, the painter Wilhelm von Kaulbach would create dioramas, and a not-yet chosen author would produce the poetry. While the "Dante" Symphony (see Chapter 5) may also have begun with similarly lofty goals, the only extant material from this specific project is his eleventh symphonic poem, *Hunnenschlacht*. Liszt draws on Kaulbach's painting of the Battle of the Catalaunian Plains in 451 (Figure 4.2) in order to produce "the impression of the two supernatural and contrasting lights, by means of two motives, of which one should represent the fury of the barbarous passion, which drove the Huns to the devastation of so many countries and to the slaughter of so many people; while the other represents the serene powers, the virtues irradiating from Christianity."[32] Historically, the battle was important in weakening Attila the Hun and his invading forces. It also marked one of the first military confrontations between Christians and pagans.

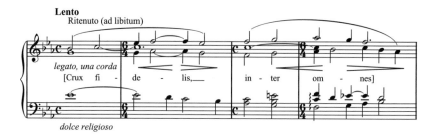

**Example 4.9** Liszt, *Hunnenschlacht*, mm. 271–274, arr. Stradal

Liszt emphasizes the "divine truth, universal charity, progress of humanity, and a hope beyond the world" of these Christians of late antiquity by assigning them a slightly altered rendition of the plainchant melody "Crux fidelis," the eighth stanza from the sixth-century Latin hymn "Pange lingua gloriosi proelium certaminis." Stanzas 1–7 relate how Jesus has fulfilled God's promise of salvation, while stanzas 8–10 valorize the cross on which he died as the vehicle through which that salvation was secured. Thus Liszt's invocation of the "Crux fidelis" tune in *Hunnenschlacht* helps to move the listener to the time period of the historical battle itself while also contextualizing the battle in terms of Christian – that is, nominally European – salvation history.

This message is in fact built into the form of *Hunnenschlacht* itself. The work begins with Liszt's note to the conductor that "The whole coloring must at first be very sombre and all the instruments must sound ghostlike [geisterhaft]." This direction suggests that, unlike, say, more traditional battle pieces like Beethoven's *Wellingtons Sieg* (see Chapter 1), Liszt begins the work mid-battle. This decision may have been influenced by a legendary account, and emphasized in Kaulbach's painting, that the ferocity of the event caused even the dead warriors to continue the fight post-mortem. Thus melodies emerge piecemeal, with fragments of the "Crux fidelis" appearing at mm. 98, 127, and 247. And in an effort to present an impression rather than full comprehension of the scene, Liszt jumps around Kaulbach's enormous canvas (137.5 × 172.5 cm) by re-enacting the same fight in different keys (e.g., mm. 77–105 in C minor and mm. 106–134 in G minor). Liszt had already used this technique in earlier symphonic poems, and it would be taken up by other composers attempting to quickly and frugally render vast images in music, including Balakirev, Musorgsky, and Debussy.

Only at m. 271, Example 4.9, does Liszt identify the hymn by name in the score and present it in full; appropriately, via an organ. What better way to beat Attila, "The Scourge of God" ("Flagellum Dei"), than with godly music? Indeed, the introduction of this instrument makes the Christian victory patent, and the addition of a pentatonic accompaniment in the first violins thirty-three bars later returns the

Catalaunian Fields to a modicum of tranquility. Like *Wellingtons Sieg*, Liszt's symphonic poem concludes with a variation and bombastic, militant coda. In keeping with Liszt's overall concept, it is the organ alone which sounds and sustains the final C major chord of triumph.

Liszt's symphonic poems represent the most important collection of program music between Carl Ditters von Dittersdorf and Richard Strauss. Their importance is arguably even stronger, however, since they – alongside accompanying essays by Liszt and his supporters – aspire to articulate artistic perspectives on "big" topics – humanity, civil society, nature, death, religion, myth, art, and the artist – through techniques and structures which were heralded as novel. (In fact, continuity of technique and structure also explain why Liszt designated two non-programmatic orchestral works, *Héroïde funèbre* and *Festklänge*, as symphonic poems.) Indeed, the development of program music between about 1860 and the First World War can be told as a series of responses to Lisztian program music.

## Chapter 5

# The New German School and beyond

## Toward a "Beethoven of the future": Liszt's "Dante" Symphony

In early 1839, Franz Liszt began to plan symphonic compositions based on Dante Alighieri's *Divine Comedy* and Johann Wolfgang von Goethe's *Faust*. By the end of the year, he had written in a public letter to Hector Berlioz that "Dante has found his pictorial expression in Orcagna and Michelangelo, and someday perhaps he will find his musical expression in the Beethoven of the future."[1] The ensuing decade of intense concertizing meant that he would not be able to realize his plans in earnest until the 1850s, but in the interim he was able to devote considerable energy to a piano piece eventually published as "Après une lecture du Dante – Fantasia quasi Sonata" in Book 2 ("Italy") of the *Années de pèlerinage* (1858). During its long gestation, Liszt assigned it various titles: "Fragment dantesque" (1839); "Paralipomènes [Postscript] à la Divina Commedia: Fantaisie Symphonique pour Piano" (*c*.1848); and "Prolégomènes [Preliminary Discourse] … " (*c*.1852).

In good programmatic fashion, the work references, but does not directly cite, two ostensibly incompatible models: Victor Hugo's poem, "Après une lecture de Dante" ("After Reading Dante"), and Ludwig van Beethoven's two piano sonatas, op. 27, each a "sonata quasi fantasia." Hugo distills the thirty-three cantos of Dante's Hell into almost as many lines of poetry (see Text Box 5.1), and Beethoven – especially in op. 27, no. 1 – infuses sonata structures with spontaneous, improvisational outbursts. Along the same lines as its models, Liszt's "Dante" Sonata is both poetic and musical gloss, offering "a reading of the Dante" – note the definite article – by way of elaborate thematic transformations and elastic formal structures akin to the Piano Sonata in B minor and *Les Préludes*.

Similarly, the indefinite article of Liszt's *A Symphony to Dante's "Divine Comedy"* (*Eine Symphonie zu Dantes Divina Commedia*) indicates another subjective reading of Dante's poetic masterpiece, what Liszt described to Richard Wagner as "a kind of commentary to this work."[2] With over fourteen thousand lines of poetry at his disposal, Liszt understandably focuses on only a small fraction of Dante's world. (Even Dante admits early on that his observations must remain fragmentary, as he

**Text Box 5.1  Victor Hugo, "After Reading Dante"**

Quand le poète peint l'enfer, il peint sa vie,
Sa vie, ombre qui fuit de spectres poursuivie;
Forêt mystérieuse où ses pas effrayés
S'égarent à tâtons hors des chemins frayés;
Noir voyage obstrué de rencontres difformes;
Spirale aux bords douteux, aux profondeurs énormes,
Dont les cercles hideux vont toujours plus avant
Dans une ombre où se meut l'enfer vague et vivant!
Cette rampe se perd dans la brume indécise;
Au bas de chaque marche une plainte est assise,
Et l'on y voit passer avec un faible bruit
Des grincements de dents blancs dans la sombre nuit.
Là sont les visions, les rêves, les chimères;
Les yeux que la douleur change en sources amères;
L'amour, couple enlacé, triste et toujours brûlant,
Qui dans un tourbillon passe une plaie au flanc;
Dans un coin la vengeance et la faim, soeurs impies
Sur un crâne rongé côté à côté accroupies;
Puis la pâle misère, au sourire appauvri;
Et la luxure immonde, et l'avarice infâme,
Tous les manteaux de plomb dont peut se charger l'âme!
Plus loin, la lâcheté, la peur, la trahison
Offrant des clefs à vendre et goûtant du poison;
Et puis, plus bas encore, et tout au fond du gouffre,
Le masque grimaçant de la haine qui souffre!

Oui, c'est bien là la vie, ô poète inspiré,
Et son chemin brumeux d'obstacles encombré.
Mais, pour que rien n'y manque, en cette route étroite,
Vous nous montrez toujours debout à votre droite
Le génie au front calme, aux yeux pleins de rayons,
Le Virgile serein qui dit: Continuons!

When the poet painted Hell, he was painting his life,
His own life, a harried shade fleeing phantoms;
A darkling wood where fearful steps
Grope forward, away from the trail;
A passage barred by monstrous forms;
The spiral's crumbling sides and plunging depths,
Its frightful rings circling down
Into the gloom where a shifting, living Hell stirs!
The slope dissolves in a foggy blur;
At the base of each step a sufferer sits,
And as you pass you can hear the sound
Of white teeth grinding in the dark night.
There are visions here, dreams, illusions;
Eyes that pain turns to bitter streams;
An entwined couple—love!—sad and still aroused,
Who pass in a gust with a wound in their side;
In a corner are vengeance and hunger, unholy sisters,
Crouching side by side over a gnawed skull;
And pallid woe with her withered smile;
And filthy pride, and shameful greed,
Leaden cloaks, all of them, that weigh down the soul!
Farther still, baseness, fear, and treason
Offer their balm and its reeking poison;
And deeper yet, in the depths of the pit,
The grimacing mask of hatred and pain!

Yes, farsighted poet, this is our life,
With its blurred, blocked, burdened way.
Yet, so that this narrow path should lack nothing,
You show us, there on your right and always present,
A guardian whose brow is calm and eyes are lucid,
Virgil, who says with serenity, Let us go on!

–Translated by James H. Johnson

"cannot give account of all of them, / For my main theme is such it hurries me on, / So that I often have to tell less than I saw" [Canto IV, ll. 145–147].)[3] Here Hugo may have come to Liszt's aid, for his poem bears tantalizing parallels to the various musical episodes of the symphony's first movement.[4]

Liszt had at one point hoped the German painter Giovanni Genelli would create a slideshow containing scenes from the *Divine Comedy*, and while the collaboration did not pan out, something of the filmic remains in the "Dante" Symphony. For example, Liszt uses the harp as an aural dissolve to the "Francesca da Rimini" episode (see mm. 280–283, 295–298) and as fade-in to the brief Capaneus scene (mm. 393–394), described below. The episodic nature of the movement is heightened by the return of a severe theme in the brass at mm. 12, 260, 388, and 637, whose appearance is always marked in the score with a portion of the famous inscription over the Gates of Hell from Canto III, l. 9: "Lasciate ogni speranza, voi ch'entrate!" ("Abandon every hope, you who enter [here]"). Still other moments do not directly cite lines from Dante's poem, but are nevertheless so strongly pictorial that a representative passage can be tentatively advanced: the brief storm music (mm. 269–278), with characteristic chromatic flutes, piccolos, and two timpani, suggest the place in Canto V where "every light is silenced, / Which roars just as the sea roars in a storm, / When it is beaten by conflicting winds" (ll. 28–30). (Liszt had also planned on utilizing a wind machine to heighten these atmospheric effects, but like the Genelli slides, it came to naught.) Likewise, Liszt's instruction in the score at m. 395 that "The entire passage is intended to be a blasphemous mocking laughter, very sharply accentuated in the two clarinets and the violas," gels well with the punishment in Canto XIV of the arrogant Capaneus, whom Zeus struck down at the siege of Thebes. Even in Hell, Dante's guide Virgil explains that "he held and seems to hold / God in contempt, and treats him as not worth much" (ll. 69–70).

The episodic nature of thematic material and orchestral effects fails to produce a sonata with development. To be sure, a case can be made for an exposition, although where the introduction ends and the exposition begins is unclear. Regardless, the section that follows the intense storm, focusing on the illicit lovers Francesca da Rimini and her brother-in-law Paolo, bears so little resemblance to what came before that it cannot function as a development. Furthermore, its thematic independence precludes a second exposition, as perhaps is the case in *Les Préludes*. And unlike that symphonic poem, which has also been read as a condensed four-movement symphony (see Chapter 4), the brevity (forty measures) of the Capaneus episode in the "Dante" Symphony is too short to function as a structural scherzo. At the same time, much of the earlier material returns, but it is gradually effaced by the descending motive that dominated the introduction. Indeed, the effect of this false recapitulation is twofold: of descent without development – the souls in Dante's Inferno, after all, have no hope of salvation; and by means of a circular (ABA) rather than teleological structure, a sense of hellish endlessness (as opposed to heavenly timelessness).

Liszt impresses this latter point on the listener even further throughout the movement by emphasizing the tritone, the only interval that remains the same in inversion. Associated with the diabolical since around the time of its prohibition by the eleventh-century theorist Guido d'Arezzo, the tritone is also a key building block of the diminished seventh chord, which contains two tritones a minor third apart. It, too, does not lose its definition when inverted. The sonority is so prominent in Liszt's "Inferno" movement that it conditions the listener to hear it as an aimless "tonic." To illustrate Hell's endless harmonic instability, Liszt juxtaposes D and G♯ throughout the movement. The line of Example 5.1 acts as a type of subglobal

**Example 5.1** Liszt, "Dante" Symphony, I, mm. 22–24, arr. August Stradal

positioning system that moves ever lower. And the composer deftly sums up the non-developmental nature of the diminished seventh sonority by juxtaposing a D–A dyad (i.e., without major or minor leanings) against a G♯ minor triad at the end of the movement (Example 5.2). This last bombastic outburst is a tough blow, for as a recomposition of the introduction, especially mm. 9–17, it betrays its hollow core by failing to redirect the movement's never-ending downward spiral.

Liszt explained to Wagner his intention to write a three-movement symphony corresponding to Dante's "Inferno," "Purgatorio," and "Paradiso," but Wagner countered that depicting Paradise in music was impossible. Liszt dropped the idea, instead opting to fashion a two-movement symphony whose conclusion featured a choral setting of the Canticle of Mary sung at Vespers, the Magnificat, a text that does not appear at all in the *Divine Comedy*. Liszt may have followed Wagner's advice, but did not necessarily share his argument. Indeed, a work like the piano piece "Bénédiction de Dieu dans la solitude" ("Benediction of God in Solitude") from the *Harmonies poétiques et religieuses* suggests that Liszt was quite comfortable depicting eternal bliss, a profile he bolsters by appending Alphonse de Lamartine's eponymous poem, whose last four lines read: "Scarcely have a few days brushed past my brow, / And it seems that a century and a world have passed away, / And that, separated from them by an immense abyss, / A new man is reborn and begins again in me."[5]

Perhaps an even stronger motivation for constructing a two-movement symphony stems from Liszt's demands for maximum programmatic contrast. In particular, the two movements of the "Dante" Symphony make an interesting juxtaposition between two female figures, Francesca da Rimini and Mary, the Mother of God. The two could not be more different: Francesca is the epitome of carnal lust, infidelity, and frustration. Liszt gives her scene decadent musical treatment, but her music neither develops nor concludes; it is perpetually locked in a state of irresolution. To be sure, Francesca is pitiable – Dante faints at the conclusion of her story (Canto V, ll. 141–142) – but she is beyond salvation.

However, Mary is the emblem of Christian hope and fidelity, a virgin who fully commits herself to God, a feature Liszt underscores by citing Mary's own words

**Example 5.2** Liszt, "Dante" Symphony, I, mm. 630–646, arr. Stradal

from Luke 1:46–55: "Magnificat anima mea Dominum, / Et exsultavit spiritus meus in Deo salutari meo" ("My soul glorifies the Lord, / And my spirit rejoices in God my Savior"). This text's appearance at the end of the second movement is the ultimate expression of a type of humility necessary for entrance into Heaven that begins with the Annunciation, mentioned by Dante in the First Terrace of Purgatory (Canto 10), in which Mary tells the angel Gabriel, "Behold the handmaid of the Lord; be it unto me according to thy word" (Luke 1:38). In Canto 28, Beatrice replaced Virgil as

Dante's guide. Liszt's selection of this Marian text to conclude the "Dante" Symphony replaces Beatrice with a more legitimate Christian figure of universal salvation, Mary.

Whereas Francesca was a way station in the episodic "Inferno," Mary the intercessor is the goal of "Purgatorio," which operates with considerable direction and confidence. With an effect similar to Act II of Gluck's *Orfeo ed Euridice*, the suffocating circles of Hell give way to a serene, almost pastoral scene. But the beauty is tempered by the sections that follow: the plaintive recitative at m. 55, a chorale with heavily chromatic inner and bass lines at m. 68, and, most importantly, a five-part fugue marked "Lamentoso" that begins at m. 128. While Liszt does not supply any citations from Dante's poem, the fugue is "particularly effective in creating a sense of the multiplicity of souls undergoing the same process [of spiritual transformation]."[6]

In following the penitent up the slope of Mount Purgatory, stopping just short of the entrance to Paradise, Liszt promotes a spatial reorientation by:

- Repeating entire passages up a half step (e.g., mm. 1–27 and 28–54);
- Prioritizing the higher registers of the orchestra (the contrabasses, for instance, make few appearances in the "Magnificat");
- Modulating from D major to B major over the course of the whole movement, a process known as progressive tonality.

Perhaps the most famous illustration of ascent comes at the end of the movement. Following the fugue and recapitulation of earlier themes (m. 237ff), an extraordinary transition at m. 288 introduces an off-stage, "invisible" (according to Liszt's directions) boys' or women's choir that sings the first two lines of the "Magnificat" and a volley of "Hosanna!" and "Hallelujah!"

While firmly in B major throughout, the final progression passes through some unusual harmonic territory. As Liszt explained it to Julius Schaeffer in a letter of 20 August 1859, "At the end of my 'Dante' Symphony I attempted to bring liturgical intonations into my *Magnificat*. You might also be interested in the triads built over a whole-tone scale, which – as far as I know – until now has never been done in its entirety."[7] The citation Liszt provides in his letter, reproduced in Example 5.3a, is not quite reflective of the score as published, since it lacks the ante-penultimate A♭ major chord in root position. However, Liszt did include in the same score a second, ebullient ending (Example 5.3b) which uses the other whole-tone scale in its entirety. While the quiet, celestial ending is preferred by conductors today, both versions are programmatically legitimate and historically innovative.[8]

With its shared key, interplay between B, B♭, and D, and use of chorus in the finale, the "Dante" Symphony shares much in common with Beethoven's "Choral" Symphony. Add to that the poetic stimulus, programmatic episodes, progressive

**Example 5.3a** Liszt, "Dante" Symphony, II, final chord progression, first ending

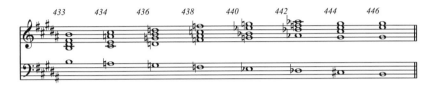

**Example 5.3b** Liszt, "Dante" Symphony, II, final chord progression, second ending

tonality, modern modulations, and avant-garde use of the whole-tone scale, and the symphony positions itself as viable successor to Beethoven's symphonic legacy.

## The New German School

Deciding the future direction of the symphony after Beethoven had been a chief concern of German composers who followed in his wake, but despite important contributions to the genre by Mendelssohn, Schumann, and Louis Spohr during the 1830s and 1840s, it was not until the 1850s that the controversy came to a head. Guided by the same artistic spirit that Liszt had used to prophesy a "Beethoven of the Future" years earlier, in Weimar he and his pupils started to describe themselves haughtily as "Zukunftsmusiker" ("Musicians of the Future") and their products as "Zukunftsmusik" ("Music of the Future"). Wagner, in exile in Switzerland, was ambivalently drawn into the group,[9] as was an even less interested Berlioz. With plenty of ink being spilled in the feuilletons but precious little music being performed outside of Weimar, Robert Schumann could legitimately wonder, "Where are Liszt's brilliant achievements? Where are they hiding? Perhaps in his desk [or under the conductor's stand]? Maybe he is so fixated on the future because he is afraid that he will be misunderstood in the present?"[10] Schumann further claimed that it was sacrilegious of Liszt to usurp the name of "Zukunftsmusiker," since that title properly belonged to Bach, Handel, and Beethoven, whose music displays as much novelty today as the day it was written. In his last piece of public criticism, entitled "New Paths" ("Neue Bahnen") from 1853, Schumann championed a group of musicians who followed a similar respect for tradition, including Woldemar Bargiel, Julius Schaeffer, and Johannes Brahms – the last of whom Schumann christened in private correspondence as "the true apostle who will write [musical] revelations that the Pharisees – just as in ages past – will not be able to unravel even after centuries of scrutiny."[11]

With the controversy showing no sign of dying down, in the summer of 1859, the editor of the *Neue Zeitschrift für Musik*, Franz Brendel, addressed a group of musicians at Leipzig to propose an ostensibly neutral appellation for the Musicians of the Future: the New German School. Anticipating objections, especially about non-Germans Liszt and Berlioz, Brendel explained that

> The birthplace cannot be decisive in matters of the mind, no more than exact chronology in other cases; for it often occurs that someone living and working in one era can really better be assigned, spiritually, to an earlier style, and vice versa … Neither artist would have become what he is if at an early point he had not been nourished and strengthened by the German spirit. As a result, Germany eventually had to become the locus of their career, and in this sense I have recommended the designation *New German School* for the entire post-Beethovenian development. Through this we gain both clarity of arrangement and a simpler, more consistent nomenclature. Protestant sacred music up to and including Bach and Handel has already long borne the name *altdeutsche Schule* (Old German School). The Italian-influenced epoch of the Viennese masters is the age of Classicism, the perfectly balanced interpenetration of the ideal and the real. Beethoven extends his hand to the specifically Germanic North and so establishes the New German School.[12]

On the surface, Brendel merely substituted one helpless term for another, but the description of the Liszt / Wagner movement as a "school" gave it a weight on par with the Leipzig Conservatory and a sense of tradition that was decidedly nationalistic. By extension, it also claimed for its own Bach, Handel, and Beethoven, whom it used to validate the existence of Liszt's symphonic poems and Wagner's music dramas. Finally, it not only set a precedent for other like-minded groups across Europe to emulate, but it stands as a flagship example of how the presence of an umbrella term like "school" rarely results in stylistic and ideological unanimity among its members.

## Hanslick on music and meaning

Until the second half of the 1850s, when Liszt began releasing his symphonic poems and programmatic symphonies, these debates on the future of (German) music – its membership, its aesthetics, and its connections to the past – were waged almost exclusively in the press, not the concert hall. Wagner's triptych of extended essays – *Art and Revolution* (1849), *The Artwork of the Future* (1849), and especially *Opera and Drama* (1851) – laid the groundwork for a type of symphonic opera, or "music drama," that would simultaneously:

- Recapture the artistic sophistication of ancient Greek drama by unifying ostensibly disparate media like dance, visual art, music, and poetry – the so-called "Total Work of Art" ("Gesammtkunstwerk");
- Tap into enduring mythological subjects that embody the Folk and exalt man in his most natural, unspoiled state;
- Extend the German – in other words, Beethovenian – symphonic tradition to its ultimate fulfillment.

While Wagner took issue with almost every aspect of music's development over the last century (Gluck and Beethoven survive his criticism, although not without wounds), he did not deny the enduring notion that music expresses. In fact, that was its chief job, although according to Wagner only recently had such a realization become possible: "Through [Beethoven's] undaunted toil, to reach the artistically Necessary within an artistically Impossible, is shown us Music's unhemmed faculty of accomplishing every thinkable task, if only she consents to stay what she really is – an *art of Expression.*"[13]

Eduard Hanslick sought to counter this ubiquitous claim in his *Vom Musikalisch-Schönen: Ein Beitrag zur Revision der Aesthetik der Tonkunst* (*On the Musically Beautiful: A Contribution to the Revision of Musical Aesthetics*), first published in 1854. Early on he distinguishes between objective, scientific perception or intellect ("Empfindung") and subjective feeling or emotion ("Gefühl"): "Perception is the true apprehension of a quality of the senses, such as of a pitch or a color. Feeling is the growing awareness of an improved or restrained frame of mind, that is, of well-being or displeasure."[14] According to Hanslick, whereas previous authors had freely mixed the two terms, this distinction allows him to explain precisely music's limits of representation: "Music can whisper, storm, roar, but love or anger can only exist subjectively inside of us. The representation of feelings and emotions is not within music's purview" (p. 13). And later: "Music can only endeavor to imitate external phenomena [äußere Erscheinung], never the specific feelings that they provoke" (p. 24). For Hanslick, then, beauty and expressive specificity operate in inverse proportion to each other.

Hanslick does not deny music's ability to create emotional responses in its listeners, but he explains that these emotions are not intrinsic to the music itself: Listeners supply their own meaning. True, "meaning" can be aided by a text, but texted music – broadly defined – is not what Hanslick has in mind:

> In vocal music, the effect of music cannot be separated from the words, plot, or scenery, such that it is impossible to define exactly how each has contributed to the production of the whole. We must also exclude compositions with specific

titles or programs that relate to the "content" of the music. The unification of music with poetry expands its power, but not its limits. (p. 20)

Instead of conveying emotion, Hanslick asserts that music's true beauty and artistic value reside in its dynamic properties, its "forms moved by tones" ("tönend bewegte Formen"). Instrumental music exists completely unto itself, devoid of externals. Thus, "just as the beauty of a composition is rooted in its musical disposition, so too does this determine the laws of its construction" (p. 43). The composer first imagines an abstract, ontologically ambivalent musical idea, and then develops it piece by piece into a satisfying musical structure. From this perspective, an intellectual listener can quantify music's quality: "The sensible coordination of intrinsically attractive sounds, their consonance and antagonism, their flight and striving, their soaring and falling – it is this which, in free forms, presented itself to our mental outlook and pleases as beautiful" (p. 32).

Hanslick's book went through ten editions between 1854 and 1902, two years before his death. While the 1854 edition primarily challenged music philosophers – *Tristan und Isolde*, Wagner's first patent example of a music drama, would not completely appear in print until 1860 – or long-dead practitioners, the 1858 edition was aimed squarely at Wagner and especially Liszt.[15] In the years between the first and second edition of Hanslick's book, Liszt had published his essays on Robert Schumann and Hector Berlioz's *Harold en Italie*, in which he explored the history, aesthetics, and current viability of program music, and to which supporters like Peter Cornelius, Felix Draeseke, and Richard Pohl offered spirited supplementary essays and reviews. The fiery Pohl, for instance, surely had Hanslick in his crosshairs when he fired off the assertion in an 1855 essay that a composer obviously had a program in mind when fashioning his music, assuming "he meant to produce anything beyond a mere play of forms and colors – which can hardly be considered a valid objective for a composer of *our time*."[16] Indeed, as Hanslick asserts in the preface to his second edition, his argument – the basic gist of which remained unaltered – is even more timely than three years before, given the appearance of pieces like Liszt's "Dante" and *Faust* Symphonies and the onslaught of pro-programmatic propaganda in the press:

> During the preparation of this second edition, Liszt's program symphonies have since appeared as complements to Wagner's writings. So far, these have only succeeded in antagonizing the self-sufficient meaning of music by presenting the listener with little more than formally inchoate fluff. I am sure that no one will rebuke me for not shortening or diluting the polemical aspects of my position in light of these developments. If anything, I would think it even more important to demonstrate the singular and eternal in musical art as it pertains to beauty, as practiced by our masters Bach, Haydn, Mozart, Beethoven, and Mendelssohn, and as it should be fostered in the future by true musical innovators.[17]

## Forging a tradition: Liszt's programmatic protégés

Hanslick was not alone in claiming that Lisztian program music was both aesthetically and historically inauthentic; critics in Berlin and Leipzig were particularly hostile toward the New Germans. Yet while Liszt's programmatic output remains the most important expression of his musical aims during the 1850s, the program music and criticism written by his sizable group of students who had moved to Weimar – including Hans Bronsart von Schellendorff, Hans von Bülow, Felix Draeseke, Joseph Joachim, Carl Tausig, and especially Joachim Raff and Alexander Ritter – specifically for concentrated musical study with the famous pianist and controversial composer also contributed significantly to the propagation of the genre.

Whereas their most vehement criticism against program music's detractors came from the 1850s, these disciples found their own compositional voice only in the following decades (see Table 5.1). Thus while they offered a fairly unified vision of how program music worked in theory through the lens of Liszt's program music, their own compositions – programmatic symphonies, suites, incidental music, and other generic hybrids – extend rather than mimic the music of their teacher. And from a practical point of view, Liszt's students – many of whom embarked on careers as performers, conductors, and/or music directors – had to placate the progressivist and conservative camps in order to succeed professionally, the result being that several questioned strongly or altogether abandoned the direction that New German music was taking, particularly after Liszt left Weimar in 1861 and Brahms's career began to take off about the same time. As a result, between about 1860 and Richard Strauss's first tone poems from almost thirty years later, there emerged no undisputed leader to follow in Liszt's programmatic footsteps.

Among the pianists to study with Liszt, Carl Tausig ranks as one of the most gifted of the century. He came to Weimar in 1855, and in early 1858 – at age sixteen – made his public debut in Berlin. That same year he met Wagner, hard at work on the second act of *Tristan und Isolde*, and became a lifelong devotee. Yet he formed a more even-sided friendship with Brahms, with whom he concertized and whose two books of "Paganini" Variations, op. 35, from 1863 speak to Tausig's formidable technique. Tausig spent the rest of his short life teaching at his School for Advanced Piano Playing in Berlin, touring, and producing piano music – many arrangements, a few original pieces, and his posthumously published *Tägliche Studien* (*Daily Studies*).

While Tausig's compositions mellowed with each passing opus, his earliest pieces proudly show equal influences of Liszt and Wagner. This is clearly the case in *Das Geisterschiff* (*The Ghost Ship*), which Tausig published as part of his Opus 1 in 1860. Based on the poem of the same name by Moritz von Strachwitz, *Das Geisterschiff*

**Table 5.1** *Selected programmatic works by Liszt's students*

| Composer | Subject (Author) | Genre | Composed / Published |
|---|---|---|---|
| Hans Bronsart von Schellendorff | *Melusine* (pno.) | Fairy tale (Märchen) | ? / 1881, op. 9 |
| | *Frühlings-Fantasie* (*Spring Fantasy*) | | 1857–1858 / 1880, op. 11 |
| | *In den Alpen* (*In the Alps*) | Symphony, with choir | 1889–1896 / – (lost) |
| | *Schicksalsgewalten* (*Choice of Fate*) | Symphony | 1897 / – (lost) |
| | *Bella Napoli* | Program suite, with solo singer and choir | 1902–1903 / – (lost) |
| Hans von Bülow | *Nirwana* | Mood picture (Stimmungsbild) (1866), fantasy in overture form (1881) | 1854 / 1866, rev. 1881 |
| | *Julius Caesar* (Shakespeare) | Heroic overture | 1851 / 1867, op. 10 |
| | *Des Sängers Fluch* (Uhland) | Ballad | 1863 / 1863, op. 16 |
| Felix Draeseke | *Frithjof* (*Frithiof's Saga*) | Symphonic poem | 1859–1865 / – |
| | *Julius Caesar* (Shakespeare) | Symphonic poem | 1860, rev. 1861, 1865 / – |
| | *Das Leben ein Traum* (*Life is a Dream*) (Calderón) | Prelude | 1868–1888 / 1888, op. 45 |
| | *Penthesilea* (Kleist) | Prelude | 1888 / 1889, op. 50 |
| | *Der Thuner See* (*Lake Thun*) | Scenic tone painting | 1903 / – |
| | *Der Traum ein Leben* (*Dream is a Life*) (Grillparzer) | Prelude | 1904 / – |
| Joseph Joachim | *Hamlet* (Shakespeare) | Overture | 1853 / 1854, op. 4 |
| | *Demetrius* (H. Grimm) | Overture | 1855 / –, op. 6 |
| | *Henry IV* (Shakespeare) | Overture | 1855 / 1902 (arr. Brahms), op. 7 |

| Composer | Title | Type | Date |
|---|---|---|---|
| Joachim Raff | *An das Vaterland* | Symphony | 1859–1861 / 1864, op. 96 |
| | *Im Walde* | Symphony | 1869 / 1871, op. 153 |
| | *Lenore* (Bürger) | Symphony | 1870–1872 / 1873, op. 177 |
| | *Gelebt: Gestrebt, Gelitten, Gestritten – Gestorben – Umworben* | Symphony | 1873 / 1874, op. 189 |
| | *In den Alpen* | Symphony | 1875 / 1876, op. 201 |
| | *Frühlingsklänge* | Symphony | 1876 / 1877, op. 205 |
| | *Im Sommer* | Symphony | 1878 / 1879, op. 208 |
| | *Zur Herbstzeit* | Symphony | 1879 / 1882, op. 213 |
| | *Der Winter* | Symphony | 1876–1882 (inc.) / 1883, op. 214 |
| | *Ein' feste Burg ist unser Gott* | Heroic dramatic tone piece in the form of an overture | 1854, rev. 1865 / 1866, op. 127 |
| | *Tempest, Macbeth, Romeo and Juliet, Othello* (Shakespeare) | Preludes | 1879 / 1891 |
| | *Die schöne Müllerin* (Müller) (string quartet) | Cyclical tone poem | 1874 / 1876, op. 192b |
| Alexander Ritter | *Erotische Legende* (Erotic Legend) | Symphonic poem | 1890 / – |
| | *Olaf's Hochzeitsreigen* (Olaf's Wedding Round Dance) | Symphonic waltz | 1891 / 1892, op. 22 |
| | *Sursum Corda!* | Storm and stress fantasy | 1894 / 1896, op. 23 |
| | *Kaiser Rudolfs Ritt zum Grabe* (Emperor Rudolph's Ride to the Grave) (Kerner; M. von Schwind) | Symphonic poem | 1895 / 1895 |
| Carl Tausig | *Das Geisterschiff* (The Ghost Ship) (Strachwitz; pno.) | Ballad | 1860 / 1860, op. 1 |

recreates an encounter on the high seas between a passenger ship and a phantom vessel. Strachwitz's quasi-ballad features three characters, a helmsman, the narrator, and the ghost ship, whose description and history take up the middle portion (ll. 13–48) of the text.[18] As is typical of this popular Romantic story line – Wagner's *Der fliegende Holländer* is a contemporary model – it is a dark, stormy night, and the waves are whipping the ship to and fro (ll. 1–4). Ultimately, the narrator chalks up the close encounter (the ships never actually meet) to travel fatigue – "my heart is travel-weary," he explains – rather than acknowledge its underlying cause of that equally popular Romantic trope, world-weariness ("Weltschmerz").

Like most of Liszt's symphonic poems, which Tausig knew inside and out, in *Das Geisterschiff* narrative depiction takes a back seat to atmosphere and expression. To be sure, there are legitimate depictions of the storm, such as the five-octave arpeggio at m. 5, the tempestuous chromatic descent at m. 33, or the famous chromatic glissando at m. 158. These passages are impressive but arguably less original, as they draw heavily on a tradition of characteristic "tempest" music that began with Vivaldi, Haydn, Beethoven, and Rossini and would continue to expand in John Knowles Paine's *The Tempest* Overture, Zdeněk Fibich's *Bouře*, and George Whitefield Chadwick's *Aphrodite*, among other orchestral essays. Indeed, far more dramatic is the recreation of the narrator experiencing the ship pass and gradually identifying its crew. Tausig spends long portions of this virtuosic piano piece building up material, such as the tritone volley at mm. 63–87 (see Example 5.4), which runs almost the entire expanse of the keyboard. The section climaxes with a truly surprising whole-tone scale (mm. 87–89) that marks the first, albeit fleeting, sighting of the phantom Vikings. That this scale is part of their exclusive sonic habitat is corroborated by mm. 182–185, which descends C–B♭–A♭–G♭ and which Tausig instructs the pianist to play "geisterhaft": "ghostly." (An equally arresting passage appears at mm. 424–440, where Tausig ascends the keyboard by means of an octatonic scale.) Yet in keeping with Strachwitz's characterization of these undead Swedes, Goths, Norwegians, and Danes as "heroes" – which also reinforces the Wagnerian mythos surrounding Scandinavia – Tausig provides two short episodes (mm. 214–245, 372–403) of martial music, albeit in far distant keys of D♭ major and A♭ major.

The most prominent theme, however, is of the ship itself, Example 5.5. Tausig endows it with a simple though demonstrative melody that uncompromisingly demands its i–vii°⁷ harmonization. The theme appears in several transformations (such as the "lamentoso" section at m. 312ff) while the ship is still in view, but its most significant reincarnation occurs in the extended coda (mm. 486–538), that is, after the vessel has vanished. The narrator, now alone and with his fear subsiding, begins to empathize with the phantom crew, to which Tausig supplies a theme that is dignified and even heroic (see m. 521ff in Example 5.6). Yet as the bass line at mm.

**Example 5.4** Tausig, *Das Geisterschiff* (*The Ghost Ship*), mm. 79–92

**Example 5.5** Tausig, *Das Geisterschiff*, mm. 99–104

526–527 or the modal mixture at mm. 534–536 suggests, the narrator remains hesitant, torn between the "real" world and that to which the ghost ship has set sail.

*Das Geisterschiff* is an exceptional Opus 1. Unfortunately, despite several tantalizing references to the composition of symphonic poems and programmatic symphonies on subjects like Byron's *Manfred* or Peter Cornelius's painting of the Four Horsemen of the Apocalypse, Tausig's sudden death in 1871 at the age of twenty-nine meant that the piano showstopper did not turn out to be a foretaste of more ambitious and enduring program music.[19] Some of Liszt's longer-lived students seem to have been stymied by the programmatic challenge: Hans Bronsart von Schellendorff contributed a single programmatic piece in the mold of Beethoven's Sixth Symphony. And Alexander Ritter, despite being one of the earliest New German adherents, did not

**Example 5.6** Tausig, *Das Geisterschiff*, mm. 521–538

begin the composition of symphonic / tone poems until 1890 – that is, after his mentee, Richard Strauss, had begun to revolutionize the genre. Still others actively chose to divest themselves of Lisztian program music altogether.

## Disillusioned disciples: Joachim, Bülow, and Raff

Brendel's suggestion to found a New German School did little to sway partisans; if anything, it further ostracized those who did not embrace the ideas and music coming primarily out of Liszt's Weimar. Alongside Hanslick's calculated responses, a short but famous document to take issue with Brendel's claims appeared in the Berlin journal *Echo* on 6 May 1860:

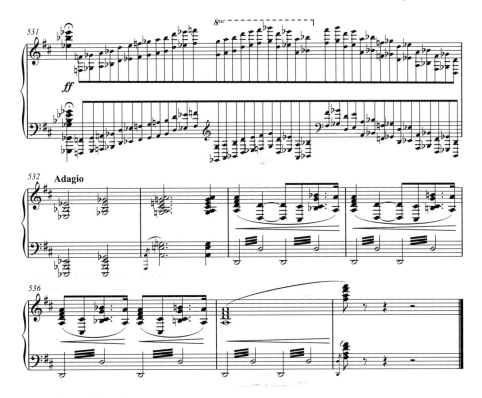

**Example 5.6** (*cont.*)

> [Brendel's] periodical constantly disseminates the opinion that seriously striving musicians are fundamentally in accord with the tendencies it champions and recognize the compositions of the leaders of this movement as works of artistic value. [. . . The undersigned] do not recognize the principles which find expression in Brendel's *Zeitschrift*, and can only deplore or condemn as contrary to the most fundamental essence of music the productions of the leaders and disciples of the so-called New German School, some of whom put these principles into practice, while other keep trying to impose the establishment of more and more novel and preposterous theories.[20]

Leaked prematurely, the document included only four signatures: Johannes Brahms, Joseph Joachim, Julius Otto Grimm, and Bernhard Scholz. Liszt was probably not surprised by any of these names, but seeing Joachim's attached to such a public document surely dredged up unpleasant memories. Following Mendelssohn's death, Joachim had studied with Liszt at Weimar, and in 1853 left for Hanover to become principal violinist for the court orchestra, at which time he also befriended Brahms and the Schumanns. Around 1855 he composed three overtures, including the *Hamlet* Overture discussed in Chapter 2, that extended

Mendelssohn's practice in ways not incompatible with Liszt's early experiments in the symphonic poem. Yet within only a few short years, such a great rift had grown between him and his former teacher that Joachim felt compelled to write to Liszt in 1857 that "Your music is entirely antagonistic to me; it contradicts everything with which the spirits of our great ones have nourished my mind from my earliest youth . . . I can be of no assistance to you, and I can no longer allow you to think that the aims for which you and your pupils are working are mine."[21]

 Although by far the most public defection, Joachim's was not unique among Liszt's pupils. In particular, Raff and Bülow – Joachim's closest friends at Weimar and also two of Liszt's most gifted pupils – also wavered in their commitment to the New German School in practice and principle. (Even Draeseke, whose defense of the New German School in the 1850s was without parallel, would end up criticizing the direction that Richard Strauss's modernist music was taking in the early twentieth century.) Consistent among these composers is the conscious emulation of the musico-poetic approaches of Schumann and especially Mendelssohn, an almost neo-classical dependence on traditional symphonic forms to undergird their programmatic musical essays, and a facility with orchestral writing that stems from their significant experience as conductors and concertmasters.

Bülow's *Nirwana*, his most ambitious programmatic composition, offers an excellent example of how the war of words that reached a fever pitch during the 1850s left deep scars on the resulting musical products for decades to come. Bülow first conceived of the work in early April 1854 as an overture in B minor, which by the end of the month he reported to Liszt as having had become "a musical daguerreotype of myself." On 30 September, Liszt wrote to his student that he has just finished reading through "your Fantasy for Orchestra ([on Carl Ritter's five-act tragedy,] *Ein Leben im Tode*)," and believes it to be "noble, profound," and rich in poetry, with musical ideas that move in an elevated spiritual plane.[22]

Sometime before the piece's premiere at the Berlin Singakademie on 27 February 1859 under the composer's baton, Liszt, thinking it wise to attach to the work a weighty literary analogue, suggested two possible titles: *Symphonic Prologue to [Schiller's] "The Robbers"* or *Symphonic Prologue to Byron's "Cain."*[23] Bülow chose the latter for the premiere, but when he published the composition in 1866, he dispensed with the literary allusion and christened the work *Nirwana: Symphonisches Stimmungsbild* (*Extinction: Symphonic Mood Picture*). That Bülow intended *Nirwana* to be heard as an outlet for Arthur Schopenhauer's philosophy is clear from the program note he distributed to audiences at a performance at Meiningen in August 1867:

> The fervent desire for deliverance from the pain and suffering of individual existence, at constant odds with the powerful will to live, and struggling to hold

**Example 5.7** Bülow, *Nirwana*, mm. 1–10

on to the dream of a means of salvation other than the ethical one, which can only be achieved through the nullification of self and the denial of the will to live.[24]

In its quest for nullification, Bülow's subject relentlessly reinvents itself. The opening three bars (Example 5.7) generate almost all of the ensuing thematic material, none of which can viably be termed "melodic." Indeed, melody seems tantamount to the alluring, "powerful will to live" from which the motive and its several permutations seek escape. The relentlessly stark orientation of Bülow's symphonic poem might explain why Liszt suggested the two dramas by Schiller and Byron as useful models: Not only are they bound by destructive fraternal conflict, but both also focus on similarly broad issues, such as personal freedom and the nature of good and evil. In the case of *Cain*, for instance, it is the anti-hero Lucifer who begs Paradise's inhabitants to challenge inherited wisdom about their Maker: "Think and endure, – and form an inner world / In your own bosom – where the outward fails; / So shall you nearer be the spiritual / Nature, and war triumphant with your own" (Act II, scene 2, ll. 463–466).

Bülow republished the work in 1881. To a listener familiar with the original, the revised version would have sounded the same; but the printed score revealed two important differences: (1) all performance directions were changed from German to Italian; and, more importantly, (2) Bülow gave the work a new subtitle: "Orchesterfantasie in Ouvertürenform" ("Orchestral Fantasy in the Form of an Overture").

Bülow's early musical life revolved around Liszt and Wagner: he had studied with the former in the 1850s and married his daughter, Cosima, in 1857; he conducted for the latter in the 1860s – premiering both *Tristan und Isolde* and *Die Meistersinger von Nürnberg* to great acclaim – and lost his wife, the very same Cosima, to Wagner in late November 1863. To be sure, Bülow's soap opera of a life in the late 1860s accounted for his haphazard relationship with members of the New German camp, but his activities as conductor since the Franco-Prussian War also seem to have prompted him to consider the divisive form-versus-content question anew. By the 1880s he had grown convinced that the New German position was flawed, and that it

*organicism*

had been Felix Mendelssohn who represented the decisive link in the symphonic chain between Beethoven and Brahms. In fact, echoing a claim that A.B. Marx had made more than fifty years earlier (see Chapter 2), Bülow had become convinced that it was Mendelssohn, not Liszt, whose programmatic instrumental music represented the most promising development of Beethoven's symphonic revolution.

The Mendelssohn connection is even stronger with Joachim Raff, who moved from Hamburg to Weimar in January 1850 in order to serve as Liszt's amanuensis. His talents as a polemicist were highly regarded by Liszt and his circle, and his compositions from the early part of the decade – indebted to Liszt and Wagner, as well as Schumann and Mendelssohn, with whom Raff had originally hoped to study – were given sympathetic hearings. But by the middle of the decade, he had become thoroughly disillusioned at Weimar, and in 1856 moved to Wiesbaden.

At the time of his death twenty-six years later, his compositional catalogue included numerous orchestral overtures, nine concertante works, six operas, nine string quartets, fifteen song collections, and over one hundred piano pieces. Indeed, with over three hundred works in all, Raff stands as Liszt's most prolific student. Despite, or perhaps due to, his disdain for the New German School, he is also the most prolific composer of program music to emerge from Liszt's circle. Nine of his eleven symphonies are programmatic, with topics ranging from landscapes (nos. 3 and 7) and the seasons (nos. 8–11) to literature (no. 5), philosophy (no. 6), and the German nation (no. 1). Many of these interests also permeate his overtures (e.g., Shakespeare), orchestral suites (Italy, Hungary, and Thuringia), and piano music.

From a conceptual point of view, Raff's program music demonstrates a thorough schooling in and attempted extensions of Liszt's practices. For instance, the Third Symphony, entitled "Im Walde" ("In the Woods"), features the traditional four movements but is divided programmatically into three parts, with movement one covering "Daytime," movements two and three "Twilight," and movement four "Night"; an elaborate program further divides "Night" into three parts. Despite such programmatic abundance, however, most individual movements or sections within his programmatic works remain at heart character pieces, such as the Seventh Symphony's inner movements, "In the Inn" and "At the Lake," the Eclogue of the Ninth, the hunt finale of the Tenth, or the Schumannesque "By the Fireside" of the Eleventh.

Such is the nature of Raff's Fifth Symphony, first performed in late 1872 and published one year later. Although named after Gottfried August Bürger's ballad *Lenore*, released a century earlier, only the symphony's finale addresses Bürger's material (see Figure 5.1). The first three movements offer a prequel to the action by addressing, as Raff explained,

> the happiness of two lovers . . . interrupted by war. The time has come when he must go forth with his fellow soldiers and she remain behind alone. In this

**Figure 5.1** *Lenore*. Steel engraving, probably by Carl Mayer of Nuremberg, in *Panorama der deutschen Klassiker*

solitude, evil forebodings take possession of her. She falls into a fever, in which her hallucinations represent to her the return of her lover. But these hallucinations prepare, in reality, only her own death.[25]

Raff's program for the Fifth Symphony moves from the generic to the specific via decidedly "New German" techniques, such that the finale is a symphonic poem in all but name. The excellent first movement bristles with the same vivacity of the first movement of Mendelssohn's "Italian" Symphony and Wagner's Act III Prelude to *Lohengrin*, rarely losing sight of the lovers' passion. Indeed, the second movement, which with the first constitutes a section Raff dubs "Love's Joy" ("Liebesglück"), is in A♭ major, a key favored by Wagner for intense love scenes. The symphony as a whole moves by thirds from E major, through A♭ major and C major, and back to E minor / major – keys associated generally with Liszt's practices, but also specifically with *Les Préludes* and the gothic *Faust* Symphony. (Raff's previous three symphonies explore alternative tertiary relationships among movements.) The recollection of themes from the first three movements in the finale also points to the *Faust* Symphony, as well as Beethoven's Fifth and Ninth Symphonies. Whereas the first three movements tout traditional symphonic forms (sonata, rondo, march, respectively), the fourth movement is through-composed according to its program, not unlike the finale of Berlioz's *Symphonie fantastique*, with which it also shares many orchestral effects. Finally, Raff is not above changing his source material to better suit the program. Thus Lenore's death around m. 390, the event that concludes Bürger's ballad, is followed at m. 403 by a chorale. The chorale returns the work to its true home of E major, an act associated with Lenore's salvation through love – yet another theme dear to Liszt and especially Wagner.

Besides writing symphonies and avoiding the term "symphonic poem," Raff's most distinctive anti-New German trait is harmonic conservatism, a sticking point in which his conceptual ideas usually break down in practice. In 1857, Draeseke distilled New German harmonic procedures into two basic principles:

*strange*

*he wanted to write a book on harmony*

1. "Any consonant chord can follow any other consonant chord if the progression of the individual intervals is stepwise or the intervals are common to both triads."
2. "Any dissonant chord can resolve to any consonant chord whose intervals are separated from its own by one step or are partly contained within it, with the obvious caveat that no interval of the dissonance can move to a tone belonging to the harmony of the same dissonance."[26]

Following these rules severely destabilizes a sense of tonic, and Raff's music follows them only in extremely rare circumstances. Indeed, most of his music is tonally certain, even in transitional passages and development sections. Rather than offer an enhanced harmonic palette, then, he relies heavily on sequences and dense counterpoint. Sometimes this approach is effective, as in the Overture to *Ein' feste Burg ist unser Gott* from 1865, in which a contentious fugue functions as transition to the recapitulation. When the moment of thematic return comes, Raff superimposes the Protestant melody, "Ein' feste Burg ist unser Gott," above the primary theme. Like Mendelssohn's Second Symphony ("Lobgesang") and the still unpublished "Reformation" Symphony, the message of Raff's overture is clear: the struggle of the faithful in the development has made possible their religious freedom in the recapitulation and beyond. But more often than not, Raff's tactics expose "an insoluble problem in [his] larger works – prolixity. His attempt . . . to reconcile the demands of his program and the traditions of sonata form results in sections that are necessary for one, but irrelevant to the other."[27]

## Liszt's New German legacy

If most of Liszt's early pupils set out on their own programmatic paths, others invoked his name in order to justify their own musical aims. Perhaps the most colorful devotee not directly affiliated with Liszt's circle was Hugo Wolf. Based in Vienna, Wolf railed against what he saw as the city's antiquarian tastes, which were having a deleterious effect on the progress of modern, poetic composition. Liszt became a powerful antidote to such a pandemic: "If you want symphonies today as Beethoven wrote them," Wolf opined in a review from April 1884,

> then turn the clock back a century, wake the master from the dead, but don't place beside him our epigones, these impotent contemporary symphonists decked out in classical garb and flirting with the classical spirit ... As for Liszt's music, it is more intelligent than deeply felt, but vividly and warmly fanciful, and always plastic. Are the themes in our celebrated new symphonies plastic? As a rule, not.[28]

Wolf clearly saw the symphonic poem as the next step in music's evolution, as being "for modern music what Haydn's symphonies were for that master's contemporaries and successors," and he drove this point home by concluding his review with a provocative statement that pitted symphonic poet against symphonist: "The very idea of comparing Liszt with Brahms! Genius with the epigone of an epigone, the eagle with the wren. Enough!"[29]

Wolf's fanatical defense of the original New Germans at the expense of Hanslick and Brahms explains the humiliating reception of his only symphonic poem, *Penthesilea*, completed one year later with encouragement from Liszt himself. Clocking in at close to thirty minutes in length, the single-movement, three-part piece is uncharacteristic of Wolf for its size. Its scope, however, is entirely consistent with the highly emotive, psychologically intense songs for which he is justifiably famous.

Less colorful but arguably more long-lasting connections with the New Germans were made elsewhere. As discussed in Chapter 9, Camille Saint-Saëns cited Liszt's symphonic poems as possible springboards for French musical innovation in the wake of the Franco-Prussian War. And in Hungary, Ödön Mihalovich, whose training included classes with Moritz Hauptmann and Peter Cornelius at the Leipzig Conservatory and Hans von Bülow for piano studies, produced symphonic poems in the 1870s and early 1880s on thoroughly New German subjects, including *The Ghost Ship* (cf. Wagner, Tausig), *The Mermaid* (cf. Liszt's *Loreley*), *Hero and Leander*, *Sabbath Round* (cf. Berlioz), as well as a symphonic poem and separate orchestral fantasy on Goethe's *Faust*. His professional relationship with Liszt led to many of these works being performed abroad, and his commitment to Hungarian music – he viewed himself as a synthesizer of New German and Hungarian musical traditions – made him a shoo-in for the directorship of the Budapest Music Academy after Liszt's death, a position he held for the next thirty-two years.[30]

## The New Russian School

The most direct emulation of the ideas and environment of the New German School came from Russia in the 1860s. Not only did the New Russians share a similar organizational structure with the New Germans, but they also focused heavily on the production of program music and opera, which they aggressively promoted in the press in the shadow of an ostensibly artistically stifling conservatory. And like the New Germans, their battles revolved around misunderstandings, misrepresentations, and a propagandistic effort to justify their positions and products through vaguely defined notions of tradition, nation, and progress.

The debate began in May 1855, when the celebrated pianist, promising conductor, and active composer Anton Rubinstein published an article entitled "Russia's Composers" in the Viennese arts journal *Blätter für Musik, Theater und Kunst.* Seeking to provide Western European readers with an overview of "the development of musical art in Russia with particular attention to the practice of this art in recent times,"[31] Rubinstein explained that music in his native land had long since found outlets in the church, but only recently had it practiced "music as art" by tackling the genres of opera and Lied.

It was Mikhail Glinka who hit upon the "bold but unhappy idea" of composing national opera, the results being *A Life for the Tsar* (1836) and *Ruslan and Lyudmila* (1842). Distinguishing between legitimate folk music and illegitimate folk opera, Rubinstein criticized Glinka's decision to use a "folk tone" ("Volkton") instead of a "world tone" ("Weltton"). Rubinstein was not singling out Glinka per se, for such national enterprise is bound to fail regardless of country. Thus "from a general aesthetic perspective," Rubinstein proposed that any attempt at a specifically national work would fail.

Rubinstein continues his survey by highlighting the dominance of Italian opera in St. Petersburg post-Glinka, which in his opinion has effectively squelched operatic innovation among his countrymen. In fact, the only genre in which composers in Russia have demonstrated any distinction is the Lied, since "the Lied is the only type of music that has a fatherland." Rubinstein concludes with the hope that these composers receive well-deserved approval from the rest of Europe, and encourages foreign publishers to issue "at the very least the Lieder (in dual-language editions), since they would offer the public much that is new, open up promising paths for other artists to consider, and expand the usefulness of the artistic circle overall."

This article was only a foretaste of the impact that Rubinstein would make on Russian music. By the end of the decade, he would found the Russian Music Society, which "has among its goals the performance of works from all composers, all schools, and all times."[32] And in the early 1860s he began to lay the groundwork for the founding of a local music institution where professional musicians could be trained – the ultimate result being the St. Petersburg Conservatory. It was during this campaign that he published another article, this time only in the Russian press, entitled "On Music in Russia," in which he complained that dilettantism had stymied musical progress in the motherland.

Rubinstein's characterization of music in Russia met with fierce hostility at home, primarily from a group of composers associated with the pianist and composer Mily Balakirev. This group, whom the critic Vladimir Stasov would later christen "The Mighty Handful" and "The New Russian School," sought to counter Rubinstein's claims that national or folk music could never be suitable bases for universal art music, as well as the more general contention that Russian music must adhere to German standards and tradition. (Rubinstein's Conservatory, the xenophobic New Russians believed, was just another one of the many "foreign products [that] have been grafted onto us.")[33] Balakirev had met Glinka only a few months after Rubinstein's article appeared, and soon set out to prove the viability of "folk tones" as proper art subjects in his two Overtures on Russian Themes (1858, revised 1881; 1864, revised 1884), both modeled on Glinka's *Kamarinskaya* from 1848. Indeed, Balakirev derided Rubinstein as much for his criticism of the venerable Russian master as he did the characterization of his fellow Russian musicians as amateurs.

In truth, the steadfast members of his circle were just that. Balakirev was a virtuoso pianist with spotty formal musical training, but Aleksandr Borodin, César Cui, Modest Musorgsky, and Nikolai Rimsky-Korsakov were not professional musicians. Nevertheless, Balakirev's strong leadership – critics would characterize it as authoritarian control – of the New Russians in the 1860s resulted in a relatively uniform aesthetic, stylistic identity, and set of consistent practices among its members, including:

- The advancement of Russian and/or exotic styles in both instrumental and vocal (especially operatic) genres;
- An interest in East-European folk music (e.g., Serbian, Czech, Russian);
- A strong distrust of establishments, such as the German symphonic tradition or the conservatory system;
- Passing interest in the symphony;
- An identification with Liszt and his progressive New German School, as well as an attachment to his program music for orchestra and for piano;
- Intense collaboration, such that "new idioms" developed by individual members "became shared property" by all;[34]
- A typically slow compositional pace, resulting in many unfinished compositions. Moreover, pieces were revised many years later.

By the end of the century the New Russians had responded to Rubinstein's challenge by producing operas in a quantity that rivaled any other country in the world, with *Boris Godunov*, *Eugene Onegin*, and *Prince Igor* being the most famous tip of the iceberg. However, one unintended consequence of their answer to Rubinstein's position was the production of equally enduring pieces of program music.

In fact, Rubinstein had remained silent regarding instrumental music, but his output from the period suggests that Russian symphonic music was as much an oxymoron as Russian opera. For example, less than a year before his article appeared, Rubinstein performed his Second Symphony, subtitled "Ocean," for the first time in Germany. Despite the tantalizing programmatic title and near ubiquitous tremolos and wave-like contours heaped on all but the third movement, Rubinstein's programmatic concern was at best the evocation or depiction of a topical event. Thus aesthetically he positioned himself in the lineage of Beethoven and Mendelssohn, the latter a composer of especially dubious character according to the New Russians.[35] Indeed, the C major Symphony's four discrete movements[36] betray numerous structural and characteristic debts to bygone German models; the fourth movement even recalls material from the second in order to revisit the Beethovenian narrative of struggle and victory.

Few works from the New Russian School follow such a traditional path. Neither Cui nor Musorgsky published any symphonies. Balakirev began one in C major in the mid-1860s, but left it unfinished until the late 1890s, which he then followed up with a second symphony in D minor in 1908. Borodin's two completed symphonies convey many characteristic "Russian" qualities (especially the Second), while Rimsky-Korsakov's nominal Second Symphony – which exists in four versions as either symphony or suite – is related programmatically to a "Persian tale" ("conte arabe") by the popular orientalist author Osip Senkovsky. (Rubinstein, by contrast, would compose six symphonies.)

Indeed, most of the other large-scale orchestral works to come from this group programmatically stress their Russianness – that is, their distance from German art music – by utilizing folk material (melodies, tales, etc.) or projecting "oriental" features. In this sense, they stand apart from the mainstream of German art music, including New German musicians, who tended to take masterpieces of world literature or art as their compositional starting points. Yet especially from technical and structural points of view, the New Russians nevertheless could legitimately and did often credit their music as developing models already put forth by Glinka, Liszt, and Berlioz.

Balakirev's *Tamara* is a case in point. Composed between 1867 and 1882 and published in 1884 with a dedication to Liszt, the orchestral work is based on Mikhail Lermontov's poem of the same name, in which the Queen Tamara – a Lorelei-like figure whose "beautiful face was angelic, / Her spirit demonic and

**Example 5.8** Balakirev, *Tamara*, mm. 136–139

mean" (ll. 7–8)[37] – lures lost pilgrims to her ancient abode. A night of passion ensues, but at daybreak Tamara is the only one to awake.

True to the nature and actions of its heroine, Balakirev's symphonic poem is an exercise in musical seduction and evocation of the landscapes of the Caucasus. The former is achieved through generous use of timpani, triangle, cymbals, and other percussion, as well as select use of two harps and solo wind instruments. Example 5.8

**Example 5.9** Balakirev, *Tamara*, m. 2

suggests how Tamara uses multiple methods of attracting her ill-fated lovers: the oboe coquettishly darts around B minor and its dominant pitch F♯ by here landing on G♮, there G♯. Choosing neither, it instead wends its way down the chromatic scale. Under this elusive line bounce the strings in carefree open fifths, while a snare drum repeats a hypnotic eighth-note rhythmic pattern. The flute above, sitting on the same F♯ as the oboe, builds tension that will not release until m. 146. Balakirev avails himself of other opportunities throughout the work to develop Tamara's exotic appeal, and nowhere does she display stronger confidence – doubtlessly bolstered by the outcomes of countless previous engagements – than during moments of erotic counterpoint between her and her newest catch (see, e.g., mm. 379–402).

Fittingly, such moments appear in developmental sections, reminders that Balakirev shaped the structure of his symphonic poem according to sonata principle, albeit after Liszt's heavily distorted fashion. Likewise, he also employs Liszt's technique of thematic transformation. Tamara's siren song grows out of the work's first gesture (Example 5.9), in which a twelve-note wave figure vacillates between Phrygian and Aeolian modes. At this point, however, it divulges nothing of its exotic potential. Instead, it follows a course that moves from B minor to D major to F♯ major. The chain of thirds is typically Lisztian, and the specific key choices may also point to the opening gambit of Mendelssohn's "Hebrides" Overture, discussed in Chapter 8. After the two-part introduction (mm. 1–71), however, Balakirev reveals the piece's true harmonic confrontation: D♭ major vs. D major. In 1869, Balakirev would survey this territory again in *Islamey*, a solo piano piece of near superhuman virtuosity, which also employs music that the composer had heard while vacationing in the Caucasus. Rimsky-Korsakov remembered that Balakirev "had an exclusive predilection for [these two keys] in those days,"[38] a predilection which also helps to explain a similar harmonic structure that governs Rimsky-Korsakov's "musical tableau," *Sadko* (1867; revised 1869, 1892), which may have been written, per Balakirev's request, as "a Russian alternative" to Rubinstein's "Ocean" Symphony.[39]

Balakirev's second overture on Russian themes also demonstrates that, like Liszt and his New German students, a work's program was as much subject to revision as its pitches. At an early point in its life, Balakirev identified the composition with nationalist sentiments akin to those that inspired Sibelius's *Finlandia* (see Chapter 8), but the composer released the work to the public in 1869 as *1,000 Years: A Musical Picture*. The program no longer concerned the unsettled present, but rather celebrated Russia's first millennium in order to bid welcome to its hopeful, modern future. Yet when Balakirev returned to the piece in the 1880s, he had enough doubts about the title to reissue the piece as a symphonic poem entitled *Rus'*, the name for Russia in the Old Slavonic tongue. The composer justified the name change by referencing the piece's historical character in a new preface:

> I selected the themes of three folk songs from my own anthology,[40] by which I wished to characterize three elements in our history: the pagan period, the Muscovite order, and the autonomous republican system, reborn among the Cossacks. Strife among these elements, expressed in the symphonic development of these themes, has furnished the content of the instrumental drama, to which the present title is far better suited than the previous one, since the author had no intention of drawing a picture of our thousand-year history but only a wish to characterize some of its constituent elements.[41]

If Balakirev was primarily responsible for shaping the aesthetic profile of the New Russian School in its early years, then it was Rimsky-Korsakov who updated and canonized it for later generations of composers that included Aleksandr Glazunov and Igor Stravinsky in Russia, as well as Debussy, Ravel, and Ottorino Respighi abroad. Rimsky-Korsakov put many New Russian works into their definitive versions, including Borodin's *Prince Igor* and Second Symphony, Aleksandr Dargomïzhsky's *The Stone Guest*, and much of Musorgsky's music.

Many of his editorial interventions, in fact, raise his status to that of co-author, as a comparison of Musorgsky's *Night on Bald Mountain* from 1867 and Rimsky-Korsakov's version of 1886 makes clear. Musorgsky had explained to Rimsky-Korsakov after completing the work that "the general character of the thing is hot; it doesn't drag, the transitions are compact and dense without any Germanic approach, which really freshens things up . . . [It] is something new and should make a satisfactory impression on the thinking musician."[42]

Musorgsky's composition divides cleanly into two sections of almost equal length: the first, mm. 1–260, involves three theme groups, by far the most prominent of which is a turning figure that rises and falls through a perfect fourth (see Example 5.10). The impish character of this theme makes it prone to severe metric distortions (e.g., mm. 109–112), which abate only upon the appearance of a new

**Example 5.10** Musorgsky, *St. John's Night on Bald Mountain* (1867), mm. 109–112

set of related ideas at m. 142. This section features some of Musorgsky's most avant-garde music, including an original use of the whole-tone scale in contrary motion at m. 246ff. This climactic moment ends the first half of the work; the second half (mm. 261–545) features seven variations on the main theme. Connection to the earlier half of the work is made by a hazy recollection of the opening section (mm. 1–86) during the extended fourth variation (mm. 358–443) and a repurposed contrary-motion whole-tone scale at mm. 514–529.

Musorgsky showed his coming-of-age work – then titled *St. John's Night on Bald Mountain* – to Balakirev, who refused to program it. Rather than cool the piece down, so to speak, in order to secure a performance, Musorgsky let it sit until he found a place for some of its material in two stage projects from the 1870s. Thus when Rimsky-Korsakov turned to the piece soon after Musorgsky's death in 1881, three versions were at his disposal. After summarizing the work's complicated compositional history in a preface to his edition, Rimsky-Korsakov explained his approach to the music: "I took from the materials left behind after the composer's death everything he considered to be the best and most suitable for giving coherence and integrity to the work."[43]

Although the editor / reviser had known this work and its subsequent transformations intimately, it is impossible to verify Rimsky-Korsakov's claims of Musorgsky's blessing. Rimsky-Korsakov retouched and re-orchestrated much of the original material and drastically cut its length by almost twenty percent, but the furthest-reaching changes involve structure. The *Night on Bald Mountain* of 1886 strongly projects sonata form by replacing Musorgsky's sequence of variations with a shortened recapitulation (mm. 260–380) of the opening one hundred and sixty-three bars. Indeed, a clear development section materializes at the new key change from one flat to three sharps at m. 164, which also features a new theme in the winds and a transformation into barks and grunts of material from the early part of the exposition. Rimsky-Korsakov's version is also more self-aware tonally: nowhere, for instance, are there bald presentations of – or even allusions to – the whole-tone scale, nor do the capricious, non-functional chord progressions of the original make an appearance.

To be sure, Rimsky-Korsakov's emendations could be viewed as giving into the very "Germanic approach" against which Musorgsky railed, but they just might as easily reflect an attempt to honor Musorgsky's program, which the composer had left on the manuscript of the earlier version:

> Subterranean noises of supernatural voices. Appearance of spirits of darkness, and, after them, Chernobog (the Black God). Celebration of Chernobog and the Black Mass. [Witches'] Sabbath. At the height of the Sabbath, the bell of the little village church reverberates in the distance and disperses the spirits of darkness. Daybreak.

Its Russian source material notwithstanding, Musorgsky's [*St. John's*] *Night on Bald Mountain* owes much conceptually to Berlioz's *Symphonie fantastique*, Mendelssohn's *Die erste Walpurgisnacht*, Liszt's *Totentanz*, *Faust* Symphony, and "Mephisto" Waltz, and the more recent *Danse macabre* by Camille Saint-Saëns. This last work might even have been an inspiration for *Night on Bald Mountain*'s new coda, mm. 381–458.

These connections helped bring music of the New Russian School to the attention of the West, but it came with a price, one which Rubinstein predicted almost a half-century earlier. When Rimsky-Korsakov took the music of his kinsmen – including the recently renovated *Night on Bald Mountain* – to the stages of Paris's *Exposition Universelle* in 1889, audiences were equally enamored and put off. One French critic determined that Glazunov's symphonic poem *Stenka Razine*, about a rebellious seventeenth-century Cossack, possessed

> all the essential qualities and the incontestable faults of the Russian musical school: a very clever and frequent use of popular motives, such as the song of the Volga boatmen, on which this entire musical tableau is built; a rare instinct for combining the strangest rhythms and for extracting from them effects of extraordinary violence and relief; an expressive and tender melancholy; a rare ability to describe through sounds all the episodes of a small imaginary drama; but also an exaggerated search of color, of the picturesque effect; a veritable abuse of developments or orchestral combinations; and above all, the absence of an underlying plan.[44]

Composers of program music who affiliated themselves with "new" schools in the second half of the century were often criticized for foisting artifice instead of producing art. Problems only multiplied once borders were crossed: Liszt's *Hungaria* may have been written by a nation's self-professed rhapsodist, but it was at best marginally Hungarian, and would be increasingly denounced as inauthentic as the century wore on. And although Musorgsky's *St. John's Night on Bald Mountain* sported a level of unabashedly Russian rawness that arguably would not be eclipsed until Stravinsky's *The Rite of Spring* almost fifty years later, it was deemed by Balakirev too aloof of Beethoven and the cosmopolitan Glinka to warrant further artistic consideration.[45] Nor did these upstart schools replace earlier traditions and institutions – if anything, partisans became more divided on the central issues of music and meaning, particularly as more ideologically minded individuals entered the compositional fray.

## Chapter 6

# *Excursus:* Faust

As the surrounding chapters chronicle, Homer, Ovid, William Shakespeare, Lord Byron, and dozens of other writers produced hundreds, probably thousands, of works of literature that enjoyed second lives in music during the common practice period. However, arguably no single literary work has attracted a greater number of musicians than Johann Wolfgang von Goethe's closet drama *Faust*. While it has inspired several operatic adaptations since its publication in the early nineteenth century, along with numerous scores of incidental music written to accompany the play, *Faust* is notable for its manifold transformations – in whole or part – into overtures, symphonies, symphonic poems, sonatas, ballets, cantatas, choruses, and solo songs by composers as stylistically diverse and chronologically separate as Franz Schubert, Hector Berlioz, Robert Schumann, Franz Liszt, Charles-Valentin Alkan, Gustav Mahler, Ferruccio Busoni, Lili Boulanger, Igor Stravinsky, and Alfred Schnittke. Moreover, in attempting to assimilate and occasionally depart from Goethe's complex stage drama and other elements of the Faustian legend, many of these composers also expanded the limits of music's programmatic potential. This chapter identifies common strands and divergent paths taken in that pursuit.

## Goethe's *Faust*: origins, themes, legacy

Goethe did not invent the tale of Faust, but rather drew upon a corpus of Faustian stories and legends – some of which went back more than two centuries – that had long since become part of German and, to a lesser extent, European folklore.[1] In fact, the crux of Goethe's play can be traced back to the anonymous *Historia von D. Johann Fausten*, published by Johann Spies at Frankfurt am Main in 1587. Here the brilliant physician and theologian Doctor Faustus, motivated by a "godless and reckless resolve,"[2] enters into a pact with a devil named Mephistopheles.[3] In exchange for his soul, Faustus receives twenty-four years of limitless abilities, allowing him to accumulate (forbidden) knowledge, wealth, success, and companionship. Toward the end of the book, with his life almost at an end, Faustus attempts reconciliation with God but fails. At the appointed hour, a tempest descends on his locked chambers. The next day, friends and students find Faustus's still twitching mangled corpse strewn across a dung heap outside.

The popularity of this unassuming chapbook (so-called for its easily portable size) is evidenced by numerous expanded revisions in the late sixteenth and early seventeenth centuries, in which Faustus's sensational but blasphemous exploits are given over to increasingly lengthy and sententious editorial commentary, generally in the form of admonishing "Prefaces to the Christian reader" ("Vorreden an den Christlichen Leser"). Such interpretive aids are largely superfluous, however, since the story concludes not only with Faustus's spectacularly gruesome demise, but also with an unambiguous warning and path to salvation. Readers are instructed to:

> learn to fear God, to flee sorcery, conjuration of spirits, and other works of the Devil, not to invite the Devil into their houses, nor to yield unto him in any other way, as Doctor Faustus did, for we have before us here the frightful and horrible example of his pact and death to help us shun such acts and pray to God alone in all matters, love Him with all our heart and with all our soul and with all our strength, defying the Devil with all his following, that we may through Christ be eternally blessed.[4]

Faustus is endowed with a far more nuanced personality in the first literary treatment of his life and legend, Christopher Marlowe's *The Tragical History of the Life and Death of Dr. Faustus*, published posthumously in 1604.[5] A product of the late sixteenth century, Marlowe's Dr. Faustus is distinguished from his predecessor by his exploratory nature. Although he has mastered philosophy, logic, medicine, law, and divinity, Faustus must admit to himself that "Yet art thou still but Faustus, and a man" (i.25).[6] In other words, he has exhausted all noble, earthly professional options. His only recourse, blasphemous though it might be, is to delve into the dark arts. He issues himself a new challenge: "A sound magician is a mighty god. / Here Faustus, try thy brains to gain a deity" (i.62–63).

Although Marlowe's Faustus ultimately shares the same fate as his German counterpart, his route to damnation is far more tragic. He is not predestined for Hell, as he appears to be in Spies's *Historia*. Marlowe's devils manipulate Faustus by increasingly distancing him from God, as when Lucifer reminds Faustus that, per the rules of the contract, "We come to tell thee thou dost injure us. / Thou talk'st of Christ, contrary to thy promise" (vi.264–265). At the same time, they offer no suitable substitute: Even the appearance of Helen of Troy, the personification of beauty, in scene xii only reinforces the ephemeral nature of life and Faustus's growing despair with it. Finally, perhaps the most tragic element of Faustus's fate is communicated through the antagonist Mephistopheles: "Think'st thou that I, who saw the face of God, / And tasted the eternal joys of heaven, / Am not tormented with ten thousand hells / In being deprived of everlasting bliss!" (iii.78–81).

As Mephistopheles's pathetic remark makes clear, characters in the Faustian universe need not necessarily be pigeonholed into medieval binaries of good and evil. To be sure, the monochromatic moralizing of the earliest Faust stories continued on the European continent for centuries via new written adventures, puppet-plays, and folkloristic verse like "Doktor Faustus" from the early nineteenth-century collection *Des Knaben Wunderhorn*. But whereas Faust had traditionally served as a warning to those with overly inquisitive minds or defiant personalities, by the late eighteenth century such characteristics had become not damnable, but enviable, even essential. Goethe's *Faust* problematizes traditional Christian theodicy by reveling in an ambiguous, perhaps even absent, moral framework. Indeed, while the eponymous protagonist still remains accountable for his actions, it is his Romantic ability to persevere despite failure that ultimately redeems him in the eyes of God, who even notes in Goethe's "Prologue in Heaven" that "Man ever errs the while he strives" (l. 317).[7] Far from a condemnation, then, the observation – made immediately after God's bet with Mephistopheles – makes clear that he who stops striving ceases to be human.

Faust's journey toward salvation occupied Goethe almost sixty years, nearly the whole of his professional career. Sometime in the early 1770s he composed what has come to be known since its discovery and publication in 1887 as *Urfaust* (*Early Faust*), a tale that shares many points in common with the final version of Goethe's conception but, among other differences, leaves the eternal fate of Faust's lover, Gretchen, unanswered. While there is evidence to suggest that Goethe circulated his *Urfaust* among select acquaintances, it was only in 1790 that he published *Faust. Ein Fragment* (*Faust. A Fragment*), which featured expanded coverage of Faust's situation but tamped down the severity of Gretchen's tragedy. Goethe again resumed work on the story near the end of the century, releasing *Faust. Eine Tragödie* (*Faust. A Tragedy*) in 1808. For the next twenty-four years, this would serve as Goethe's definitive statement. However, in 1831 he completed *Faust. Der Tragödie zweiter Theil* (*Faust. The Second Part of the Tragedy*), which upon its posthumous publication in 1832 expanded the Faustian universe to include the court of the Holy Roman Emperor, the palace of Menelaus at Sparta, and Arcadia, among other locales and characters. (Incidentally, some of its episodes realign Goethe's *Faust* with the tradition of the earliest Faust stories and Marlowe's play.) The first and second parts of *Faust* unfold over twelve thousand lines of mostly rhymed poetry, arguably constituting one of the most epic feats of nineteenth-century German literature. However, composers (and general readers) have routinely favored the first part – with its set of core characters, tight construction, and accessible style – over the second, due in large part to the latter's rich allusions, sprawling storylines, and extreme length.

Since the publication of *Faust. A Fragment*, Goethe's readers had asked him to clarify the ideas within its pages, and requests only intensified after the appearance of *Faust. A Tragedy*. Goethe rarely obliged in providing interpretations, however, since, as he related to his amanuensis Johann Peter Eckermann on 6 May 1827, *Faust* possessed no overriding theme:

> A man continually struggling from difficult errors towards something better, should be redeemed, is an effective – and, to many, a good enlightening – thought; but it is no idea at the foundation of the whole, and of every individual scene. It would have been a fine thing indeed if I had strung so rich, varied, and highly diversified a life as I have brought to view in *Faust* upon the slender string of one pervading idea. It was, in short . . . not in my line, as a poet, to strive to embody anything *abstract* . . . I am rather of the opinion, that the more incommensurable, and the more incomprehensible to the understanding, a poetic production is, so much the better it is.[8]

Goethe's *Faust* materializes through three main characters: Faust, Gretchen, and Mephistopheles. Faust begins the play world-wearied, contemplating suicide as much as the cosmos, before Mephistopheles and Gretchen independently rekindle his waning passions. The naïve, pious, and pure Gretchen is a completely new addition to the Faust tradition, and it is her precipitous downfall that comprises the play's most tragic elements: she inadvertently kills her mother, her affair with Faust leads to her brother's death, and she is sentenced to the gallows for infanticide. As it turns out, her faith in God saves her at the end of Part I, just as her intercession from beyond redeems Faust in Part II. Mephistopheles is Goethe's most nuanced of the three main characters, providing everything from philosophical insight, ribald humor, and appropriate ambiguity in almost every scene in which he appears. As he explains to Faust at their first meeting, he is "Part of that force which would / Do ever evil, and does ever good . . . The spirit that eternally denies!" (ll. 1335–1336, 1338).[9] In epitomizing the inseparability of good and evil, Mephistopheles's presence in *Faust* severely problematizes the tale's time-tested moral lesson. While Mephistopheles is at his most productive – and usually destructive – when he is able to negatively refract the thoughts and actions of his victims, events he facilitates occasionally result in unforeseen outcomes that end up bolstering the good. (The play's scenic divisions are given in Table 6.1.)

Indeed, Goethe's characterizations of Faust, Gretchen, and especially Mephistopheles fundamentally shift the emphasis of *Faust* from the dynamics of "good and evil" or "right and wrong" to what Jane K. Brown has characterized as the "epistemological and aesthetic." As a result, Goethe allows themes to proliferate and overlap at almost dizzying speed: instinct and institution; creation and destruction; spirit and flesh; comic and serious; separation and synthesis; literal and figurative; time and vision; statement and meaning; art and nature; real and ideal; subject and object; earthly confusion and celestial order; and tradition and (subversive)

**Table 6.1** *Goethe,* Faust I, *scenes*

Dedication (ll. 1–32)
Prelude in the Theatre (ll. 33–242)
Prologue in Heaven (ll. 243–353)
Night (ll. 354–807)
Before the City Gate (ll. 808–1177)
Study (ll. 1178–1529)
Study (ll. 1530–2072)
Auerbach's Cellar (ll. 2073–2336)
The Witch's Kitchen (ll. 2337–2604)
Street (ll. 2605–2677)
Evening (ll. 2678–2804)
Promenade (ll. 2805–2864)
The Neighbor's House (ll. 2865–3024)
Street (ll. 3025–3072)
Garden (ll. 3073–3204)
A Garden Bower (ll. 3205–3216)
Wood and Cave (ll. 3217–3373)
Gretchen's Room (ll. 3374–3413)
Martha's Garden (ll. 3414–3543)
At the Well (ll. 3544–3586)
City Wall (ll. 3587–3619)
Night (ll. 3620–3775)
Cathedral (ll. 3776–3834)
Walpurgis Night (ll. 3835–4222)
Walpurgis Night's Dream (ll. 4223–4398)
Dismal Day (*prose*)
Night. Open Field (ll. 4399–4404)
Dungeon (ll. 4405–4612)

innovation.[10] And instead of presenting such binaries as irreconcilable, Goethe tends to explore them dialectically.

Music in *Faust* constitutes an essential element in conveying many of these themes. The first extended introduction to Gretchen as a simple and innocent maiden is highlighted by her singing "Es war ein König in Thule" (ll. 2759–2782), a ballad about a king whose lifelong fidelity to his deceased queen prefigures Gretchen's fidelity to Faust. The spinning song, famously set by Schubert as "Gretchen am Spinnrade," D118, in 1814, is a scene unto itself (ll. 3374–3413), in which she is overcome by recollections of her absent lover. But music also preys on her anxieties, as in the exceptional "Cathedral" scene, where her guilt is fueled by the whisperings of an Evil Spirit in one ear, and the most fire-and-brimstone verses of the sequence "Dies irae" in the other (ll. 3776–3834). And despite her madness in the

"Dungeon" scene, she is able to cobble together some verses (ll. 4413–4420) and recall how the townspeople sang degrading songs at her (l. 4448).

Not surprisingly, it is Mephistopheles who exploits music as a vehicle for manipulation. He ingratiates himself to the tavern folk in Auerbach's Cellar by singing a "Song of the Flea" (ll. 2211–2218, 2223–2237), whose subject matter contrasts sharply with Gretchen's discerning king, discussed above. Later, Mephistopheles offers Faust a "moral song" that is anything but (ll. 3682–3697), the performance of which quickly leads to the murder of Valentin, Gretchen's brother. Unlike Gretchen and Mephistopheles, Faust never sings spontaneously, and his only musical moment occurs in a narrative trio (ll. 3871–3911) that heralds the Walpurgis Night.

Choruses are prevalent in *Faust*, and while the majority of ensembles are given to creatures affiliated with Mephistopheles, two important sacred choruses bookend Goethe's two-part story. The first occurs in Faust's chambers, in which the dejected Faust seeks to end his life by imbibing poison. As he raises the bowl to his lips, church bells ring out and a choir of angels sings the Easter hymn "Christ is arisen!" ("Christ ist erstanden!"; ll. 737–741), an announcement which prompts Faust to question his own decisions as well as Heaven's intentions. These will not be revealed until the final eight lines of *Faust II* (ll. 12104–12111), in which a "Chorus mysticus" – in its only appearance – explains that:

| | |
|---|---|
| Alles Vergängliche | All that is changeable |
| Ist nur ein Gleichnis; | Is but reflected; |
| Das Unzulängliche, | The unattainable |
| Hier wird's Ereignis; | Here is effected; |
| Das Unbeschreibliche, | Human discernment |
| Hier ist's getan; | Here is passed by; |
| Das Ewig-Weibliche | The Eternal-Feminine |
| Zieht uns hinan. | Draws us on high. |

Notable for its numerous allusions, evasions, and ambiguities, *Faust* loomed large in the imagination of the Romantic artist, to say nothing of the cultured (German) reader, for whom it represented nothing less than a "worldly Bible" ("Weltliche Bibel"). Ludwig van Beethoven, Schubert, and others had set some of the most lyrical passages from *Faust* to music soon after the publication of *Faust I* in 1808, and Hector Berlioz sought to offer a comprehensive overview of such moments in his *Huit scènes de Faust* of 1829. But it was not until well after the publication of *Faust II* that composers began to grapple with the broader aesthetic, philosophical, and dramatic dimensions of Goethe's sprawling play, with many of them turning to the medium of instrumental music for solutions. Yet despite the chronological proximity shared by many of these compositions, each operates under remarkably independent notions of genre, topic, and program.

## Symphonic metamorphoses (I): Wagner, Liszt

In December 1839, Wagner began work on a symphony based on *Faust*. He completed the first movement one month later, but its premiere was delayed for several legitimate reasons, including Wagner's move from Paris to Dresden and his newest operatic project, *Der fliegende Holländer*. By the time he premiered the movement at Dresden on 22 July 1844, Wagner had abandoned the multi-movement symphonic plan and heavily revised the score, along the way settling on the ambitious title *Ouvertüre zu Göthes Faust (erster Theil)* (*Overture to Goethe's Faust I*). Following a performance under Liszt's baton at Weimar eight years later, Wagner turned his attention again to the work, retitling it *Der einsame Faust (oder: Faust in der Einsamkeit). Ein Tongedicht* (*The Lonely Faust [or: Faust in Solitude]. A Tone Poem*) in November of the same year. However, it was only in January 1855, upon learning that Liszt had completed a three-movement *Faust* Symphony, that Wagner thoroughly rewrote the work, which he ushered into print in October 1855 as *Eine Faust-Ouvertüre* (*A Faust Overture*) with the following epigraph from *Faust I* (ll. 1566–1571):

| | |
|---|---|
| Der Gott, der mir im Busen wohnt, | The lord within my bosom bowered |
| Kann tief mein Innerstes erregen; | Can stir me to the inmost kernel; |
| Der über allen meinen Kräften thront, | The one past all my powers empowered, |
| Er kann nach außen nichts bewegen; | He cannot alter anything external. |
| Und so ist mir das Dasein eine Last, | Existence seems a burden to detest, |
| Der Tod erwünscht, das Leben mir verhaßt. | Death to be wished for, life a hateful jest. |

Wagner jettisons the ubiquitous, Romantically ambivalent characterization of Faust as lonely or isolated in favor of a world-weary, near-nihilistic protagonist. Indeed, in Goethe's play, Faust follows these six despairing lines with a string of increasingly brazen epithets that climaxes with curses on the Christian virtues of faith, hope, and patience (ll. 1605–1606) before cadencing in his famous wager with Mephistopheles. Wagner, who since the early 1850s was living in exile in Switzerland for his participation in the May Uprising, had been similarly laid low, lacking friends, funds, and professional prospects.

As seen in Example 6.1, the gloomy atmosphere that pervades long stretches of the overture – and invites autobiographical associations – owes itself to a series of angular, chromatic motives generated from material in the work's first three measures. The dramatic leap of a minor seventh in m. 1, followed by an even more precipitous drop of an octave in the next measure outlines a half-diminished seventh chord. The chromatic slippage from B♭ to A to G♯ between measures two and three suggests the equally unstable sonority of the German augmented sixth. Already by measure three, Wagner begins to develop these interrelated motives and sonorities:

**Example 6.1** Wagner, *Faust* Overture, mm. 1–9, arr. Hans von Bülow

the interval of the augmented sixth is inverted to that of the diminished third in the motive that first appears in the first half of measure three, while the diminished seventh and augmented sixth are arpeggiated in the second half. The evasive nature of these motives and sonorities provides the momentum for the increasingly dramatic introduction, which divulges neither theme nor key. Yet once both are established at m. 31 (Example 6.2a), marked Allegro molto agitato, the hoped-for surprise is mitigated by surprising familiarity: the main melody is but a rhythmically augmented transposition of the melody first heard in mm. 8–10, while its continuation at mm. 34–36 references the accompanimental figure at m. 3, obscured only slightly by slower rhythm and octave displacement. In retrospect, what seems to be the introduction in fact turns out to be the beginning of the exposition; the fast section thus constitutes an important stage of development.

Yet despite its several different generic designations over a fifteen-year period, the *Faust* Overture never abandoned its sonata form. Although Wagner began working on the *Faust* Overture while steeped in French grand opera, it is worth emphasizing that Wagner's compositional procedures emanate more from the German – that is, Beethovenian – symphonic than the Franco-Italian operatic tradition. As such, his

**Example 6.2a** Wagner, *Faust* Overture, mm. 31–36, arr. Bülow

**Example 6.2b** Wagner, *Faust* Overture, mm. 63–66, arr. Bülow

dramatic compositions prioritize motive over melody and organic development over dogmatic formalism. Moreover, Wagner's increasingly precise programmatic focus – a symphony on and, shortly thereafter, overture to *Faust I* (*c.*1840), a tone poem on Faust (1852), an overture that examines a particular aspect of Faust's personality (1855) – necessitated important musical changes. Indeed, the relationships between elements in the slow and fast sections discussed above highlight several compositional devices that Wagner uses throughout the overture to efface the sonata's tidy tripartite structure of exposition, development, and recapitulation:

- Continuous motivic development
- Mutual thematic dependency
- Ambiguity between melody and accompaniment
- Thematic counterpoint.

It is the overwhelming sense of continuous thematic development despite no real dramatic or narrative progress that expertly captures Faust's situation and endears the overture to the programmatic. As seen in Example 6.2b, an even more assertive,

**Example 6.3** Wagner, *Faust* Overture, mm. 118–125, arr. Bülow

homophonic theme appears at m. 63, but its modal deviance from and chromatic extension of earlier material do little to distinguish its individuality. In short, the Faust of Goethe's play and Wagner's overture feels trapped.

Relief comes in the form of an ardent melody in F major that soars through two octaves (Example 6.3). However, it is hardly foreign to its environment, for while the melody is innocently diatonic, its accompaniment features the most chromatic harmonization yet heard in the overture – as if melody and accompaniment have swapped roles between primary and secondary theme groups. Moreover, this and the next theme (mm. 167–176) share the same contour, although the latter is segmented by a passionate accompanimental figure that prominently showcases the overture's tonic center of D. But more importantly, the correspondence between the themes at mm. 118 and 167 helps to jar the memory of mm. 19–20 – another instance in which expectation of the new disappointingly yields to settling for the old.

The continuous development of interrelated themes also makes locating the recapitulation problematic. A theme that follows the contour and rhythms of the theme at m. 31 appears at m. 276, but it is ambiguously perched between D minor and A minor and sandwiched in the orchestra's middle register. As if to downplay the possibility of this passage being the true formal point of return, Wagner develops it through several different keys, none of which approaches the tonic. Only at m. 309 does a sincere dominant pedal emerge, which at m. 325 resolves to a theme first heard at m. 63 (recall Example 6.2b). Wagner brings the full might of the orchestra to bear on this moment of home-key return, instructing it to play the descending chromatic motive as loudly and with as much abandon as possible. Despite an impressive number of chromatic passages that follow this arrival, the remaining measures rarely leave D minor or D major, with the secondary themes from the exposition making only the briefest of appearances.

Although the *Faust* Overture borders on monothematicism, there are nineteen measures (Example 6.4) that remain almost completely independent from their surroundings. Measures 148–153 exude simplicity: the melody in the upper registers contentedly arpeggiates the sonorously alternating F major and B♭ major harmonies

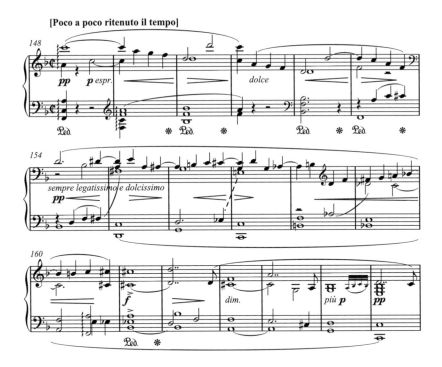

**Example 6.4** Wagner, *Faust* Overture, mm. 148–166, arr. Bülow

below; counterpoint is sparse; rhythms are square; and repetition, not development, generates forward momentum. What follows, however, can hardly be more different. The easy leaps of an octave from d″ to d‴ in m. 150 and d′ to d″ in m. 152 give way in m. 154 to a tortuous chromatic ascent that moves in fits and starts. The unsettled quality of line is magnified by the supporting harmonies, which, while initially suggesting a move through the circle of fifths, break down at m. 158 via a diminished seventh chord. When the German augmented sixth materializes in the next measure, the dramatic leap of an octave in m. 164 harks back to the same chordal interplay that characterized earlier moments like Example 6.1 and m. 31ff. But in the context of the chromatic melody and other harmonically enriched moments (especially mm. 160–161 and m. 163), these two chords shed their pessimistic connotations. Rather, they contribute to the aspirational nature of this passage, as if they have been given a second lease on life. Indeed, some intangible force leads this old material in new directions. The augmented chord at m. 163 is a case in point: Wagner voices it to lead the ear toward a resolution in D minor, but instead creates a ii–V$^9$–I cadence in F major through motion by step.

Fleeting as this nineteen-bar passage may be, it nevertheless represents a significant moment in the work's programmatic development. Although the overture nominally deals exclusively with Faust, Wagner recognized that this focus was

**Example 6.5** Wagner, *Faust* Overture, mm. 423–447, arr. Bülow

dramatically unsustainable. As he wrote to Theodor Uhlig on 27 December 1852, when the *Faust* Overture was still conceived as a tone poem, "Here Faust is the subject, and *woman* hovers before him only as an indefinite, shapeless object of his yearning; as such, intangible and unattainable. Hence his despair, his curse on all the torturing semblance of the beautiful, his headlong plunge into magical, maddening pain."[11] The "Chorus Mysticus" at the end of *Faust II* had provided an explanation – albeit a cryptic one – for Faust's salvation, in which the "Eternal-Feminine" urges her aspirant to strive ever higher. In the *Faust* Overture, Wagner conflates the agent of aspiration with its goal, so that "woman" ("das Weib") – with her own melodies, contrapuntal procedures, and harmonic vocabulary – remains apart from Wagner's protagonist. At the same time, the work's conclusion (Example 6.5) clearly suggests a rosier outlook thanks to her intervention: Faust's transformation from D minor to

D major by means of the progression $V^{6/4}/III$–iii–I is one of those moments in the overture that opens up new programmatic vistas that beg for a second movement.

Wagner's changes to the *Faust* Overture that focus on the "woman" also speak to a topic that interested him throughout his professional life: redemption, especially redemption through love. During the first half of the 1850s, he composed little new music, instead essaying theoretical tomes like *Oper und Drama* (*Opera and Drama*; 1851) and the libretto for *Der Ring des Nibelungen*. The second half of the decade, however, saw a number of important new musical projects get off the ground: he completed the music to *Das Rheingold* in September 1854, composed the whole of *Die Walküre* between June 1854 and March 1856, turned to Act I and parts of Act II of *Siegfried* soon thereafter, and began work on *Tristan und Isolde* in October 1857. In early 1855 Wagner returned to the *Faust* Overture, adding the passage in Example 6.4, altering several others, and giving special attention to mm. 118–166. While the *Faust* Overture might pale in scope to these ambitious theatrical works, like Tannhäuser, Tristan, and Amfortas, its title character is in need of redemption, even before he enters into his wager with Mephistopheles. In fact, it is this thematic emphasis – which became something of an obsession in Wagner's oeuvre after he was introduced to Arthur Schopenhauer's *Die Welt als Wille und Vorstellung* (*The World as Will and Representation*) in 1854 – coupled with the epigraph from *Faust I*, that explains why Wagner cannot depict Faust's redemption, but only suggest its possibility. That the definitive version of the *Faust* Overture exhibits two stages of Wagner's musical development is in fact completely appropriate from a programmatic point of view, since Faust's wavering, allusive style[12] is thrown into relief by the confident, futuristic style of his better half.

Liszt's support of Wagner's *Faust* Overture – Wagner had made the score available to Liszt in early 1849, and Liszt gave a successful performance of it on 11 May 1852 – reflected his desire to equip the small ducal town of Weimar with sophisticated literary music that drew on the legacies of Beethoven and Goethe, as well as a special interest in *Faust* that he had harbored for decades. In December 1830, Hector Berlioz, the eventual dedicatee of Liszt's *Faust* Symphony, introduced the young pianist to Goethe's work in Gérard de Nerval's famous translation, which quickly became one of Liszt's favorites. The idea of engaging *Faust* musically took hold a decade later, when Liszt set some of the vocal numbers and began drafting material for a planned instrumental work. In 1850, Nerval approached Liszt about the possibility of collaborating on a *Faust* opera, and while the project never got off the ground, Weimar hardly lacked *Faust*-inspired offerings in the early 1850s: Liszt conducted or programmed examples by Berlioz, Schumann, and Wagner. Thus when he began concentrated work on a *Faust* Symphony sometime around 1854, Liszt had considered, or at least been exposed to, Goethe's play from a number of generic perspectives, including symphonic overture, cantata, and opera.

Liszt's final result, premiered in 1857 and published with revisions in 1862, betrays debts to several predecessor works, especially earlier incarnations of Wagner's *Faust Overture* and Berlioz's *Symphonie fantastique*. At the same time, however, Liszt considerably expanded upon his models. For example, its title – *Eine Faust-Symphonie in drei Charakterbildern* (*A Faust Symphony in three Character Pictures*) – realizes Wagner's earlier ambitions of producing a symphony whose movements take inspiration from specific characters from Goethe's universe. And while Liszt's title might suggest three single-movement symphonic poems loosely strung together, there are important motivic correspondences and thematic transformations that create psychological depth and narrative thrust across the entire symphony in ways far different than Berlioz's *idée fixe* or Harold theme. Even the introduction of the chorus toward the end of the work redirects the listener away from the ubiquitous teleological paradigm of Beethoven's Ninth Symphony.

Liszt left no preface to the *Faust* Symphony that explains his compositional decisions. However, the New German propagandist Richard Pohl produced a study of the symphony upon its publication that remained unsurpassed in terms of insight and scope for a century. Pohl's observations and interpretations are especially valuable, as they may have come from Liszt himself, with whom Pohl was in close contact during the 1850s. Indeed, the programmatic specificity he gives to the symphony's numerous motives (see Text Box 6.1), and – even more important – the myriad ways in which they act and interact over the course of the entire composition, likely reveal insight from the privileged mind of the composer. It was in Liszt's *Faust* Symphony that Pohl found a worthy musical

---

**Text Box 6.1  Richard Pohl's description of Faust's themes in the first movement of Liszt's *Faust* Symphony.**

First Main Motive – The marrow of the Faust character, his entire being at its most succinct. Doubt, grief, sullenness, and disaffection; contempt for the world, for science, as well as his own pursuits; inside him a hopeless desert.

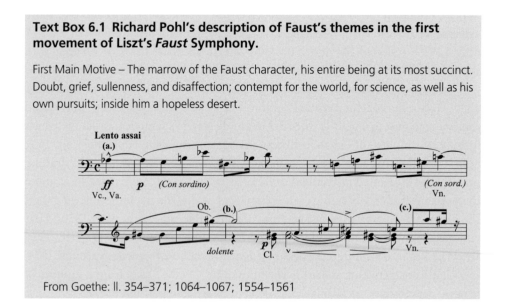

From Goethe: ll. 354–371; 1064–1067; 1554–1561

## Text Box 6.1  (continued)

Second Motive – That of impassioned impulse toward higher knowledge, toward mighty deeds; of restless forward striving without inner fulfillment; of the fight for freedom.

From Goethe: ll. 410–413, 418; 302–303, 306–307; 1694–1697

Third Motive – The aching longing for unknown joy; cry for deliverance from inner torment.

From Goethe: ll. 33–34, 39–40, 43–44; 455–459; 1074–1075

Fourth Motive – That of love, as general divine and human love. A wondrously beautiful motive.

From Goethe: ll. 775–778; 1182–1185

**Text Box 6.1  (continued)**

Fifth Motive – That of pride, of the powerful awareness of the highest insight. Faust, in sublime self-assurance, rising to the realms of the Earth Spirit.

From Goethe: ll. 109–112; 499–500; 1224; 1784

**Source:** Richard Pohl, "Faust-Symphonie," in *Franz Liszt. Studien und Erinnerungen* (Leipzig: Bernhard Schlicke, 1883), 277–283.

analogue to Goethe's play, which he proudly judged to be "the greatest revelation of our greatest German poet."[13]

Liszt, he argued, succeeded in wedding Beethoven's abstract compositional practices of motivic manipulation and formal logic to the dramatic needs of Goethe's characters. Thus Liszt's musical motives "are carriers of specific thoughts. Sometimes they function in a general way, but always as the most succinct characterization of the selected subject ... Sometimes they are like the echo of special, poetic moments, and with such incisive expression that [Liszt's] motives can only be dubbed 'speaking.'"[14] The organization of these motives across the symphony's three movements of "Faust," "Gretchen," and "Mephistopheles" reflects not so much specific scenes in Goethe's play, but rather the shifting psychological states of its protagonist Faust. Indeed, Gretchen and Mephistopheles present themselves in the symphony as antipodal paths for Faust to follow: a "faithful, unspoiled soul" for the former; the latter a "principle" – not even a legitimate character – of negation.[15]

Faust is psychologically split by the choice. In the second movement he shares with Gretchen motives identified by Pohl as numbers three ("aching longing") and four ("divine and human love"), both of which grow in richness and nobility as their intimacy deepens. The third motive, for instance, frames a duet between three cellos and two first violins (mm. 139–163) that is made even more incandescent by a chamber-like accompaniment of divided flutes, harp, tremolo second violins, and occasional homophonic punctuations by the woodwinds. Yet even Gretchen is not able to satisfy Faust's restless spirit, and fragments of motives one (section b) and two intrude on their affair. Her themes remain immune to this grief-stricken assault, however, but by the third movement these themes, along with the fifth motive, enter Mephistopheles's domain. Here they appear as perversions, as mockeries of already fragile themes, some of which have not been heard since the first movement. Pohl argues that Mephistopheles does such violence to Faust's themes because he worries about losing his prey to Gretchen and, by extension, to the Lord who comes to her spiritual rescue at the end of *Faust I*. Indeed, Gretchen's theme, undisturbed by the din of the devilish scherzo, enters abruptly in D♭ major at m. 419, planting a seed of hope that gradually overshadows Mephistopheles's persistent and admittedly impressive coercions.

Liszt's original ending for "Mephistopheles" – and thus the entire symphony – made a short reference to Gretchen's theme in C major (mm. 678–681) before concluding with an orchestral fanfare. Wagner was impressed, writing in his autobiography that "If anything convinced me of the masterly powers of poetic conception he possessed, it was the original finale of the *Faust* Symphony, which ended delicately and sweetly with a last, utterly compelling reminiscence of Gretchen, without any attempt to arouse attention forcibly." In 1857 Liszt revisited this solution and added more than one hundred bars of an Andante mistico. Here a male choir joins the orchestra to chant the "Chorus Mysticus," while a tenor sings the line "das Ewig-Weibliche" to a rhythmically augmented version of Gretchen's theme that starts out in "her" home key of A♭ major. When Wagner happened upon this revision, he was disappointed and accused Liszt of introducing "choruses in a manner calculated to produce a more ostentatious effect."[16] Wagner is correct that the effect is far less understated than Liszt's original. But as this movement is still about Mephistopheles, Liszt's addition provides an understandable corrective. Just as Faust is a part of Gretchen's movement, so too is she a part of Mephistopheles's. And once it becomes clear that Mephistopheles cannot negate her, he evaporates. Gretchen is revealed at the end of Mephistopheles's movement to be his own negation: her theme is diatonic, her orchestra is homophonic, her choir the ensemble so favored by Liszt in his religious music and Wagner in his quasi-religious chorales from *Tannhäuser*, *Lohengrin*, and – later – *Parsifal*. In "Mephistopheles," Gretchen emerges as a true adversary and, ultimately, victor. Thus Liszt stayed true to painting Mephistopheles's "character picture" while also wrapping up his *Faust* Symphony in a programmatically compelling manner.

## Symphonic metamorphoses (II): Rubinstein, Mayer

Despite its epic proportions, Liszt's *Faust* Symphony received little attention in the wake of its premiere under the composer's baton at Weimar on 5 September 1857. Wagner's criticism of Liszt's misguided poetic judgment – notwithstanding the fact that Liszt's earlier version of the *Faust* Symphony aligned better with Wagner's *Faust* Overture – was also belatedly shared by several members of Liszt's Weimar circle, including Joachim Raff, Hans von Bülow, and Anton Rubinstein. Among this group, Rubinstein was the only one to create a work based on *Faust*, which he probably got to know as a young man through Mikhail Mikhaylov's 1848 Russian translation. However, Rubinstein's initial conception of a symphonic transformation of Goethe's tale came during a tour of Germany in July 1854, when the twenty-four year old reported to his mother an ambitious new symphonic project: "The first movement will be called 'Faust,' the second movement – 'Gretchen,' the third movement – 'Mephistopheles,' the fourth – 'The Poet.' The subject is excellent but difficult."[17] Rubinstein worked steadily on his *Faust* Symphony during the second half of 1854, but he left it unfinished. How far he actually came with the work is unclear, for he destroyed all but the first movement, which he published ten years later as *"Faust." Ein musikalisches Charakterbild* (*Faust. A Musical Character Picture*), op. 68. While certain parallels to Liszt's *Faust* Symphony – which the older composer would begin drafting in earnest about one month after Rubinstein mentioned the topic to his mother – are undeniable, his orchestral work bears an equally strong affinity to Wagner's *Faust* Overture (a personal favorite of Rubinstein's) and owes its stylistic profile primarily to Beethoven's Ninth Symphony and the "Leipzig" school of Mendelssohn and Niels Gade, its dedicatee.

The composition begins with a demonstrative show of B♭ major, the tonic, in which the interval of a fifth is prominently featured (Example 6.6). Indeed, eight bars later a solo horn picks up the motive, to which a solo clarinet in B♭ and oboe respond in turn. Under their interplay, Rubinstein effects a modulation to A♭ major and introduces at m. 17 an important rhythmic motive of ♩ ♩ ♩. After some counterpoint between the main intervallic and rhythmic motives, the solo clarinet returns in m. 29 to present a melancholy melody (Example 6.7) that descends under the weight of its dotted rhythms. The Allegro assai that follows picks up immediately where this melody left off, passing the dotted figure up through the strings. The orchestra pauses on the pitch B♭, but while the theme that follows clearly owes its content to Example 6.6, its harmonization destabilizes B♭ major as tonic. D minor seems to be the likeliest candidate, but it too is overruled by the E♭ major chords at mm. 58–61. Only at m. 65 does a theme appear that not only preserves the important interval of a fifth but also unambiguously asserts D minor as the new tonic.

**Example 6.6** Anton Rubinstein, *Faust*, mm. 1–2, arr. August Horn, adapted

Playing off the tension between B♭ major and D minor – each of whose tonic chords have two pitches in common – was not Rubinstein's invention. Beethoven had exhaustively explored it in his Ninth Symphony, most famously in the opening chord of the fourth movement. Rubinstein owed even more to this composer and especially this work, however: the opening of his *Faust* has the same recitative-like quality, melodic design, and even orchestration as the finale of Beethoven's last symphony; Rubinstein repeats motives with a brute force technique (e.g., mm. 386–403) that is rhetorically compelling; and he often strips the orchestra down to unisons when making sudden modulations.

There are also crucial ways, however, in which Rubinstein's *Faust* strays from Beethovenian models and practices; many of these deviations probably stem from Rubinstein's programmatic conception of Faust. First, his composition is through-composed. What might be tentatively identified as the "Faust" theme (Example 6.6) and its permutations (Examples 6.8 and 6.9) almost never return in tonic – be it B♭ major or D minor. Instead, their quality – key, intervallic makeup, instrumentation, and so forth – often responds defensively to some external pressure. For instance, Example 6.9 returns almost verbatim at m. 187 in D minor, signaling what could be a premature recapitulation. However, from what follows (Example 6.10), it quickly becomes clear that Rubinstein is presenting another event in Faust's life, most likely his crushing depression and imminent suicide – witness the descending bass line in mm. 190–198 and altered dominant prolongation in m. 198ff with C♯ and C♮ frequently at odds. Faust's plan is thwarted by a full brass contingent in F major (mm. 206–212), whose joyful chorale of "Christ ist erstanden" turns Faust's musical motive toward the idyllic days of his childhood. Indeed, while the moment is ultimately temporary, its effect on Faust is strong enough to keep his motive from ever appearing again in D minor.

The through-composed nature of Rubinstein's *Faust* also allows for another disarming event: Gretchen's appearance. Of course, Rubinstein does not identify her in the score; and lacking his destroyed (or unwritten) second movement, it is not possible to identify her definitively as Faust's future lover. Like the introduction of

**Example 6.7** Rubinstein, *Faust*, mm. 29–34, arr. Horn, adapted

Gretchen's music into the fabric of Wagner's *Faust* Overture (recall Example 6.4), Rubinstein's music in Example 6.11 seems to come from out of nowhere, having no precedent in Faust's musical world: an affective, limber melody; colorful – though diatonic – harmony, such as the half-diminished chord at m. 364; static key; moderate tempo; and a lush yet intimate orchestration of solo oboe, solo horn, and strings. But unlike Wagner's interpretation, this interaction yields no redemption. Quite the opposite, in fact, for when Faust comes out of his momentary reverie,

**Example 6.8** Rubinstein, *Faust*, mm. 45–48, arr. Horn

**Example 6.9** Rubinstein, *Faust*, mm. 65–68, arr. Horn

he has become harmonically unmoored, and only with significant effort is he able to direct his sights on the unheard-of key of B minor. But even that pursuit collapses, and by the end of the movement Faust has been diminished psychologically and motivically. Indeed, the last strains of his once-proud perfect fifth now assume the (diabolical) interval of a tritone (m. 427ff), fueling a pessimistic worldview that only intensifies with the slow coda (mm. 441–457; excerpted in Example 6.12).

The musical depictions of Wagner, Liszt, and Rubinstein gel with Ary Scheffer's portrait of Faust (Figure 6.1), in which a highly flawed but eminently relatable figure captures the quandary of the Romantic artist. But it is not a foregone conclusion that a musical elaboration on *Faust* need necessarily prioritize its male protagonist. Indeed, at least one contemporary composer, Emilie Mayer (1812–1883), seems instead to have focused on Gretchen's tragedy in her *Faust-Ouverture*, op. 46, of 1880. That a female would even attempt such a compositional feat surprised at least one (anonymous) critic, whose chauvinistic review of Mayer's score is worth quoting in full:

**Example 6.10** Rubinstein, *Faust*, mm. 190–213, arr. Horn.[18]

The world has been turned upside down! Our young male composers indulge themselves in lyrical outpourings, singing of the spring and of love, while the women commit musical treatments of weighty and sublime matters to 16-stave music paper. One of these resolute and entrepreneurial ladies is Emilie Mayer (Mrs. or Miss?), who came up with a "Faust" Overture for her op. 46 that isn't half bad. With respect to the actual content, the piece makes an admittedly bald impression; the little Adagio introduction turns out to be vacuous, and the themes that follow likewise exhibit little fundamental meaning. Yet the instrumental writing is uniformly good, at times even praiseworthy. In this respect the composer has played it safe albeit well, writing down what the whole world already knows to be feasible and effective.[19]

**Example 6.10**  (cont.)

What the reviewer fails to mention is that, despite rehearsing a *Faust* that everyone evidently knows inside and out, Mayer's overture is not primarily about Faust. Instead, her focus is on the second half of Part I of Goethe's play, often referred to as Gretchen's Tragedy. As shown in Example 6.13, although three themes make up her overture, its true subject only emerges near the end of the work, when Theme 1, originally in an unsettled B minor, returns in a triumphant B major below the words "Sie ist gerettet!" – "She is redeemed!" More than a poetic afterthought, this citation, adapted from the final Dungeon scene of *Faust I*, helps to explain some of the characteristic elements of Mayer's themes. On the one hand, infatuation with Faust has brought about the death of her mother, brother Valentin, and child – events orchestrated by Mephistopheles,

**Example 6.11** Rubinstein, *Faust*, mm. 362–369, arr. Horn, adapted

**Example 6.12** Rubinstein, *Faust*, mm. 441–443, arr. Horn, adapted

whose alluring yet dangerous melody comes across as Theme 2. (In the context of Mayer's relatively conservative harmonic world, the augmented seventh chord on the downbeat of m. 81 and elsewhere is terrifying.) On the other hand, the penitent Gretchen places her trust in God's grace, particularly in the Cathedral and Dungeon scenes, a characteristic embodied in the chorale, Theme 3.

The only figure redeemed in Part I of *Faust* is Gretchen, and Mayer's interpretation of Gretchen's struggle may have been shaped by practices local to Berlin, where she had been based since 1847. In particular, the Singakademie had performed Prince Antoni Henryk Radziwiłł's *Faust Compositionen* yearly from 1830 until 1860, an ambitious collection of arias, choral numbers, melodramas, and other vocal genres that concludes with a choir of angels singing "Gloria, Gloria in excelsis Deo, gerettet, gerettet, gerettet!" ("Glory, glory to God in the highest, saved, saved, saved!")

**Figure 6.1** Ary Scheffer, *Faust with the Cup of Poison* (1852)

## Faust for one: Gregoir, Alkan

Although no longer a household name, Joseph Gregoir (1817–1876) was a well-known composer and virtuoso pianist who, along with the composer and cellist Adrien François Servais, was a chief representative of the Belgian school. Most of his piano works bear the influence of his principal teacher, Henri Herz, but his most ambitious work, *Faust (d'après Goethe). Poême musical en deux parties*, premiered by the composer in Antwerp on 27 January 1847, also touches on the formal and stylistic innovations of Beethoven, Chopin, and Schumann.

Gregoir's work spans twelve movements, divided into two unequal parts, as given in Table 6.2. While he does not furnish the pianist with an explicit narrative, from

**Example 6.13** Mayer, *Faust-Ouverture*, major themes

the given titles and occasional summaries it is clear that Part I deals primarily with Faust and Gretchen (or Marguerite, as she is always called in French translation), Part II with Faust's salvation. Moreover, as Table 6.3 demonstrates, Gregoir develops five motives over the course of the piece to provide structural and programmatic integrity. Movement one introduces four of the motives. Movements two and three, while partially having precedent in Goethe's play and being substantially worked out musically, are incidental to Part I's primary emphasis, which picks up speed in movement four. After an extended introduction that recalls Schumann's tender settings of "Du bist wie eine Blume" and "Mondnacht," Faust appears by way of a signature ninth chord (motive 2). Following an anguished modulation from G

**Table 6.2** *Gregoir,* Faust (d'après Goethe), *divisions and author descriptions*

**Part I**

1  Night. (Faust meditates, lost in gloomy thoughts, which overpower him. He summons infernal powers to his aid. The sound of bells announces the Easter celebration, which the choir of angels celebrates in Heaven.)

2  Promenaders leaving town. Peasants dancing and singing.

3  Chorus of soldiers.

4  Vision.

5  Marguerite's song.

6  Ecstasy!

7  "... He loves me!"

8  Love.

9  Dies irae. (Heaven's wrath falls upon you; the trumpets sound, the tombs are shaken; and the ashes of your body, resuscitated by flames, tremble with terror.)

**Part II**

10  The Sabbath. [A] Introduction and [B] Witches' dance.

11  Dance of the spirits. (In the midst of their romp, Hell opens and demons drag Faust down into the abyss, arguing over their prey.)

12  Apotheosis.

major to F♯ major, he commences with a diatonic transformation of motive 4 in the tenor register that soars above the accompaniment at m. 24. It is this version of the melody that Gregoir develops for the remainder of the movement, and while its lush harmonization and wide gamut tamp down its infernal origins, the unprepared dissonance of motive 5 illustrates the awkward and even disingenuous beginning to his relationship with Marguerite. In Goethe's play, Marguerite is unaware of Faust's gaze in her chamber. Indeed, the protagonist's musical motives go uncited in movement five, a wordless rendition of "Es war ein König in Thule" in F♯ minor whose mazurka melody is labeled *con tristezza*. The sixth movement – in the "visionary" key of A♭ major – follows without pause, and while none of the previous themes here appear, Gregoir's setting, especially the lush middle section in D♭ major, clearly references the two lovers. Marguerite's joy spills over into the seventh movement, a waltz which begins with a dominant trill that recalls the opening of Chopin's Waltz in A♭ major, op. 42. The culmination of their relationship comes in movement eight, which not only returns to A♭ major but recapitulates mm. 23–43 of movement four. An even more rhythmically square and emotionally charged rendition of motive 4 at this point further cements the impression that Marguerite has purged Faust's infernal inclinations and, by extension, secured his salvation.

Given Part I's sustained treatment of his relationship with Marguerite over five movements, Part II's resolution of Faust's fate in three movements – the first two of

**Table 6.3** *Recurring motives in Gregoir,* Faust *(d'après Goethe)*

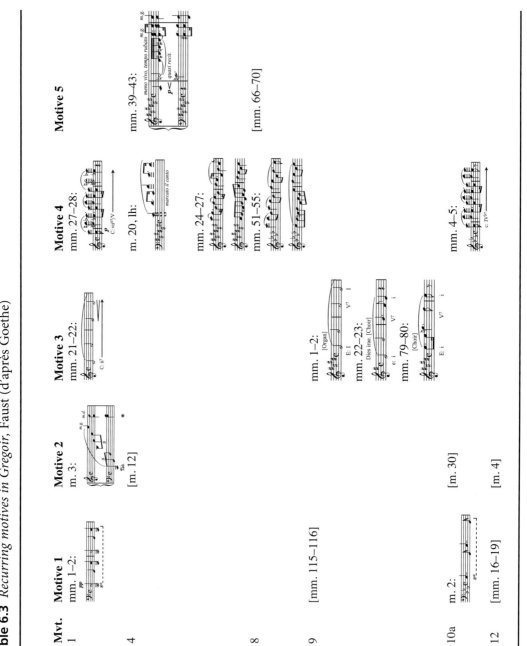

which barely reference him, while the last one is the shortest of the entire set – is anticlimactic. In fact, movements ten and eleven recall the two dance movements of Part I (all are in a quick duple time, for instance, and sport similar formal designs), which further distance their participants from the protagonist. Similarly, movement ten begins with several promising transformations of earlier motives, but these are abandoned once the Witches' dance formally begins. Instead Gregoir culls super-natural effects from outside his environment: the Sabbath mimics Schubert's "Die junge Nonne," D828; the Witches' dance appropriates figures from the finale of Beethoven's "Appassionata" Sonata, op. 57; and the Dance of the Spirits quotes almost verbatim (mm. 62–72) the music that follows the forging of the second bullet in the famous "Wolf's Glen" scene from Weber's *Der Freischütz*. These references are not necessarily inappropriate per se, but they interrupt what has been, up to this point, a viable programmatic rendition. Indeed, Faust's apotheosis in movement twelve, while justified according to the conclusion to *Faust II*, destabilizes the action; that Gregoir's setting ends this way – incidentally, Faust's great foil, Mephistopheles, is nowhere to be found – ultimately disappoints musically, poetically, and dramatically.

In a retrospective of *Faust* settings from 1886, the composer and critic Frederick Corder came down hard on Gregoir's musical poem:

> Of this composer we confess to knowing little beyond his name. Of his works, if they at all resemble his "Faust," we certainly desire to know nothing at all. This queer composition, or series of compositions, only deserves notice for its ludi-crousness, consisting, as it does, of twelve *morceaux*, which for pretentiousness and utter feebleness it would be hard to surpass.[20]

Having just covered Wagner's *Faust* Overture and Liszt's *Faust* Symphony, Corder understandably judged Gregoir's piano piece to be second-rate. But it is neither ludicrous nor pretentious, at least if its target audience is taken into account. Gregoir almost certainly did not seek to make a grand philosophical statement out of his twelve *morceaux* on the same level as his more remembered contemporaries; rather, he designed his *Faust* with an eye toward a bourgeois audience that consumed sheet music ravenously, read widely and discussed literature frequently, and routinely attended balls where mazurkas and waltzes – the two dances in Gregoir's set explicitly associated with Marguerite – were popular fare. As discussed in Chapter 1, character pieces and sentimental subjects were popular with this large segment of the musical public, with Stephen Heller, Alfred Jaëll, Louis Moreau Gottschalk, and countless others meeting the demand. Gregoir's *Faust* encompasses many of these domestic genres, while aspiring – like the piano cycles of Schumann or Liszt – toward weightier poetic topics, dramatic scenarios, and even philosophical insights.

Gregoir's emphasis on Faust and Marguerite at the expense of Mephistopheles and his cohort also speaks to a larger cultural divide vis-à-vis *Faust* between Germany and France. The former tended to highlight the philosophical and grandiose aspects of Goethe's drama, as examples by Schumann, Liszt, and even Rubinstein show. The latter focused on the personal and intimate. Indeed, Charles Gounod's operatic adaptation from 1859 owes as much, if not more, to Michel Carré's play *Faust et Marguerite* as it does to Goethe's *Faust I*. Richard Pohl's dismissive assessment of this work neatly sums up the two approaches: "Gounod took such artistic liberties with the work of art, that in making his *Faust* so gracious, he might as well have called it *Robert* or *Romeo!*"[21]

An exception to this elastic rule is Charles-Valentin Alkan (1813–1888), one of the most enigmatic composers of the nineteenth century. His technique, as his music and reviews of his sporadic appearances in concert and private attest, was phenomenal, perhaps only challenged by Liszt in the 1830s and 1840s and Carl Tausig or Anton Rubinstein later in the century. Like many of these contemporaries, he wrote primarily for the piano, issuing variations, sketches ("Esquisses"), études, songs without words, and humble characteristic gems; but also massive multi-movement works such as the Sonata, op. 33, Sonatina, op. 61, and his magnum opus, the *Douze études dans les tons mineurs*, op. 39, which contains a four-movement symphony, three-movement concerto, overture, and variations apparently designed to mimic animals from Aesop's fables. However, as Hugh Macdonald observes, "Alkan was a man of deeply conservative views, whose style of life, manner of dress and faith in the traditions of earlier music marked him off from other musicians and from the world in general."[22] Indeed, Alkan's music is a recipe of Liszt, Felix Mendelssohn, Gioachino Rossini, and Erik Satie.

As its title implies, "Quasi-Faust" – the second movement of the sonata – hovers between a literal rendering of the Faust story and the more general characteristic of its elemental themes.[23] The former is easily recognizable through Alkan's identification of two key participants: a plainsong citation, and a collection of motives that appear in new and transformed guises as the movement progresses. "Quasi-Faust" begins with a series of three motivic gestures (see Table 6.4): a rising and falling third, rising and falling fourth, and four repeated quarter notes. Development of this programmatically nondescript material soon heralds the arrival of the Devil (explicitly labeled), whose theme inverts the first two motives of segment A. The theme that emerges first at m. 57 in G♯ minor (segment C) also harks back to the opening, but proceeds to shape a melody that is eerily attractive and altogether new. A triumphant transformation at m. 101 in G♯ major throws caution to the hellish wind that provided it with energy, and the exposition concludes with a soaring, affirmative melody (segment D).

**Table 6.4** *Characters and correspondences in Alkan, "Quasi-Faust"*

At this point, Alkan begins to rewrite the basic narrative of sonata form, for the increasingly violent interactions between these themes in the development effaces a sense of triumphant return in the recapitulation. And for good reason: the movement's true conflict has yet to begin. Only at m. 227 does Alkan expose its cosmic scope by means of four lusciously voiced chords (segment E). The struggle between Heaven and Hell commences with a fugue on the plainsong subject "Verbum supernum prodiens" at m. 231, swells to eight distinct voices by m. 255, and resolves only through the intercession of the Lord at m. 259.[24] The fugue subject – thoroughly transformed in a wash of thick, four-part piano textures – turns to support Faust's theme at m. 275 in the bright key of F♯ major. The Devil's theme, enfeebled by the preceding events, fails at m. 304 to redirect the thematic momentum. The movement ends triumphantly, as if enacting the promise of salvation described in the penultimate verse of "Verbum supernum prodiens":

|  |  |
|---|---|
| O salutaris hostia, | O saving victim, |
| Quæ cæli pandis ostium, | Who throws open the gate of Heaven, |
| Bella premunt hostilia; | Hostile wars are raging; |
| Da robur, fer auxilium. | Grant us strength, deliver help. |

Parallels abound between Alkan's "Quasi-Faust" and Goethe's *Faust*: Mephistopheles's mandate to deny or invert; Faust's complicated relationship to him; heavenly salvation. And the themes of striving, development, and transformation are inherent to sonata forms. But perhaps the most original aspect of Alkan's interpretation is the manner in which the performer must become Faust. Without a doubt, the movement represents one of the pinnacles of nineteenth-century piano music, demanding a performer of almost superhuman stamina, drive, and character. (The conclusion of the fugue is a case in point.) But the pianist must also invest in Alkan's themes a phenomenal range of personalities, as the composer's performance instructions fuel the narrative considerably. Faust must be passionate, fiery, even diabolical, but also reticent, despairing, and verging on self-destruction. While the two antipodal figures of the Devil and God have important narrative roles to play in "Quasi-Faust," it is for Faust that Alkan reserves the most programmatically pregnant directions. In this sense, "Quasi-Faust" blends Berlioz's narrative focus with Liszt's (as yet unwritten) symphonic character study.

This is only fitting, since "Quasi-Faust" also features a program-within-a-program, belonging to a piano sonata entitled "The Four Ages" ("Les quatre âges") in which each movement corresponds to a decade of human life. The opening movement illustrates a man in his twenties by means of a limber, optimistic Chopinian scherzo. Nevertheless, Alkan sows the unsettled seeds of the next decade's "Quasi-Faust" by concluding the first movement with a theme whose shape prefigures the opening of the second.

"A Happy Family" ("Un heureux ménage"), complete with scampering children, is the subject of the third movement. (If Gretchen / Marguerite is to be found anywhere in the sonata, it is here.) The sonata concludes with "Prometheus Bound" ("Prométhée enchaîné"), an uncompromisingly dark, somber depiction of the protagonist in his fifties as he waits for death to deliver him. His anguish is more psychological than physical, however, as motives from the three previous movements return fleetingly to intensify – and which Alkan presses even further by citing the final line from Aeschylus's poem – "these torments which I endure" ("les tourments que j'endure!"). Finally, the programmatic journey is mirrored by the sonata's progressive tonality, with each movement drifting further from the previous – thus it moves from D major to B major in the first; D♯ minor to F♯ major in the second; G major in the third; and G♯ minor in the fourth. As the protagonist looks back on his life, the tritone he has traversed since the first movement could not be more distant.

Despite his conservative aesthetic leanings and reliance on traditional large-scale forms, Alkan saw no inherent problem in the use of programmatic procedures. Like Liszt, a program was a point of departure, not an interpretive foregone conclusion. Preempting potential criticism regarding his use of "particular titles to these four movements and sometimes . . . quite unusual terms," Alkan explains that

> Imitative music does not concern us here; still less is this music that seeks to justify itself at an extra-musical level. Each of the four movements corresponds in my mind with a given moment of existence, to a particular mode of thought or imagination. Why not make this clear? The musical content remains unaffected while the performer, without forfeiting his own individuality, is stimulated by the same ideas as the composer; a fact which must surely deepen his understanding of the work.[25]

In transforming the legend of Faust into a work of world literature, Goethe opened the door for musicians to follow suit. While his work served as the basis for several ambitious realizations across a variety of genres, it by no means inhibited other writers and musicians from exploring alternative contexts for Faust and his cohort. In 1862 Liszt scored a pianistic hit with his "Mephisto" Waltz, based on Nikolaus Lenau's poem *Faust* (1836), in which Mephistopheles and Faust make merry at a country inn. The hypnotic second movement of Maurice Ravel's *Gaspard de la nuit* captures a reading of *Faust* filtered through the mind of the French poet Aloysius Bertrand. Like Alkan's sonata, both of these works put a premium on virtuosity, whose connection to the Devil was already centuries old. (Faustian readings of Liszt's explicitly non-programmatic Sonata in B minor are indebted to this tradition of pitting the religious against the sacrilegious.) A parallel Romantic fascination with the fantastic helped to elevate Mephistopheles's popularity, evidenced by Arrigo Boito's only opera, *Mefistofele*, from 1868 (revised 1875).

In the twentieth century, Goethe's *Faust* largely lost its appeal to composers of instrumental music. Sergei Rachmaninov drafted his first piano sonata after it, but wavered in the decision to publicize his literary source. He summed up his misgivings to his friend Nikita Morozov in May 1907:

> The sonata is certainly wild and interminable. I think it takes about 45 minutes. I was lured into this length by its guiding idea. This is – three contrasting types from a literary work [*Faust*]. Of course no program will be indicated, though I begin to think that the sonata would be clearer if the program were revealed. Nobody will ever play this composition, it's too difficult and long and possibly – and this is the most important – too dubious musically.[26]

Ultimately, Rachmaninov suppressed his program; perhaps understandably, given its parallels to those of Wagner, Rubinstein, and especially Liszt.

This early twentieth-century desire to break with the nineteenth century also accounts for Ferruccio Busoni's unfinished opera *Doktor Faust*, based on the always-popular puppet plays; Mikhail Bulgakov's politically incendiary novel *Master and Margarita* (c.1939; published 1966–1967); and Thomas Mann's *Doktor Faustus* of 1947, in which the alchemist Faust has been replaced by the serialist composer Adrian Leverkühn, whose downfall mirrors that of his own Nazi Germany. Having witnessed atrocities of an almost unimaginable scale, Mann and his colleagues could no longer identify with Goethe's optimistic tale of redemption through struggle, a tale that had left an indelible stamp on some of the most important artistic and musical creations of the preceding century.

## Chapter 7

# Programmatic paths around the *fin de siècle*: Mahler and Strauss

Writing of the contemporary Austro-German musical landscape in 1912, the Munich-based critic and theorist Rudolf Louis posited three competing tendencies among composers of instrumental music: "the first, program-musical tendency leads via Berlioz and Liszt to Richard Strauss; the second, diametrically opposed direction leads via Schumann to Max Reger; and the third, which in a certain sense mediates between them, leads to Gustav Mahler."[1]

Louis's valiant efforts in creating a stylistic taxonomy of music fall short vis-à-vis program music. His Strauss–Reger–Mahler trichotomy seeks to extend the philosophical divisions of the 1850s, which, as Chapter 5 contends, were at best practiced inconsistently by composers who often fled from one camp to the other – a situation perhaps implicitly acknowledged by Louis, who enlists Schumann on Reger's behalf. Similarly, none of the contemporary composers mentioned by Louis (including Mahler, who had recently died) can be confined to any single category. Even Strauss, the public face of program music by the century's end, routinely equivocated on the degree to which his music should assert programmatic agendas. Perhaps the single element that binds together composers active around the *fin de siècle* is an uneasy sense of place in history, for their compositions are as much about breaking away from tradition as they are about maintaining it.

## Strauss as heir to the New German School

Between 1888 and 1899, Strauss composed seven tone poems that established him as Germany's leading avant-garde composer. Growing up under the watchful eye of his father Franz, a famous horn virtuoso, Richard was exposed to the pantheon of German orchestral composers from the century-long period of Haydn and Mozart to Mendelssohn and Schumann. New German composers like Liszt and Wagner – whose *Tristan und Isolde* Franz had reluctantly helped premiere in 1865 – were off limits. Thus Richard's compositions through the mid-1880s, which include two symphonies and four works for soloist and orchestra, took only passing interest in contemporary music, save for the music of Johannes Brahms, under whose spell

195

**Example 7.1** Raff, *Orchestral-Prelude to Shakespeare's Macbeth*, mm. 26–29

Strauss fell hard in 1885. However, despite latent Wagnerian sympathies as early as 1881, a full-blown New German obsession gripped Strauss beginning in 1886, when he moved to Meiningen to work with Hans von Bülow and his renowned orchestra. There he met Liszt's former pupil Alexander Ritter. As Strauss related in an autobiographical sketch from around 1898, it was Ritter who turned the twenty-one-year-old composer–conductor into "a confirmed *musician-of-the-future*" by introducing and explaining Liszt, Wagner, and Schopenhauer. Strauss credited Ritter with "put[ting] me on the way that I now walk independently."[2]

Strauss's first cautious attempt at program music, *Aus Italien*, bears witness to his compositional reorientation under Ritter's teachings, but in terms of form it remains heavily indebted to the traditional orchestral suite. Indeed, the compositional and ideological aligned definitely only around 1888, when Strauss completed the initial draft of *Macbeth*, his first tone poem. That year he came clean to Bülow, whose passion for the New German School had long since cooled:

> If you want to create a work of art that is unified in its mood and consistent in its structure, and if it is to give the listener a clear and definite impression, then what the author wants to say must have been just as clear and definite in his own mind. This is only possible through the inspiration by a poetical idea, whether or not it be introduced as a program. I consider it a legitimate method to create a correspondingly new form for every new subject, to shape which neatly and perfectly is a very difficult task, but for that very reason the more ... The exact impression of my artistic thinking and feeling, and in style the most independent and purposeful work I have yet done, is "Macbeth."[3]

Few composers of instrumental music took on Shakespeare's *Macbeth*, tending to focus instead on *Hamlet* (see Chapter 2), *Romeo and Juliet*, or the comedies. One notable exception that may have been on Strauss's radar in the late 1880s came from another of Ritter's mentors, Joachim Raff, whose *Orchestral-Prelude to Shakespeare's Macbeth* received its premiere at Wiesbaden in early January 1882, only five months before the composer's death.[4] For a score that runs about twelve minutes, Raff's *Macbeth* is densely populated, with five distinct themes. And while Raff left no program for the prelude, the ubiquity of the unison theme shown in Example 7.1 – and its absence in the final thirty-five bars of the piece – suggests Macbeth himself. By extension, Macbeth's theme is in frequent dialogue with two other diametrically

**Table 7.1** *Raff,* Macbeth, *structure and principal themes*

| I. mm. 1–61 | II. 62–168 | V. 253–351 |
|---|---|---|
| 1: Witches | 71: Lady Macbeth | 261: Battle music |
| 26: Macbeth (Ex. 7.1) | 77: Bellicose | 269: Macbeth |
| 31: Banquo | 91: Battle music | 288: Macduff, transition (cf. m. 241) |
| 36: Bellicose music | 107: Macbeth | 300: Macbeth, fragmented |
|  | 125: Banquo | 317: Macduff, triumphant |
|  |  | 340: Apotheosis |
| **III. 169–206** | **IV. 207–252** |  |
| 169: Witches | 207–218: Interlude |  |
| 188: Macbeth | 218: Lady Macbeth |  |
| 192: Macduff (Ex. 7.2) | 229: Bellicose |  |
|  | 241: Transition |  |

**Example 7.2** Raff, *Orchestral-Prelude to Shakespeare's Macbeth*, mm. 192–198

opposed melodies. The first appears immediately after his, at m. 31, in another meter (3/4) and in warmer colors provided by flutes, oboes, bassoons, and horns – probably Banquo. The second comes much later, at m. 71, this time in select winds and lower strings. Its chromatic maneuvering and serpentine profile, characteristically antithetical to Banquo's material, suggests Lady Macbeth. Finally, Example 7.2, a theme that first appears during the second visit to the witches (Act IV) quickly gains prominence in the middle section of the *Orchestral-Prelude*, and is the only theme left standing by the end of the piece. Its wide ambitus, harmonic confidence, and regal character point to Macduff, slayer of Macbeth and hero of Shakespeare's play.

As Table 7.1 shows, three large sections of characteristic music help anchor Raff's *Macbeth* structurally and allow for the dramatic and psychological development of its characters. The three witches, whose prophecies motivate so much of the play's action, appear in mm. 1–62 and mm. 169–206, in which divided flutes flitter up and down altered minor and chromatic scales, oboes and clarinets provide palpitating accompaniment, and the strings present overlapping arpeggiated lines and quirky trills – yet another approach to calling forth the supernatural that, considering only non-operatic music, responds to Berlioz, Liszt, and Saint-Saëns. Just as ubiquitous is

**Example 7.3a** Strauss, *Macbeth*, mm. 6–18, Macbeth theme

**Example 7.3b** Strauss, *Macbeth*, mm. 67–73, Lady Macbeth theme

the music that introduces and accompanies the battle between Macbeth and Macduff. At m. 253, the tempo changes to Allegro guerriero and a solo military drum enters. The call to arms is answered by trumpets and timpani at m. 260, and the combatants enter nine bars later. In short, Raff attempts to depict simultaneously the psychological and the narrative.

Strauss may have originally taken an approach closer to Raff's in his *Macbeth*, but the final version of his aggressively dissonant tone poem avoids characteristic scenes and instead focuses almost exclusively on the eponymous subject and his wife. Strauss charts their respective descents into paranoia and madness with modified brands of Lisztian thematic transformation and Beethovenian–Brahmsian sonata form. After a brief curtain-raising orchestral fanfare on the dominant, Macbeth – whom Strauss names in the score – appears at m. 6 with an acrobatic leap in the oboes, clarinets, and upper strings. As shown in Example 7.3a, the theme's first four-bar phrase ends on A♭ with support from an F minor chord; four bars later, on a high G to a first-inversion E♭ major chord. Only at m. 18, following another blitz ascent in the strings and winds, is the tonic, D minor, established.

The non-diatonic harmonies, irregularly repeating rhythmic cells, and cumulative orchestration mark Macbeth as a character already changing from within and, more ominously, subject to manipulation from without. The greatest external pressure comes from Lady Macbeth, explicitly identified in the score at m. 67, whose profile Strauss enhances with a quotation from Friedrich Schiller's 1801 translation of Act I, scene 5, ll. 26–31: "Hie thee hither, / That I may pour my spirits in thine ear; / And chastise with the valour of my tongue / All that impedes thee from the golden round, / Which fate and metaphysical aid doth seem / To have thee crowned withal."[5]

Lady Macbeth, having just been apprised of the prophecies given by the witches to her husband, swiftly determines to make him king despite his being "too full o' the milk of human kindness" (l. 18). Strauss's Lady Macbeth, Example 7.3b, is as terse and confident as her husband is sprawling and indecisive. These two characters lay out the primary and secondary themes of the sonata's exposition, but their formal development is thwarted by two unrelated, adjacent episodes (mm. 123–259, 260–323). Yet when Macbeth's theme returns at m. 324 in the tonic, it has contracted and fragmented, and lost most of its orchestral support and registral buoyancy. His wife's material is even more severely fractured, with a struggling rising figure at m. 371 in the oboes only able to eke out the first four notes of her original theme at m. 387. Soon after, however, she fades away entirely – save for the retrospective epilogue, mm. 515–558 – and the tone poem focuses its remaining energy on eliminating its title character.

Destruction is a powerful theme that runs through Strauss's first batch of tone poems, of which *Don Juan* is arguably the clearest embodiment. The character had been a favorite of authors and audiences since the mid-seventeenth century, resulting in numerous plays and adaptations from the 1630s right up to Strauss's day. In music, however, the dominant image of Don Juan as a rake who gets his just reward had been fixed since Mozart's *Don Giovanni* of 1787. When Strauss turned to the subject a century later, he decided not to model his subject on the famous epic poem by Lord Byron (1818–1824), the darling of Liszt's generation, but rather Nikolaus Lenau. Lenau's portrait of Don Juan, published posthumously, is episodic and incomplete, a feature which may have endeared the work to Strauss, who at the time was struggling to find the right balance of narrative and character depiction in his tone poems. Moreover, while Lenau's Don Juan remains the famous lover, it is his near-nihilistic insouciance – similar to Lenau's Faust – that distances him from Mozart's Enlightenment depiction and situates him squarely in the late Biedermeier, if not early modern period.

As explanation for Don Juan's world-weariness, Strauss prefaces his full score with three excerpts from Lenau: the first speaks to the character's promiscuity; the second, the insatiability of his lust; the third, his emptiness and confusion – "It was a beautiful storm that drove me on," reflects Lenau's and Strauss's Don Juan, but

> it has subsided and a calm has remained behind. All my desires and hopes are in suspended animation; perhaps a lightning bolt, from heights that I contemned, mortally struck my amorous powers, and suddenly my world became deserted and benighted. And yet, perhaps not – the fuel is consumed and the hearth has become cold and dark.[6]

Thematically, Strauss works even harder to transform the Don's theme than in *Macbeth*: the primary and secondary themes are cut from the same cloth, the former (mm. 1–40) potent and vigorous, the latter (mm. 90–148, with adumbration in the solo violin at m. 73ff) sweet and seductive. It is between these two characteristic poles that the Don's exploits play out, including his death in a duel. Formally, *Don Juan* shares with *Macbeth* two episodes that work dialectically with the expected development (mm. 197–307) and that recollect themes very late in the piece, but the end product is not easily fitted to sonata form. Indeed, while a legitimate case has been made for an initial rondo form that transforms into a sonata upon the appearance of the "Heldenthema," several passages still remain for which neither schematic fully accounts.[7]

In contrast to Don Juan, so disgusted with life that he throws down his weapon and lets himself get shot, the subject of *Tod und Verklärung* (*Death and Transfiguration*) perseveres – and for that, he is rewarded. Strauss's first of two tone poems not drawn from literature, *Tod und Verklärung* nevertheless follows a programmatic trajectory, albeit one devised by Strauss himself: A dying man, alone in a desolate room, recalls the joys and tribulations of his life. Despite the seemingly endless obstacles, however, a deep longing kept him, and continues to keep him, going. Death finally comes, and the man is provided with a glimpse of fulfillment, of "world redemption, world transfiguration" ("Welterlösung, Weltverklärung!"). Upon the completion of the composition, Strauss entrusted Ritter to transform his prose scenario in a four-part, sixty-two line poem.

The tone poem pays its respects to Wagner and Liszt. Its title reflects Wagner's *Tristan und Isolde*, whose famous prelude Wagner originally designated as a "Liebestod" ("Love Death"), and whose equally famous concluding scene, Isolde singing "Mild und leise" over Tristan's corpse, Wagner called "Isoldens Verklärung" ("Isolde's Transfiguration"). More fundamental to the philosophy of *Tod und Verklärung* is Arthur Schopenhauer's ideas on the phenomenon and noumenon as laid out in his influential treatise *Die Welt als Wille und Vorstellung* (*The World as Will and Representation*; 1818, rev. 1844). Phenomenon roughly corresponds to the world as comprehended by the senses, noumenon to the unknowable or indiscernible world.

Wagner focused large sections of *Tristan und Isolde* – especially Acts II and III – on tensions between the phenomenal and noumenal, and Strauss seems to do the same in *Tod und Verklärung*. As Table 7.2 suggests, while the tone poem works as a type of sonata form, the most important structural signposts appear when the phenomenal breaches the noumenal and vice versa. In the context of Ritter's poem, the noumenal links to events that occur out of time. In the development section, for example, the "palpitation" theme violently brings the dying man out of his memories between mm. 270 and 325; and in one remarkable passage, Example 7.4,

**Table 7.2** *Strauss,* Tod und Verklärung, *structure*

| Poem | Location | Structural Event | Temporal Location |
|---|---|---|---|
| ll. 1–14 | mm. 1–15: Palpitations | Introduction | Present |
| | 16–20: Reminiscence | | Past |
| | 21–29: Palpitations | | Present |
| | 30–45: Reminiscence, "Childhood" | | Past |
| | 46–66 | | Present |
| 15–22 | 67: Growling theme in bass clarinets, bassoons, cellos, basses | Exposition | |
| | 96: "Determination" | | |
| | 121: +Palpitations | | |
| | 163–164: "Ideal" | | |
| | 165–185: ?? | | |
| 23–46 | 186: Childhood | Development | Past |
| | 206: Transition | | ? |
| | 214: Childhood | | Past |
| | 230: Stormy transition | | ? |
| | 235: Prime of his life | | Past |
| | 270–271, 278, 282, 287: Palpitations | | Past ↔ Present |
| | 319, 333, 354: "Ideal" | | |
| | –365: Transition | | |
| 47–54 | 366–395 | Recapitulation | Present |
| 55–58 | 395–429 | Transition to Coda | |
| 59–62 | 430–499: "Ideal" and "Childhood" | Coda | Transfiguration: Past ↔ Future |

movement between present and past is so quick that the two are essentially operating simultaneously.

Homage to Liszt comes primarily in Strauss's handling of the coda, the site of full transfiguration. Liszt had referred to this type of section in *Die Ideale* as the apotheosis, and its presence in many of his large-scale instrumental works, such as *Les Préludes* or the "Dante" Sonata, made it a defining feature of his compositional style.[8] Strauss's treatment, with a long buildup from m. 395 to m. 429 is likely modeled on Liszt's *Faust* Symphony, a work which made Strauss "vividly aware that Liszt is the only symphonist, the one who had to come after Beethoven and represents a gigantic advance upon him. Everything else is drivel, pure and simple."[9] But perhaps the biggest correspondence between Strauss's transfiguration and Liszt's apotheosis is the perfection of two themes that have been participating in what David Larkin calls "the ongoing process of teleological genesis."[10] The first is

**Example 7.4** Strauss, *Tod und Verklärung*, mm. 306–310

sometimes called the "ideal" theme. It initially appears at mm. 163–164, pops up in remote keys toward the end of the development (mm. 319–321, 333–335, 354–355), and serves as a basis for the transition in its final, perfected version at m. 429. The second theme appears briefly in the introduction (mm. 30–45), opens the development at m. 186, and is associated with youth, that is, a time of carefree innocence. (Perhaps this characteristic accounts for its relative stability during the stormier parts of the development.) During the sonata-proper, there appears to be little connection between these two themes. But in the coda, their close proximity reveals a shared motivic connection (see Example 7.5), a noumenal event in which, as Strauss put it in a personal letter of 1895, "the soul leaves the body, in order to find perfected in the most glorious form in the eternal cosmos that which he could not fulfill here on earth."[11]

Strauss's guiding principle for his first cycle of tone poems can be summarized by four lines from Ritter's poem for *Tod und Verklärung*: "To take everything that ever

**Example 7.5** The connection between the "Ideal" and "Childhood" themes in Strauss, *Tod und Verklärung*

seemed transfigured and to mold it into an even more transfigured shape: this alone is the noble impulse that accompanies him through life" (ll. 35–38).[12] Like Liszt, Strauss brought literary and philosophical weight to his symphonic music, and structured them accordingly. Yet his employment of Liszt's process of thematic transformation is prominent only in *Tod und Verklärung*. Wagner is in fact a better model for the types of melodies favored by Strauss, whereby an individual line is sublimated into another contrapuntally, yielding a complex of music in the orchestra that can sustain incredibly long moments of tension. Indeed, the musico-dramatic framework toward which Strauss reaches in his early tone poems is distinctly Wagnerian, and his experiments in writing wordless, quasi-operatic scenes positioned him well for *Guntram*, the opera that occupied most of his compositional energy in the first half of the 1890s.

## Mahler and the end of the programmatic symphony

Against the backdrop of Strauss's rise to preeminence in the 1890s as avant-garde tone poet, his friend and rival Gustav Mahler composed and copiously revised his First Symphony, a work exemplary for the various programmatic positions it adopted between its premiere at Budapest on 20 November 1889 and its publication a little more than nine years later. Mahler first presented the symphony to the Hungarian public as a five-movement, two-part symphonic poem without any programmatic apparatus. Its failure caused the composer to shelve the symphony until early 1893, when he carried out a major overhaul of the second, third, and fifth movements, and less drastic changes to the other two (only the odd-numbered movements of the Budapest version have survived.) This revision received its premiere at Hamburg, where Mahler was employed as chief conductor of the City Theatre, on 27 October 1893. Now dubbed "*Titan*, a Tone Poem in Symphonic Form," the symphony was heard with the aid of a long prose program that provided not only titles for its two main sections and its five movements, but also elaborate descriptions of the happenings of movements one, five, and especially four (see

**Text Box 7.1  Mahler's program for his First Symphony, 1893–1894**

*Titan*, a Tone Poem in Symphonic Form
   Part 1. From the Days of Youth, Flower-, Fruit-, and Thorn-Pieces
   I. *Spring and No End* (Introduction and Allegro comodo). The introduction pictures the awakening of nature from a long winter's sleep.
   II. *Blumine* (Andante)
   III. *Under Full Sail* (Scherzo)
   Part 2. "The Human Comedy"
   IV. *Stranded! (Funeral March in the Manner of Callot)*. The following may serve as an explanation for this movement: The author received an overt suggestion for it from *Des Jägers Leichenbegängnis* (*The Hunter's Funeral Procession*), a parodistic picture that is well known to all Austrian children and is taken from an old book of children's fairy tales. The animals of the forest escort the coffin of a deceased hunter to the gravesite. Rabbits carrying a banner follow a band of Bohemian musicians accompanied by music-making cats, toads, crows, and so on; stags, does, foxes, and other four-legged and feathered animals of the forest follow the procession in amusing poses. At that point the piece in some ways expresses an ironic, humorous mood and in other ways expresses an eerie, brooding mood, followed immediately by
   V. *From Hell* (Allegro furioso). As the sudden outburst of despair from a deeply wounded heart.

**Source:** Adapted from Constantin Floros, *Gustav Mahler: The Symphonies*, trans. Vernon and Jutta Wicker (Portland, OR: Amadeus Press, 1993), 29–30.

Text Box 7.1). The work in this guise seems to have been received well enough for Mahler to plan a repeat performance, which he conducted at Weimar – the cradle of Liszt's New German School – in early June 1894 with small tweaks to the prose program, including retitling the fifth movement as "From Hell to Paradise." (It is unclear whether this title serves as defiant reference to Liszt's own "Dante" Symphony, which, as discussed in Chapter 5, stopped short of Paradise.) Yet at the next performance almost two years later in Berlin, Mahler jettisoned the program, descriptive titles, and second movement, "Blumine," and presented the hour-long orchestral piece as a four-movement symphony in D major.

   The symphony is a conspectus of both Mahler's compositional oeuvre through about 1890 and his Austro-German-Hungarian-Bohemian cultural heritage. The exposition of the first movement (m. 62ff) begins with an instrumental setting of Mahler's song, "Ging heut' Morgens über's Feld," from his four-song cycle, *Lieder eines fahrenden Gesellen*, of 1885. The "Blumine" movement harks back to one year before that, when Mahler composed incidental music to Joseph Viktor von Scheffel's epic poem, *Der Trompeter von Säkkingen*. The middle section of the funeral march, m. 83ff, owes a significant debt to the last verse of the fourth song from the *Lieder eines fahrenden Gesellen*, "Die zwei blauen Augen von meinem Schatz." The programmatic use of this material in the First Symphony strongly reinforces Theodor Adorno's observation that "The link between the novelesque and the ductus of Mahler's music are the songs. Their function in relation to his symphonic writing cannot be subsumed . . . under the facile concept of preparatory studies."[13]

The symphony is also replete with references beyond Mahler's own music. The introduction to the first movement instrumentally dramatizes the "principle of mobile spatial deployment" that Mahler transported from the opera house into the concert hall using Beethoven's *Fidelio* and Wagner's *Tristan und Isolde* as particular models.[14] The second movement replaces the traditional scherzo or minuet with a series of ländler and waltzes, thus acting as a compendium of folk dances. The opening melody of the funeral march is the ubiquitous children's song "Bruder Martin" ("Frère Jacques"), and many listeners have heard a parodistic take on a rural Bohemian folk or Klezmer band at m. 39. But Mahler also invokes "high" culture, particularly by referencing E.T.A. Hoffmann's influential seventy-year-old novel, *Fantasiestücke in Callot's Manier* – the same source that inspired Robert Schumann's *Fantasiestücke*, op. 12, and *Kreisleriana*, op. 16 (see Chapter 3), and which also bore a preface by Jean Paul Richter, author of *Siebenkäs* and *Titan*, whose title Mahler lent to his First Symphony for a time. The fifth movement commandeers several "high" pieces of German music for programmatic effect, including bits from the "Inferno" movement of Liszt's "Dante" Symphony, the "Grail" motive from Richard Wagner's recent festival drama *Parsifal*,[15] and appropriately, by way of victorious conclusion, the famous "Hallejujah" Chorus from George Frideric Handel's *Messiah*. That this theme bookends the symphony – appearing in the first movement "like a sound of nature" ("wie ein Naturlaut") and ending the fifth with a promise of divine oversight and personal deliverance ("and He shall reign for ever and ever") – illustrates both a historical and a programmatic dimension to Mahler's First Symphony that makes it unique not only within his own output, but also among late nineteenth-century symphonic music altogether.

The funeral march is worth examining in greater detail, for while it has been routinely praised for living up to Mahler's description of it as "harrowing in its sharp irony and reckless polyphony,"[16] it also belongs to a small group of overlooked programmatic symphonic pieces that subjectify and delimit movement through space or time. Mahler's choice of funeral march might point to Beethoven's "Eroica" Symphony or the Allegretto movement of his Seventh Symphony as models, but the extreme juxtaposition of sacred and profane elements suggests a genealogy that probably starts with Hector Berlioz and Felix Mendelssohn.

As discussed in Chapter 3, in the "Marche des pèlerins," the second movement of *Harold en Italie*, Berlioz constructs a procession of pilgrims around the fixed point of the protagonist Harold, in order to highlight his aloofness, indifference, or anti-heroicism – features all drawn from Byron's narrative poem. About the same time, Mendelssohn was working on what would become his "Italian" Symphony.[17] The drama of its second movement, Andante con moto, hinges on the juxtaposition of modal and tonal systems; or put another way, of sacred and secular traditions. One plausible interpretation that overlaps with the Italian leg of Mendelssohn's Grand Tour of 1830–1832 concerns the composer's impressions of Rome and Naples. In a letter from Rome to his parents, he admitted that although Rome was a city stuck in the past, it was nevertheless "singular and beautiful and great" for the sincerity of its adherence to tradition. By contrast, he was turned off by Naples, which he found "more lively, more diverse, more cosmopolitan," and, by extension, he was unable to embrace its "diversity" ("Vielseitigkeit").[18] By referencing the topic of the processional through an active walking bass that begins in the second half of m. 2, Mendelssohn thus may have attempted to highlight "the contrasting ambience of the two geographical axes of [his] Italian journey."[19]

Yet these axes intersect at important moments, the most prominent of which occurs at m. 57 (see Example 7.6), when the modal theme wrenches control away from the tonal theme and reasserts A minor, not the tonal theme's E minor. Yet this power play is short-lived, as it fails to result in a full statement of the modal theme; only its consequent phrase materializes. Moreover, it cannot maintain control, for despite efforts by the oboes, bassoons, and violas at m. 67 to resurrect the complete modal theme (with the walking bass now transferred to the violins), the next full presentation of a theme comes at m. 74, where the tonal theme appears in D major. Indeed, after this long section (through m. 86), the modal theme eventually appears in the tonic (m. 96), but never again fully assembled. Instead, it slowly decays into a rhythmically augmented version of the A–B♭–A reciting tone that originally (mm. 1–2) called the theme to order.[20]

Ceremony and grandeur stand at the heart of the processional movement of Schumann's Third Symphony, op. 97, which as a whole has long been associated with the Rhine River and with the "local color" of its towns. That association has given the fourth movement a programmatic life of its own, with Schumann's friend, colleague, and first biographer, Wilhelm Joseph von Wasielewski, claiming its direct connection to the elevation of a Cologne archbishop to the rank of cardinal. The closest documented remark by Schumann to such an event – which the composer never witnessed – occurred at the symphony's premiere at Düsseldorf on 6 February 1851, where he listed the movement in the printed program as being "in the character of an accompaniment to a solemn ceremony." Yet when Schumann published the score in October of that year, this description was reduced to "solemn" ("feierlich").

**Example 7.6** Mendelssohn, "Italian" Symphony, op. 90, III, mm. 55–75, arr. unidentified

Despite his suppression of its earlier title, however, Schumann retains the processional character primarily in the subtle manipulation of the pseudo-archaic melody – tellingly given to a choir of horns and trombones – that dominates each of the movement's three sections. As Table 7.3 shows, the main melody never establishes a definitive rhythmic guise: its first presentation at m. 1 routinely avoids the downbeat; its counterpart at m. 24 seems to find a metric footing around m. 26, but abruptly disintegrates one bar later in order to let the episode commence; and the melody does return in rhythmic augmentation at m. 44, but the complementary change of meter from common time to 4/2 means that nothing substantially has

**Table 7.3** *The metric augmentation of the main melody in Schumann's Third Symphony, III, mm. 1–7, 24–27, 44–50*

changed. At the same time, the metric modulation from common time to 3/2 to 4/2 militates against hearing the movement exclusively as a three-part, ABA' structure coda. Instead, it gives an impression – if only at an abstract level – of movement toward a specific event, which comes at m. 52. At this juncture the movement replaces dense, independent lines of counterpoint with lush, coordinated homophony; subdominant–tonic–dominant harmonic relationships with a foray into the submediant; and intervals of fourths – perfect and altered – and minor seconds for thirds and sixths.

The authenticity of religious experience is the subject of one of Liszt's most underrated orchestral compositions, *Der nächtliche Zug* (*The Nocturnal Procession*), completed in 1861. A symphonic poem in all but name, its literary source is Nikolaus Lenau's *Faust. Ein Gedicht* of 1836. In contrast to Goethe's ultimately optimistic tale of redemption through striving (see Chapter 6), Lenau's Faust is a nihilist who, after traveling with Mephistopheles through a variety of stations, commits suicide. As preface to his score, Liszt reproduces the whole of Lenau's eleventh, same-named chapter of seventy-two lines, which follows Faust as he happens upon a group of the faithful taking part in a procession on the eve of the Feast of St. John. Although a dark night, the woods have come alive in anticipation, yet the damaged Faust can only retreat from the celebratory strains.

As Table 7.4 shows, however, Liszt prioritizes select passages of Lenau's poem by employing them as epigraphs to the composition's six main sections. (He does something similar in his symphonic poem *Die Ideale*.) The first four sections take

**Table 7.4** *Poetic epigraphs in Liszt's* Der nächtliche Zug

| Section | Epigraph* | Music |
|---|---|---|
| 1 | Heavy and dark clouds hang in the sky / And wait, listening to the forest below / Far into the night. (ll. 1–3) | mm. 1–27 |
| 2 | But a sweet spring breeze is blowing / In the forest, a warm tender murmur, / The blossom-filled skies sway and swell, / One can hear all life-sources flow. / Oh Nightingale, oh dear one, call out, sing! / So that your blissful tune pierces every leaf! (ll. 3–8) | 28–111 |
| 3 | But Faust rides further through the night / And in his gloomy displeasure, does not take notice / Of the wonderfully moving voices of spring. / He lets his horse trot / Along the path towards the forest edge. (ll. 13–17) | 112–151 |
| 4 | What shines so brightly within the forest / So that bush and sky glow in a gleam of purple? / What sings so gently in such joyful tones, / As if it could appease all earthly misery? / That distant, dark and yearnful song / Sways with sweet emotion through the calm sky. (ll. 25–30) | 152–192 |
| 5 | A festive procession approaches. (l. 40) | 193–334 |
| 6 | As Faust stands alone in the darkness once again; / He madly grasps his trusty steed / Pressing his face deep within its mane / He sheds burning tears / So bitter, as he never before had wept. (ll. 68–72) | 335–380 |

*Translations from Mary Angela Hunt, "Franz Liszt: The Mephisto Waltzes" (DMA diss., University of Wisconsin-Madison, 1979), 21–22

turns establishing sharply contrasting environments: the first, labeled Andante moderato e mesto, is a stereotypically foreboding Romantic forest in the dead of night, where brooding motives barely survive on a diet of half-step intervals and where harmonic and metric development is foreign; here Faust makes his first appearance in section 3. By contrast, the second section teems with life, with confident melodic lines and sonorous, often enriched, harmonies giving rise to the equally stereotyped calls of the nightingale (m. 43ff) and creating the *misterioso* effects that fashion the romanticized portrait of nature as an idealized oasis untouched by modern life; in section 4, a man-made song – or, as Liszt describes the effect in the score, "like a peal of bells from afar" – gradually infiltrates this opulent wood. With the two antithetical landscapes now fully profiled, the procession proper begins in section 5, which culminates in the presentation of the plainchant melody, "Pange lingua gloriosi corporis mysterium." Initially, the English horn acts as cantor, the flutes and bassoons as respondents. But as more members of the train materialize, so too does the melody pass and develop through the entire orchestra, which reaches maximum proximity to the voyeuristic Faust at m. 296, the first of only two points in the score where Liszt calls for a triple *forte* dynamic.

**Example 7.7** Liszt, *Der nächtliche Zug*, mm. 307–334, arr. Liszt

Liszt's handling of the procession's departure, excerpted in Example 7.7, is deft. Over the course of almost forty measures, the orchestra descends more than three octaves, the tempo slows, dynamic levels recede, and instruments gradually go silent until only the violas and cellos remain to intone the chant. Berlioz's Harold responded to similar events with aloofness. Faust, however, knowing full well that he will be forever removed from the spiritual exercises that are now out of earshot, responds with tears – which explode with the other triple *forte* dynamic at m. 356, and which Liszt directs the orchestra to play as if it were "profusely crying" ("heftig

**Example 7.8** Schumann, Symphony no. 3, op. 97, V, mm. 99–105, arr. August Horn

weinend"). In a crucial earlier scene from Lenau's *Faust* called "The Commitment" ("Die Verschreibung"), Faust is given the opportunity by a monk to renounce his ways and turn to the church. Instead, he embraces Mephistopheles's promise to show him "truth" ("Wahrheit"). As an affirmation of his new affiliation, he dramatically renounces God by throwing his bible into a fire and proclaiming, "Faith will never attract me. / It burns; its magic has been conquered; / The consolation it offered has fled, / Scattered in gray flecks of ash."[21]

The "Pange lingua" melody that Liszt selected – Lenau does not specify the song's title in his poem – offers an ideal foil to Faust's actions and their spiritual consequences. The melody is sung during processions on the Feast of Corpus Christi and Maundy Thursday, and its thirteenth-century text speaks of the transubstantiation of Christ at the Last Supper. The fourth stanza ends with the allowance that when the senses fail, faith alone strengthens the sincere heart ("et si sensus deficit, / ad firmandum cor sincerum / sola fides sufficit"). Having renounced his faith for truth, Faust can only watch the procession with growing anguish.[22]

While the musical processions by Mendelssohn, Schumann, and Liszt exhibit numerous internal levels of juxtaposition, such as modal versus tonal or genuine versus feigned solemnity, external contrasts contribute just as significantly to their individual profiles. The finale of Mendelssohn's "Italian" Symphony is explicitly labeled a saltarello, which adds a new locale to the symphony's map, introduces a raucous folk dance that is neither reified nor refined, and offers a different solution to the modal–tonal question by ending the A major symphony in its parallel minor. Schumann purposefully harnesses the music of the folk in the second and fifth movements of his Third Symphony, but the sudden appearance of material from the fourth movement in the finale (Example 7.8) seems to draw attention to the difference between modes of celebration, with one taking place inside a claustrophobic,

**Figure 7.1** Moritz von Schwind, *How the Animals Buried the Hunter* (*Wie die Tiere den Jäger begraben*; 1850), in Otto Weigmann, ed., *Schwind. Des Meisters Werke in 1265 Abbildungen* (Stuttgart and Leipzig: Deutsche Verlags-Anstalt, 1906), 296

man-made church, the other a revelry under the clear blue skies of nature. Liszt remained adamant that *Der nächtliche Zug* should always be played before *Der Tanz in der Dorfschenke*, commonly known as the first "Mephisto" Waltz, since they "*belong together* through the contrast of feeling."[23] Indeed, the waltz shows Faust throwing his life away in pursuits of the flesh while being urged on by the Bacchic melodies of Mephistopheles's infernal violin.

These are some of the traditions with which the funeral march from Mahler's First Symphony engages – but not without significant personalization. Indeed, Adorno's conclusion about Mahler's mimetic handling of the external world can also be applied to his handling of tradition: "Even where Mahler's music arouses associations of nature and landscape," he writes, "it nowhere presents them as absolutes, but infers them from the contrast to that from which they deviate."[24] One stark deviation from his predecessors has to do with Mahler's choice of melody. By selecting one that works as a round, he is able to terrace entries in a way that allows each instrument to maintain its identity while still allying it to the larger group – in other words, a means by which to order chaos. If Figure 7.1, Moritz von Schwind's *How the Animals Buried the Hunter* (*Wie die Tiere den Jäger begraben*), served as inspiration for certain elements of Mahler's march, then the funeral cortège is at best semi-organized; likewise, the "Bruder Martin" melody appears in the contrabasses at m. 3, bassoons at m. 9, cellos at m. 11, bass tubas at m. 15, and B♭ clarinets at m. 17. Only at m. 19 do entries at every second bar become the norm, the last occurring in the horns and harp at m. 29.

One instrument that does not participate in the round is the oboe. However, its melody at m. 19 is clearly indebted to the children's song, as the profiles, range, and even pitches of both melodies overlap. The oboe's melody and the deceptive return

**Example 7.9** Mahler, Symphony no. 1, III, mm. 135–145

in E♭ minor instead of D minor at m. 113 constitute two major mishearings of "Bruder Martin." To be sure, these alterations are part of Mahler's general penchant for irony and distortion, but in the context of a procession, these mishearings might also be attributed to the physical distance separating the participants – an understandable occurrence, given that there appears to be no musical leader in Schwind's picture. Such spatial musical reasoning also helps to account for the decisive return to D minor at m. 138 (Example 7.9). Not every animal in the train has caught up, it seems, since one bar later the conductor is told to move the orchestra "suddenly much faster" and to keep the flutes, oboes, and clarinets "extremely rhythmic." The movement's opening tempo is finally re-established at m. 145, yet all that remains of the "Bruder Martin" melody is its skeletal accompaniment in the harp, contrabasses, and, later, timpani. Even its derivative oboe melody has splintered.

While the topical elements and technical features of Mahler's First Symphony can be found throughout his remaining eight completed symphonies, its programmatic abundance cannot. Indeed, Mahler tries various alternatives to communicate meaning and guide interpretation: the Second, Third, Fourth, and Eighth Symphonies, for instance, trumpet the importance of song by setting texts from the Catholic liturgy, Goethe's *Faust, Des Knaben Wunderhorn*, and Mahler himself for various ensembles of voices. However, the Fifth, Sixth, and Seventh Symphonies downplay song – the Fifth's famously melodic Adagietto notwithstanding – but do not compensate with explicit extra-musical referents. Still, Mahler's tendency, à la Berlioz, to invest deeply personal experiences and philosophies into his music has led to numerous programmatic interpretations of these ostensibly non-programmatic works, interpretations which are often based on the composer's own conversations and correspondence. Finally, it would have behooved critics to programmatize the Ninth Symphony as Mahler's musical valediction, given its world premiere under Bruno Walter's baton in Vienna thirteen months after the composer's death.[25]

Yet the fact remains that Mahler never returned to the instrumental programmatic symphony after the mid-1890s. His uphill battles with critics who failed to understand his intentions certainly account for this abandonment, but so might the realization that this particular artistic union of poetry, literature, painting, and music was destined to remain an unhappy one. Indeed, Mahler's First Symphony marks one of the last major programmatic symphonies of the century. By contrast, the more formally flexible and less tradition-bound symphonic / tone poem continued to attract attention, in large part due to a second set produced by Strauss at the twilight of the nineteenth century.

## Strauss and the end of the characteristic

After the failure of *Guntram* in 1894, Strauss would not return to the operatic stage until 1901. And while he composed several sets of songs toward the end of the century, his major focus was on the tone poem, of which he produced four massive exemplars in as many years. In these later pieces, Strauss largely avoids structures associated with Liszt's symphonic poems, such as the modified sonata and the apotheosis coda. In fact, Strauss denies the latter altogether through the inclusion of retrospective epilogues rather than transformative finales, and even parodies the idea in *Till Eulenspiegel*, which concludes with an "apotheosis of eternal humor" ("Apotheose des unsterblichen Humors," m. 650ff).

Likewise, the episodic developments found in the first set of tone poems grow in stature, resulting in complex and often ambiguous variation (*Don Quixote*), rondo (*Till Eulenspiegel*), and through-composed (*Also sprach Zarathustra, Ein*

*Heldenleben*) forms. Strauss's turn to self-serving, iconoclastic heroes and humorous, parodistic anti-heroes in his second set further separates his later tone poems from the idealistic subjects preferred by Liszt and Wagner. In fact, their music – and by extension the entire German symphonic tradition – serves to illustrate significant stylistic and philosophical differences that now exist between Strauss and his former masters: hence the transposed "Tristan" chord at m. 47 of *Till Eulenspiegel*, or the metrical mishearing of *Les Préludes* halfway (mm. 529–583) through *Also sprach Zarathustra*.

Entire compositional techniques also come under fire. Fugue, for instance, makes its first formal appearance in a Strauss tone poem in *Also sprach Zarathustra*, yet it does not function as a symbol of struggle, as it had for Mendelssohn[26] and Liszt. Instead, Strauss relegates the device to a small section entitled "On Science" (mm. 201–238), in which academic posturing only further solidifies fugue's contemporary irrelevance. Even the work's subtitle, "freely after Friedrich Nietzsche," speaks to a tension between tradition – dependence on Nietzsche – and innovation – but only to a point – that courses through Strauss's second series of tone poems. Indeed, the most pathbreaking feature of Strauss's tone-poetic "enterprise lies in its openness to a multiplicity of allusive possibilities without insisting on any of them as objective fact."[27]

These pieces also sound the death knell for the chief building blocks of program music since the last quarter of the eighteenth century: the topic and character piece. Particularly in *Till Eulenspiegel* and *Don Quixote*, Strauss's ability to depict narrative content through music reached an almost filmic level, in which sound, gesture, and color collaborated in creating not saccharine gondola songs or routine military marches, but rather Quixote's voyage in an enchanted dinghy (Variation 8) or Till's graphic execution. That neither of these works bears the designation "tone poem" in its title also speaks to the genre's identity crisis near the turn of the century.

Like Puck, Petrushka, or Harlequin, the rascally Till Eulenspiegel had been a staple in north European literature since the sixteenth century, and almost certainly in its oral history before that. By the nineteenth century, several versions of his exploits were in circulation. The tradition embraced by Paul Geisler in his symphonic poem *Till Eulenspiegel* painted Till – according to the prefatory poetic epigraph – as a man of "free heart and good sense, / saucy tongue and daring love, / singing, fighting, / drinking, lady-loving." Geisler, who modeled his music after the techniques and philosophies of the New German School, published his first symphonic poem in 1877 on the subject of Heinrich von Ofterdingen, the medieval Minnesanger whose famous though highly fictionalized life provided Wagner with substantial material for the character of Tannhäuser. His most regarded piece of program music, on the legend of the Rat-Catcher of Hamelin came in 1880, and *Till Eulenspiegel*, published a year later with a dedication "to the Master Franz Liszt,"

**Example 7.10a** Geisler, *Till Eulenspiegel*, mm. 9–12

**Example 7.10b** Geisler, *Till Eulenspiegel*, mm. 31–34

attempted to duplicate the success and increase his renown beyond northern Germany, where he would be based until his death in 1919.

Geisler's passage is a modification of a passage from Julius Wolff's *Till Eulenspiegel redivivus: Ein Schelmlied* (*Till Eulenspiegel Reborn: A Roguish Song*), whose original reads: "free heart and good sense, / youthful vigor and courage to love, / drinking, lady-loving, / singing, magic." Geisler's transformation of Till into a harmless Biedermeier bon vivant carries over to the music, although a wisp of the picaresque remains in the harmonically deceptive opening of both phrases of his balanced main theme (Example 7.10a), which initially point to D minor instead of the work's home key, C major. A secondary theme that initially appears as accompaniment to the first (m. 18) blossoms into an important variation of Till's theme (Example 7.10b), and upon these two themes Geisler builds a transparent, almost neo-classical sonata form. Likewise, the poetic epigraph seems to have been included in order to draw attention to moods, not deeds, since Geisler responds with stereotyped bold, bellicose outbursts in the brass at mm. 168–176, a cantilena on a solo violin at mm. 56–73, a contrapuntally tipsy permutation of the second theme at mm. 109–114, and a pastoral siciliano at mm. 131–145. A playful element underwrites the character of all these themes and their various permutations, resulting in a light-hearted work that lacks the philosophical weight that tradition had foisted upon the symphony and its offshoots. In short, Geisler's Till is neither New German mythic hero nor its antithesis.

The wide-ranging music critic and biographer Bernhard Vogel was non-plussed by the work. With expectations high after the success of Geisler's *Der Rattenfänger von Hameln*, Vogel questioned Geisler's decision to call *Till Eulenspiegel* a symphonic poem, which should have "much stronger contrasts and demands a more logical development."[28] Instead, Vogel hears Geisler's piece as a series of variations, that is, without the connective motivic tissue and transformation procedures that make music cohere on the large-scale level. Most intriguing is Vogel's implicit understanding of Till Eulenspiegel as a uniquely German figure, and, by extension, Vogel's equation of the symphonic poem with German music. Thus Geisler's use of "Bellini-esque" melodies and expression marks written in Italian insult the work's nominal genre and its ostensible subject: "Why the composer is so fixated on this . . . is unclear. Even our good old Till Eulenspiegel, who clearly spoke and understood only his beloved German, would have made a perplexed face about it."[29]

While Geisler's symphonic poem falls short on several accounts, its design and reception highlight several important considerations in dealing with the transferal of folk material into music:

1. There is usually no definitive characterization or narrative of the subject. In the case of Till Eulenspiegel in the nineteenth century, there was a literary treatment by Wolff and an edited volume by Karl Simrock that featured beautiful illustrations by Adolf Schrödter. And in his review Vogel fondly recalls a short poem by the mid-eighteenth-century author Christian Fürchtegott Gellert in which Till is more philosopher than rascal.
2. This plurality of depictions also opens the door for composers like Geisler and Strauss, acting on models by Liszt,[30] to mix and match sources, or even to add their own narrative supplements or character traits.
3. Since folk figures are almost always built upon a collection of multi-authored, incidental vignettes rather than a bounded, deliberate, and extended literary treatment, the structures of the resulting musical works tend to tip toward the episodic.

Geisler cautiously exploits these features to create a gemütlich hero. Strauss, by contrast, hyperbolizes them to create a hero completely outside of tradition. The full title of his piece admits as much: *Till Eulenspiegel's Merry Pranks. According to the Old Rogue's Manner, in Rondeau Form.* The kinship to Wolff's "reborn" Till is clear enough; but by taking the prank as his work's guiding philosophical and stylistic principle, Strauss goes much further.

The first prank Strauss pulls is in shaping an expectation of a structure that does not materialize; in this case, a rondeau, the most structurally complicated of the fourteenth- and fifteenth-century *formes fixes*. Strauss's music contradicts this claim. Its more contemporary but still dated homophone, the rondo, comes closer, but its form does not account for important sections of thematic recapitulation, discussed below, which point to a possible sonata structure. At best, *Till Eulenspiegel* offers some features of one, some of the other; that is, what James Hepokoski posits as a "sonata-rondo deformation."[31]

Part of the work's formal ambiguity rests on its wily protagonist, whose character is split across two themes. The first, which appears in the horn at m. 6, is metrically dissonant, playfully longing, and acrobatic; the second theme is sounded by clarinets in its most characteristic form at m. 46. These two themes form the primary musical material of mm. 1–111, a section that might be heard as the exposition of a sonata form. Such reasoning is bolstered by mm. 112–429, in which Strauss sends his themes off into the world, away from the tonic F major. At m. 429, the horn's theme returns exactly as before, but a sense of urgency hovers over the affair: another horn picks up the theme in D major, and the second theme quickly jumps in at m. 443, only one beat before other members of the orchestra pick it up. From here, the tonic is only strongly asserted briefly at m. 500, and the version of Till's second theme that corresponds to m. 46 does not occur until m. 582, during a section dominated by menacing brass and low winds and strings, as if Till is tempting fate.

*Till Eulenspiegel* is the first of Strauss's tone poems not to include specific extramusical references. The composer may have envisioned this omission as another type of prank, but he soon thought better of it, and ended up providing what would turn out to be the most detailed program of any of his tone poems.[32] The program not only contradicts hearing mm. 1–111 as a sonata exposition, since it "develops" Till Eulenspiegel by prematurely sending him "off to make new pranks" at m. 75ff, but it contradicts the wider literary tradition. Till's second-theme outburst at m. 582 occurs in the midst of his trial, and his execution at mm. 615–624 swiftly follows. However, Strauss plays one final prank in the epilogue by revisiting the introduction (cf. mm. 1–5) and Till's second theme in its unadulterated state (mm. 651–652) – as if to say that Till, or at least what he stands for, cannot be silenced by the philistines who thought they had put him down.

Till may be disruptive, but in Strauss's conception he remains genuine and consistent. The same cannot be said for the other comic subject to be featured in Strauss's second set of tone poems, Don Quixote. Cervantes's *Don Quixote* had served as a basis for ballets and comic operas since the early seventeenth century, and Georg Philipp Telemann wrote perhaps the first programmatic work based on the wayward hero, the *Ouverture Burlesque de Quixotte*, in the second half of the 1720s. Over the course of a traditional two-part French overture and seven titled sections, Telemann recreates Quixote's most infamous deeds, including his charging at the windmills and poor wooing of Dulcinea, and also leaves plenty of room for the antics of Sancho Panza, Quixote's trusty steed, Rosinante, and Panza's mule – all while mocking convention through generic distortion and topical overuse.[33]

Telemann primarily latched on to the satirical elements of Cervantes's tale while avoiding the darker though equally prominent theme of a psychologically damaged man lost in his own misguided fantasies. This was remedied at the turn of the nineteenth century, as young German authors were increasingly drawn to the dramatic implications of the Don's psychosis. Chief among them was Ludwig Tieck, who began a celebrated translation in 1799 of *Don Quixote* and modeled many of his own comic plays on his Spanish predecessor. By donning the Quixotean mantel, Tieck sought to "taunt the pedantry of the theatrical establishment and the philistine tastes of the average audience, to shock expectations and break down stage illusion."[34] Indeed, *Don Quixote* became a model work for those seeking emancipation from stale Enlightenment literary doctrines. Tieck's colleague, Friedrich Schlegel, while in no way downplaying the novel's biting satire, stood in awe of its perfect generic balance: "jocular and serious, witty and poetic"[35] – in other words, the product of a true Romantic genius.

Romantic composers were also intrigued by Cervantes's book. Anton Rubinstein's "musical character picture" on *Don Quixote* from 1870 is a cautious essay in music humor. A page-long preface to the orchestral score introduces Don Quixote as a dreamer who, under the influence of "chivalric romances," undertakes three adventures: (1) dispersing a flock of sheep (Part I, ch. 18); (2) meeting three peasant women and choosing Dulcinea as his true love (II, 10); (3) and falling in with a group of bandits who turn on him (II, 60–61). Now in a state of despair, Quixote recognizes his foolishness and dies.[36]

While Rubinstein subtitles his *Don Quixote* a "Humoreske," its content verges on the tragicomic. As a character study, too many of Quixote's themes share qualities with those of Rubinstein's brooding Faust (see Chapter 6), making the Don's setbacks and death lamentable. (It is telling, for instance, that the composition begins in C major and ends in C minor.) However, Rubinstein's handling of Quixote's encounters is often technically original, humorously executed, and programmatically apt.

A standout example comes during Quixote's attempt to find a suitable maiden to whom he can dedicate his great deeds. A passionate melody appears in the bassoons at m. 149, and a jaunty dance running over a prolonged F♯ diminished seventh chord commences at m. 181. At m. 197 (Example 7.11), the dance melody continues in the flutes, oboes, and bassoons, with the lower strings providing accompaniment. Simultaneously, the passionate melody reappears in the first violins, but instead of fitting itself to the dance's triple meter, it sticks to its original duple pulse. Thus not only does Rubinstein create two separate groups of characters – three women and

**Example 7.11** Anton Rubinstein, *Don Quixote*, mm. 197–204

one Quixote, each with separate accompaniment à la the finale to the first act of Mozart's *Don Giovanni* – but he also highlights their ultimate incompatibility. Indeed, the scene changes by m. 213, where brass fanfares and Quixote's "travel" music appear to accompany him on his next misguided quest.

Rubinstein's "Humoreske" does not unfold according to models that take motive, melody, or harmony as their chief structural elements. Instead, it exhibits a three-part structure (ABA') where the outer sections focus on Quixote's emotional responses, and where the middle section strings together narrative incidents with strong characteristic components – such as dances, laughter, or the infernal – from Cervantes's novel. The melodic variety that this unorthodox structure necessitates led even supporters like Tchaikovsky to complain of the composition's episodic feel. A contemporary reviewer was even less persuaded by Rubinstein's experiment, calling it "program-music carried to the verge of lunacy." While Rubinstein succeeds in channeling Quixote's madness, the reviewer faults the middle section, in which the composer "attempts to express by music what is quite beyond its province." To be sure, this is a position that had been taken against program music for decades, but in this instance, the satirical subject matter made Rubinstein's failure something of a foregone conclusion:

> We cannot help regarding the work as a failure – a most interesting failure, it is true, because it is the work of a really talented man; but none the less unsuccessful, because in search of novelty he has gone on what we may most appropriately call a Quixotic adventure, and attempted the impossible. Herr Rubinstein is not a Beethoven; but even had Beethoven tried to treat such a subject, he must, from its very nature, have failed.[37]

Rubinstein ostensibly overreached in his attempts to express the inexpressible according to earlier music-aesthetic principles. Strauss largely avoided aspects of expression, and instead focused on depiction with an almost phonographic precision. As a series of highly visceral, "Fantastic Variations," Strauss respects the episodic structure of Cervantes's novel (especially Part I) and the idiosyncrasies of its protagonist. Moreover, his *Don Quixote* returns to the fissure between Renaissance order and modern chaos that Cervantes sought to capture in

> a vision for a world which, for all its aberrant qualities, appears generally to be more colorful and more thrilling, and also, incidentally, to be inspired by more honorable rules of conduct, than the world of ordinary people, "realism," current affairs, private interests, easy jibes, and petty pranks. It is a world in which actions are performed out of a sense of their beauty and excitement, not for the sake of their usefulness.[38]

Strauss's *Don Quixote* is beautiful and exciting according to its own delimited, self-absorbed terms. Rubinstein had depicted the Don's charging toward and scattering of the sheep by staggering several entries of a falling, deceptively accelerating line across the strings over six short measures. That this act of depiction should be understood as separate from Quixote's emotional state is confirmed by the abrupt harmonic turn toward A♭ major that the piece makes; previously, all signs pointed to C major, but after the sheep scatter, the Don's theme returns in C minor – a clear sign that he has been affected by the brief encounter.

Strauss, however, primarily relegates Quixote's psychological upheavals to the introduction, where he loses his mind reading novels of chivalry (mm. 1–122), and the finale (mm. 688–750), where he comes to his senses, spends his remaining days in meditation, and dies (mm. 740–745). Thus, in Strauss's recreation of the sheep-scattering scene, Quixote dissolves into the environmental frame. Marked *bellicose* ("kriegerisch"), the second variation (mm. 211–245) begins with three solo cellos calling the orchestra to arms in D major. The sheep come into view, the key changes to F♯ minor, and the attack commences at m. 230 (Example 7.12), again with a bold assertion of D major, which the violins maintain despite the intensely dissonant bleating in the brass and winds. Thankfully, the attack is over quickly, and the orchestra, this time led by the cellos and first violins, celebrates its victory with a slightly modified version of the variation's introduction.

Strauss does not employ traditional characteristic material to create this vivid and famous scene, nor does he rely on topical or characteristic precedent in most of the other variations, especially 7 through 10. Variations 7 and 8 illustrate the scope of Strauss's depictive virtuosity, whereby the former explores the heavens (complete with wind machine), the latter the Venetian canals. Variation 9 follows a structure similar to the sheep-scattering scene, and like *Also sprach Zarathustra* uses fugue with purposeful artifice. Indeed, in keeping with the ambivalent attitude toward tradition displayed in the earlier tone poems from his second set, Strauss gives the listener plenty of characteristic misreadings: the first half of variation 3 features a

**Example 7.12** Strauss, *Don Quixote*, mm. 230–233

series of conversations between Quixote and Sancho Panza that develops through thematic fragmentation à la Beethoven; the fifth variation is a hyperextension of Liszt's style of instrumental recitative; the next variation totters in and out of quintuple time (2 + 3) – hardly an appropriate meter for a country dance tune, as Sancho Panza finds out the hard way; and the final variation, at mm. 654–658, pays mock-homage to the musical pastoral tradition by citing a bucolic theme reminiscent of Rossini's *Guillaume Tell* Overture as Quixote is beaten by the Knight of the White Moon and subsequently forced to return home (Part II, chap. 64).

**Example 7.12** (cont.)

The narrative and depictive structure of *Don Quixote* dovetails nicely into Strauss's last tone poem of the century, *Ein Heldenleben*. In elucidating its title, Strauss divulged a familiar narrative and depictive structure in the score:

1. The Hero (mm. 1–117)
2. The Hero's Adversaries (118–191)
3. The Hero's Companion (191–369)
4. The Hero's Battlefield (368–710)
5. The Hero's Works of Peace (711–812)
6. The Hero's Retreat from the World and Fulfillment (812–926)

*Ein Heldenleben* is a worthy swansong for Strauss, the incomparable tone poet caught between nineteenth-century tradition and twentieth-century innovation. First, the ongoing tension between program music as psychological portrait or narrative recreation remains, with the first three sections tilting toward the former, and the fourth and fifth sections suggesting the latter; the final section, like the introduction and finale to *Don Quixote*, draws on both. At the same time, that very structure has yielded divergent judgments of its form: Is *Ein Heldenleben* a through-composed piece, or does a trio of character expositions, confrontation, and resolution suggest the principle of either a heavily altered sonata form or a subcutaneous multi-movement form?

Despite legitimate criticisms of rampant displays of egotism, a biographical element undeniably courses through *Ein Heldenleben*, with Strauss's new wife, the singer Pauline de Ahna, providing the stimulus for the third section's half-voluptuous, half-shrill violin solos and snippets of Strauss's previous music – drawn primarily from the other six tone poems and *Guntram* – feeding the fifth section. Yet this thematic mining was not new, and in fact harks back to some of the earliest programmatic pieces in Strauss's performance repertoire, particularly Hector Berlioz's *Symphonie fantastique*. Finally, while *Ein Heldenleben* almost always appears on English-speaking programs as *A Hero's Life*, a more accurate rendition is *A Heroic Life*. The adjective calls to mind not only a small collection of heroic works by Beethoven, Liszt, Anton Rubinstein (op. 110, 1884), and Edward MacDowell (op. 50, 1895), but also, more generally, one of the most cherished philosophical narratives and analytical metaphors of musical Romanticism – struggle and victory.

The wide-ranging influence of Strauss's first and second cycles of tone poems, as well as his *Symphonia Domestica* (1903) and *Eine Alpensinfonie* (*An Alpine Symphony*; 1915), can be seen in the number of Austro-German musicians who took to the genre between the last decade of the nineteenth century and the First World War. As discussed in Chapter 1, Béla Bartók modeled *Kossuth* on *Ein Heldenleben*. Arnold Schoenberg extended the orchestral effects of *Don Quixote* to his symphonic poem, *Pelleas und Melisande*, in 1905, and formalized the Strauss-indebted technique of "Klangfarbenmelodie" ("sound-color melody") in the *Fünf Orchesterstücke* four years later. Even the "diametrically opposed" Max Reger would put Louis's book out of date in 1913 with the *Vier Tondichtungen nach Arnold Böcklin* (*Four Tone Poems after Arnold Böcklin*), op. 128, whose haunting third movement, "Die Toteninsel" ("The Isle of the Dead"), drew on the same painting – actually five separate paintings – that inspired symphonic essays by Heinrich Schulz-Beuthen, Hans Huber, and Sergei Rachmaninov, among others.

However, after Strauss turned his attention to opera in the new century, no composer emerged to replace him as the torchbearer of the New German programmatic tradition. Many of the most important tone poems to come from Austro-Germans were one-off experiments, stylistic anomalies, or stopovers on the path to more promising musical developments. Instead, the concentrated production of program music shifted from the traditional cultural centers of Europe to its hinterlands, where Jean Sibelius, Mieczysław Karłowicz, Josef Suk, and others interrogated the genre with one final burst of program-musical creativity.

*Chapter 8*

# Programming the nation

## Mendelssohn's Scottish complex and Liszt's German *Hungaria*

On 7 August 1829, from the town of Tobermory in the Scottish Inner Hebrides, Felix Mendelssohn dispatched a letter to his family that contained the first twenty-one measures of what would become his "Hebrides" Overture. The next day he and his traveling companion, Karl Klingemann, sought out Fingal's Cave, a picturesque destination made popular by James Macpherson's "translations" from the 1760s of the ancient Scots-Gaelic bard Ossian. Composition and revision occupied Mendelssohn for more than five years after his visit to the Hebrides, and he never did settle on a definitive title for one of his most admired orchestral works: On 11 December 1830 he described the work as an *Ouverture zur einsamen Insel* (*Overture to the Solitary Island*), five days later as *Die Hebriden* (*The Hebrides*); it was premiered by the Philharmonic Society in London on 14 May 1832 as *The Isles of Fingal*, a title Mendelssohn also sanctioned for the London publication sixteen months later of the four-hand piano arrangement. On the continent, however, that same edition appeared as *Ouverture aux Hébrides (Fingals Höhle)* (*Overture to the Hebrides [Fingal's Cave]*). Orchestral parts appeared in June 1834 for *Die Hebriden*, while the full score from April 1835 advertised itself as *Die Fingals-Höhle*. However, one constant among the myriad titles Mendelssohn vetted is his subject matter's exotic distance from its intended European audience. Indeed, few figures captivated readers (and listeners) as forcefully in the late eighteenth and nineteenth centuries: A long-dead, quasi mythic poet (Ossian) chronicles the deeds of his father (Fingal) in a mysterious, long-abandoned realm (Fingal's Cave) in a remote part of the Western world (the Hebrides).

Soon after the publication of Macpherson's Ossian text, visual responses appeared, first from Scottish, Irish, and English artists in the 1760s and 1770s, then Germans and Scandinavians about twenty years later, and finally from the French during the Napoleonic era. Thus when Mendelssohn began drafting the "Hebrides" Overture in the late 1820s, Ossianic depictions by Nicolai Abildgaard (Caspar David Friedrich's teacher), Thomas Girtin, François Gérard, Anne-Louis Girodet, and Jean-Auguste-Dominique Ingres, among others, were in wide circulation. Given this rich visual culture, it is not surprising that Mendelssohn's overture has long been discussed not so much as a musical recreation of Ossian or the Hebrides, but rather a blending of elements from genre, history, and landscape painting that provide a listener with the tools to create a personally meaningful Ossianic narrative or series of poetic tableaux. But Mendelssohn perhaps even goes one step further: If the first theme, m. 1ff, with its grand, sequential rise through the tonic triad of B minor, helps establish the components of this Ossianic world of yore, then the D major second theme at m. 47 "records," according to Thomas Grey, "the *act* of viewing this landscape (albeit a highly stylized act), in which the spectator not only contemplates the scene before him – with all its changing effects of wind and wave, light and shade, and so on – but also invests it with shades of an imagined mythic history."[1] In other words, Mendelssohn's "Hebrides" Overture does not create a new picture of his subject, but rather validates and reinforces a conception of Ossian and his historical-poetic environment that had been cemented for more than two generations.

From Mendelssohn's German perspective, his "Hebrides" Overture also doubles as "Scottish" music in a specific context, one that engenders an imagined, foreign authenticity. On the one hand, the harmonic progression of the overture's opening – B minor, D major, F♯ minor – determines key structural events in the work, an approach that Mendelssohn's symphonic predecessors had put to good use. But the progression also serves as an exotic or mythopoetic harmonic emblem of the foreign. As Matthew Gelbart has noted, Mendelssohn's "consistent use of these three resting points in order in his Scottish music suggests an apparent abstraction from the locally Scottish into a *German* approach to modality – one that was a part of Mendelssohn's education and that he would probably have considered immediately universal."[2] If Mendelssohn thought in these terms, then not only his "Hebrides" Overture, but also his Third Symphony, op. 56 (1829–1843), and piano Fantasy, op. 28 (1833), were Scottish.

Dictating from without rather than receiving from within in order to establish authenticity of a national style meant that, despite an unparalleled familiarity with the music of their homeland, Scottish, Russian, or other "ethnic" composers who hoped to enjoy European success were ironically held to an almost impossible standard. As Richard Taruskin describes it, those hailing from outside the Franco-German orbit

> are in a double bind. The group identity is at once the vehicle of their international appeal (as "naifs") and the guarantee of their secondary status vis-à-vis the unmarked "universal." Without exotic native dress such composers cannot even achieve secondary canonical rank, but with it they cannot achieve more. However admiringly it is apparently done, casting a composer as a "nationalist" is preeminently a means of exclusion from the critical and academic canon.[3]

A complicated example of how this double bind plays itself out is *Hungaria*, Liszt's ninth published symphonic poem. The work's roots extend as far back as 1840, when Liszt was given a hero's welcome in Hungary after an absence of almost two decades. In the wake of Liszt's visit, the poet Mihály Vörösmarty, seeing an opportunity to capitalize on a rare moment of national solidarity, penned "To Franz Liszt" ("Liszt Ferenczhez"), whose fourteen sestets implore the virtuoso pianist and aspiring composer to provide his native country with a music in which "occupants of magnificent thrones and humble cottages / [can] Unite in yearning for courage and joy" (ll. 23–24).[4] According to the poet, after centuries of patient waiting and unfortunate setbacks, Hungary was primed for a leader whose art could be both ethnically authentic and competitive on the Western European stage. Thus he argues that "Now ... art wanders illumined halls / Lending inspired images to a new age; As thoughts of a thousand minds ascend, / The nation's giant hands are at work" (ll. 33–36).

By the mid-1840s, Liszt had collected and transcribed dozens of folk tunes. As he wrote to his mistress in 1846, during the zenith of his fame as concert pianist, with this material

> one could fairly well recompose the musical epic [Épopée] of that strange land, of which I constitute the Rhapsodist. The six new volumes ... that I have just published in Vienna under the collective title of *Mélodies hongroises* ... form an almost complete cycle of this fantastic, half-Ossianic (for there is the sense of a vanished heroic race in these songs) and half-Bohemian epic.[5]

Liszt's explicit reference to Ossian, and the juxtaposition he makes between the Irish bard and the stereotypical roaming gypsies, reveals a universalizing, Germano-centric perspective similar to Mendelssohn's. At the same time, Liszt envisions himself as a modern Hungarian Ossian who can lend "inspired images to a new age." Thus from a stylistic point of view, *Hungaria* is Liszt's most eclectic symphonic poem; in terms of form, his most ambiguous. Two of its themes (see themes 1 and 4 in Example 8.1) are based on Liszt's *Heroischer Marsch in ungarischem Stil* (*Heroic March in the Hungarian Style*), a solo piano piece from around the time of the pianist's triumphant return to Hungary. The profiles of the themes are such that, given the right context, they may be heard as either ethnically neutral (on account of the march rhythms, regular phrasing, and diatonic harmonies and melodies) or distinctly Hungarian (the constant dotted march rhythm or the three-note melodic emphasis with anacrusis).

When Liszt extended the *Heroischer Marsch* into *Hungaria*, he clearly chose to extend and deepen the latter characterization. Almost all of his added themes convey Hungarian-gypsy elements, such as theme 2, whose melody prominently features a choriamb that reflects the stress patterns of the Hungarian language, or theme 3,

**Example 8.1** Liszt, *Hungaria*, major themes

with its improvisatory flourishes anchored by the affective augmented second. Such additions also programmatize the two themes held over from the *Heroischer Marsch*. When the heroic theme 4 appears as a funeral march at m. 428, it is not hard to hear Vörösmarty's appeal that "if your song recalls tragedy, / Veil its power: / It should sing the breath of flutes, / A bitter sound, / That of autumn winds stirring fallen leaves, / Whispering sorrow and loss" (ll. 49–54). Likewise, Liszt's introduction of Jozsef Rizner's popular song *The Bridal Dance of Tolna* as the apotheosis of *Hungaria* at m. 604 (theme 6) seems tailored to Vörösmarty's recommendation that "if you would inspire patriotism, embrace the present / That it may cradle the past in reverent remembrance / While heralding the future" (ll. 61–63).

The disastrous revolution of 1848, in which many of Hungary's political and cultural elite were either executed or went into exile, put the country's future in peril. But while Liszt clearly composed *Hungaria* as a response to Vörösmarty's poem,[6] he downplayed its potential political messages. Thus he provided no program or written description of the symphonic poem, and rarely performed it. Furthermore,

**Example 8.1** (cont.)

his decision to give the work a Latin instead of German ("Ungarn") or Hungarian ("Magyarország") title focuses attention on the country's cultural history and its mytho-poetic imagination rather than its contentious political reality, just as "Britannia" is both a historical name for the land and a mythicized conception as female goddess figure. Most importantly, the cooperation of Germanic and (pseudo-) Hungarian musical materials shows respect for and idealized rapprochement of both traditions.

Works like the "Hungarian" Rhapsodies, *Hungaria*, and other select programmatic works for piano or for orchestra endeared Liszt to a generation of composers in the second half of the nineteenth century who were looking to fashion a national style of music based on homegrown material, including Edward MacDowell in the United States, Bedřich Smetana in Bohemia, Jean Sibelius in Finland, Edvard Grieg in Norway, and the New Russians. The appeal of the symphonic poem to these potential Rhapsodes was twofold: Unlike the symphony, there was no Western

European "critical or academic canon" of program music – in other words, the double bind was slightly less acute. At the same time, the premises of Lisztian program music made the symphonic poem an extremely flexible medium for creating a sense of shared identity, as it could synthesize a diverse range of indigenous music, local narratives, and other material into an autonomous structure that projected cultural meaning – even political action – through its layered programmatic associations. The following discussion identifies ways in which a region, "school," and individual composer poeticized indigenous cultural material in music during the last third of the nineteenth century.

## Bohemia

In a letter to Liszt from 1858, Bedřich Smetana proudly named himself "one of the most fervent disciples of our artistic direction, who in word and deed will champion and enable its sacred truth."[7] Smetana proved his loyalty by producing three symphonic poems in as many years that were directly modeled on Liszt's recently published examples: *Richard III* (Shakespeare), on Liszt's *Tasso*; *Wallenstein's Lager* (Schiller), on *Mazeppa*; and *Hakon Jarl* (Adam Oehlenschläger), on *Hunnenschlacht*.[8] At this point in his career, Smetana – living in self-imposed exile in Göteborg, Sweden – was not the face of Bohemian music. Yet certain elements of these "Swedish" symphonic poems point to Smetana the latent musical nationalist. For instance, Schiller's *Wallenstein* trilogy, completed in 1799, takes place in Bohemia during the Thirty Years War, a locale Smetana tries to capture with a Czech-like bagpipe motive (m. 187), and more blatantly and anachronistically, a polka (m. 354). More importantly, although Wallenstein is assassinated, the reverential apotheosis he is given in Smetana's musical translation is both personal and overtly political: Wallenstein was not only a Bohemian from the same community where Smetana grew up, but in the 1860s he had also been praised by Bohemians as a model patriot for his heroic resistance to the Habsburg Emperor Ferdinand II.

Bohemian nationalists would likely have similarly cheered the downfall of Håkon Jarl's oppressive regime as depicted in Smetana's symphonic poem. As Smetana put it in a program note for the work's premiere in Prague on 24 February 1864,

> For a long time the subjugated [Norwegian] people yearn for freedom. The violent leader's measure is full and his heathen trappings, which had surrounded him with godly splendor, have been undermined. The Irish king Olaf Tryggvason ... approaches in order to free the oppressed, suffering people. With the cross of Christ leading the way, followed by priests singing psalms, Olaf enters his native country. The shouts of joy of the inhabitants greet him as

the liberator and Håkon Jarl, the last shield of heathendom, falls in battle as a hero, even though he had sacrificed his only son to the gods in order to achieve a victory. The cross of Christ emerges victorious in Norway.[9]

After the composition of his three symphonic poems, Smetana vitalized Czech opera with *The Brandenburgers in Bohemia, Dalibor, Libuše*, and *The Bartered Bride.* All but the latter draw on subjects from Czech history or mythology, an interest which carries over to his most enduring instrumental work, *Má vlast* (*My Country*).

Especially when considered alongside the exceptionally detailed description provided by Smetana (see Text Box 8.1), the six movements of *Má vlast* are quintessential products of the Czech National Revival (*obrození*), a period in which Czech intellectuals sought to recover components of "Czechness" that had been outsourced, suppressed, or forgotten following the political upheavals of the sixteenth and seventeenth centuries, in which "predominantly Czech, Protestant, and recalcitrant" nobles were replaced with a smaller group that was "'German,' Catholic, and loyal to the Habsburgs."[10] The first step undertaken by Czech revivalists in the early nineteenth century was to resuscitate the native language, which had survived for centuries primarily on the tongues of rural peasants. In the 1820s, linguist and author Josef Jungmann produced a history of the Czech language, a dictionary, and translations of seminal German, French, and English dramas – that is, publications aimed at introducing Czech to the literate, predominantly German-speaking native populace. Collections of Slavic folk songs soon followed, and in 1836 František Palacký released the first of what would be six volumes on the history of the Czech nation, for which he sought to provide "a faithful account of its past, in which it would recognize itself as in a mirror and regain consciousness of what it needs."[11] (Notably, Palacký's final volume, published in 1867, ends with the ascension of the Habsburg dynasty in 1526.)

## Text Box 8.1 Smetana's program for *Má vlast*

I. *Vyšehrad.* The harps of the bards begin; a bard sings of the events that have taken place on Vyšehrad, of the glory, splendor, tournaments and battles, and finally of its downfall and ruin. The composition ends on an elegiac note.

II. *Vltava.* The composition depicts the course of the river, from its beginning where two brooks, one cold, the other warm, join a stream, running through forests and meadows and a lovely countryside where merry feasts are celebrated; water-sprites dance in the moonlight; on nearby rocks can be seen the outline of ruined castles, proudly soaring into the sky. Vltava swirls through the St. John Rapids and flows in a broad stream towards Prague. It passes Vyšehrad and disappears majestically into the distance, where it joins the Elbe.

**Text Box 8.1  (continued)**

III. *Šárka*. This poem depicts not the landscape but the story of Šárka. It begins with a portrayal of the enraged girl swearing vengeance on the whole male race for the infidelity of her lover. From afar is heard the arrival of armed men led by Ctirad who has come to punish Šárka and her rebel maidens. In the distance Ctirad hears the feigned cries of a girl [Šárka] bound to a tree. On seeing her he is overcome by her beauty and so inflamed with love that he is moved to free her. By means of a previously prepared philter, she intoxicates Ctirad and his men who finally fall asleep. As she blows her horn (a prearranged signal), the rebel maidens, hidden in nearby rocks, rush to the spot and commit the bloody deed. The horror of general slaughter and passion and fury of Šárka's fulfilled revenge form the end of the composition.

IV. *Z českých luhů a hájů* (*From Bohemia's Woods and Fields*). This is a painting of the feelings that fill one when gazing at the Bohemian landscape. On all sides singing, both gay and melancholic, resounds from fields and woods: the forest regions, depicted on the solo horn; the gay, fertile lowlands of the Elbe valley are the subject of rejoicing. Everyone may draw his own picture according to his own imagination; for the poet has an open path before him, even though he must follow the individual parts of the work.

V. *Tábor* (*Ktož jste Boží bojovníci* [*Ye Who are God's Warriors*]). The whole composition is based on this majestic chorale. It was undoubtedly in the town of Tábor, the seat of the Hussites, that this stirring hymn resounded most powerfully and most frequently. The piece depicts the strong will to win battles, and the dogged perseverance of the Táborites, and it is on this level that the poem ends. It cannot be analyzed in detail, because it expresses the glory and renown of the Hussite struggle and the indestructible character of the Hussite warriors.

VI. *Blaník*. *Blaník* begins where the preceding composition ends. Following their eventual defeat, the Hussite heroes took refuge in Blaník Mountain where, in heavy slumber, they wait for the moment when they will be called to the aid of their country. Hence the chorale, which was used as the basic motive in *Tábor*, is used as the foundation of this piece, namely, *Ye who are God's warriors*. It is on the basis of this melody, the Hussite chorale, that the resurrection of the Czech nation, its future happiness and glory, will develop. With this victorious hymn, written in the form of a march, the composition ends, and with it the whole cycle of *Vlast*. As a brief intermezzo we hear a short idyll, a description of the Blaník region where a little shepherd boy plays a piece while the echo gently floats back to him.

**Source:** Brian Large, *Smetana* (New York and Washington: Praeger, 1970), 270, 273, 276–277, 279–280, 282, 284.

*Má vlast* explores three overlapping interests and concerns of the Czech revivalists:

- *Myth.* Smetana's description of *Vyšehrad* references Bohemia in its former, pre-Habsburg glory, corroborated musically by citing material from his earlier opera, *Libuše*, a legend centered on the eponymous elven queen of Bohemia who goes on to found the city of Prague. *Šárka* is a gruesome Bohemian legend that is first documented in the early twelfth century. *Blaník* refers to the legend of the tenth-century Duke Wenceslaus I of Bohemia and his army, who will arise from their slumber when needed. Referencing one of Prague's most historic sites, *Vyšehrad* is less specific, although one of the events described may be the Battle of Vyšehrad, which took place at the beginning of the Hussite Wars.

- *Place.* Five movements take specific Bohemian locations or landmarks as starting points. Vyšehrad, the ancient seat of Bohemia's rulers, appears in the first movement, to which *Vltava* adds the St. John Rapids, Prague, and the Elbe river. Likewise, the fourth movement specifically poeticizes Bohemian woods and fields. *Tábor* is named after the seat of the Hussite army, which lies in wait at Blaník, 34.5 kilometers to the northeast. In fact, all of the places mentioned by Smetana in *Má vlast* had been singled out by revivalists for their cultural and symbolic import to the pining nation.

- *Obrození.* Smetana does not mince words when he explains that the concluding movement's victory march is a sign of things to come. But *Má vlast* is also a compendium of the types of materials that will enable "the resurrection of the Czech nation" and make possible "its future happiness and glory." Moreover, while movements of *Má vlast* are typically performed independently, the cycle as a whole displays an important sense of development by entrusting the auditor with more interpretive independence; or put another way, forcing him to take more interpretive control. A type of prelude to the whole, *Vyšehrad* serves as a powerful reminder of what once was. *Vltava* is unusually specific, but in the following nature piece, *Z českých luhů a hájů* (*From Bohemia's Woods and Fields*), Smetana allows "Everyone [to] draw his own picture according to his own imagination." The next movement is beyond analysis, because it channels the "glory," "renown," "struggle," and "indestructible courage" of the country's true defenders.

Smetana's music underscores these programmatic associations. The nobility and determination of the Czech people is given expressive weight in several wordless songs and dances, such as the main theme of *Vyšehrad*, the major-mode version of *Vltava*'s famous tune, and the polkas of *Vltava*, *Šárka*, and *From Bohemia's Woods and Fields*. The cycle's ongoing tension between presenting this idealized material and acknowledging stark reality plays out over diatonic and chromatic confrontations, such as in

**Example 8.2**  Smetana, *Má vlast*, I, mm. 208–222, arr. Karel Šolc

Example 8.2 from *Vyšehrad*, where the bardic songs are interrupted by a depiction of Vyšehrad's destruction. But true to the spirit of the cycle, the Vyšehrad theme is not annihilated; rather, it returns at m. 235 in a debilitated minor-mode version over a promising dominant pedal.

Smetana extends this effect in the final two movements, which adopt the fifteenth-century Hussite song "Ye who are God's warriors," whose Dorian mode and ionic meter handily separate it from contemporary Western European musical practice. In the extended fantasy of *Tábor*, the bellicose melody appears as a symbol of Bohemian tenacity and determination, while *Blaník* transforms it into a rousing call to action. Along the way, reference to the central theme of the first movement and a nod to the idyl of the fourth constitute one final survey of all that Smetana holds dear about his homeland. In a work like *Má vlast*, Smetana "created an 'eternal present' of the Czech people through the use of local subjects"[12] – its music, literature, legends, and landscapes. His model was taken up by most subsequent composers from the region, including the most internationally renowned Bohemian composer of the century, Antonín Dvořák.

A short-lived affair with the music of Liszt and Wagner likely resulted in Dvořák's op. 14, a symphonic poem from 1874 on an unknown or perhaps non-existent topic. Nevertheless, program music only played a marginal role for Dvořák until close to the end of the century. One outlier example is the "Husitská" Overture from 1883, a commission from the Prague National Theatre. The overture draws on two ancient Czech melodies, "Svatý Václave" ("St. Wenceslaus") and "Ktož jste Boží bojovníci" ("Ye who are God's warriors") to tell the story of the Hussite uprising in the fifteenth century. However, unlike Smetana's vision of this event in *Tábor* and *Blaník* as one which might inspire national pride in his countrymen, Dvořák allows it to play out in the distant, politically safe past. A trio of concert overtures appeared in the early 1890s under the collective title *Nature, Life, and Love*, which included *V přírodě* (*In Nature's Realm*), op. 91, *Karneval* (*Carnival*), op. 92, and *Othello*, op. 93. And a smattering of pieces from the same period, such as the *Poetické nálady* (*Poetic Mood Pictures*), op. 85, of 1889 and the Ninth Symphony, "From the New World," espoused various programmatic associations.

However, programmaticism and nationalism only merged decisively in a set of four symphonic poems that Dvořák began within a year of returning from America in the spring of 1895. These works draw on a common literary source, Karel Jaromír Erben's *Kytice z pověti národních* (*A Garland of National Myths*). Although published in 1853 in a heavily censored edition, by the end of the century Erben's collection of folk ballads had become a foundational source of Czech identity, akin to *Grimm's Fairy Tales* in Germany or Aleksandr Nikolayevich Afanasyev's Russian folk- and fairy-tale collections.

The four tales that Dvořák selected from Erben's anthology share with Smetana's *Šárka* a penchant for unhappy relationships that often involve extreme violence, shadowy interlopers, and supernatural goings-on. Unlike Smetana's scorned lover, however, all of Dvořák's characters are stock figures – unspecified maidens, kings, wizards, peasants, and the like – and none exhibits any specifically Bohemian characteristics. In fact, the prefaces to *Der Wassermann* (*The Water Goblin*), op. 107, and *Das goldene Spinnrad* (*The Golden Spinning Wheel*), op. 109, downplay the Czech roots of their stories by citing narrative parallels with other folk traditions, while the preface to *Die Waldtaube* (*The Wild Dove*), op. 110, presents the story in five discrete sections in the manner of Beethoven's Sixth Symphony or Berlioz's *Symphonie fantastique*.

These prefaces stem from Dvořák himself, who likely felt compelled to provide them in order to avoid being misunderstood by the public. In this regard, his concerns were no different than those of Mahler, Strauss, or other *fin-de-siècle*

**Example 8.3** Dvořák, *The Noon Witch*, some transformations of the mother's theme

composers of program music who also struggled to present listeners with just the right amount of explanatory cues. Surviving letters from Dvořák to the Viennese critic Robert Hirschfeld demonstrate that the composer sought to follow the stories quite closely in his musical renditions, and that he attached a great deal of faith in music's ability to convey specific objects and events, chart the emotional trajectory of its characters, and reflect a detailed, changing narrative.

For instance, his description of the final scene of *Die Mittagshexe* (*The Noon Witch*), op. 108, reveals an extreme level of specificity:

> It is midday – the father prays, without any knowledge of what has happened [m. 457ff]. He opens the door [m. 463] and discovers his wife unconscious on the floor. The mother's motive appears again [in the oboe, mm. 465–466]. The father tries to revive her, and gradually she begins to breathe again [m. 477ff]. She regains consciousness. Modulation to A major [m. 481]. The figure [in mm. 484–486] and a sudden crescendo lead to the motive that follows [at m. 487], where the father, in despair at the loss of the child, displays the *greatest agitation*. The witch vanishes [m. 498].[13]

Dvořák's manipulation of thematic content sits between Brahms's developing variations and Liszt's thematic transformations. The mother is the only character present throughout *The Noon Witch*, and it is her emotional state that undergoes the most substantial change (see Example 8.3). Her anger is the first to show in m. 51, where she mocks her child's noisy cockerel and rampages down a diminished seventh chord that modally disrupts the serenity of the first scene's C major. Even though she remains quarrelsome at m. 86, she has calmed down, as evidenced by a more composed line and the harmonically agreeable key of A minor. However, according to Dvořák, after the surprising appearance of the witch, she moves from "desperate" (mm. 274ff, 304ff) to hysterical (m. 344) to unconscious (m. 402), the state in which the woman's husband finds her at m. 465. Once revived, she trips over herself at m. 484 trying to explain what has transpired; once she gets through to her husband, they share a moment of grief through her theme (mm. 487–494) that is cut short by the departure of the Noon Witch from the stage.

Dvořák's thematic transformations can impact characters and events. One of the most chilling moments in *The Noon Witch* comes after the innocent first scene between mother and child, when Dvořák depicts "The appearance of the witch as she opens the door slowly and walks up to the mother" at mm. 252–264. Without a doubt, this is theater music, akin in style and quality to Othello's famous tiptoeing around Desdemona's chamber at the beginning of Act III in Giuseppe Verdi's *Otello*. Dvořák gives the witch's entrance extraordinary color and dimension with hypnotic half-step oscillations played by muted strings, a static bass clarinet solo, subterranean brass and timpani, and a rhythmic augmentation at m. 261ff. Moreover, in *The Noon Witch*, this motive appears in various guises as an emblem of scenic advancement and as an emblem of the witch's power. Thus it functions as a short transition section to the recapitulation of the first scene (m. 110ff), and it graphically depicts the mother coming out of her stupor (m. 476ff) right before she delivers the devastating news to her husband.

The theatrical conventions, compositional procedures, and dramatic structures found in *The Noon Witch* can be extended to the other three Erben-inspired symphonic poems. While these orchestral essays represent important contributions to the nourishment of Bohemian program music, their mimetic richness and characteristic depth also helped foster Dvořák's operatic ambitions. Indeed, his heavy investment in the symphonic poem at the end of the century would pay handsome dividends when he turned to the composition of *Čert a Káča* (*The Devil and Kate*) in 1899 and *Rusalka* a year later.

## The Boston Six

In a lengthy review from 1873 of Richard Wagner's recently published *Gesammelte Schriften* (*Collected Writings*), the American composer, critic, and educator John Knowles Paine lamented that in their pursuit of "poetic ideas," Liszt, Berlioz, and Wagner had seriously neglected Bach, Mozart, and Beethoven. Recently appointed to the faculty of Harvard College, Paine was in fact less concerned about the future direction of music in Germany – where he had received the majority of his formal training – than he was about the current state of music at home. Seeing an opportunity to capitalize on what Paine saw as a Wagnerian contagion that threatened Germany's artistic preeminence, Paine calls his readers to action: "As art-loving Americans let us hope that it will be the mission of our own country to rejuvenate the life of music; may it be vouchsafed to her to lift the veil that now shrouds the future of this beautiful art!"[14]

Within a generation, the United States would be able to count several composers capable of carrying out Paine's mission. Boston, having benefitted from campaigns by Paine, the editorial and critical acumen of John Sullivan Dwight, and the founding of the Boston Symphony Orchestra in 1881, offered a hub for a group of composers that has come to be known by historians as The Boston Six: Arthur Foote, Horatio Parker, Amy Beach, George Whitefield Chadwick, Edward MacDowell, and Paine, the last four of whom produced substantial programmatic compositions. Their examples illustrate that the development of American program music can be divided into two periods: the first, running from the late 1870s (with Paine's *As You Like It* and *The Tempest* Overtures) to the mid-1890s, in which European models predominate; in the second period, which began in the early 1890s and still touted an unmistakable European influence, composers produced program music whose thematic content and poetic expression sounded – at least to foreign ears – as if it were of the New World.

Next to Paine, MacDowell represents the most direct link between Europe and the United States. He enrolled in Paris's Conservatoire in 1876, moved two years later to Germany, where he studied composition under Joachim Raff, was heard by Liszt several times, and composed more than two dozen works in the European mold. He returned to Boston in 1888 with all four of his programmatic symphonic works either completed or well underway. The first, entitled *Hamlet, Ophelia: Zwei Gedichte* (*Hamlet, Ophelia: Two Poems*) is in two movements, a structure that recalls Liszt's character-driven *Faust* Symphony. MacDowell originally planned to issue one opus on Shakespeare's male characters (Hamlet, Benedick, Othello, and perhaps Falstaff) and one sequel on the female characters Ophelia, Beatrice, and Desdemona. Similarly, his *Two Fragments after the Song of Roland* features a first movement on "The Saracens," and a second movement that depicts Roland's faithful fiancée, Auda.

*Hamlet, Ophelia* is an unusually direct literary source, for MacDowell typically draws on myths and legends filtered through contemporary poets to populate his program music. Take *Lamia*, his third symphonic poem, completed in 1888 but not performed and published until after his death in 1908. MacDowell summarizes John Keats's same-named epic poem, just shy of four hundred lines long, in a short preface:

> Lamia, an enchantress in the form of a serpent, loves Lycius, a young Corinthian. In order to win him she prays to Hermes, who answers her appeal by trans-forming her into a lovely maiden. Lycius meets her in the wood, is smitten with love for her and goes with her to her enchanted palace, where the wedding is celebrated with great splendour. But suddenly Apollonius the magician appears; he reveals the magic. Lamia again assumes the form of a serpent, the enchanted palace vanishes, and Lycius is found lifeless.

The story as MacDowell tells it gives him ample opportunity to infuse his musical rendition with supernatural effects, amorous encounters, explosive orchestral tuttis,

**Example 8.4a** MacDowell, *Lamia*, mm. 1–5, arr. MacDowell

**Example 8.4b** MacDowell, *Lamia*, mm. 250–256, arr. MacDowell

and mournful strains. Yet like most of the models provided by Liszt and Raff, these devices appear in order to better highlight Lamia's emotional state as she encounters Hermes, Lycius, and Apollonius. Her theme is strongly colored by the interval of the augmented second, which for at least a century had been a superficial marker of exoticism, or difference. Thus, in order for Lamia to make herself more attractive to

Lycius – to make herself more like him – she adapts her melody to his vanilla diatonicism. In fact, MacDowell purposely exaggerates Lycius's tonal certainty by supporting his aggressive melody (m. 68ff) exclusively with tonic, dominant, and subdominant harmonies in order to highlight the extent of Lamia's transformation.

It is convenient that MacDowell's title character is a shape-shifter, as it allows him to create a symphonic portrait of her along two different axes. The first focuses on the physical and environmental: here the depiction of the "true" Lamia in serpent form versus her transformed image follows the degree to which the augmented second pervades her melody. Alone she is exposed to the listener in genuine form, as in the opening line in the bassoons and cellos (Example 8.4a), the spun out flute melody at mm. 26–53, the return of the opening material following the gracious pastoral duet between Lycius and Lamia (mm. 171–182), or the trumpet punctuation at m. 294 that gradually infects the remaining brass instruments and sets the stage for the symphonic poem's final catastrophe. However, when the enchantment is at full power, such as during the wedding scene, her augmented second call sign evaporates, replaced by a melody that is as passionate as it is contrived (Example 8.4b).

The second axis of depiction, the emotive, draws heavily on models by members of the New German School. MacDowell considered this component the most fundamental of his style, calling music a "language of the intangible, a kind of soul-language."[15] MacDowell's emotional portrayal of Lamia suggests that she is the real victim, even though Lycius dies. (Lycius, in fact, whose melody never shakes its militant rhythm, is something of a prop.) To be sure, the symphonic poem begins Lento misterioso, a clear reference to the fantastic nature of its subject. But it is also to be performed *con tristezza*. Sadness turns into hope at m. 26ff, a sentiment which carries into the scene of Lycius's appearance. Hope quickly turns to affection ("tenerezza," m. 125), and the central portion of the piece witnesses Lamia at her most content. But cracks in the facade start to show soon after the wedding, and by about m. 308 Lamia's world is beginning to crumble around her. By m. 332, a solo clarinet line cries out ("dolent"), stifled further by closed position augmented sixth chords. The discovery of Lycius's body – corresponding to the pompous G minor outburst by the orchestra at m. 354 – is MacDowell's addition; Keats simply has him vanish with her, but not without ominously concluding that "For truth's sake, what woe afterwards befel, / 'Twould humour many a heart to leave them thus" (ll. 395–396).

By 1895, MacDowell abandoned the symphonic poem, but continued for the rest of his life to produce songs and piano music that evoked the poetic, such as the third ("Norse") and fourth ("Keltic") piano sonatas – each of which contains a poetic epigraph – and his well-received collections of piano miniatures. In the latter genre he was joined by many American composers, including Amy Beach. Her first published keyboard cycle, *Four Sketches* (1892), illustrates how French and German programmatic pianism could blend without incident. The third piece, entitled

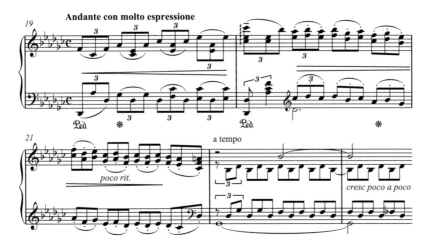

**Example 8.5a** Beach, *Four Sketches*, "Dreaming," mm. 19–23

**Example 8.5b** Liszt, *Harmonies poétiques et religieuses*, "Bénédiction de Dieu dans la solitude," mm. 18–23

"Dreaming," includes an epigraph from the first line of Victor Hugo's poem "A celle qui est voilée" ("To the Veiled One"): "You speak to me from the depths of a dream." In the lush key of G♭ major, Beach unfolds stacks of triplet eighth notes undulating in thirds across a spacious 4/4 meter. The melody materializes at m. 3 over a $V^7/I$ sonority, and after briefly cadencing in the tonic at m. 13 and more definitively at m. 22, does not emphatically return to the tonic until m. 71, the piece's penultimate bar. This technique of harmonic "veiling" utilizes common and neighboring tones in order to move through a variety of keys, all of which are further softened by an extended harmonic vocabulary that derives from Chopin, Liszt, and Debussy (see Example 8.5). Yet despite this strong French connection, the accompaniment harks back to Schubert's famous G♭ major Impromptu, D899/3, while the piano writing incorporates figurations and textures made famous by Brahms.

As *Lamia* and "Dreaming" demonstrate, early programmatic compositions to come from members of the Boston Six do not overtly project any clear "American" traits, and are arguably indistinguishable stylistically and aesthetically from their European counterparts. In the last decade of the century, however, American composers had received advice on how to change this situation from Dvořák, who had arrived in New York in late 1892 expressly to "show [the Americans] the way into the Promised Land, the realm of a new, independent art, in short a national style of music!"[16] Dvořák tried to lead by example, producing the haunting String Quartet in F major, an extended suite in A major for piano, and the sensational Ninth Symphony, "From the New World," in which critics praised the skillful intermingling of indigenous – that is, "American," "Negro," and "Indian" – music and moods. Two months before he returned to his native Bohemia for good, he penned an article for *Harper's New Monthly Magazine* that instructed American composers to look for musical inspiration inside their own borders:

> Undoubtedly the germs for the best in music lie hidden among all the races that are commingled in this great country. The music of the people is like a rare and lovely flower growing amidst encroaching weeds. Thousands pass it, while others trample it under foot, and thus the chances are that it will perish before it is seen by the one discriminating spirit who will prize it above all else. The fact that no one has as yet arisen to make the most of it does not prove that nothing is there.[17]

At least initially, MacDowell did troll his homeland's countryside for compositional stimulus in a manner not unlike the famous Bohemian. The same year that Dvořák's article appeared in *Harper's*, MacDowell completed his second orchestral suite, subtitled "Indian," whose five movements turn generic Romantic themes into imagined American experiences by quoting Native American music as presented by Theodor Baker in his 1882 study, *Über die Musik der Nordamerikanischen Wilden* (*On the Music of North-American Savages*) – a book which had also furnished Dvořák with material during his American period. However, MacDowell did not see Dvořák's "American" music as authentic because it was created by an outsider: "America needs absolute freedom from the restraint that an almost unlimited deference to European thought and prejudice has imposed upon us. Masquerading in the so-called nationalism of Negro clothes cut in Bohemia will not help us."[18] MacDowell would lightly dust much of his later piano music with titles that evoked American locales and customs, but only rarely would he include authentic Native American music. One example of both streams can be found in the ten-movement piano cycle *New England Idyls*, op. 62, whose "Indian Idyl" carries the following poetic epigraph: "Alone by the wayward flame / She weaves broad wampum skeins / While afar through the summer night / Sigh the wooing flutes' soft strains." Even though this is nominally a Native American piece, MacDowell creates one melody from scratch, borrows another from an anthology, and wraps both in a decidedly transatlantic style of dreamy American nostalgia and soft French Impressionism.

Dvořák's status ensured that his American colleagues would take his challenge seriously. If MacDowell ultimately demurred to it, Amy Beach reoriented its focus: "We of the North," she wrote in 1893,

> should be far more likely to be influenced by old English, Scotch or Irish songs inherited with our literature from our ancestors, than by the songs of a portion of our people who were kept for so long in bondage, and whose musical utterances were deeply rooted in the heart-breaking griefs attendant upon their condition. It seems to me that, in order to make the best use of folk-songs of any nation as material for musical composition, the writer should be one of the people whose songs he chooses, or at least brought up among them.[19]

Her definition of an American style as one governed by shared art, tradition, and association feeds directly into her "Gaelic" Symphony, begun within a month of the Boston premiere of Dvořák's "New World" Symphony on 29 and 30 December 1893. The timetable is important to keep in mind, for even though Beach was impressed by Dvořák's symphony, she lamented how it "represent[ed] only the peaceful, sunny side of the negro character and life. Not for a moment does it suggest their suffering, heartbreaks, *slavery*."[20] Thus her "Gaelic" Symphony draws on melodies of wide chronological and emotional range but limited geographical distance. The focus throughout is on a people whose experiences, joys, and setbacks come to life in a vernacular instrumental song with which her audience could identify. Thus in the third movement, which arguably sits at the greatest remove from Dvořák's "New World" Symphony, noble laments sound forth in finely wrought orchestral colors, such as the solo cello setting of the Gaelic lullaby "Paisdin Fuinne" at m. 20, to which a solo violin adds further dramatic counterpoint. Yet shortly thereafter, the entire character of the movement changes, the grief personified by the solo strings now giving way to bombastic, hopeful outbursts in the winds and brass at m. 40. This same sense of struggle resounds in another symphonic work from across the Atlantic Ocean, Augusta Holmès's *Irlande* (1885), which merges the composer's Irish heritage and Ireland's contemporary political upheavals into a symphonic poem of proud defiance and cautious optimism.

Yet another approach to exploring and exhibiting America in music appears in Chadwick's *Symphonic Sketches*. Completed in 1904 after ten years of labor, it is a four-movement program symphony in all but name, and it succeeds in painting a portrait of America through a stylistic defiance of European standards that MacDowell advocated but never achieved. The first movement, "Jubilee," is a case

**Example 8.6** Chadwick, *Symphonic Sketches*, "Jubilee," mm. 21–32, strings

in point. The two stanzas that precede the movement seem to encourage a rapprochement between the traditional sounds of the slightly stodgy, old-world symphony orchestra and the vivacity and communal inclusivity of the town marching band: "Pale flutes and oboes" sit beside "a cornet and a tambourine," the "gray tones" of the former blending with the "warmest red and green" of the latter and "the violets and the May" to "paint MY Jubilee!"

True to its word, the movement is an explosion of color and energy, and while Chadwick's orchestra is almost quaint compared to that of Strauss, the special attention he gives to the brass and percussion sections tips his large ensemble more to the town square than the concert hall. The infectious opening careens forward in duple meter, but already in the first two measures Chadwick hints at the theme's triple-meter potential. Indeed, this metrical play is not featured solely for show, but also to smooth transitions in an otherwise structurally boxy movement. Example 8.6 shows the conclusion of the first theme and the beginning of the second. Although the orchestra fully cadences in A major and falls silent for two quarter notes immediately

**Table 8.1** *The structure of "Jubilee," from Chadwick,* Symphonic Sketches

| Section | Exposition | | | | Development | | | |
|---|---|---|---|---|---|---|---|---|
| Location | 1 | 29 | 59 | 97 | 111 | 127 | 146 | 153 |
| Key | A | c♯ | C | V/C♯ | c♯ | E | E | |
| Theme | 1 | 2 | 3 | Trans. | 1 | 4 | 2 | Retrans. |

| | Recapitulation | | | Coda | | | | |
|---|---|---|---|---|---|---|---|---|
| | 158 | 187 | 225 | 239 | 255 | | 275 | 316 |
| | A | F | V/F♯ | f♯ | A | | A | A |
| | 1 | 3 | Trans. | 1 | 4 | | 3 | 1 |

after, it has prepared the meter of the second theme by moving from a predominantly compound duple (6/4) to triple (3/2) meter. A similar metrical smoothing occurs between mm. 126 and 127, in which a version of the first theme transitions in the first presentation of the fourth theme, which although in cut time, features accents that give a hypermetric impression of the first's theme compound duple meter.

While Chadwick's metrical effects have a storied precedent in the music of Beethoven, Schumann, and Brahms, his sense of form is not typical of contemporary European music. Table 8.1 suggests how the movement might project a sonata form: An exposition of three themes, each in a different key, is followed by a development that introduces a new theme in the dominant. The recapitulation begins in the tonic, but tonal fulfillment is delayed until the appearance of the "new" theme in the coda. But there are problems with this model. The recapitulation, for instance, does not feature the second theme at all; in fact, Chadwick restricts it to a single appearance in the development. Furthermore, the third theme appears in far distant keys in both the exposition and the recapitulation, and like the fourth theme, finds tonic only in the coda.

Binary form is another option for "Jubilee," since each half is roughly the same length. However, while the first half modulates to the dominant, the second half begins uncharacteristically back in tonic. Moreover, the presence of theme 2 exclusively in the first section imbalances the two sections from a thematic perspective. In short, "Jubilee" does not provide an adequate structural solution, at least when read against European *Formenlehre.* "A Vagrom Ballad," the final movement of the *Symphonic Sketches,* clearly demonstrates Chadwick's intentional ambivalence to traditional structures. After all, this was a movement that celebrated America's anti-heroes: "A tale of tramps and railway ties, / Of old clay pipes and rum," as its preface states, "Of broken heads and blackened eyes / And the 'thirty days' to come!"

Chadwick followed the *Symphonic Sketches* with four symphonic poems, each of which approaches technical issues of form, tonal planning, and motivic transformation and melodic development in ways that respond to their widely diverse source material, be it myth, poetry, or sculpture. To be sure, compositions like *Tam O'Shanter*

(1914–1915), on an Anglo-Celtic topic of which MacDowell and Beach would have approved, reflect the American experience as it was understood by Chadwick's Boston colleagues in the first decades of the twentieth century. But only the *Symphonic Sketches* were designed at the outset to adhere to principles that were "*American in style – as I understood them.*"[21] To be sure, Americans like Charles Martin Loeffler, Henry Hadley, and Charles Griffes would continue to produce significant works of program music in the first two decades of the new century that nonetheless bore strong European imprints, including Strauss and Debussy. But Chadwick's particular understanding of how American music could operate through a programmatic filter gained momentum with the next two generations of composers who came into artistic maturity during the interwar years, including George Gershwin, Ferde Grofé, and Horatio Parker's most brilliant student, Charles Ives.

## Sibelius

On 4 June 1914, having been invited by Parker to concertize on the East Coast while the Western world was readying for catastrophic war, Jean Sibelius premiered his tone poem *Aallottaret* (*The Oceanides*) in Norfolk, Connecticut. The understated work gradually transforms two themes, both introduced in the winds, over three rotations on the high seas, whose waves form in D major, crest in D minor and F major, and break in D major. Indeed, while the title of the works suggests a focus on aquatic nymphs from Greek and Roman mythology, there is as little formal development as there is drama. Instead, Sibelius's muted colors and delicate counterpoint, especially in the lower half of the orchestra, dramatize the play of the water by invoking the Romantic sublime and celebrating the awe-inspiring power of nature – not unlike what Debussy had attempted to capture ten years earlier in *La mer*, to which *Aallottaret* may be Sibelius's answer. At the very least, the work neither makes an overt nationalistic claim nor even espouses what Rosa Newmarch had identified eight years earlier as "the echo of [Sibelius's] national spirit," which accounted for "much that seemed weird and wild in his first works."[22]

Indeed, Sibelius's first works came about at a transformative time in the history of his native country. Schooled primarily in Swedish-speaking Finland but with two important stints in Berlin and Vienna, by the early 1890s Sibelius had embraced the Finnish language through its most ancient source of myth and legend, *The Kalevala*. *The Kalevala* had already served as an important source for Sibelius's slightly older colleague Robert Kajanus, whose two "Finnish" Rhapsodies and symphonic poems *Aino* and *Kullervo's Funeral March* appeared in the 1880s. Sibelius's debt to Kajanus is patent in his first major "Finnish" orchestral work, *Kullervo*, a programmatic choral symphony based on the tragic life of the eponymous character as told in

**Example 8.7** Sibelius, *Finlandia*, mm. 24–38, arr. Sibelius

*The Kalevala.* Deep study of Liszt, Wagner, Bruckner, and contemporary Russians followed, culminating in several tone poems and suites, and around 1900, in *Finlandia*, the tone poem for which he is best known.

Although Finland had been under Russian control since 1808, it had been allowed a high degree of political autonomy from the empire. That relationship changed in February 1899, however, when Tsar Nicholas II began a campaign of "Russification," in which Russian rule, currency, language, religion, and military service were forced on the Finns. In late 1899, Sibelius had written over a half-hour's worth of music to accompany a set of six tableaux vivants that reflected Finland's turbulent history, including its conversion to Christianity (Tableau II) and the Russian invasion of Finland in the early eighteenth century (Tableau IV). The last tableau, entitled "Finland Awakens," showcased the still oppressed but promising country poised to make the leap into modernity. Soon after the exhibition, which had been put on to criticize recent censorship laws, Sibelius reworked the material from "Finland Awakens" into *Finlandia*.

*Finlandia* is yet another reinvention of the nineteenth-century battle piece (see Chapter 1). To be sure, there are clear adversaries depicted, but the victor of the music – in keeping with the spirit of the tableau that inspired the symphonic poem – does not "win" so much as undergo an awakening. By analogy, *Finlandia* avoids traditional symphonic structures in favor of "a process of tonic- and structure-building."[23] The home key of A♭ major, for instance, is not affirmed until the very end of the piece (m. 209), although it has been tentatively reached in earlier sections (e.g., m. 129). The famous hymn also gradually awakens through a process of crystallization that had been a hallmark of Sibelius's style since *Lemminkäinen's Return* (1896). As shown in Example 8.7, its contours are anticipated in the winds at mm. 24–29, but the melody cadences decisively in F minor. By m. 100 a more definitive shape and militant character appear, but in the context of a transitional phrase. Finally, the hymn emerges – again in the woodwinds – at m. 132, although its second section still maintains a hint of F minor (m. 147). At the final apotheosis, however, room is made only for A♭ major. Indeed, the process of melodic transformation – mirroring the narrative of a Finnish awakening – is cemented by the sequential presentation of this material. Put another way: no earlier version of the hymn ever appears after its next incarnation. Bearing the heroic struggles of Beethoven's middle-period music, the nationalist suggestion of Liszt's *Hungaria*, and the self-awareness of Strauss's *Tod und Verklärung*, *Finlandia* acts on numerous programmatic levels simultaneously.

Despite *Finlandia*'s complete lack of Finnish melodies or other local reinforcements, its enduring success as the definitive musical document of Finland's struggle and Sibelius's ardent nationalism has eclipsed his other programmatic music on Finnish subjects (to say nothing of those on non-Finnish or more cosmopolitan subjects). In particular, *The Kalevala*, Finland's national epic, provided the composer with material for the four-piece *Lemminkäinen Suite* of the mid-1890s, *Pohjola's Daughter* (1906), *Luonnotar*, a tone poem from 1913 for soprano voice and orchestra, and *Tapiola* (1926), his last completed piece of orchestral music. And although *En Saga* (*A Saga*, 1892) does not cite a specific source, it is imbued with a "neo-primitivist musical language [that] is the hallmark of Sibelius's early 'epic' discourse."[24] Indeed, the tone poem even adopts an epic mode of delivery that blends sonata form and strophic presentation of its two theme groups (initially given at mm. 96 and 202, respectively).[25] Its conclusion, which chooses E♭ minor as final tonal resting place over the previously dominating keys of C minor and E♭ major, adds a strong element of melancholy, a feature that carries over to *Skogsrået* (*The Wood Nymph*) from 1895, based on Viktor Rydberg's same-named poem, in which a wood nymph, aided by some unscrupulous dwarves, enchants a wanderer named Björn. As a consequence, he loses his soul to her and becomes forever trapped in the Otherworld.

The *Lemminkäinen Suite*, sometimes also referred to as the *Legends Suite*, brings together Sibelius's folk modeling and symphonic ambitions. The composer premiered the four movements on 13 April 1896 at Helsinki as follows:

1. Lemminkäinen and the Maidens of the Island (based on *The Kalevala*, Runo 29)
2. Lemminkäinen in Tuonela (Runo 14)
3. The Swan of Tuonela (Runo 14)
4. Lemminkäinen's Return (Runo 30).[26]

The preface in the first edition of *The Swan of Tuonela*, probably written by Sibelius's German publisher in an effort to acclimatize foreign audiences to the Finnish legend, only scratches the surface of the scene, which finds the hero Lemminkäinen pursuing the sacred swan in an effort to win the fairest virgin

**Example 8.8** Sibelius, *The Swan of Tuonela*, mm. 1–22, reduction and analysis

daughter of the witch-queen Louhi: "Tuonela, empire of death, Hell in Finnish mythology, is bounded by a wide river with black water and torrential course, upon which the singing Swan of Tuonela drifts by majestically."

The key of A minor begins and ends the movement, whose bleakness rises up through the heavily divided strings. An English horn solo punctuates these mists, which smoothly but unsettlingly move through a succession of non-functional common-tone and neighbor-note harmonies (see Example 8.8). Indeed, the unpredictable harmonic trajectory, inconsistent entries of the English horn, and ebbing and flowing of the orchestral apparatus makes for a disorienting, otherworldly aural experience. Thus when the entire color of the orchestra changes at m. 65 (Poco allargando) with the appearance of harp, bass drum, and timpani in a resplendent C major, the scene momentarily comes into focus. By m. 69, however, it has faded completely, replaced by the same bleak material that preceded it. It is of secondary importance whether this ephemeral moment represents a rare sighting of the swan (which does not technically appear in *The Kalevala*) or Lemminkäinen (the dirge at

m. 75ff might make him a candidate). Instead, Sibelius's chief interest is bringing to life landscapes and what they represent psychologically and emotionally. Thus it is not surprising that the devices used to create Tuonela in all its bleakness crop up in many of his later orchestral essays – programmatic or otherwise.

At the risk of mixing metaphors, most of the music discussed in earlier chapters might be called absolute program music, as it operates in a closed system of referents that includes text, music, and – occasionally – image. But when a piece of program music becomes saturated with "non-universal" referents – a depiction of a local castle, the retelling of a regional tale, the employment of a peasant melody – then the result can quickly skew toward the national, if not nationalistic. Thus at least from a Germano-centric perspective, it becomes yet another manifestation of the double bind. Is it not easier to hear or be convinced of a national message or even a nationalistic / imperialist agenda in Tchaikovsky's Second Symphony than in the finale of Beethoven's first "Razumovsky" Quartet, op. 59, no. 1, even though Beethoven explicitly highlights a "thème russe," whereas Tchaikovsky keeps mum on his sources?[27] It is not just a matter of a double bind at work, but a double standard: Central composers like Beethoven and Mendelssohn can choose to adopt a national style for a limited time or for a specific effect; peripheral composers, however, do not seem to have the same luxury. And those on the fence, like Liszt, are easily misinterpreted or misrepresented.

Indeed, there is something viral in the identification of national styles and schools that can easily mask other avenues of inquiry and analysis. Sibelius is easily written off as a national composer despite a prodigious catalogue of non-national music, and it is tempting to do the same for those in similar situations, like Edvard Grieg or Mieczysław Karłowicz. As for the propagation of a particular school, Smetana and Dvořák heavily influenced Czech composers who came into prominence in the early twentieth century, but it would be misleading to use the same criteria of analysis on the program music of Josef Suk, Leoš Janáček, or Vítězslav Novák. Indeed, Suk's massive cycles of program music – *Pohádka* (*Fairy Tale*, 1900), *Pohádka léta* (*Summer's Tale*, 1909), and the five *Symphonic Poems from Czech History* completed in 1917 – either strike a cosmopolitan middle ground or consciously challenge indigenous programmatic juggernauts like *Má vlast*.[28] Janáček's fantastic *Taras Bulba* nominally draws on a novel by the Ukrainian-Russian author Nikolai Gogol, but it and his other two symphonic poems actually misread their literary models severely. In fact, misreading also helps to explain one of the most concerted, zealous, and ambiguous efforts to create a cohesive national school of music in the last decades of the nineteenth century: France.

## Chapter 9

# "Ars Gallica"

On 19 July 1870, the Second French Empire, led by Napoleon III, declared war on the Kingdom of Prussia and its German allies. Tensions between the two groups had escalated dramatically in the last ten years, in which France, whose general geographical boundaries had remained unchanged for centuries, grew increasingly wary of Prussia's aggressive efforts in expanding its borders, particularly following its success against the Austrians in the short-lived Austro-Prussian War of 1866. Despite such omens, Napoleon III thought that a war against the Prussians would be quick and decisive. Yet his defeat and capture at the Battle of Sedan on 1 September 1870 ended his reign, his empire, and any prospects for French military success on the continent for a generation to come. Indeed, while fighting would continue into the next year, the Prussians had won the war at Sedan, which paved the way to German unification on 18 January 1871. For the French, the irony was bitter: Napoleon I's military campaigns had destroyed the First Reich in 1806; Napoleon III's miscalculations two generations later helped to create the Second.

Many of France's musicians had also been concerned by another German threat: the rising tide of interest in Richard Wagner's operas. Wagner himself had overseen a production of his opera *Tannhäuser* that flopped at the Paris Opéra in March 1861, and his grand opera *Rienzi* was featured at the Théâtre-Lyrique in 1869 with only slightly better results. Nevertheless, while these two operas hardly represented Wagner's more recent fare (especially the music drama *Tristan und Isolde*), they were enough to plant the seeds of French Wagnerism, the shoots of which threatened to choke almost every new French opera for the remainder of the century. On top of that, Hector Berlioz's death in 1869 meant that France was without a major composer of orchestral instrumental music.

The perception among many French composers of an internal artistic vacuum and external musical threats could only be strengthened in the wake of France's defeat by the Prussians. Thus, five weeks after the German Empire was born, Henri Duparc, Camille Saint-Saëns, César Franck, Jules Massenet, and a half-dozen other French musicians drew up plans for a "National Society of Music" ("Société Nationale de Musique"). Yet while the group adopted the motto "Ars Gallica," it was not actively xenophobic, as the preamble to its statutes makes clear:

> The goal of the Society is to further the production and popularization of all serious musical works; to encourage and to bring to light, as much as is in its power, all musical endeavors, in whatever form they may take, on condition that they reveal elevated and artistic aspirations on the part of the author. It is in brotherhood, with absolute disregard for self-interest, with the firm intention to help one another with all their power, that the members should, each within the sphere of his action, work toward the study and performance of the works that they are called to choose and to interpret.[1]

For the members of the Société Nationale, France had at one time been a home for "serious" music, as evidenced by the operas of Jean-Baptiste Lully, Jean-Philippe Rameau, and Christoph Willibald Gluck, or the keyboard music of Jacques Champion de Chambonnières (1602–1672) and François Couperin (1668–1733). The period following the 1789 Revolution, however, had been dominated by foreigners, including Luigi Cherubini as head of the Conservatoire, Giacomo Meyerbeer at the Opéra, and Gioachino Rossini at the Théâtre-Italien. Even the most celebrated pianists, such as Franz Liszt, Sigismond Thalberg, and Frédéric Chopin, had come from abroad.

Thus, creating a new French school of music ("la nouvelle école") meant looking outside of – both geographically and historically – the domestic musical practices of the previous two generations. But what differentiated genuinely serious, French music from its competition across the Rhine was the means by which cutting-edge musical genres, techniques, and theories were imbued with seventeenth- and eighteenth-century elements of clarity, restraint, and order. While specific definitions of these characteristics were continually shaped and contested, they nevertheless led to important advancements in French song (*mélodies*), opera, operetta, incidental music, ballet, solo piano music, and orchestral composition. The symphonic poem was especially well cultivated during this period, which in the wake of France's cultural self-scrutiny is not as surprising as it may first seem. Indeed, as Timothy Jones has noted, it

> presented a relatively blank slate on which composers could inscribe a new type of French instrumental music. With its emphasis on dramatic incident, instrumental colour, and non-standard forms, the symphonic poem provided composers with the opportunity to draw on the rich orchestral style associated with French stage music. And, not least, the discipline of working to the demands of a literary or dramatic programme undoubtedly had the paradoxical effect of freeing the imaginations of composers.[2]

The novelty of the symphonic poem, the historically strong French attachment to dramatic music, and the stability of the Third Republic – lasting from 1870 to 1940, it remains France's longest-lasting government since the fall of the *ancien régime* – created an ideal environment for program music to flourish, with Saint-Saëns, Franck, Claude Debussy, Augusta Holmès, Vincent d'Indy, Maurice Ravel, and others producing outstanding examples. In the first two decades of the twentieth century, the programmatic works of these composers would heavily influence a generation of American composers, including Charles Griffes, George Antheil, Charles Ives, and Aaron Copland, who sought radical alternatives to the German-American music discussed in the previous chapter.

## Saint-Saëns and the symphonic poem

Like Wagner's stage works, Franz Liszt's symphonic poems were passionately debated more than they were actually heard in France in the 1860s and 1870s. One important French musician to advocate for Liszt was Saint-Saëns, who organized a concert of Liszt's orchestral and choral music at the Théâtre-Italien in Paris on 18 March 1878. Saint-Saëns staged the concert in part to repay Liszt for making possible the premiere of his opera *Samson et Dalila* at Weimar three months earlier. But his debt to Liszt went back more than a decade, when Saint-Saëns encountered Liszt's symphonic poems in four-hand piano arrangements. Taking the unfashionable position of privileging Liszt the composer over Liszt the virtuoso pianist, Saint-Saëns would claim that Liszt's "brilliant and influential creation" of the symphonic poem "will be his title to immortality and, when time has removed the vivid trace of the greatest pianist who ever lived, it will inscribe on its roll of honour the name of the man who set instrumental music free." Reflecting on the program of his all-Liszt concert from 1878, Saint-Saëns was struck by how "it is in the truth and intensity of expression that Liszt is truly incomparable. His music speaks, and to avoid hearing its words you have to stuff your ears with the cotton wool of prejudice, which unfortunately is always to hand. His music describes the indescribable."[3]

Saint-Saëns had written several orchestral works in traditional genres during the 1850s and 1860s, including seven symphonies – although only the First Symphony in E♭ was published in 1855 – and an extended concert overture on the subject of the Roman gladiator Spartacus that earned him an accolade from the Société Sainte-Cécile in 1863. In the 1870s, however, he largely abandoned these genres and became one of the first among French composers to embrace the symphonic poem. In terms of subject matter (see Text Box 9.1), Saint-Saëns's four orchestral works support his glowing assessment of Liszt, as they share much in common with the twelve symphonic poems that the elder composer had published up to that point: an affinity for heroic subjects; a deference to classical literature; and strong confrontations between protagonist and antagonist(s). However, Saint-Saëns is far less forthcoming than Liszt as to his motivations for composing his program music, and

## Text Box 9.1  Saint-Saëns's prefaces to his symphonic poems

### Phaéton

Phaethon was allowed to drive the chariot of the Sun, his father, in the sky. But his inept hands led the steeds astray. The fiery chariot, thrown off course, veered toward earth. With the whole universe about to perish in the blaze, Jupiter struck down the foolhardy Phaethon with his lightning.

### Le rouet d'Omphale

The subject of this symphonic poem is feminine seduction, the triumphant struggle of weakness against strength. The wheel is only a pretext, in the sense that it was chosen solely for rhythm and general allure of the piece.

   Those in search of details might be interested to know that at rehearsal letter J, Hercules bemoans the chains that he cannot break; and at rehearsal letter L, Omphale mocks the hero's vain efforts.

### La jeunesse d'Hercule

The fable explains that upon his entry into the world, Hercules saw open before him two paths: that of pleasure and that of virtue.

   Indifferent to the seductions of the nymphs and Bacchants, the hero commits himself to the way of struggle and combat, after which he glimpses – through the flames of the pit – the reward of immortality.

### Danse macabre

> Zig and Zig and Zig, Death in time
> Strikes his heel on a grave,
> Death at midnight plays a dance tune,
> Zig and Zig and Zag, on his violin.
> The winter wind blows, and the night is dark,
> The linden trees whimper,
> White skeletons move to the shade,
> Running and leaping under their large shrouds.
> Zig and Zig and Zig, everyone moves and grooves,
> The bones of the dancers are heard clattering.
> . . . . . . . . . . . . . . . . . . . . . . . . . .
> . . . . . . . . . . . . . . . . . . . . . . . . . .
> But look! All at once they leave the circle,
> They jostle and flee, the cock has crowed.
> . . . . . . . . . . . . . . . . . . . . . . . . . .
> . . . . . . . . . . . . . . . . . . . . . . . . . .

**Example 9.1** Saint-Saëns, *Phaéton*, mm. 45–60

nowhere does he shift to a first-person voice. Instead, his prefaces do little more than introduce the characters, their dramatic context, and the moral, if any. Rarely do specific plot points merit his attention; even his identification of Hercules's efforts and Omphale's mocking in the preface to *Le rouet d'Omphale* is motivated by a desire to direct the reader/listener as unambiguously as possible to the real crux of his first symphonic poem. Indeed, as he reiterated in a letter of 6 March 1899:

> in principle I do not favour pieces which tell a story. In the *Danse macabre* there are the terrors and ironies of death; in *Le rouet d'Omphale*, seduction; in *Phaéton*, pride; in *La jeunesse d'Hercule*, the struggle between heroism and sensual pleasure … If there is no sentiment to express, I do not see what purpose music serves unless it is pure music, limited to the cultivation of form and the expression of an aesthetic idea.[4]

The expression of sentiment and idea through an expert cultivation of form occurs in *Phaéton*. Although Saint-Saëns does not divulge it, his source was probably Ovid's *Metamorphoses*. At the end of Book I, it is revealed that Apollo is Phaethon's true father. In Book II, he confronts the sun god, who offers to grant him any wish. Phaethon chooses to drive Apollo's chariot, and despite the father's best efforts to change his son's mind, Phaethon takes the reins. The journey begins promisingly, but Phaethon's inexperience sends the chariot off course, forcing Zeus to intervene with a preemptive strike. Phaethon falls from the sky into the Po River, from which Hesperian nymphs pull his body and ceremoniously bury it. Apollo, robbed of his newfound son, plunges the world into darkness before reluctantly mounting his chariot.

Saint-Saëns references only a small portion of Ovid's sprawling narrative (433 lines) in his preface to *Phaéton*. The music, however, is more comprehensive. To be sure, Phaethon's pride is on full display, thanks to a heroic, though slightly uncertain, melody that first appears in the trumpets and trombones at m. 45 (Example 9.1). A transformation comes after Phaethon's initial round with the horses, its circulatory profile suggesting a groove (Example 9.2) that, unfortunately, the young driver cannot maintain. The theme returns in a third guise at the work's conclusion, although its

**Example 9.2**  Saint-Saëns, *Phaéton*, mm. 175–182, arr. A. Benfeld

once proud diatonic profile has been replaced by targeted intervallic alterations that skew Phaeton's story toward the tragic.

Indeed, Saint-Saëns gives the eponymous hero of his symphonic poem a level of dignity not unlike Jean-Baptiste Lully's treatment of the same subject almost two centuries earlier. For instance, Saint-Saëns's decision to destroy Phaethon "off-stage," as it were, is not only dramatically effective, but also true to Ovid's retelling:

> And Phaethon, flames ravaging his auburn hair, / Falls headlong down, a streaming trail of light, / As sometimes through the cloudless vault of night / A star, though never falling, seems to fall. / Eridanus receives him, far from home, / In his wide waters half a world away, / And bathes his burning face.[5]

The spatial properties of *Phaéton* also help pinpoint the appearance of the crowd that witnesses Phaethon's horrific ride from afar. As Example 9.3 shows, Saint-Saëns presents an affective theme in the horns on *terra firma*, while bare octaves flitter far above. The horn theme is far more tuneful, but the drama of this section (mm. 123–174) rests completely on the rise and fall of pitches in the violins. Phaethon's recklessness threatens both heaven and earth, and Saint-Saëns manages to capture both planes simultaneously in his symphonic poem.

Liszt may have inspired such a conception. In 1872, Saint-Saëns published a pseudonymous review of Liszt's symphonic poems, in which he had the following to praise in *Mazeppa*:

> Toward the middle of the composition, one gets the impression of an immensity without boundaries; horse and rider flee into the unlimited steppes, and the

**Example 9.3** Saint-Saëns, *Phaéton*, mm. 123–136, arr. Benfeld

man's sight becomes disoriented, as the thousand details of the expanse are more than he can take in. There is at that point a marvelous orchestral effect. The strings, divided to the utmost, make heard from the height and depth of their range a mass of little sounds of all types.[6]

Saint-Saëns is surely alluding to Example 4.5, in which the first and second violins are each divided into three voices, and the violas and cellos each into two. And just as Byron goes to great length to capture the particulars of the landscape swirling and blurring around Mazeppa, so too does Ovid use Phaethon's doomed ride as a pretext to traverse the known world. Thus Ovid's readers visit countless cities, hear of the Nile's retreat to an unknown source, and learn how the Sahara turned into an expansive desert wasteland.

To be sure, these details are secondary to Phaethon's tale, but Saint-Saëns nevertheless cultivates them for formal clarity. As Table 9.1 suggests, *Phaéton* is a through-composed work in which altitudinal changes, coupled with key, create important interpretive signposts. The short introduction, mm. 1–4, adumbrates the harmonic tensions to come by means of the chord progression E♭–E°–Em–G whose G pedal

**Table 9.1** *Saint-Saëns,* Phaéton, *dimensional structure*

| | | |
|---|---|---|
| | 111: Ascent, V/E♭ | |
| | 123: Observers (Ex. 9.3), E♭ | |
| | 175: Phaethon (Ex. 9.2), E♭ | |
| | 197: Horses + Phaethon, C → X | |
| | 227: Phaethon, fragmented in bass | |
| | 249: Zeus strikes, E♭ | |
| 1–4: Intro, E♭ → G | | |
| 5: Horses, C → V/G | | |
| 45: Horses, Phaethon (Ex. 9.1), G → F → B → V/C | | |
| 79: Horses, C | | |
| 95: Phaethon, E♭ | | |
| | | 249: Descent, E♭ → V/C |
| | | 265: Nymphs (≈ Observers), C |
| | | 277: Phaethon, mourned (Ex. 9.4), C |

also suggest a dominant prolongation in the key of C. (The Phrygian, Dorian, and Lydian augmented scales on beat four of each measure further obscure this passage's intent.) As they leave Mount Olympus, the horses pound out a dactylic motive modeled on "The Ride to the Abyss" from Hector Berlioz's *La damnation de Faust*, shortly after which they gracefully modulate toward G to accommodate their pilot. However, this fleeting moment is the only time that G major makes a substantive appearance; from this point forward a combat between E♭ (Phaethon, his sympathizers) and C major (the horses) take center stage. Likewise, Phaethon's theme becomes increasingly fragmented and diatonically undone. In particular, the second half of his theme appears disoriented at m. 227, sickly rocking between D♭ and B♮ in the bassoons, tubas, and low strings. Zeus strikes at m. 249, and Phaethon begins his fall to earth. Saint-Saëns transfers the theme of the observers to the nymphs who collect Phaethon's body, and his theme gets one last solemn presentation. Yet the augmented sixth at m. 283 (see Example 9.4), the augmented dominant at m. 286, and the descending natural minor scale at m. 290 conspire against an unambiguous C major conclusion, as if Saint-Saëns is echoing Ovid's conclusion that no one benefitted from Phaethon's demise.

The *Danse macabre*, composed in October 1874 and published one year later, employs a different set of tactics in order to invigorate the shopworn Romantic topic of the supernatural. Modeled in part on Liszt's first "Mephisto" Waltz and Berlioz's *Symphonie fantastique*, and in turn inspiring later diabolical symphonic poems by Charles Martin Loeffler (*La villanelle du diable*, 1901; an arrangement of an earlier

**Example 9.4** Saint-Saëns, *Phaéton*, mm. 277–293, arr. Benfeld

song of the same title) and Henry Hadley (*Lucifer*, 1910), Saint-Saëns's work succeeds in large part due to its phantasmagorical scoring and external references, such as the "devilish" tritone, the harp's twelvefold toll of the church bell, the detuned solo violin, the clarinet's imitation of the cock's crow, and the presence of the xylophone – all delivered as a waltz, the most popular social dance of Saint-Saëns's day. But as its transformation from poem to song to symphonic poem illustrates, the *Danse macabre* is also a perfect example of the Parnassian doctrine of "art for art's sake," to which Saint-Saëns subscribed.

Much of the symphonic poem is based on a song entitled "Danse macabre" that Saint-Saëns had set in 1872 to Henri Cazalis's recent poem, "Égalité, Fraternité." Cazalis imagines a clearing at midnight. At the stroke of twelve, Death appears and plays a dance song ("air de danse") on the violin. Skeletons soon join the party, as does a "lascivious couple." As the dancing gets more heated, Cazalis reveals that the two are of different social stations: she, a noble lady; he, a nobody from town. But their status matters not, for as Cazalis happily proclaims, "O! What a beautiful night for the poor world! / And long live death and equality!" (ll. 27–28).

Saint-Saëns set Cazalis's complete poem as song, but shows himself to be more discriminating in his symphonic poem. Its preface provides lines 1–10 of Cazalis's poem, followed by two lines of ellipses, and concludes with lines 25 (slightly altered) and 26. In other words, Saint-Saëns either expects his listeners to fill in the missing lines that mostly deal with the lascivious couple, or excises them because they are no longer relevant to the symphonic poem's construction and programmatic goals. At the very least, he denies his orchestral piece the political and arguably nihilistic moral that Cazalis – who wrote his poem in the wake of the disastrous Paris Commune of 1871 – hoped to convey; namely, that death is the great equalizer. From this perspective, Saint-Saëns's *Danse macabre* is far less serious, though no less artistic. Indeed, the composer compensates for his editorial suppressions by increasing the size of his symphonic poem by more than 340 bars, or 70 percent, over the song, with newly composed material that effaces the work's strophic origins and improves its thematic development. The net result is an expansive character piece that seems to masquerade as *memento mori* but never relinquishes its ironic tone. (Saint-Saëns amplified these parodistic elements in citations of the *Danse macabre* in the twelfth movement, "Fossils," of his *Carnival of the Animals* from 1886.)

The novelty of the symphonic poem in France during the 1870s cannot be blamed for Saint-Saëns's reluctance to imbue it with political and moral weight. Instead, looking back to models from the seventeenth and eighteenth centuries, he saw his primary role as composer in the Third Republic to save an endangered French tradition – currently threatened to the point of extinction by a cultish Wagnerian style that thrived on overabundance – by reviving music as a medium for direct and pointed expression.

## César Franck and the "Bande"

Saint-Saëns's position as co-founder of the Société Nationale and innovations as composer made him one of the most powerful men in, and one of the most important symbols of, the revitalization of French music in the decade that followed the Franco-Prussian War. By the early 1880s, however, that status was being challenged by a sizable group of Society members who believed that French music was lapsing into an all-too-familiar provincialism. In the summer of 1881, those musicians led a massive coup, electing César Franck, Vincent d'Indy, Gabriel Fauré, Henri Duparc, Émile Bernard, and Antoine Lascoux to the Society's executive committee. One year later, Ernest Chausson and Camille Benoît were elected to replace vacancies made by d'Indy and Duparc. The group then bided its time until it sloppily ousted co-founder Romain Bussine in 1886, whereupon it revised the Society's statutes to allow performances of works by foreign composers. The change was radical and far-reaching: Saint-Saëns, unable to reconcile the paradox of a National Society supporting non-nationals, severed ties with the group entirely; the departure of both co-founders in as many months allowed for the consolidation of power by this "Bande à Franck," that is, those who looked to Franck as their musical leader and would keep his name alive long after his death in 1890.

Despite being active as a composer in a wide variety of genres and performer on piano and organ since the early 1840s, Franck did not begin to garner a notable following until the early 1870s, when he was appointed professor of organ at the Paris Conservatoire. Over the next two decades, he would compose the large-scale works for which he is best known today, including the oratorio *Les béatitudes*, the Symphony in D minor, the *Prélude, choral et fugue* for piano, and three powerful chamber works. His résumé from this period also includes five symphonic poems, which place him alongside Saint-Saëns as the most important French purveyor of the genre in the last third of the nineteenth century.

In terms of structure and drama, Franck's symphonic poems follow the definition as laid down and practiced by Saint-Saëns:

> The symphonic poem, in the form that Liszt gave it, is usually a collection of different movements which depend on each other and stem from an initial idea, and which connect together and create a single piece ... In order to obtain the greatest possible variety, Liszt most often chose a musical phrase that he transformed by means of rhythmic techniques in such a way as to aid in the expression of the most dissimilar sentiments.[7]

Important differences do exist, however. Whereas Saint-Saëns drew on classical literature or depoliticized contemporary poetry in order to give it something of a timeless quality, Franck turned to contemporary poets like Victor Hugo, Leconte de Lisle, and, in *Psyché*, a mysterious "S. Sicard" and perhaps Louis de Fourcand; and while the poetic source of *Le chasseur maudit*, Gottfried August Bürger's ballad *Der wilde Jäger*, had been published in 1786, it remained a storyteller's staple throughout the nineteenth century. Second, while Franck characterized each of the works in Table 9.2 as a symphonic poem or, in the case of *Rédemption*, a "poème-symphonie," the presence of a continuous, virtuosic solo piano part in *Les djinns* or the four-part chorus in *Psyché* tests the limits of what it meant for a composition to be "symphonic." Finally, Franck's harmonic language, influenced by Wagner, Liszt, and Brahms, is far more chromatic than that of Saint-Saëns, allowing him to ratchet up the intensity of expression – be it for the supernatural of *Le chasseur maudit*, the (racially coded) terror of *Les djinns*, or the eroticism of *Psyché* – in ways that seemed unprecedented to most contemporary French composers of orchestral music.

As with so much of Victor Hugo's poetry, "Les djinns" (loosely translated as "The Genies" or "Evil Spirits"), from his 1829 collection, *Les orientales*, takes sound as its primary subject. In this case, the cyclic progression from silence to cacophony and back to silence reflects the attempted Armageddon brought on by diabolical djinns, which the fearful narrator thwarts at the last minute by appealing to Muhammad.

**Table 9.2** *Franck's symphonic poems*

| Title | Composition / Prem. / Pub. | Source | Instrumentation |
|---|---|---|---|
| *Ce qu'on entend sur la montagne* | c.1847 / 1987 / – | Victor Hugo | Orch. |
| *Rédemption* | 1871–72 / 1873 / 1872 rev. 1874 / 1875 / 1875 | E. Blau | Orch., Sop., Female Choir, Speaker |
| *Les éolides* | 1875–76 / 1877* / 1893 | Leconte de Lisle | Orch. |
| *Le chasseur maudit* | 1882 / 1883* / 1884 | G.A. Bürger, *Der wilde Jäger* | Orch. |
| *Les djinns* | 1883–84 / 1885* / 1893 | Hugo | Orch., pno. solo |
| *Psyché* | 1887–88 / 1888* / 1903 | S. Sicard; L. de Foucard? | Orch., SATB Choir |

* = premiered by the Société Nationale

**Table 9.3** *Hugo, "Les djinns," structure and content*

| *Stanza* | 1 | 2 | 3 | 4 | 5 | 6 | 7 | 8 |
|---|---|---|---|---|---|---|---|---|
| *Syllables* | 2 | 3 | 4 | 5 | 6 | 7 | 8 | 9 |
| *Content* | Silence | Sound emerges | | | Djinns approach | Djinns arrive | Description of hideous creatures | Imminent destruction |

| *Stanza* | 9 | 10 | 11 | 12 | 13 | 14 | 15 |
|---|---|---|---|---|---|---|---|
| *Syllables* | 8 | 7 | 6 | 5 | 4 | 3 | 2 |
| *Content* | Appeal to holy prophet | Djinns retreat | Djinns disappear | | | Sonic echo | Silence |

This stay of destruction in "Les djinns" is unusual for *Les orientales*,[8] as is the poem's structure of fifteen stanzas, eight lines apiece, organized in what Franck's student d'Indy referred to as a "lozenge."

As Table 9.3 demonstrates, Hugo produces a disorienting, compartmentalized poetic Doppler effect in which the number of syllables per line grows through the first eight stanzas and then contracts in the remaining seven. Franck responds with a fine musical analogue in the opening of his symphonic poem (Example 9.5a), which the solo piano personalizes and substantially develops shortly after its initial entry (Example 9.5b). D'Indy maintained that Franck's piece was neither "a musical adaptation of" nor "very closely connected with" Hugo's poem,[9] yet the appearance of a new theme at m. 347 in the new and surprisingly stable key of B minor and played *fortissississimo* – the loudest dynamic marking given in the entire score – suggests

**Example 9.5a** Franck, *Les djinns*, mm. 1–12

**Example 9.5b** Franck, *Les djinns*, mm. 135–138

otherwise. Not only does this music respond fittingly to the eighth stanza's talk of "infernal cries," "wailing and weeping voices," and "the horrible swarm," but so does the piano's response at m. 357 (Example 9.6) to Hugo's ninth stanza, which reads:

> Prophet, if thy hand but save me / From these foul demons of the night, / I will bow my head and lave me / And fulfill thy holy rite. / On these ever-faithful portals / Make their breath to burn in vain, / And let the claws of these immortals / Vainly scratch this darkened pane.[10]

In like fashion, Franck instructs the pianist to play the expressive, almost prayer-like melody "pleadingly, but with anxiety and a little bit of agitation." Indeed, the presence of the djinns remains strong in this passage, as their hypnotic, four-bar bass line still threatens in the bowels of the orchestra. Upon the return of the opening material at m. 368 in the home key (albeit rhythmically transformed), its diabolical character starts to fade, and by m. 409 it is completely extinguished.

## The challenge of the instrumental ballad

*Phaéton*, *Danse macabre*, and *Les djinns* illustrate how French composers of program music tended to allow greater flexibility than their German counterparts in fashioning descriptive and evocative stories in music. In particular, Franck may have

**Example 9.6** Franck, *Les djinns*, mm. 353–360

been willing to stretch such boundaries, given that his non-narrative, atmospheric, "French" instrumental setting of de Lisle's poem "Les éolides" ("The Æolides"), although initially well received when it was premiered at a Société Nationale concert on 13 May 1877, failed miserably when it was revived in February 1882; that is, eight months before Franck put the finishing touches on *Le chasseur maudit*. Yet Franck could not claim credit for reviving the genre, for his students[11] had preceded him in this respect by almost a decade: Duparc produced a symphonic poem based on Bürger's famous ballad, *Lenore*, in 1875; and d'Indy followed three years later with *La forêt enchantée*, a "Légende-Symphonie" based on Ludwig Uhland's *Harald*. The Franckists' interest in turn-of-the-nineteenth-century German ballads would culminate in one of the most enduring orchestral works of the period, Paul Dukas's *L'apprenti sorcier* (*The Sorcerer's Apprentice*).

As extended narrative poems, ballads would seem to be ideal source material for the composer of program music. Yet while Liszt, Sigismond Thalberg, Edvard Grieg, Gabriel Fauré, Claude Debussy, Amy Beach, Carl Reinicke, Adolf von Henselt, and Louis Moreau Gottschalk contributed enduring examples of the nineteenth-century piano ballade, none publicly discloses a firm poetic source. Of Frédéric Chopin's four ballades for piano, the first, op. 25, and second, op. 38, have been associated with the poetry of Adam Mickiewicz since the early 1840s, leading many commentators to hear not just those two but all four of Chopin's ballades as being "Polish," despite Chopin's silence to the contrary. The piano ballades of Hans von Bülow, op. 11, and Johannes Brahms, op. 10, are on somewhat firmer programmatic ground, although the contemplative poetry attached to the former (a two-line excerpt from Victor Hugo's *Voix intérieures*) and the compactness of the latter challenge the genre's narrative ambitions. In fact, only a handful of piano works from the century, such as Theodor Kullak's *Lenore*, op. 81 (1853), or Carl Tausig's *Das Geisterschiff*, op. 1 (1860; see Chapter 5), qualify as full-fledged narrative musical ballades. The trio of orchestral ballades by Franck and his two pupils thus represent a small but concerted effort to form a genuinely new contribution to the burgeoning French programmatic tradition during the early years of the Third Republic.

A notable feature of *Le chasseur maudit* is its depopulation of Bürger's supernumerary characters. In Bürger's telling, the Count is met by the proverbial "good" and "bad" angels as the sun rises. The good angel pleads with the Count to return, the bad angel – stoking the Count's ego – urges him to continue. After considering his options, the Count, recognizing a kindred spirit in his sinister companion, redoubles the pursuit of his prey. Along the way, he rebuffs the pleas of a poor field laborer, his dogs feast on the choice heifer of a distraught farmer, and he laughs in the face of a hermit preaching repentance. Suddenly his two companions depart, and he finds himself completely alone. After a voice from above ("Donnerstimme") condemns the Count to be pursued by agents of Hell for all eternity, Bürger explains in the final stanza how the Count can still be heard in the woods at night, by pious and sinners alike.

Save for "a gloomy, implacable voice" and the Count, Franck eliminates all references in his preface to the horsemen, narrator, laborer, farmer, and hermit:

> It was Sunday morning; far away reverberated the joyful sound of bells and the religious songs of the crowd . . . Sacrilege! The savage Count of the Rhine has sounded his horn.
>
> Hello! Hello! The chase rushes over fields, moors, and meadows. – "Stop, Count, I beg you; hear the pious songs." – No! Hello! Hello! – "Stop, Count, I implore you; be on guard." – No, and the rider rushes on like a whirlwind.
>
> Suddenly the Count is alone; his horse refuses to go any further; the Count would blow his horn, but it no longer sounds . . . A gloomy, implacable voice curses him: "Sacrilegious man," it cries, "be forever hunted by Hell!"
>
> Then flames erupt from every direction . . . The Count, mad with terror, flees faster and faster, pursued by a swarm of demons: by day across abysses, by night through the air.

**Example 9.7** Franck, *Le chasseur maudit*, mm. 129–136

In their stead he creates a motive of appeal – Example 9.7, exhibiting Franck's characteristic bar form – that attempts to sway the Count, whose self-destructive arrogance and intransigence is embedded in a resolute, rhythmically charged four-bar theme that returns to the tonic at each measure's downbeat but prominently features two tonically destabilizing sonorities (VI⁺, ♭vii). The interplay of these two voices characterizes the second section of Franck's symphonic poem (mm. 77–231), which moves, with characteristic Lisztian sequences, from G minor to B minor, and which superimposes themes contrapuntally instead of developing them sectionally – an approach not too far removed from Wagner's application of leitmotives. At m. 203, the announcement of the Count in E♭ major – a traditional key of heroism and victory – is mitigated by a narrowing gap between the Count's theme and that of his would-be intercessors. Upon a return to G minor at m. 223, the Count finds himself abandoned; the ensuing appearance of the bass drum at m. 232 and cymbals one bar later leads to a more dramatic loss at m. 248. Franck instructs the horns to plug their bells ("bouchée"), which results in an eerie timbre designed to mimic the Count's own suddenly obstinate instrument.

As Table 9.4 suggests, *Le chasseur maudit* is a semi-ballade, in that two of its four sections seek to approximate narrative elements of Bürger's story. Along with the second section, the fourth follows the damned Count through the countryside by means of a parodistic/satirical transformation akin to the third movement of Liszt's *Faust* Symphony, discussed in Chapter 6. However, sections one and three are primarily atmospheric. The former highlights the pastoral character of the Count's realm and the piety of its people, features which are thrown into even greater relief by the contrasting trochaic rhythms of the pastoral and the iambs of the horn. The latter draws on models like Carl Maria von Weber's *Der Freischütz* and Hector Berlioz's *Symphonie fantastique* to create sinister, foreboding woods.

**Table 9.4** *Franck,* Le chasseur maudit, *structure*

| Section I: Pastoral | II: Open Countryside | → | III: Closed Woods | IV: Chase |
|---|---|---|---|---|
| **mm. 1–76** | **77–231** | **232–272** | **273–311** | **312–542** |
| Introduction of topics, G: 1ff: hunt 17, 37ff: pastoral 33ff: church bells → | 77: Count's theme, g | 232: Bass drum, cymbals | 273–309: Sequence without notable melody; transformation of opening horn motive 273: b 285: d 292: f → | 312–335: Continued transformation of opening horn motive; development of wave figure from section III; chromatic and half-step motion predominates |
| 49ff: Superimposition of all three | 114: Count, *tutti,* g | 248: "Bouchée" horns | 310: f♯ | 336: Count, transformation, G pedal |
| 61: Development of pastoral theme → | 129: Theme of appeal, E♭ → f | 249ff: Count, fragmented, vii°4/2/d → vii°4/2/b | | 392, 400; 450, 458: Pastoral, fragmented in low strings |
| 69: Pastoral, *fff* | 140: Count + whirling violins, b 177: Count, b → D 192: Appeal, G → a 203–223: Count ↔ Appeal 203: E♭ ↔ c♯ 211: F ↔ b 223: Count, g | | | 478: Bells |

The widespread popularity of Bürger's ballads during the nineteenth century also helps explain Duparc's instrumental setting of *Lénore*, written in 1875. Duparc's treatment of his source material is far less specific and comprehensive than in the third part of Joachim Raff's near-contemporary Fifth Symphony (see Chapter 5). Whereas Raff, having spent an earlier movement delving into the ill-fated couple's relationship, focuses on the frenetic plot of Lenore's wild ride, Duparc uses it as

**Example 9.8** Duparc, *Lénore*, mm. 21–33, arr. Saint-Saëns

pretext for charting Lenore's increasing emotional distress. Indeed, Duparc glosses over the consequences of Lenore's sacrilegious actions by transforming Bürger's story into a full-fledged Wagnerian tale of redemption through self-sacrificial love, an approach hinted at in the program provided in the full score:

> Lenore mourns her betrothed, William, who has fallen in battle. Suddenly he appears as an apparition riding a black horse and abducts Lenore. They set out with the fury and speed of a tempest. "Hurrah! The dead are keeping up with us. Are you afraid of them, my love?" "No," she responds, "but let them be at peace." Shrieking spirits pursue. At the stroke of midnight, rider and steed crumble to dust. Lenore dies.[12]

The Wagnerian theme is reinforced by Duparc's musical language, which, like *Tristan und Isolde*, features passionate outbursts in the upper strings that gradually rise in register, dynamic level, chromatic saturation, and impatiently appear to accelerate, as in Example 9.8. Moreover, the ride that begins at m. 42 and really starts to move at m. 54 bears more than a passing resemblance to Wagner's

**Example 9.8** (cont.)

"Walkürenritt" ("Ride of the Valkyries"), the Prelude to Act III of *Die Walküre* that – at least to Duparc and his colleagues in the early 1870s – would have constituted some of Wagner's most modern and advanced depictive music.

While Duparc's musical vocabulary is indebted to Wagner and to a lesser extent to Franck – for instance, in the oscillating chord pairs at mm. 76–77 and 112–113 – his structural design for *Lénore* points more to Liszt and Saint-Saëns. As Table 9.5 suggests, the "Tristan" material sits alongside a sonata-like structure. In the exposition, two themes are introduced in the closely related keys of G major and B minor, and a third appears in the development in C♯ minor. All three return in order in the second half of the work, although neither the second nor the third theme returns in tonic.

This sonata is not working in isolation, however, as it is clearly being influenced by the interrupting slow episodes. The first episode, for instance, can be heard as an introduction to the sonata, while the second might serve as the real beginning of its development. Likewise, the key areas of the first three episodes are closely related to

**Table 9.5** *Duparc,* Lénore, *structure*

| | |
|---|---|
| 1–41: Andante sostenuto, G | *(Introduction)* |
| | *(Exposition)* |
| | 54: I, G |
| | 69: II, b |
| 86–104: Più largamente, E | *(Development)* |
| | 124: III, c♯ → X |
| | *(Recapitulation)* |
| | 146: I, G |
| 163–188: Più largamente, B | |
| 173: + III | |
| | 189: + II, X |
| | *(Coda / Development II)* |
| | 199: + III, e → X |
| | 223–228: Più largamente, G ↔ III, g |
| | → 229–256: Tempo primo (248–257: V/G) |
| | *(Synthesis)* |
| | 256–282: Andante → Più lento → Adagio |
| | III', g + material from Andante sostenuto |

those of the sonata's three principal themes: G major; B major / B minor; E major / C♯ minor. At the same time, the episodes also weaken the structural integrity of the sonata. The appearance of a portion of the third theme at m. 173, for instance, undermines the recapitulation, as does the second theme's failure to find a definitive key. In fact, the symphonic poem seems to head away from sectional divisions and more toward synthesis. Thus what might be construed as a coda in sonata space at m. 199ff is in fact the beginning of the merger of the emotional and narrative worlds of Duparc's piece. The tonic, for instance, is only achieved at m. 274, and its modal defection to G minor is no doubt due to the increasingly strong presence of theme III, whose transformation at m. 257 achieves a funereal quality in the hands of the bassoons and trombones. Duparc's collapsing of the narrative and psychological frames in *Lénore* makes for a compelling, original reading of his well-known source material.

Like Duparc's *Lénore,* Vincent d'Indy's *La forêt enchantée* (completed in 1878) draws on a German ballad – this time by Ludwig Uhland from 1811 – whose hero enters a supernatural world from which he does not return. In d'Indy's case, the knight Harald is riding home with his companions after a successful campaign. The woods start to stir, and suddenly the group is accosted by elves, whose charms ensnare all but brave Harald. In making his way out of the "savage forest," he stops for refreshment. Removing his helmet in order to drink some water from a rock-side

**Example 9.9** D'Indy, *La forêt enchantée* (*The Enchanted Forest*), mm. 145–151

fountain, the parched Harald falls into a petrified sleep that continues into the present day.[13]

D'Indy's decision to title his symphonic legend *The Enchanted Forest* instead of *Harald* speaks to the composer's primary focus: environment, not character. D'Indy's treatment of the latter tends to expose his overreliance on, rather than development of, tradition. One example is Harald's theme, Example 9.9, whose contours, rhythms, and orchestration are kindred to the eponymous subject of Saint-Saëns's *Phaéton*. Even the theme's transformation in the final third of the piece, which traces Harald's descent into the dream world, mirrors the fate – and the music – of Apollo's overconfident son. However, d'Indy succeeds admirably in adding to the soundscape of the ubiquitous Romantic forest as practiced by Carl Maria von Weber in *Der Freischütz*, Berlioz in the *Symphonie fantastique*, and Wagner in "Waldesrauschen" ("Forest Murmurs") from Act II of *Siegfried*, whose premiere d'Indy witnessed at Bayreuth in 1876. The elves are introduced in the middle of *La forêt enchantée*, at which point d'Indy divides the orchestra into several chamber-like ensembles. Example 9.10 offers a rich palette of colors, from shimmering first violins, a plucked harp that doubles a solo horn, and solo flute. The restricted intervallic range – no instrument jumps more than a major third – gives this passage a hypnotic quality, which is momentarily broken by a trio of strings that bubbles up from below at mm. 295–297 – an adumbration of the pent-up energy that this group will soon release on Harald and his fellow knights. Notwithstanding the uneven treatment he gives to his materials in *La forêt enchantée*, d'Indy's orchestral sensitivity would pay dividends in later, more mature compositions that take a physical site or geographical region as inspiration, including the *Symphonie sur un chant montagnard français* (1886), *Jour d'été à la montagne* (1905), *Le poème des rivages* (1921), and *Diptyque méditerranéen* (1926).

## A return to musical painting? Debussy and Ravel

Reflecting after the turn of the century on the historical development of the symphonic poem and orchestral fantasy, d'Indy identified three "schools": (1) Berliozian; (2) Russian; and (3) Franckist. It was Berlioz who had brought about a

**Example 9.10** D'Indy, *La forêt enchantée*, mm. 283–298

"renaissance of the symphonic poem" that not only impacted instrumental music but (Wagnerian) opera as well. From Berlioz followed Liszt, Saint-Saëns, Gustave Charpentier (*Impressions d'Italie*, published in 1892), and especially Claude Debussy, whose descriptive music "has notably boosted … the genre of the symphonic poem."[14]

Like Liszt, Debussy developed his compositional style primarily through the piano and, slightly later, the orchestra. Yet despite d'Indy's attempt to categorize his colleague's music as the product of a proud, French tradition that emanated from Berlioz, Debussy himself remained deeply ambivalent about the programmatic status of his music, a position stemming from a more general disdain for all things orthodox (e.g., the symphony), academic (the Franckists), or cultish (Wagnerism). Consider three examples:

- Debussy met Stéphane Mallarmé in 1890 and began attending his Tuesday salon regularly in 1892. The Symbolist poet encouraged the young artist to compose music to his "L'après-midi d'un faune" ("The Afternoon of a Faun"; 1876), which Debussy completed in 1894. Mallarmé's eclogue considers a half-awake faun who cannot clearly perceive the difference between his dreams and reality. Debussy immediately blurs these lines of perception by presenting the famous flute melody over three starkly contrasting supporting harmonies: a D major seventh at m. 11, C♯ minor 6/5 at m. 21, and E ninth at m. 26. The *Prélude* develops and returns to this theme throughout its one hundred and ten measures, a number that corresponds exactly to the lines of Mallarmé's poem. Yet shortly after the work's premiere at a Société Nationale concert in December 1894, Debussy emphasized in a program note that his *Prélude* constituted "a very free illustration" of the poem, and "does not purport to be a synthesis of it."[15]

- In 1903 Debussy described to his publisher a plan for a symphonic work entitled *La mer* (*The Sea*), which would comprise three movements: I. "Beautiful Sea by the Bloodthirsty Islands," a title derived from a short story by Camille Mauclair from 1893; II. "Play of the Waves"; and III. "The Wind Makes the Sea Dance." When he premiered the work two years later, only the title of the second movement had survived intact. The first now bore the non-literary title, "From Dawn to Midday on the Sea," while the third movement featured a dialogue instead of a dance between wind and waves. And despite its three movements of contrasting character, *La mer* was not to be construed as a symphony or symphonic poem, but a trio of "symphonic sketches." Finally, the composer insisted that the published music's cover feature Katsushika Hokusai's *The Great Wave off Kanagawa* (Figure 9.1).

- Less than a decade later, Debussy released two books of preludes for the piano. Each of the twenty-four pieces bore a title, such as "The Sunken Cathedral," "The

**Figure 9.1**  Katsushika Hokusai, *The Great Wave off Kanagawa*

Girl with the Flaxen Hair," "Ondine," and "Fireworks." But instead of placing the titles in the usual position, Debussy withholds their appearance until the final bar-line, suggesting that interpretation, or at least programmatic interpretation, of a work should begin only *after* its performance has ended. Indeed, as if delighting in the ambiguous nature of the entire programmatic enterprise, Debussy concludes the second prelude from Book I with the pendant "Voiles," which means either "veils" or "sails" – expansive and transparent, or mysterious and opaque? And both images were favorites of the Symbolists: Veils call to mind exotic women, both Eastern and ancient Greek, while sails evoke imagery of the sea and maritime voyages.

To be sure, Debussy's style underwent significant change over the thirty or so years of his professional life. An ardent and uncompromising Wagnerian in the 1880s, by about 1900 he had abandoned the sage of Bayreuth; in the last years of his life, he became militantly devoted to the idea of producing "French" music (see Chapter 1). Consistent over his career, however, is his promotion of a deeply personal form of musical expression: "I live in a world of imagination," he divulged during an interview in 1908, "which is set in motion by something suggested by my intimate surroundings rather than by outside influences . . . I find an exquisite joy when I search deeply in the recesses of myself and if anything original is to come from me, it can only come that way."[16]

Since his own time, Debussy's music has routinely been linked to Impressionist painting (e.g., Claude Monet) or Symbolist poetry (e.g., Mallarmé), and his remark indeed stresses the intimacy of one's surroundings demanded by the former group and the mystery prized by the latter. Both positions are encapsulated in his review of a concert in which Beethoven's "Pastoral" Symphony and Liszt's *Mazeppa* were performed. He complains that "The popularity of the *Pastoral Symphony* is due to the widespread misunderstanding that exists between Man and Nature." Exact imitation, he continues, of babbling brooks and chirping birds is ludicrous: "Can the mystery of a forest be expressed by measuring the height of the trees? Is it not rather its fathomless depths that stir the imagination?" By contrast, Debussy grants *Mazeppa* more latitude for the indirectness of its emotional gestures, such that "the stormy passion that rages throughout captures us at last so completely that we are content to accept it without further reasoning."[17]

While Debussy and Ravel invariably charted out significantly different musical paths, Debussy's recommendation to accept without recourse to reason is an appropriate way to approach Ravel's greatest and most explicit programmatic composition, *Gaspard de la nuit*. The three-movement piece for solo piano draws its title from Aloysius Bertrand's same-named collection of poems, published post-humously in 1842 but largely unknown until Charles Baudelaire brought it to the attention of his readers in the preface to his own posthumously published prose poem collection, *Le spleen de Paris* (1869). For the rest of the century the renown of *Gaspard de la nuit* grew, particularly among Symbolist poets like Stéphane Mallarmé, who saw Bertrand as a kindred spirit.

For Ravel, who sought in his *Gaspard de la nuit* "to say with notes what a poet expresses with words,"[18] the attraction of Bertrand's collection partially lay in its kaleidoscope of characters, particularly the way in which they so strongly assert their vagueness and instill a sense of doubt in the reader. In "Ondine," the source of Ravel's first movement, Bertrand Gothicizes a figure long part of European folklore with descriptions of a "vague harmony," of windows "lighted by the moon's dismal [*mornes*] rays," of water both fluid and "croaking" ["*coassante*"]. The reader's perspective becomes further skewed when Bertrand switches from Ondine speaking in the first three paragraphs to the narrator being spoken to in the fourth – the point, in other words, where objective subject becomes subjective object. And this new subject, who begins to speak in the first person in the fifth and final paragraph, has no back story or context, save that "I love a mortal [woman]." Indeed, while the scene ends with Ondine fleeing, it would be a gross exaggeration to say that it ends conclusively. Deception is encoded in the movement's DNA.

Ravel spoke of *Gaspard de la nuit* as "three romantic poems of transcendental virtuosity." The clear allusion to Liszt's "Transcendental" Études of 1852 (see

**Example 9.11** Ravel, *Gaspard de la nuit*, "Ondine," mm. 80–82

Chapter 4) certainly suggests that he wished his programmatic triptych to represent a new stage in piano technique, although it is routinely less flamboyant about its virtuosity than Liszt's études. The outer movements are the most demanding. A major challenge in "Ondine," for instance, is balance, as the accompaniment – Bertrand's "dismal" rays or "croaking" waters? – remains extremely active, changes frequently, and often infringes upon the melody (see Example 9.11). The hyper-charged "Scarbo," about a mischievous goblin, is a toccata in all but name. Although its fast repeated notes and volleys of arpeggios demand an extraordinary, limber technique, the irregular stopping and starting of phrases makes it difficult to get comfortable with the material. Put another way, Ravel programmatizes the uncanny, the strangely familiar, just as Bertrand's narrator in "Scarbo" begins each of the first three lines with the ironic phrase, "How many times . . . " ("Que de fois . . . ").

Indeed, *Gaspard de la nuit* also represents a new stage in programmatic thinking. Whereas the overwhelming majority of programmatic compositions take a single perspective of a subjective experience as their aesthetic basis, *Gaspard de la nuit* attempts to juggle multiple perspectives simultaneously. This approach comes to the fore most prominently in the non-narrative second movement, "Le gibet" ("The Gallows"). An epigraph from Goethe's *Faust* either serves as memory aid or moment of poetic inspiration: "What do I see moving about the gallows?"[19] Bertrand's poem proper then begins:

> Ah! Is what I hear the howling night north wind or a hanged man giving forth a sigh on the gibbet's fork?

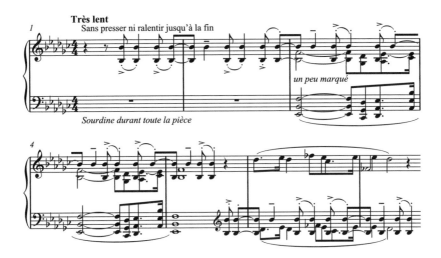

**Example 9.12** Ravel, *Gaspard de la nuit*, "Le gibet," mm. 1–7.

Would it be some cricket that sings nestled in the moss and the sterile ivy that the woods wear in pity?

Would it be some fly on the hunt sounding its horning with a fanfare of tallyhos about these deaf ears?

Would it be some beetle who plucks in its uneven flight a bloody hair from its bald skull?

Or else would it be some spider embroidering a half-ell of muslin to put a cravat on that strangled neck?

It is the bell that tolls to the walls of the city under the horizon, and the carcass of a hanged man that the setting sun reddens.[20]

The bells are omnipresent in the ostinato (long–short–long–short–long) B♭ octave that remains moored to the piano's middle register. In connection with the movement's key signature of six flats and the emphasis given to E♭ on the downbeats of mm. 3–5 and 8–9, the pitched bells should function as a component of a tonic, mediant, or dominant sonority. Yet Ravel avoids all three and chooses instead to focus on enriched sonorities, in which ninths, elevenths, and even thirteenths destabilize tonic leanings. In fact, many of these sonorities, especially at the outset (see Example 9.12), lack the third, so that at least at the local level they give the impression of being an assemblage of stacked primary and secondary dominants. The introduction of a short melody at m. 6 with a prominent F♭ not only further erodes tonic opportunities for E♭, but diminishes options in G♭ as well. In short, Ravel is playing with groups of sonorities that allude, but never commit, to a specific key or tonal center.

Bertrand's poem does the same. The narrator does not want to admit what he hears, and so he concocts a series of increasingly unbelievable sounds in a vain attempt to allay his growing fears. Ravel gives away the ending by introducing the bell's ostinato at the outset of "Le gibet" – no cricket, fly, beetle, or spider is so monotonically dependable. But just because the bells frame the movement and might even legitimately stand in as its "subject," there is substantial development in terms of form and program. "Le gibet" intermingles characteristic and musical figures of denial, paranoia, and perversion to chart a slow descent into madness. It gains further expressive power when considered in the context of the more active outer movements, in which erotic desire, ambivalence, mockery, and self-doubt contribute to *Gaspard de la nuit*'s long-range goal of fracturing the subjectivity of its narrator and listeners.

By no means did the production of new program music cease after the First World War, in France or abroad. However, a strong backlash that pervaded the arts in general against nineteenth-century approaches and ideologies meant that an increasing number of musicians no longer practiced – or at least no longer disclosed practicing – programmatic composition. Igor Stravinsky is emblematic of this change. Early works like the *Scherzo fantastique* or *Feu d'artifice*, both from 1908, extend late nineteenth-century Russian program music alongside examples by less famous contemporaries like Anatoly Lyadov or Aleksandr Skryabin. As a composer for the Ballets Russes in Paris in the years leading up to the war, Stravinsky produced a trio of masterpieces – *The Firebird*, *Petrushka*, and *The Rite of Spring* – whose amalgam of word, music, and gesture speaks to a concerted effort in the early twentieth century to raise the poetic status of ballet, as evidenced by the "poèmes dansés" of Dukas (*La péri*; 1911) and Debussy (*Jeux*; 1912) and Ravel's "symphonie choréographique" *Daphnis et Chloé* (1912). Yet by the next decade, Stravinsky had abandoned this super-programmatic style for a "neo-classical" one, in which a work like his Octet was in no way to be construed as "emotive," but rather as "a musical composition based on objective elements which are sufficient in themselves."[21] Similar reorientations by major composers like Béla Bartók, Paul Hindemith, and Arnold Schoenberg during the interwar years decidedly turned the aesthetic tide toward objective, ostensibly non-expressive music, and thus closed the door on a tradition of programmatic composition that had come to characterize a major stream of music of the preceding century.

# Notes

## Introduction

1. Igor Stravinsky, *Chronicle of My Life*, trans. Anon. (London: Victor Gollancz, 1936), 91–92. Original emphases.
2. An extended consideration of this piece and its attendant philosophies is Daniel Albright, *Untwisting the Serpent: Modernism in Music, Literature, and Other Arts* (University of Chicago Press, 2000), 185–197.
3. Quoted in Julian Rushton, "Music and the Poetic," in *The Cambridge History of Nineteenth-Century Music*, ed. Jim Samson (Cambridge University Press, 2001), 151–177, at 151.
4. Carl Dahlhaus, *The Idea of Absolute Music*, trans. Roger Lustig (University of Chicago Press, 1989), 128.
5. Susan McClary, "The Impromptu That Trod on a Loaf: Or How Music Tells Stories," *Narrative* 5, 1 (1997): 20–35, at 29.
6. James Hepokoski, "Back and Forth from *Egmont*: Beethoven, Mozart, and the Nonresolving Recapitulation," *19th-Century Music* 25, 2–3 (2002): 127–154, at 135.
7. See Matthew Guerrieri, *The First Four Notes: Beethoven's Fifth and the Human Imagination* (New York: Alfred A. Knopf, 2012). This story served Tchaikovsky well, when he elaborated on it significantly for a program to his Fourth Symphony that he provided to a patron. The program is reproduced in Richard Taruskin, *On Russian Music* (Berkeley and Los Angeles: University of California Press, 2009), 136–138.
8. Jean-Jacques Nattiez, "Can One Speak of Narrativity in Music?" trans. Katherine Ellis, *Journal of the Royal Musical Association* 115, 2 (1990): 240–257, at 249.
9. This term has long been associated with a conception of music advocated by Eduard Hanslick, discussed in detail in Chapter 5. Yet this is not technically how "absolute music" as a term got its start. Richard Wagner apparently first used it in an analysis of Beethoven's Ninth Symphony from 1846. According to Wagner, whereas the first three instrumental movements manifested "infinite and indecisive expression," it was at the beginning of the finale that Beethoven introduced a "moving recitative, which ... nearly abandon[s] the confines of absolute music." Thus the question was not ever about instrumental music as lacking the potential for expression, but rather its forms of expression. See Sanna Pederson, "Defining the Term 'Absolute Music' Historically," *Music & Letters* 90, 2 (2009): 240–262, esp. 243–244, which considers Wagner's contribution.

10. James Hepokoski, "The Second Cycle of Tone Poems," in *The Cambridge Companion to Richard Strauss*, ed. Charles Youmans (Cambridge University Press, 2010), 78–104, at 92.
11. See, for example, Carlo Caballero's discussion of Saint-Saëns's *Le rouet d'Omphale* in "In the Toils of Queen Omphale: Saint-Saëns's Painterly Refiguration of the Symphonic Poem," in *The Arts Entwined: Music and Painting in the Nineteenth Century*, ed. Marsha L. Morton and Peter L. Schmunk (New York: Garland Publishing, 2000), 119–141.

## 1 Characters, topics, and the programmatic battlefield

1. Heinrich Christoph Koch, *Musikalisches Lexikon* (Frankfurt am Main: August Hermann, 1802), cols. 1384–1385.
2. This and all further citations of this review come from Anon., "Gegenwärtiger Zustand der Musik in Paris ... Zweyter Brief," *Allgemeine musikalische Zeitung* 2, 43 (23 July 1800): cols. 745–747.
3. Leonard G. Ratner, *Classical Music: Expression, Form, and Style* (New York: Schirmer, 1980), 9.
4. For an overview of the contents of and contexts for Couperin's keyboard pieces, see David Tunley, *François Couperin and "The Perfection of Music"* (Aldershot: Ashgate, 2004). In the second half of the 1750s, Bach composed twenty-eight character pieces, which are discussed in detail by Peter Wollny in the introduction to *C.P.E. Bach: The Complete Works*, series I, vol. 8.2 (Cambridge, MA: Packard Humanities Institute, 2006), xiv–xvii. A conspectus of the character piece since *c.*1500 is Willy Kahl, *Das Charakterstück* (Laaber-Verlag, 2005).
5. V. Kofi Agawu (*Playing with Signs: A Semiotic Interpretation of Classic Music* [Princeton University Press, 1991], 137) memorably describes this phenomenon as one of "morphological continuity and a referential discontinuity."
6. Anon., "Douze Etudes Caractéristiques de Concert ... par Adolphe Henselt," *The Musical World* 112 [New Series 18] (3 May 1838): 19.
7. Agawu, *Playing with Signs*, 34.
8. Translation made from the original German document in John Rice, "New Light on Dittersdorf's Ovid Symphonies," *Studi musicali* 29, 2 (2000): 453–498, at 479–480.
9. In an overview of the "Ovid" Symphonies, F.E. Kirby identifies marches, dialogues, pastorals, and other musical events that tip Dittersdorf's collection toward the theatrical, and specifically the operatic. See Kirby, "Expression in Dittersdorf's Program Symphonies on Ovid's 'Metamorphoses'," *Revista de musicología* 16, 6 (1993): 3408–3418.
10. The subjective, rhetorical nature of Kuhnau's sonatas is on full display in the prefaces he provides.
11. A catalogue of eighteenth- and early nineteenth-century programmatic orchestral music grouped by subject can be found in Richard Will, *The Characteristic Symphony in the Age of Haydn and Beethoven* (Cambridge University Press, 2004), 299–303.
12. J. B. Logier, *The Battle of Trafalgar ... Opus 6* (Dublin: W. Power and Cos, n.d.), 1. Original emphases.

13. The popularity of battle music in nineteenth-century domestic spaces might also be linked to what John M. Picker has identified as "the development of Victorian self-awareness [through] ... sonic environments." See Picker, *Victorian Soundscapes* (Oxford University Press, 2003), 11.

14. *Louis Spohr's Autobiography*, trans. unknown, 2 vols. (London: Longman, Green, Longman, Roberts, and Green, 1865), II:178.

15. Robert Schumann, "Die Weihe der Töne ... Symphonie von Spohr," *Neue Zeitschrift für Musik* 2, 16 (24 February 1835): 65–66, at 66. Overall, Schumann was unimpressed with Spohr's symphony, but in an effort to provide a balance of opinion in his journal, he soon published Ignaz von Seyfried's detailed analysis and positive endorsement of the score in *Neue Zeitschrift für Musik* 2, 27–28 (3 and 7 April 1835): 107–109 and 111–112.

16. Eduard Hanslick, *Aus dem Concert-Saal* (Vienna and Leipzig: Wilhelm Braumüller, 1897), I:83.

17. *Louis Spohr's Autobiography*, I:213–214.

18. Camille Saint-Saëns, "Art for Art's Sake [1913]," in *On Music and Musicians*, ed. and trans. Roger Nichols (Oxford University Press, 2008), 12–15, at 13.

19. Quoted in William H. Parsons, "Tchaikovsky, the Tsars, and the Tsarist National Anthem," in *Tchaikovsky and His Contemporaries: A Centennial Symposium*, ed. Alexander Mihailovic (Westport, CT: Greenwood Press, 1999), 227–233, at 231.

20. A summary of the sights and sounds surrounding the coronation can be found in Richard Wortman, "The Coronation of Alexander III," in *Tchaikovsky and His World*, ed. Leslie Kearney (Princeton University Press, 1998), 277–299.

21. See David Schneider, *Bartók, Hungary, and the Renewal of Tradition: Case Studies in the Intersection of Modernity and Nationality* (Berkeley and Los Angeles: University of California Press, 2006), 41–45.

22. Schneider (*Bartók, Hungary, and the Renewal of Tradition*, 53–55) notes how the symphonic poem proceeds along the lines of a typical "Hungarian" Rhapsody, with sections 1–5 functioning as the slow Lassú, and sections 6–8 as the fast Friss. However, the presence of the funeral march and section 10 – which Bartók prefaces with the words "A hopeless silence reigns" – is atypical of the genre.

23. Béla Bartók, "*Kossuth* Symphonic Poem," in *Essays*, ed. Benjamin Suchoff (London: Faber & Faber, 1976), 399–403, at 399.

24. Richard Langham Smith, ed. and trans., *Debussy on Music* (New York: Alfred A. Knopf, 1977), 233.

25. See François Villon, *Poems*, ed. and trans. David Georgi (Evanston, IL: Northwestern University Press, 2013), 208–211, which includes Villon's original late medieval French text.

26. Letter of 22 July 1915 to Jacques Durand, in Claude Debussy, *Correspondance, 1872–1918*, ed. François Lesure *et al.* (Paris: Gallimard, 2005), 1910. An elaboration of Debussy's comment can be found in Jonathan Dunsby, "The Poetry of Debussy's *En blanc et noir*," in *Analytical Strategies and Musical Interpretation: Essays on*

*Nineteenth- and Twentieth-Century Music*, ed. Craig Ayrey and Mark Everist (Cambridge University Press, 1996), 149–168, esp. 163–165.

27. Marianne Wheeldon, *Debussy's Late Style* (Bloomington and Indianapolis: Indiana University Press, 2009), 52.

28. See David Wyn Jones, *The Symphony in Beethoven's Vienna* (Cambridge University Press, 2006), 173, which also contextualizes the early history of the "Eroica" Symphony as a key document in the rivalry between Beethoven and Anton Eberl (1765–1807), a native Viennese composer who had cultivated a wide circle of admirers.

29. Carl Dahlhaus has noted that for the turn-of-the-nineteenth-century philosopher Friedrich Schlegel, "'characteristic' meant idiosyncratic rather than general or typical, the exception rather the rule, 'interesting' and 'striking' rather than 'nobly simple,' coloristic rather than statuesque." See Dahlhaus, *Nineteenth-Century Music*, trans. J. Bradford Robinson (Berkeley and Los Angeles: University of California Press, 1989), 69–70.

## 2 Expression, musical painting, and the concert overture

1. This document is reproduced in Giorgio Pestelli, *The Age of Mozart and Beethoven*, trans. Eric Cross (Cambridge University Press, 1984), 274–275, at 274.

2. Richard Wagner, "On the Overture" (1841), in *Richard Wagner's Prose Works*, trans. William Ashton Ellis (London: K. Paul, Trench, Trübner, 1898), VII:153–165, at 155.

3. Wagner, "On the Overture," 156, 160. Emphasis original.

4. Collin's version of the story differs from Shakespeare's in several large and small details. For instance, Shakespeare has Coriolanus killed by his collaborators, the Volscians, instead of Coriolanus committing suicide. And Collin's naming of mother and wife is consistent with Plutarch, not Shakespeare, in whose drama Coriolanus's mother is named Volumnia, his wife Virgilia.

5. Heinrich Joseph von Collin, *Sämmtliche Werke* (Vienna: Anton Strauß, 1812), I:195.

6. Collin, *Sämmtliche Werke*, I:268–269.

7. Johann Wolfgang von Goethe, *Egmont. A Tragedy*, trans. Michael Hamburger, in *Early Verse Drama and Prose Plays*, ed. Cyrus Hamlin and Frank Ryder (New York: Suhrkamp, 1988), 83–151, at 150.

8. James Hepokoski, "Back and Forth from *Egmont*: Beethoven, Mozart, and the Nonresolving Recapitulation," *19th-Century Music* 25, 2–3 (2002): 127–154, at 133. Original emphasis.

9. Goethe, *Egmont*, 151.

10. Lewis Lockwood, *Beethoven: The Music and the Life* (New York and London: W.W. Norton, 2003), 267–268.

11. Several compositions by Beethoven have unsubstantiated relationships with some of Shakespeare's plays, including the "Tempest" Piano Sonata, op. 31, no. 2, the "Appassionata" Piano Sonata, op. 57, and the "Ghost" Piano Trio, op. 70, no. 1.

12. Lawrence Kramer, "The Strange Case of Beethoven's *Coriolan*: Romantic Aesthetics, Modern Subjectivity, and the Cult of Shakespeare," *Musical Quarterly* 79, 2 (1995): 256–280, at 257.

13. Victor Hugo, *Dramas*, trans. George Burnham Ives (Boston: Little, Brown, and Company, 1909), III:16.

14. Hugo, *Dramas*, III:423.

15. Johann Wolfgang von Goethe, *Wilhelm Meister's Apprenticeship*, ed. and trans. Eric A. Blackall (New York: Suhrkamp, 1989), 146. For some political activists during the Vormärz period, Hamlet was a symbol of Germany's indifference, as Ferdinand Freiligrath's poem "Hamlet" from 1844 makes abundantly clear.

16. Berlioz published the piece in 1852 as the third movement of his *Tristia* (*Sad Things*), op. 18.

17. A competing formal analysis appears in Jane Vial Jaffe, "Eduard Marxsen and Johannes Brahms" (PhD diss., University of Chicago, 2009), 294–301.

18. Schumann's support of the overture is evident in his letter of 8 June 1853 to Joachim, given in Andreas Moser, *Joseph Joachim: Ein Lebensbild* (Berlin: B. Behr's Verlag, 1898), 114–116. Tellingly, by the end of the decade, Joachim ceased composition, only to pick it up briefly again around 1900.

19. Letter of 18 January 1856 in Pauline Pocknell, ed., *Franz Liszt and Agnes Street-Klindworth: A Correspondence, 1854–1886* (Stuyvesant, NY: Pendragon Press, 2000), 81–82.

20. Thomas Grey, "The Orchestral Music," in *The Mendelssohn Companion*, ed. Douglass Seaton (Westport, CT: Greenwood Press, 2001), 395–550, at 461. Original emphasis.

21. Adapted from R. Larry Todd, *Mendelssohn: A Life in Music* (Oxford University Press, 2003), 162–163.

22. In the 1820s, Mendelssohn was one of the few composers to continue Beethoven's recent compositional experiments, producing his Piano Sonata in E major, op. 6, in March 1826 (modeled on Beethoven's op. 101 and op. 110 Piano Sonatas) and String Quartet in A minor, op. 13, a year later. This latter work not only takes cues from Beethoven's late quartets, but by drawing on melodic material from Mendelssohn's own song, "Frage" ("Question"), it also challenges the long tradition of the string quartet as the preeminent genre of abstract, self-sustaining music.

23. Adolf Bernhard Marx, *Ueber Malerei in der Tonkunst* (Berlin: G. Finckelschen Buchhandlung, 1828), 24.

24. Marx, *Ueber Malerei in der Tonkunst*, 59–60; translation modified and expanded from Judith Silber Ballan, "Marxian Programmatic Music: A Stage in Mendelssohn's Musical Development," in *Mendelssohn Studies*, ed. R. Larry Todd (Cambridge University Press, 1992), 149–161, at 159.

25. The English title given here is the traditional one, although a more accurate translation is *Quiet Sea and Fortunate Voyage*.

26. Lawrence Kramer, "*Felix culpa*: Goethe and the Image of Mendelssohn," in *Mendelssohn Studies*, ed. R. Larry Todd (Cambridge University Press, 1992), 64–79, at 76.

27. Mendelssohn to Frau von Pereira, Genoa, July 1831, in Felix Mendelssohn Bartholdy, *Letters from Italy and Switzerland*, trans. Lady Wallace (London: Longman, Green, Longman, and Robert, 1862), 197–198.

28. Cited in R. Larry Todd, *Mendelssohn: "The Hebrides" and Other Overtures* (Cambridge University Press, 1993), 77.

29. Todd, *Mendelssohn: "The Hebrides,"* 78; Grey, "The Orchestral Music," 470; Kramer, "*Felix culpa,*" 76; Douglass Seaton, "Symphony and Overture," in *The Cambridge Companion to Mendelssohn*, ed. Peter Mercer-Taylor (Cambridge University Press, 2004), 91–111, at 100.

30. Benedict Taylor, *Mendelssohn, Time, and Memory: The Romantic Conception of Cyclic Form* (Cambridge University Press, 2011), 219.

31. Letter of 7 April 1834 in Felix Mendelssohn Bartholdy, *Letters from 1833 to 1847*, ed. Paul Mendelssohn Bartholdy and Carl Mendelssohn Bartholdy, trans. Lady Wallace (New York: F.W. Christern, 1865), 31–32. Original emphasis.

32. Grey, "The Orchestral Music," 475–483.

33. A.B. Marx, *Musical Form in the Age of Beethoven: Selected Writings on Theory and Method*, ed. and trans. Scott Burnham (Cambridge University Press, 1997), 133.

## 3  Berlioz and Schumann on music and literature

1. Camille Saint-Saëns, "Berlioz I," in *On Music and Musicians*, ed. and trans. Roger Nichols (Oxford University Press, 2008), 79.

2. Saint-Saëns, "Berlioz II," in *On Music and Musicians*, 81.

3. David Cairns, ed. and trans., *The Memoirs of Hector Berlioz* (New York and Toronto: Alfred A. Knopf, 2002), 70 (chapter 18).

4. Letter to Humbert Ferrand of 6 February 1830, in Hector Berlioz, *Correspondance générale: 1803–1832*, ed. Pierre Citron (Paris: Flammarion, 1972), 306.

5. Letter to Ferrand of 16 April 1830, in Berlioz, *Correspondance*, 319. At this point, Berlioz entitled the work "*Épisode de la vie d'un artiste* (grande symphonie fantastique en cinq parties)."

6. At least one symphony preceded Berlioz's in attempting to capture a protagonist's descent into madness. In a preface to the score of his Symphony no. 33 in C minor, subtitled "Il maniatico" ("The Maniac"), from 1780, Gaetano Brunetti explained that his composition "describes as far as possible with the use of instruments alone, without the help of words, the obsession of a delirious person with a theme; and this part is performed by a solo violoncello, which the other instruments join like friends committed to deliver him from his delirium, presenting to him an infinite variety of ideas, in the variety of motives. The maniac remains for a long time fixed in the first theme until he finds a happy motive that persuades him and causes him to join the others; after that he relapses again, and at last transported by the common impulse he ends happily united with the others." Cited in René Ramos, "Gaetano Brunetti," in *The Eighteenth-Century Symphony*, ed. Mary Sue Morrow and Bathia Churgin (Bloomington and Indianapolis: Indiana University Press, 2012), 185–207, at 204.

7.  Stephen Rodgers, *Form, Program, and Metaphor in the Music of Berlioz* (Cambridge University Press, 2009), 105. This discussion is indebted to Rodgers's fifth chapter, "The *vague des passions*, monomania, and the first movement of the *Symphonie fantastique*," 85–106.

8.  François-Joseph Fétis, "Critical Analysis. Episode in the Life of an Artist. Grand Fantastic Symphony by Hector Berlioz. Opus 4. Piano-Score by Franz Liszt," in Hector Berlioz, *Fantastic Symphony*, ed. Edward T. Cone (New York: W.W. Norton, 1971), 216–220, at 217.

9.  Cited in R. Larry Todd, *Mendelssohn: A Life in Music* (Oxford University Press, 2003), 239.

10.  Cairns, *The Memoirs of Hector Berlioz*, 216 (chapter 45).

11.  Letter of 28 January 1817 to Thomas Moore in *"So Late Into the Night": Byron's Letters and Journals. Volume 5, 1816–1817*, ed. Leslie A. Marchand (Cambridge, MA: Belknap Press, 1976), 165.

12.  Mark Evan Bonds, *After Beethoven: Imperatives of Originality in the Symphony* (Cambridge, MA: Harvard University Press, 1996), 50.

13.  Quoted in Julian Rushton, *Berlioz: "Roméo et Juliette"* (Cambridge University Press, 1994), 87.

14.  Daniel Albright, *Berlioz's Semi-Operas:* Roméo et Juliette *and* La damnation de Faust (University of Rochester Press, 2001), 48.

15.  Rodgers, *Form, Program, and Metaphor*, 133. In fact, Wagner presented Berlioz with a copy of *Tristan und Isolde* on 21 January 1860 that carried the inscription: "to the dear and great author of *Roméo et Juliette*, the grateful author of *Tristan und Isolde*." Berlioz heard Wagner's concert one week later and reported that "Wagner has just given a concert that exasperated three quarters of the audience and enthused the rest. Personally, I found a lot of it painful, even though I admired the vehemence of his musical feelings in certain instances. But the diminished sevenths, the discords and the crude modulations made me feverish, and I have to say that I find this sort of music loathsome and revolting." See Berlioz, *Selected Letters*, ed. Hugh Macdonald, trans. Roger Nichols (New York and London: W.W. Norton, 1997), 385.

16.  Rushton, *Berlioz: "Roméo et Juliette,"* 87–88.

17.  Letter of 15 October 1842, excerpted in Peter le Huray and James Day, eds., *Music and Aesthetics in the Eighteenth and Early-Nineteenth Centuries* (Cambridge University Press, 1981), 457.

18.  All citations from these reviews are taken from Hector Berlioz, "A Critical Study of Beethoven's Nine Symphonies," in *The Art of Music and Other Essays (A Travers Chants)*, ed. and trans. Elizabeth Csicsery-Rónay (Bloomington and Indianapolis: Indiana University Press, 1994), 9–37.

19.  Hector Berlioz, "On Imitation in Music," in Hector Berlioz, *Fantastic Symphony*, ed. Edward T. Cone (New York: W.W. Norton, 1971), 36–46, at 37.

20.  Berlioz, "On Imitation in Music," 41. Original emphasis.

21.  Berlioz, "On Imitation in Music," 44.

22. John Daverio, *Robert Schumann: Herald of a "New Poetic Age"* (Oxford University Press, 1997), 118.

23. Robert Schumann, "Ein Opus II," *Allgemeine musikalische Zeitung* 33, 49 (7 December 1831): 805–808, at 808.

24. Robert Schumann, "[Review of Berlioz: *Fantastic* Symphony]," in *Music Analysis in the Nineteenth Century. Volume II: Hermeneutic Approaches* (Cambridge University Press, 1994), 161–194, at 192.

25. Schumann, "[Review of Berlioz]," 193.

26. Robert Schumann, *Gesammelte Schriften über Musik und Musiker*, 4 vols. (Leipzig: Georg Wigand, 1854), III:17.

27. Schumann, *Gesammelte Schriften*, III:19.

28. Schumann, *Gesammelte Schriften*, III:19–20.

29. Robert Schumann, *Music and Musicians: Essays and Criticisms*, ed. and trans. Fanny Raymond Ritter (London: William Reeves, 1877), 312.

30. Schumann, *Gesammelte Schriften*, IV:43.

31. The idea of "Witz" ("joke," "wit") has been identified by John Daverio, *Nineteenth-Century Music and the German Romantic Ideology* (New York: Schirmer, 1993), 49–88, and developed further by Erika Reiman, *Schumann's Piano Cycles and the Novels of Jean Paul* (University of Rochester Press, 2004), 15–18.

32. According to private correspondence and diary entries, Goethe and Shakespeare (*Hamlet*) figured in the composition of the second and third.

33. Schumann did, however, sketch material for a *Hamlet* Symphony between 1830 and 1832.

34. E. T. A. Hoffmann, *Musical Writings:* Kreisleriana, The Poet and the Composer, *Music Criticism*, ed. David Charlton, trans. Martyn Clarke (Cambridge University Press, 1989), 79. The citation comes from the opening paragraph of *Kreisleriana*.

35. Robert Schumann, *Tagebücher*, ed. Georg Eismann (Leipzig: VEB Deutscher Verlag für Musik, 1971), I:82.

36. Reiman, *Schumann's Piano Cycles*, 18.

37. Letter of 19 April 1832; quoted in Martin Geck, *Robert Schumann: The Life and Work of a Romantic Composer*, trans. Stewart Spencer (University of Chicago Press, 2013), 65.

38. See Eric Frederick Jensen, "Explicating Jean Paul: Robert Schumann's Program for *Papillons*, Op. 2," *19th-Century Music* 22, 2 (1998): 127–143, esp. 139–143. The chapter in question appears in translation in Daverio, *Robert Schumann*, 493–501.

39. The first edition has nine bars; the second edition, which Schumann published in 1850 (Book I) and 1851 (Book I), lacks the final bar.

40. Letter of 21 April 1838 in Clara and Robert Schumann, *The Complete Correspondence*, ed. Eva Weissweiler, trans. Hildegard Fritsch and Ronald L. Crawford (New York: Peter Lang, 1994), I:158–159. Despite several letters from Clara to Robert in the week following his letter, she seems to have stayed silent about the program of *In der Nacht*.

41. Robert Schumann, review of "Julius Rietz, Ouverture zu Hero und Leander ... zu 4 Händen eingerichtet," *Neue Zeitschrift für Musik* 18, 33 (24 April 1843): 131–132, at 132.

42. Mendelssohn concurred, as evidenced by a glowing letter he wrote to Rietz following the overture's premiere. See Felix Mendelssohn Bartholdy, *Letters from 1833 to 1847*, ed. Paul Mendelssohn Bartholdy *et al.*, trans. Lady Wallace (London: Longman, Green, Longman, Roberts, & Green, 1863), 251–253.

43. Schumann, "[Review of Berlioz]," 192.

## 4  Liszt and the symphonic poem

1. Detlef Altenburg, "Franz Liszt and the Legacy of the Classical Era," *19th-Century Music* 18, 1 (1994): 46–63, at 53.

2. Letter of 22 January 1844 to Marie d'Agoult, in *Correspondence of Franz Liszt and the Comtesse Marie d'Agoult*, ed. and trans. Michael Short (Hillsdale, NY: Pendragon Press, 2013), 369.

3. Franz Liszt, "The Overture to *Tannhäuser*," ed. David Trippett, trans. John Sullivan Dwight, in *Richard Wagner and His World*, ed. Thomas S. Grey (Princeton University Press, 2009), 251–268, at 257–258.

4. Liszt, "The Overture to *Tannhäuser*," 260.

5. Franz Liszt, "Robert Schumann (1855)," in *Schumann and His World*, ed. R. Larry Todd (Princeton University Press, 1994), 338–361, at 345 and 358.

6. All citations of this essay come from Franz Liszt, *Gesammelte Schriften*, ed. and trans. Lina Ramann, 6 vols. (Leipzig: Breitkopf & Härtel, 1880–1883), IV:1–102.

7. This and other statements made by Liszt on the subject of music and emotion suggest a close reading of Franz Brendel (see Chapter 5), who had written in 1850 that "Modern music shows a decisive striving for definiteness in expression and the greatest possible sharpness of characterization even in purely instrumental music. The common striving is to represent definitive, palpable poetic states of the soul, and to realize this goal are employed all available depictions of every sort, and painting." Quoted in Donald Mintz, "1848, Anti-Semitism, and the Mendelssohn Reception," in *Mendelssohn Studies*, ed. R. Larry Todd (Cambridge University Press, 1992), 126–148, at 144.

8. All citations of this poem in English come from *The Essential Victor Hugo*, ed. and trans. E.H. and A.M. Blackmore (Oxford University Press, 2004), 77–81.

9. On this aspect of *Also sprach Zarathustra*, see Bryan Gilliam, "Richard Strauss," in *The Nineteenth-Century Symphony*, ed. D. Kern Holoman (New York: Schirmer, 1997), 345–368, at 355. On Ropartz's Third Symphony, see A. Peter Brown and Brian Hart, *The Symphonic Repertoire. Volume III, Part B: The European Symphony from ca. 1800 to ca. 1930: Great Britain, Russia, and France* (Bloomington and Indianapolis: Indiana University Press, 2008), 673–683.

10. Anatole Leikin, "Chopin's Preludes Op. 28 and Lamartine's *Les Préludes*," in *Sonic Transformations of Literary Texts: From Program Music to Musical Ekphrasis*, ed. Siglind Bruhn (Hillsdale, NY: Pendragon Press, 2008), 13–43, at 28.

11. Quoted in Franz Liszt, *Les Préludes*, ed. Rena Charnin Mueller (Budapest: Editio Musica, 1996), 35. Three other prefaces circulating in the 1850s and early 1860s and

presumably endorsed by Liszt are given in Theodor Müller-Reuter, *Lexikon der deutschen Konzertliteratur* (Leipzig: C.F. Kahnt Nachfolger, 1909), 297–301.

12. A pithy description of the difference in approach between Liszt's thematic transformation and Brahms's continually developing variation technique ("immer entwickelte Variationen," as Arnold Schoenberg christened the process) is given in Walter Frisch, *Brahms and the Principle of Developing Variation* (Berkeley and Los Angeles: University of California Press, 1984), 49.

13. Eduard Hanslick, *Sämtliche Schriften: Aufsätze und Rezensionen 1857–1858*, ed. Dietmar Strauß (Vienna: Böhlau, 2002), 51.

14. Keith T. Johns, *The Symphonic Poems of Franz Liszt*, ed. Michael Saffle (Stuyvesant, NY: Pendragon Press, 1996), 55. Alternative conclusions using this approach can be found in Alexander Main, "Liszt after Lamartine: 'Les Préludes'," *Music & Letters* 60, 2 (1979): 133–148, esp. 142–143; and Andrew Haringer, "Liszt as Prophet: Religion, Politics, and Artists in 1830s Paris" (PhD diss., Columbia University, 2012), 241–244.

15. See Mueller's introduction to Liszt, *Les Préludes*, 21–22.

16. See Serge Gut, *Franz Liszt* (Sinzig: studiopunkt-verlag, 2009), 508.

17. Letter of 9 July 1852 in Franz Liszt, *Briefe*, ed. La Mara, 8 vols. (Leipzig: Breitkopf & Härtel, 1893–1905), I:225. Original emphases.

18. Lamartine, "Commentaire de la quinzième méditation," in *Méditations poétiques avec commentaires* (Paris: Didot, 1849), 144. In this peculiar statement, Lamartine seems to suggest that poetic inspiration came to him from music. In fact, he continues by calling himself "the most skilled of artists, playing as I did on my instrument."

19. This and other correspondences between Liszt's symphonic poem and Gluck's opera are noted in Joanne Cormac, "Liszt as Kapellmeister: The Development of the Symphonic Poems on the Weimar Stage" (PhD diss., University of Birmingham, 2012), 218–221.

20. Liszt, Preface to *Orphée*, Stradal arr. Trans. unknown.

21. Arthur McCalla, *A Romantic Historiography: The Philosophy of History of Pierre-Simon Ballanche* (Leiden: Brill, 1998), 164.

22. *Correspondence of Franz Liszt and the Comtesse Marie d'Agoult*, 45. Liszt actually misquotes Ballanche, who writes: "Le poëte est l'expression vivante de Dieu, des choses, des hommes" ("The poet is the living embodiment of God, of things, of men"). See Ballanche, *Essais de Palingénésie sociale. Orphée* (Paris: Didot, 1829), 284.

23. Letter of 4 December 1856 in Liszt, *Briefe*, I:245. Ironically, in describing *Orpheus* this way, Liszt was trying to dissuade Ritter from performing the controversial work.

24. McCalla, *A Romantic Historiography*, 230.

25. Richard Wagner, *Prose Works*, trans. William Ashton Ellis, 2nd edn. (London: Kegan Paul, Trench, Trübner & Co., 1895), I:125.

26. Translation modified from Lord Byron, *The Major Works*, ed. Jerome J. McGann (Oxford University Press, 1986), 1041–1042. The original French document is widely available, including in Voltaire, *L'histoire de Charles XII* (Paris: Didot, 1817), 162.

27. Jim Samson, *Virtuosity and the Musical Work: The* Transcendental Studies *of Liszt* (Cambridge University Press, 2003), 203.

28. When Liszt returned to revise this yet-unpublished collection in 1859, he replaced this canzone with a "new" gondolier's song from Act III of Gioachino Rossini's *Otello*, "Nessun maggior dolore" – whose text had first emanated from the mouth of the damned adulteress Francesca da Rimini in Dante's *Divine Comedy*. As discussed in the following chapter, this scene had long been on Liszt's mind, and found a particularly affective form of expression in the "Inferno" movement of his "Dante" Symphony.

29. Entry of 31 March 1877 in Cosima Wagner, *Diaries*, 2 vols., ed. Martin Gregor-Dellin and Dietrich Mack, trans. Geoffrey Skelton (New York: Harcourt Brace Jovanovich, 1978), I:955.

30. All citations in English from this play come from Johann Wolfgang von Goethe, *Verse Plays and Epic*, ed. Cyrus Hamlin and Frank Ryder, trans. Michael Hamburger (New York: Suhrkamp, 1987), 55–139. See also the helpful editorial postscript on pp. 310–313.

31. See David V. Pugh, "Goethe the Dramatist," in *The Cambridge Companion to Goethe*, ed. Lesley Sharpe (Cambridge University Press, 2002), 66–83, at 79.

32. Franz Liszt, Preface to *Hunnenschlacht*, in *Franz Liszts Musikalische Werke*, ser. I, vol. VI, ed. Eugen d'Albert *et al.* (Leipzig: Breitkopf & Härtel, n.d.), 2.

## 5 The New German School and beyond

1. Franz Liszt, *An Artist's Journey: Lettres d'un bachelier ès musique, 1835–1841*, ed. and trans. Charles Suttoni (University of Chicago Press, 1986), 187.

2. Letter of 2 June 1855 to Wagner, in Franz Liszt and Richard Wagner, *Briefwechsel*, ed. Hanjo Kesting (Frankfurt am Main: Insel, 1988), 423.

3. All citations of this text in translation come from Dante Alighieri, *The Divine Comedy*, ed. David H. Higgins, trans. C.H. Sisson (Oxford University Press, 1993).

4. Liszt did not attach a preface to the published score, but he did authorize Richard Pohl to publish an influential analysis of the work in 1858, recently republished in the *Journal of the American Liszt Society* 65 (2014): 59–64.

5. Translation by Stanley Applebaum in Franz Lizst, *Sonata in B Minor and Other Works for Piano* (New York: Dover, 1989).

6. Maria Ann Roglieri, "From *le rime aspre e chiocce* to *la dolce sinfonia di Paradiso*: Musical Settings of Dante's *Commedia*," *Dante Studies* 113 (1995): 175–208, at 177.

7. Franz Liszt, *Briefe*, ed. La Mara, 8 vols. (Leipzig: Breitkopf & Härtel, 1893–1905), VIII:148.

8. Using this scale to depict an otherworldly ascent is somewhat ironic, as it contains no perfect intervals other than the octave. Instead, it emphasizes the tritone, the same interval Liszt employed to depict the terrors of Hell in the first movement. Nevertheless, Liszt's decision to conclude his symphony in B major is consistent with his associating the key with the afterlife, as Paul Merrick has noted in "The Role of Tonality in the Swiss Book of *Années de Pèlerinage*," *Studia Musicologica Academiae Scientiarum Hungaricae* 39, 2–4 (1998): 367–383, at 367–368.

9. The most important document by Wagner concerning his views on program music is the 1857 essay, "On Franz Liszt's Symphonic Poems," published in translation and with useful commentary by Thomas S. Grey as "Wagner's Open Letter to Marie Wittgenstein on Liszt's Symphonic Poems," *The Wagner Journal* 5, 1 (2011): 65–81.

10. Letter of 6 February 1854 to Richard Pohl, in Robert Schumann, *Briefwechsel mit Franz Brendel, Hermann Levi, Franz Liszt, Richard Pohl und Richard Wagner*, ed. Thomas Synofzik, Axel Schröter, and Klaus Döge (Cologne: Dohr, 2014), 409.

11. Letter of 7 October 1853 from Robert Schumann to Joseph Joachim in Joseph Joachim, *Briefe*, ed. Johannes Joachim and Andreas Moser, 3 vols. (Berlin: Julius Bard, 1911–1913), I:84. Schumann's "Neue Bahnen" first appeared exactly three weeks later in the *Neue Zeitschrift für Musik* and has been translated often, including in Leo Treitler, ed., *Strunk's Source Readings in Music History* (New York: Norton, 1998), 1157–1158.

12. Franz Brendel, "Franz Brendel's Reconciliation Address," ed. James Deaville, trans. Deaville and Mary A. Cicora, in *Richard Wagner and His World*, ed. Thomas S. Grey (Princeton University Press, 2009), 311–332, at 328.

13. Richard Wagner, *Opera and Drama*, trans. William Ashton Ellis (London: Kegan Paul, Trench, Trübner & Co., Ltd., 1900), 71. Original emphases.

14. Eduard Hanslick, *Vom Musikalisch-Schönen* (Leipzig: Rudolph Weigel, 1854), 4. Unless otherwise noted, all further references to Hanslick's book come from this source. Unfortunately, no English translation of the first edition of Hanslick's book is available, and those that are available often conflate several editions into a composite version that Hanslick never actually wrote. In this regard, the most transparent translation into English is Eduard Hanslick, *On the Musically Beautiful: A Contribution towards the Revision of the Aesthetics of Music*, trans. and ed. Geoffrey Payzant (Indianapolis, IN: Hackett, 1986), which takes the eighth edition of 1891 as its source.

15. Hanslick was an inveterate supporter of Berlioz, and the first edition of *Vom Musikalisch-Schönen* excused his program-musical tendencies by noting that "we neither question nor underrate Berlioz's extraordinary talent" (p. 41) – a position he maintained in all subsequent editions.

16. Quoted in Thomas Grey, " . . . *wie ein rother Faden*: On the Origins of 'Leitmotif' as Critical Construct and Musical Practice," in *Music Theory in the Age of Romanticism*, ed. Ian Bent (Cambridge University Press, 1994), 187–210, at 206.

17. Eduard Hanslick, *Vom Musikalisch-Schönen*, 2nd edn. (Leipzig: Rudolph Weigel, 1858), ix.

18. The original German poem and English translation can be found in James Parakilas, ed., *The Nineteenth-Century Piano Ballade: An Anthology* (Madison, WI: A-R Editions, 1990), 43.

19. See Tausig's letters to Liszt in *Briefe hervorragender Zeitgenossen an Franz Liszt*, ed. La Mara, 3 vols. (Leipzig: Breitkopf & Härtel, 1895–1904), esp. II:93, 154–155, 173, and 191. Further subjects include the character Blanchefleur, who is variously associated in medieval literature with Tristan (as his mother) and the Grail legend, and a multi-movement "Symphony of Love" ("Liebessymphonie").

20. Quoted in David Brodbeck, "Brahms, the Third Symphony, and the New German School," in *Brahms and His World*, ed. Walter Frisch and Kevin C. Karnes, rev. edn. (Princeton University Press, 2009), 95–116, at 111.

21. Quoted in Alan Walker, *Franz Liszt: The Weimar Years, 1848–1861* (New York: Alfred A. Knopf, 1988), 347.

22. *Briefwechsel zwischen Franz Liszt und Hans von Bülow*, ed. La Mara (Leipzig: Breitkopf & Härtel, 1898), 101.

23. *Briefwechsel zwischen Franz Liszt und Hans von Bülow*, 307. La Mara's date of early 1861 for this letter is certainly incorrect; it must have been written before the work's premiere at the Singakademie in 1859.

24. Translated by Judyth Schaubhut Smith in the liner notes to *Szell, Heger, Bülow, Weingartner: Original Music by Legendary Conductors*, National Philharmonic of Lithuania, cond. Leon Botstein (Arabesque Recordings, Z 6752, 2001). The tortuous original German passage is available in Hans-Joachim Hinrichsen, *Musikalische Interpretationen Hans von Bülow* (Stuttgart: Steiner, 1999), 37.

25. Quoted in Boston Symphony Orchestra, *Season 1891–92: Programme* (Boston Symphony Orchestra, 1892), 188. According to the program note, Raff's description of the *Lenore* Symphony comes from a letter he wrote to Martin Röder in 1874.

26. Quoted in James Deaville, "Defending Liszt: Felix Draeseke on the Symphonic Poems," in *Franz Liszt and His World*, ed. Dana Gooley and Christopher H. Gibbs (Princeton University Press, 2006), 485–514, at 499–500.

27. A. Peter Brown, *The Symphonic Repertoire*, vol. III, part A (Bloomington and Indianapolis: Indiana University Press, 2007), 859.

28. Henry Pleasants, ed. and trans., *The Music Criticism of Hugo Wolf* (New York and London: Holmes & Meier Publishers, 1979), 44.

29. Pleasants, *The Music Criticism of Hugo Wolf*, 45.

30. I am indebted to Ákos Windhager for making available to me his unpublished paper, "Edmund Mihalovich's Weg von der 'Neudeutschen Schule' bis zur Ungarischen Königlichen Musikakademie."

31. All citations from this article are translated from Anton Rubinstein, "Die Komponisten Rußland's," *Blätter für Musik, Theater und Kunst* 1, 29, 33, and 37 (11 May, 25 May, 8 June 1855): 113, 129–130, 145–146.

32. Letter to Franz Liszt of 12 [24] November 1859, in *Briefe hervorragender Zeitgenossen an Franz Liszt*, II:255.

33. This according to Stasov in a highly vitriolic rebuttal to Rubinstein, quoted in in Philip S. Taylor, *Anton Rubinstein: A Life in Music* (Bloomington and Indianapolis: Indiana University Press, 2007), 93.

34. Mark Humphreys, "Rimsky-Korsakov: (1) Nikolay Andreyevich Rimsky-Korsakov," in *New Grove Dictionary of Music and Musicians*, gen. ed. Stanley Sadie, 2nd edn., 29 vols. (New York: Macmillan, 2001), XXI:400–401.

35. The only piece of Rubinstein's to score even moderate success among New Russians was his "Musical Character Picture," *Ivan the Terrible* (also known as *Ivan IV*), which Balakirev conducted for a concert of the Free Music School in November 1869.

36. Rubinstein expanded the 1851 work of four movements into six movements in 1863, to which he added a seventh in 1880.
37. Mikhail Lermontov, *Major Poetical Works*, trans. Anatoly Liberman (Minneapolis: University of Minnesota Press, 1983), 265.
38. Nikolai Rimsky-Korsakov, *My Musical Life*, trans. Judah A. Joffe, 2nd edn. (New York: Tudor Publishing Co., 1936), 72.
39. Francis Maes, *A History of Russian Music: From Kamarinskaya to Babi Yar*, trans. Arnold J. and Erica Pomerans (Berkeley and Los Angeles: University of California Press, 2002), 71.
40. In 1866, Balakirev published an anthology of forty Russian folk songs that he had collected in an expedition along the Volga River.
41. Quoted in Richard Taruskin, "How the Acorn Took Root," in *Defining Russia Musically: Historical and Hermeneutical Essays* (Princeton University Press, 1997), 113–151, at 147–148.
42. Letter of July 1867 to Rimsky-Korsakov, quoted in Caryl Emerson, *The Life of Musorgsky* (Cambridge University Press, 1999), 70.
43. Although the first edition included a French translation from the Russian of Musorgsky's program, it did not translate Rimsky-Korsakov's preface. Thus I am grateful to Matthew Kregor for his translation of this passage.
44. Quoted in Annegret Fauser, *Musical Encounters at the 1889 Paris World's Fair* (University of Rochester Press, 2005), 45.
45. Even the preface of *Stenka Razine* reveals a transcultural disconnect: the Russian preface describes the anti-hero, Stenka Razine, through copious citations from Pavel Melnikov's seminal novel, *In the Forests* (1871–1874). The French preface, however, does not mention the author at all.

## 6 *Excursus*: Faust

1. A notable precursor to the Faust tradition is the sixth-century Saint Theophilus the Penitent, whose heretical pact with the Devil helped to stoke interest in the cult of the Virgin Mary in the Middle Ages.
2. H.G. Haile, *The History of Doctor Johann Faustus* (Urbana: University of Illinois Press, 1965), 25.
3. The spelling of this character's name varies according to source: the *Historia*, for instance, has "Mephostophiles," while Marlowe's play uses "Mephastophilis." "Mephistopheles" appears in Goethe's *Faust*, and is adopted here.
4. Haile, *History of Doctor Johann Faustus*, 132–133.
5. A significantly different version that included reworked and extra material, known by scholars as the "B Text," was published in 1616.
6. Christopher Marlowe, *Dr. Faustus*, ed. Roma Gill (New York: W.W. Norton, 1989), 29. All subsequent citations of Marlowe's play come from this edition.
7. Quoted in Johann Wolfgang von Goethe, *Faust*, ed. Cyrus Hamlin, trans. Walter Arndt, 2nd edn. (New York: W.W. Norton, 2001). "Es irrt der Mensch, solang er strebt." All subsequent citations of Goethe's play come from this edition.

8. Johann Peter Eckermann, *Conversations with Goethe*, ed. J. K. Moorhead, trans. John Oxenford (London: J.M. Dent & Sons, 1930), 206–207.

9. "Ein Teil von jener Kraft, / Die stets das Böse will und stets das Gute schafft . . . Ich bin der Geist, der stets verneint!"

10. Brown elaborates on these topics vis-à-vis a virtuosic reading of *Faust I* and *Faust II* in *Goethe's "Faust": The German Tragedy* (Ithaca and London: Cornell University Press, 1986). Her discussion of the "epistemological and aesthetic" aspects of *Faust* begins on page 26 and continues through the remainder of the book.

11. Richard Wagner, *Letters to His Dresden Friends*, trans. J. S. Shedlock (New York: Scribner and Welford, 1890), 300. Translation modified.

12. Egon Voss has noted several musical and stylistic parallels between the *Faust* Overture and Beethoven's *Coriolan* Overture (1807) and Ninth Symphony (1824), Carl Maria von Weber's *Der Freischütz* (1821), and Berlioz's *Roméo et Juliette* Symphony (1839). See Voss, *Richard Wagner. Eine Faust Overtüre* (Munich: Wilhelm Fink Verlag, 1982), 5–12.

13. Richard Pohl, "Faust-Symphonie," in *Franz Liszt. Studien und Erinnerungen* (Leipzig: Bernhard Schlicke, 1883), 247–320, at 255.

14. Pohl, "Faust-Symphonie," 355.

15. Pohl, "Faust-Symphonie," 300 and 307.

16. Richard Wagner, *My Life*, ed. Mary Whittall, trans. Andrew Gray (Cambridge University Press, 1983), 537–538.

17. Cited in Philip S. Taylor, *Anton Rubinstein: A Life in Music* (Bloomington and Indianapolis: Indiana University Press, 2007), 53.

18. Bar numbers given here follow those of the orchestral score; Horn's arrangement lacks mm. 105–117.

19. Anon., "Kritischer Anhang: Emilie Mayer. Faust-Ouverture für grosses Orchester, Op. 46. Stettin, Paul Witte," *Musikalisches Wochenblatt* 12, 34 (18 August 1881): 411.

20. F. Corder, "The Faust Legend, and Its Musical Treatment by Composers. VI.," *Musical Times* 27, 520 (1 June 1886): 324–327, at 326.

21. Pohl, "Faust-Symphonie," 296. "Robert" is a reference to the title character of Giacomo Meyerbeer's grand opera, *Robert le diable*.

22. Hugh Macdonald, *Beethoven's Century: Essays on Composers and Themes* (University of Rochester Press, 2008), 57.

23. In 1841, Alkan captured the tortured sounds of Hell in "L'Enfer," the middle movement of his Grand Duo Concertante, op. 21, by placing plaintive violin lines in the remote key of C♯ major above thick, densely packed chromatic harmonies emanating from the bowels of the piano.

24. The liturgical origin of this theme is identified in Brigitte François-Sappey, "Sonates d'Alkan et de Liszt: Opéras latents," in *D'un opéra à l'autre: Hommage à Jean Mongrédien*, ed. Jean Gribenski *et al.* (Paris: Presses Universitaires de France, 1996), 55–66, at 61.

25. Quoted in Ronald Smith, *Alkan: The Music* (London: Kahn & Averill, 1987), 68.

26. Sergei Bertensson and Jay Leyda, *Sergei Rachmaninoff: A Lifetime in Music* (Bloomington and Indianapolis: Indiana University Press, 2001), 138.

## 7 Programmatic paths around the *fin-de-siècle*: Mahler and Strauss

1. Rudolf Louis, "On the Tone Poems of Richard Strauss," trans. Susan Gillespie, in *Richard Strauss and His World*, ed. Bryan Gilliam (Princeton University Press, 1992), 305–310, at 306. The quotation comes from Louis's 1912 book, *Die Deutsche Musik der Gegenwart* (*Contemporary German Music*).

2. Quoted in David Larken, "The First Cycle of Tone Poems," in *The Cambridge Companion to Richard Strauss*, ed. Charles Youmans (Cambridge University Press, 2010), 59–77, at 59–60. Original emphasis.

3. Letter of 24 August 1888 in Hans von Bülow and Richard Strauss, *Correspondence*, ed. Willi Schuh and Franz Trenner, trans. Anthony Gishford (New York: Boosey & Hawkes Limited, 1955), 82–83.

4. Henry Hugo Pierson's intriguing symphonic poem on *Macbeth* appeared in 1859, but seems to have fallen off the map by the time of Strauss's early maturity. On Pierson's *Macbeth* and *Romeo and Juliet* (1874) compositions, see Julian Rushton, "Henry Hugo Pierson and Shakespearean Tragedy," in *Europe, Empire, and Spectacle in Nineteenth-Century British Music*, ed. Rachel Cowgill and Julian Rushton (Aldershot: Ashgate, 2006), 77–98.

5. On Schiller's conception of *Macbeth*, see Wolfgang Ranke, "Shakespeare Translations for Eighteenth-Century Stage Productions in Germany: Different Versions of *Macbeth*," in *European Shakespeares: Translating Shakespeare in the Romantic Age*, ed. Dirk Delabastita and Lieven D'hulst (Amsterdam: John Benjamins, 1993), 163–182, esp. 176–177.

6. Translation by Stanley Applebaum, in Richard Strauss, *Tone Poems: Series I* (New York: Dover, 1979), n.p.

7. James Hepokoski argues for the rondo-turned-sonata approach in "Fiery-Pulsed Libertine or Domestic Hero? Strauss's *Don Juan* Reinvestigated," in *Richard Strauss: New Perspectives on the Composer and His Work*, ed. Bryan Gilliam (Durham, NC and London: Duke University Press, 1992), 135–175. Steven Vande Moortele argues instead for a two-dimensional sonata form, in which multi-movement symphony and single-movement sonata unfold simultaneously, an approach that Liszt took in many of his compositions from the Weimar period. See Vande Moortele, *Two-Dimensional Sonata Form: Form and Cycle in Single-movement Instrumental Works by Liszt, Strauss, Schoenberg, and Zemlinksy* (Leuven University Press, 2009), 81–93, esp. 90.

8. One very early – perhaps the earliest – use of the term "apotheosis" in a manner that anticipates Liszt comes in the tenth and final section of Jan Ladislav Dussek's *The Sufferings of the Queen of France*, op. 23, published in 1793 for piano.

9. Letter of 19 November 1890 to Ludwig Thuille, quoted in Willi Schuh, *Richard Strauss: A Chronicle of the Early Years, 1864–1898*, trans. Mary Whittall (Cambridge University Press, 1982), 209.

10. Larkin, "The First Cycle," 76.

11. Letter to Friedrich von Hausegger, quoted in Schuh, *Richard Strauss: A Chronicle*, 180.

12. Translation by Stanley Applebaum, in Strauss, *Tone Poems: Series I*, n.p.

13. Theodor Adorno, *Mahler: A Musical Physiognomy*, trans. Edmund Jephcott (University of Chicago Press, 1991 [orig. 1960]), 74.

14. See Thomas Peattie, "The Expansion of Symphonic Space in Mahler's First Symphony," *Journal of the Royal Musical Association* 136, 1 (2011): 73–96, at 92.

15. The Liszt and Wagner references are identified by Constantin Floros in *Gustav Mahler: The Symphonies*, trans. Vernon and Jutta Wicker (Portland, OR: Amadeus Press, 1993), 43–48.

16. Herbert Killian, *Gustav Mahler in den Erinnerungen von Natalie Bauer-Lechner*, ed. Knud Martner, rev. edn. (Hamburg: Karl Dieter Wagner, 1984), 174.

17. The popular title "Italian" does have a basis in Mendelssohn's conception of the work. Despite being published posthumously without subtitle, in November 1830 Mendelssohn wrote of toying with the idea of a symphony called "The Charms of Italy"; by spring 1831, as composition was ostensibly underway, he referred to it frequently in correspondence as his "Italian" Symphony.

18. Letter of 6 June 1831 in Felix Mendelssohn, *Briefe einer Reise durch Deutschland, Italian und die Schweiz*, ed. Peter Sutermeister (Zurich: Max Niehans Verlag, 1958), 160.

19. John Michael Cooper, *Mendelssohn's "Italian" Symphony* (Oxford University Press, 2003), 174.

20. Mendelssohn completed the symphony in late winter 1833 and revised the second, third, and fourth movements one year later. However, these revisions were not incorporated into the first edition, meaning that the "1833 version" has become the definitive version and the one used in most commentaries on the work. A modern edition of the "1834 version" of the symphony appears in Felix Mendelssohn Bartholdy, *Sinfonie A-Dur ("Italienische"), MWV N 16, Fassung 1834*, ed. Thomas Schmidt-Beste (Wiesbaden: Breitkopf & Härtel, 2011).

21. Nikolaus Lenau, *Faust. Ein Gedicht* (Stuttgart and Augsburg: J.G. Cotta'scher Verlag, 1858), 28.

22. By contrast, Henri Rabaud's symphonic poem, *La procession nocturne*, from 1910, is based on the same scene as Liszt's *Der nächtliche Zug* but seeks to create sympathy instead of disdain for Faust. Thus the procession, which forms the second of the work's three large sections, functions more as a distraction for Faust than as a reminder of the damnable decisions he has made.

23. Letter of 29 August 1862 to Franz Brendel in Franz Liszt, *Briefe*, ed. La Mara, 8 vols. (Leipzig: Breitkopf & Härtel, 1893–1905), II:25. Original emphases. It is worth noting that Liszt reverses the order in which the two episodes come in Lenau's poem.

24. Adorno, *Mahler*, 15.
25. Mahler's sketches for his incomplete Tenth Symphony tantalizingly suggest a return to program music, with a third movement entitled "Purgatorio" and a finale featuring numerous references to his wife, Alma.
26. Fugue is common in Mendelssohn's oratorios, but it also features in select instrumental works, such as the fugue from his op. 35, no. 1, written in 1827 while his friend August Hanstein was dying. According to R. Larry Todd (*Mendelssohn: A Life in Music* [Oxford University Press, 2003], 172–173), "the increasingly agitated counterpoint symbolized for [Adolf] Schubring the 'progress of the disease as it gradually destroyed the sufferer.' Climaxing with stentorian octaves, the fugue culminates with a 'chorale of release,' a freely composed hymn in E major in which soothing conjunct motion smoothes out the jarring fugal contours. A quiet epilogue, rather like a devotional organ postlude, brings the composition to a hushed close."
27. James Hepokoski, "Framing *Till Eulenspiegel*," *19th-Century Music* 30, 1 (2006): 3–43, at 42.
28. Bernhard Vogel, "Werke für Orchester. Paul Geisler. 'Till Eulenspiegel' . . .," *Neue Zeitschrift für Musik* 78, 3 and 4 (15 and 22 January 1882): 27–28, 39–40, at 28.
29. Vogel, "Werke für Orchester," 40.
30. Carl Dahlhaus writes that Liszt "did not set Shakespeare's and Goethe's dramas to music, but rather invented musical equivalents of Hamlet and Faust as the archetypes which, half released from the poetic works themselves, they had in the meantime become in the general European consciousness." See Dahlhaus, "Wagner's Place in the History of Music," trans. Alfred Clayton, in *Wagner Handbook*, ed. Ulrich Müller and Peter Wapnewski, trans. and ed. John Deathridge (Cambridge, MA: Harvard University Press, 1992), 99–117, at 110–111.
31. See Hepokoski, "Framing *Till Eulenspiegel*," 28–37.
32. The program, keyed to events in the music, is presented in Hepokoski, "Framing *Till Eulenspiegel*," 13 and n23.
33. A pithy summary of Telemann's parodistic music, including the *Don Quixote* burlesque, is found in Steven Zohn, *Music for a Mixed Taste: Style, Genre, and Meaning in Telemann's Instrumental Works* (Oxford University Press, 2008), 99–117.
34. Gabrielle Bersier, "A Metamorphic Mode of Reflexivity: Parody in Early German Romanticism," in *Parody: Dimensions and Perspectives*, ed. Beate Müller (Amsterdam: Rodopi, 1997), 27–46, at 35.
35. Friedrich Schlegel, *Geschichte der alten und neuen Litteratur*, in *Sämmtliche Werke* (Vienna: Jakob Mayer, 1822), I:106
36. A translation of the program is found in Anton Rubinstein, *Autobiography*, trans. Aline Delano (Boston: Little, Brown, and Company, 1890), 154–155.
37. Anonymous, "*Don Quixote*. Musikalisches Characterbild . . .," *The Monthly Musical Record* 2 (1 March 1872): 40.
38. Pier Maria Pasinetti, Introduction to *Don Quixote*, in *The Norton Anthology of World Masterpieces*, gen. ed. Maynard Mack, 5th edn. (New York and London: W.W. Norton, 1987), 1180.

## 8 Programming the nation

1. Thomas S. Grey, "*Fingal's Cave* and Ossian's Dream: Music, Image, and Phantasmagoric Audition," in *The Arts Entwined: Music and Painting in the Nineteenth Century*, ed. Marsha L. Morton and Peter L. Schmunk (New York and London: Garland, 2000), 63–99, at 80. Original emphasis.

2. Matthew Gelbart, *The Invention of "Folk Music" and "Art Music": Emerging Categories from Ossian to Wagner* (Cambridge University Press, 2007), 250. Original emphasis.

3. Richard Taruskin, "P.I. Chaikovsky and the Ghetto," in *Defining Russia Musically* (Princeton University Press, 1997), 48.

4. Translation of this poem taken from Patrick Rucker, "Vörösmarty's Ode to Liszt," *Journal of the American Liszt Society* 20 (December 1986): 42–49.

5. Letter 18 October 1846 to Marie d'Agoult, slightly amended from *Correspondence of Franz Liszt and the Comtesse Marie d'Agoult*, ed. and trans. Michael Short (Hillsdale, NY: Pendragon Press, 2013), 395.

6. In a letter of 10 November 1862 to Mihály Mosonyi, Liszt revealed that "with the symphonic poem *Hungaria* I believe I have already given my answer to Vörösmarty." See Franz Liszt, *Briefe aus ungarischen Sammlungen, 1835–1886*, ed. Margit Prahács (Kassel: Bärenreiter, 1966), 113.

7. Letter of 24 October 1858 in František Bartoš, ed., *Smetana in Briefen und Erinnerungen*, trans. Alfred Schebek (Prague: Artia, 1954), 60.

8. See Kenneth DeLong, "Hearing His Master's Voice: Smetana's 'Swedish' Symphonic Poems and the Lisztian Models," in *Liszt and His World*, ed. Michael Saffle (Stuyvesant, NY: Pendragon Press, 1998), 295–334.

9. Quoted, with slight modification, in DeLong, "Hearing His Master's Voice," 324.

10. Lonnie R. Johnson, *Central Europe: Enemies, Neighbors, Friends*, 2nd edn. (Oxford University Press, 2002), 90.

11. Quoted in Derek Sayer, *The Coasts of Bohemia: A Czech History*, trans. Alena Sayer (Princeton University Press, 1998), 128.

12. Michael Beckerman, "In Search of Czechness in Music," *19th-Century Music* 10, 1 (1986): 61–73, at 67.

13. Adapted from John Clapham, "Dvořák's Unknown Letters on His Symphonic Poems," *Music & Letters* 56, 3–4 (1975): 277–287, at 284. Emphases original.

14. John Knowles Paine, "The New German School of Music," *The North American Review* 116, 239 (1873): 217–245, at 241 and 245.

15. Lawrence Gilman, *Edward MacDowell: A Study* (New York: John Lane Company, 1909), 82.

16. Klaus Döge, "Dvořák, Antonín (Leopold)," in *New Grove Dictionary of Music and Musicians*, gen. ed. Stanley Sadie, 2nd edn., 29 vols. (New York: Macmillan, 2001), VII:783.

17. Antonín Dvořák, "Music in America," *Harper's New Monthly Magazine* 90, 537 (February 1895): 429–434, at 433.

18. Gilman, *Edward MacDowell*, 85.

19. H. H. A. Beach, "American Music. Dr. Antonin Dvorak Expresses Some Radical Opinions," *Boston Herald* (28 May 1893).

20. Quoted in Adrienne Fried Block, *Amy Beach, Passionate Victorian: The Life and Work of an American Composer, 1867–1944* (Oxford University Press, 1998), 88. Original emphasis.

21. Cited in Hon-Yun Lang, "Nationality versus Universality: The Identity of George W. Chadwick's Symphonic Poems," *American Music* 21, 1 (2003): 1–44, at 26.

22. Rosa Newmarch, *Jean Sibelius: A Finnish Composer* (Leipzig: Breitkopf & Härtel, 1906), 10.

23. James Hepokoski, "*Finlandia* Awakens," in *The Cambridge Companion to Sibelius*, ed. Daniel M. Grimley (Cambridge University Press, 2004), 81–94, at 82.

24. Daniel M. Grimley, "The Tone Poems: Genre, Landscape and Structural Perspective," in *The Cambridge Companion to Sibelius*, 95–116, at 97.

25. A similar structure guides Sibelius's *Nightride and Sunrise* from 1908, although here the tone poem's subject is, according to the composer, "the inner experiences of an average man riding solitary through the forest gloom; sometimes glad to be alone with Nature; occasionally awe-stricken by the stillness or the strange sounds which break it; not filled with undue foreboding, but thankful and rejoicing in the daybreak." Incidentally, Sibelius was concerned that the title alone might lead listeners "to expect in it a reflection from the older romanticism of Raff's day." See Rosa Newmarch, *Jean Sibelius* (Boston, MA: C.C. Birchard Co., 1939), 68.

26. All of the movements underwent revision soon after the premiere. The last two movements were published in 1901, yet the first two did not appear in print until 1954. Sibelius may have changed the ordering of the inner movements to better reflect the profile of the traditional symphony, in which the scherzo appears in third place. At the same time, only Sibelius's First, Second, and Sixth Symphonies follow this model.

27. Incidentally, the Second Symphony's colloquial title, "Little Russian," derogatorily references its use of Ukrainian instead of Russian folk tunes.

28. Novák's music is similarly bifurcated. Orchestral pieces such as *In the Tatras*, op. 26, and *Toman and the Wood Nymph*, op. 40, both from the first decade of the twentieth century, clearly extend the approaches taken to the symphonic poem by his Czech predecessors, especially Dvořák. However, the influence of Debussy is exceptionally strong in Novák's piano cycle, *Pan*, op. 43, from 1910, and the tone poem *Von ewiger Sehnsucht* (*On Eternal Longing*; 1905), based on the twenty-seventh chapter of Hans Christian Andersen's *A Picture-Book without Pictures*, which the composer published complete as preface: "There was a calm, – said the Moon – the water was as transparent as the pure air through which I floated. I could see, far below the surface of the sea, the strange plants which, like giant trees in groves, heaved themselves up towards me with stems a fathom long, whilst the fish swam over their tops. High up in the air flew a flock of wild swans, one of which sank with wearied wings lower and lower: its eyes followed the airy caravan, which every moment became more distant; its pinions were expanded widely, and it sank, like a soap-bubble in the still air; it touched the

surface of the water, bowed back its head between its wings, and lay still, like a white lotus upon the calm Indian Sea. The breeze blew, and lifted up the bright surface of the water, which was brilliant as the air; there rolled on a large, broad billow – the swan lifted its head, and the shining water was poured, like blue fire, over its breast and back. The dawn of day illumined the red clouds, and the swan rose up refreshed, and flew towards the ascending sun, towards the blue coast, whither had betaken themselves the airy caravan; but it flew alone – with longing in its breast, flew alone over the blue, the foaming water!" See Hans Christian Andersen, *A Picture-Book without Pictures; And Other Stories*, trans. Mary Howitt (New York: C.S. Francis & Co., 1848), 113–114.

## 9 "Ars Gallica"

1. Translation modified from Michael Strasser, "*ARS GALLICA*: The Société Nationale de Musique and Its Role in French Musical Life, 1871–1891" (PhD diss., University of Illinois at Urbana-Champaign, 1998), 136–137.
2. Timothy Jones, "Nineteenth-Century Orchestral and Chamber Music," in *French Music since Berlioz*, ed. Richard Langham Smith and Caroline Potter (Aldershot: Ashgate, 2006), 53–89, at 76.
3. Camille Saint-Saëns, *On Music and Musicians*, ed. and trans. Roger Nichols (Oxford University Press, 2008), 89 and 96.
4. Quoted in Jones, "Nineteenth-Century Orchestral and Chamber Music," 78.
5. Ovid, *Metamorphoses*, ed. E. J. Kenney, trans. A. D. Melville (Oxford University Press, 1986), 34.
6. Quoted in Lynne Johnson, "Franz Liszt and Camille Saint-Saëns: Friendship, Mutual Support, and Influence" (PhD diss., University of Hawaii, 2009), 206. The review was originally published in *La Renaissance littéraire et artistique* 1, 36 (28 December 1872): 285–286.
7. Camille Saint-Saëns, "Liszt," in *Harmonie et mélodie*, 2nd edn. (Paris: Calmann Levy, 1885), 155–172, at 163–164.
8. See Richard B. Grant, "Sequence and Theme in Victor Hugo's *Les Orientales*," *Proceedings of the Modern Language Association* 94, 5 (1979): 894–908.
9. Vincent d'Indy, *César Franck*, trans. Rosa Newmarch (London and New York: John Lane, 1910), 163.
10. Translation taken from Jacques Barzun, *An Essay on French Verse: For Readers of English Poetry* (New York: New Directions Books, 1991), 128–135, at 133.
11. Franck's students include: Henri Duparc, Arthur Coquard, Alfred Cahen, Alexis de Castillon, Vincent d'Indy, Ernest Chausson, Camille Benoît, Augusta Holmès, Pierre de Bréville, Louis de Serres, Guy Ropartz, Charles Bordes, Dynam-Victor Fumet, Gabriel Pierné, Charles Tounemire, Paul de Wailly, Sylvio Lazzari, and Guillaume Lekeu. Chabrier and Dukas, although French Wagnerians, were not Franck's pupils.
12. This program is translated from the French text in the first edition. Since it was published in the mid-1890s by the firm of Leuckhardt of Leipzig, the edition also

includes a program in German. While the German text generally follows the French text, it includes additional citations from Bürger's ballad, specifically lines 145–148 and 309–316. Whether Duparc suggested or even authorized this supplemental material is unclear.

13. An English translation can be found in Ludwig Uhland, *The Poems*, trans. Alexander Platt (Leipzig: Friedrich Volckmar, 1848), 358–360.

14. Vincent d'Indy, *Cours de composition musicale*, ed. Auguste Sérieyx, 3 vols. (Paris: Durand, 1903–1951), II:321.

15. Debussy's complete notice in the original French is provided in Arthur Wenk, *Claude Debussy and the Poets* (Berkeley and Los Angeles: University of California Press, 1976), 152. A translation of Mallarmé's poem appears on pp. 307–310.

16. Richard Langham Smith, ed. and trans., *Debussy on Music* (New York: Alfred A. Knopf, 1977), 233.

17. Claude Debussy, "Beethoven," in *Monsieur Croche the Dilettante Hater*, trans. B. N. Langdon Davier, published in *Three Classics in the Aesthetic of Music* (New York: Dover, 1962), 38–39.

18. Quoted in Stelio Dubbiosi, "The Piano Music of Maurice Ravel" (PhD diss., New York University, 1967), 78.

19. Bertrand's reference is to Faust's first line in the scene "Night. Open Field" from *Faust I*: "Was weben die dort um den Rabenstein?"

20. *Louis "Aloysius" Bertrand's Gaspard de la Nuit: Fantasies in the Manner of Rembrandt and Callot*, ed. and trans. John T. Wright, 2nd edn. (Lanham, MD: University Press of America, 1994), 123.

21. Quoted in Stephen Walsh, *Stravinsky: A Creative Spring: France and Russia, 1882–1934* (Berkeley and Los Angeles: University of California Press, 1999), 354.

# Guide to further reading

## Introduction

Albright, Daniel. *Panaesthetics: On the Unity and Diversity of the Arts.* New Haven and London: Yale University Press, 2014.

Bonds, Mark Evan. *Absolute Music: The History of an Idea.* Oxford University Press, 2014.

Brown, A. Peter. *The Symphonic Repertoire.* 5 vols. Bloomington and Indianapolis: Indiana University Press, 2002–.

Casler, Lawrence. *Symphonic Program Music and Its Literary Sources. 2 vols.* Lewiston, NY: Edwin Mellen Press, 2001.

Fink, Monika. *Musik nach Bildern: Programmbezogenes Komponieren im 19. und 20. Jahrhundert.* Innsbruck: Helbling, 1988.

Hepokoski, James, and Warren Darcy. *Elements of Sonata Theory: Norms, Types, and Deformations in the Late-Eighteenth-Century Sonata.* Oxford University Press, 2006.

Kivy, Peter. *Antithetical Arts: On the Ancient Quarrel Between Literature and Music.* Oxford University Press, 2009.

Klauwell, Otto. *Geschichte der Programmusik von ihren Anfängen bis zur Gegenwart.* Leipzig: Breitkopf & Härtel, 1910; repr. Wiesbaden, 1968.

Petersen, Peter. *Programmusik: Studien zu Begriff und Geschichte einer umstrittenen Gattung.* Laaber-Verlag, 1983.

Robinson, Jenefer. *Deeper Than Reason: Emotion and Its Role in Literature, Music, and Art.* Oxford University Press, 2007.

## Chapter 1

Arnold, Ben. *Music and War: A Research and Information Guide.* New York: Garland, 1993.

Bonds, Mark Evan. *Wordless Rhetoric: Musical Form and the Metaphor of the Oration.* Cambridge, MA: Harvard University Press, 1991.

Dickensheets, Janice. "The Topical Vocabulary of the Nineteenth Century." *Journal of Musicological Research* 31, 2–3 (2012): 97–137.

Feldman, Martha. "Music and the Order of the Passions." In *Representing the Passions: Histories, Bodies, Visions,* ed. Richard Meyer, 37–67. Los Angeles: Getty Publications, 2003.

Frigyesi, Judit. *Béla Bartók and Turn-of-the-Century Budapest.* Berkeley and Los Angeles: University of California Press, 1998.

Hatten, Robert S. *Interpreting Musical Gestures, Topics, and Tropes: Mozart, Beethoven, Schubert*. Bloomington and Indianapolis: Indiana University Press, 2004.

Loughridge, Deirdre. "Magnified Vision, Mediated Listening and the 'Point of Audition' of Early Romanticism." *Eighteenth-Century Music* 10, 2 (2013): 179–211.

Mathew, Nicholas. *Political Beethoven*. Cambridge University Press, 2013.

Mirka, Danuta, ed., *The Oxford Handbook of Topic Theory*. Oxford University Press, 2014.
    and Kofi Agawu, eds., *Communication in Eighteenth-Century Music*. Cambridge University Press, 2008.

Monelle, Raymond. *The Musical Topic. Hunt, Military and Pastoral*. Bloomington and Indianapolis: Indiana University Press, 2006.

Morrow, Mary Sue. *German Music Criticism in the Late Eighteenth Century: Aesthetic Issues in Instrumental Music*. Cambridge University Press, 1997.

Watkins, Glenn. *Proof Through the Night: Music and the Great War*. Berkeley and Los Angeles: University of California Press, 2003.

## Chapter 2

Allen, Aaron S. "Symphonic Pastorals." *Green Letters: Studies in Ecocriticism* 15, 1 (2011): 22–42.

Bonds, Mark Evan. *After Beethoven: Imperatives of Originality in the Symphony*. Cambridge, MA: Harvard University Press, 1996.
    *Music as Thought: Listening to the Symphony in the Age of Beethoven*. Princeton University Press, 2006.

Botstiber, Hugo. *Geschichte der Ouvertüre und der freien Orchesterformen*. Leipzig: Breitkopf & Härtel, 1913.

Grey, Thomas S. "Wagner, the Overture, and the Aesthetics of Musical Form." *19th-Century Music* 12, 1 (1988): 3–22.

Guyer, Paul. "Mendelssohn's Theory of Mixed Sentiments." In *Moses Mendelssohn's Metaphysics and Aesthetics*, ed. Reinier Munk, 259–278. Dordrecht: Springer, 2011.

Schmalfeldt, Janet. *In the Process of Becoming: Analytic and Philosophical Perspectives on Form in Early Nineteenth-Century Music*. Oxford University Press, 2011.

Steinkämper, Claudia. *Melusine – vom Schlangenweib zur "Beauté mit dem Fischschwanz": Geschichte einer literarischen Aneignung*. Göttingen: Vandenhoeck & Ruprecht, 2007.

## Chapter 3

Brittan, Francesca. "Berlioz and the Pathological Fantastic: Melancholy, Monomania, and Romantic Autobiography." *19th-Century Music* 29, 3 (2006): 211–239.

Colas, Damien. "Berlioz, Carpani et la question de l'imitation en musique." In *Berlioz: Textes et contextes*, ed. Joël-Marie Fauquet, Catherine Massip, and Cécile Reynaud, 221–239. Paris: Société française de musicologie, 2001.

Holoman, D. Kern. *Berlioz: A Musical Biography of the Creative Genius of the Romantic Era*. Cambridge, MA: Harvard University Press, 1989.

*The Société des Concerts du Conservatoire, 1828–1967*. Berkeley and Los Angeles: University of California Press, 2004. Accompanying website: hector.ucdavis.edu/sdc.

Johnson, James H. *Listening in Paris: A Cultural History*. Berkeley and Los Angeles: University of California Press, 1995.

Kelley, Thomas Forrest. *First Nights: Five Musical Premieres*. New Haven and London: Yale University Press, 2000.

Newcomb, Anthony. "Once More Between Absolute and Program Music: Schumann's Second Symphony." *19th-Century Music* 7, 3 (1984): 233–250.

"Schumann and Late Eighteenth-Century Narrative Strategies." *19th-Century Music* 11, 2 (1987): 164–174.

"Schumann and the Marketplace: From Butterflies to Hausmusik." In *Nineteenth-Century Piano Music*, ed. R. Larry Todd, 258–315. New York: Schirmer, 1990.

Plantinga, Leon B. *Schumann as Critic*. New Haven and London: Yale University Press, 1967.

Rosen, Charles. *The Romantic Generation*. Cambridge, MA: Harvard University Press, 1995.

Thorslev Jr., Peter L. *The Byronic Hero: Types and Prototypes*. Minneapolis: University of Minnesota Press, 1962.

## Chapter 4

Bertagnolli, Paul A. "Amanuensis or Author: The Liszt-Raff Collaboration Revisited." *19th-Century Music* 26, 1 (2002): 23–51.

*Prometheus in Music: Representations of the Myth in the Romantic Era*. Aldershot: Ashgate, 2007.

Bonner, Andrew. "Liszt's *Les Préludes* and *Les Quatre Élémens*: A Reinvestigation." *19th-Century Music* 10, 2 (1986): 95–107.

Gibbs, Christopher H. and Dana Gooley, eds. *Franz Liszt and His World*. Princeton University Press, 2006.

Hall-Swadley, Janita R., ed. and trans. *The Collected Writings of Franz Liszt*. 7 vols. Lanham, MD: Scarecrow Press, 2011–.

Hamilton, Kenneth, ed. *The Cambridge Companion to Liszt*. Cambridge University Press, 2005.

Hoeckner, Bertold. *Programming the Absolute: Nineteenth-Century German Music and the Hermeneutics of the Moment*. Princeton University Press, 2002.

Huschke, Wolfram. *Musik im klassischen und nachklassischen Weimar, 1756–1861*. Weimar: Böhlau, 1982.

Kirby, F. E. "The German Program Symphony in the Nineteenth Century (to 1914)." In *A Compendium of American Musicology: Essays in Honor of John F. Ohl*, ed. Enrique Alberto Arias *et al.*, 195–211. Evanston, IL: Northwestern University Press, 2001.

Micznik, Vera. "The Absolute Limitations of Programme Music: The Case of Liszt's 'Die Ideale'." *Music & Letters* 80, 2 (1999): 207–240.

Walker, Alan. *Franz Liszt: The Weimar Years, 1848–1861*. New York: Knopf, 1989.

## Chapter 5

Altenberg, Detlef, ed. *Liszt und die Neudeutsche Schule*. Laaber-Verlag, 2006.

Bevier, Carol Sue. "The Program Symphonies of Joseph Joachim Raff." PhD diss., University of North Texas, 1982.

Dahlhaus, Carl. "Wagner and Program Music." *Studies in Romanticism* 9, 1 (1970): 3–20.

Deaville, James. "The Controversy Surrounding Liszt's Conception of Programme Music." In *Nineteenth-Century Music: Selected Proceedings of the Tenth International Conference*, ed. Jim Samson and Bennett Zon, 98–124. Aldershot: Ashgate, 2002.

Dömling, Wolfgang. "Reuniting the Arts: Notes on the History of an Idea." *19th-Century Music* 18, 1 (1994): 3–9.

Grey, Thomas S. "Metaphorical Models in Nineteenth-Century Criticism: Image, Narrative, and Idea." In *Music and Text: Critical Inquiries*, ed. Steven Paul Scher, 93–117. Cambridge University Press, 1992.

Grimes, Nicole. "A Critical Inferno? Hoplit, Hanslick and Liszt's *Dante Symphony*." *Journal of the Society for Musicology in Ireland* 7 (2011–2012): 3–22.

Gur, Golan. "Music and 'Weltanschauung': Franz Brendel and the Claims of Universal History." *Music & Letters* 93, 3 (2012): 1–24.

Karnes, Kevin. *Music, Criticism, and the Challenge of History: Shaping Modern Musical Thought in Late Nineteenth-Century Vienna*. Oxford University Press, 2008.

Stasov, Vladimir Vasilevich. *Selected Essays on Music*, trans. Florence Jonas. London: Barrie & Rockliff, 1968.

Taruskin, Richard. *On Russian Music*. Berkeley and Los Angeles: University of California Press, 2009.

Trippett, David. "*Après une lecture de Liszt*: Virtuosity and Werktreue in the 'Dante' Sonata." *19th-Century Music* 32, 1 (2008): 52–93.

## Chapter 6

Butler, Elizabeth M. *The Fortunes of Faust*. Cambridge University Press, 1952.

Fitzsimmons, Lorna. *Lives of Faust: The Faust Theme in Literature and Music*. New York: Walter de Gruyter, 2008.

Grim, William E. *The Faust Legend in Music and Literature*. Lewiston, NY: Edwin Mellen Press, 1988.

Hamilton, Kenneth. *Liszt, Sonata in B Minor*. Cambridge University Press, 1996.

"Wagner and Liszt: Elective Affinities." In *Richard Wagner and His World*, ed. Thomas S. Grey, 27–64. Princeton University Press, 2009.

Larkin, David. "A Tale of Two *Fausts*: An Examination of Reciprocal Influence in the Responses of Liszt and Wagner to Goethe's *Faust*." In *Music and Literature in German Romanticism*, ed. Siobhán Donovan and Robin Elliott, 87–104. Rochester, NY: Camden House, 2004.

Sand, George. *The Seven Strings of the Lyre*, trans. and introduced by George A. Kennedy. Chapel Hill, NC: University of North Carolina Press,1989.

Schulte, Hans, John Noyes, and Pia Kleber, eds. *Goethe's "Faust": Theatre of Modernity*. Cambridge University Press, 2011.

Scott, Derek B. *From the Erotic to the Demonic: On Critical Musicology*. Oxford University Press, 2003.

## Chapter 7

Brosche, Günter. "Musical Quotation and Allusion in the Works of Richard Strauss." In *The Cambridge Companion to Richard Strauss*, ed. Charles Youmans, 213–225. Cambridge University Press, 2010.

Floros, Constantin. *Verschwiegene Programmusik*. Vienna: Verlag der Österreichische Akademie der Wissenschaft, 1982.

Johnson, Julian. *Mahler's Voices: Expression and Irony in the Songs and Symphonies*. Oxford University Press, 2009.

Mandel, Oscar, ed., *The Theatre of Don Juan: A Collection of Plays and Views, 1630–1963*. Lincoln and London: University of Nebraska Press, 1963.

Monahan, Seth. "'I have tried to capture you … ': Rethinking the 'Alma' Theme from Mahler's Sixth Symphony." *Journal of the American Musicological Society* 64, 1 (2011): 119–178.

Schneider, Mathieu. "*Kunstkritik* and Tonmalerei in the Tone Poems of Richard Strauss." In *Sonic Transformations of Literary Texts: From Program Music to Musical Ekphrasis*, ed. Siglind Bruhn, 173–202. Hillsdale, NY: Pendragon Press, 2008

Todd, R. Larry. "Strauss before Liszt and Wagner: Some Observations." In *Richard Strauss: New Perspectives on the Composer and His Work*, ed. Bryan Gilliam, 3–40. Durham, NC and London: Duke University Press, 1992.

Tunbridge, Laura. *Schumann's Late Style*. Cambridge University Press, 2007.

Youmans, Charles. *Richard Strauss's Orchestral Music and the German Intellectual Tradition: The Philosophical Roots of Musical Modernism*. Bloomington and Indianapolis: Indiana University Press, 2005.

## Chapter 8

Bloom, Harold. *A Map of Misreading*, 2nd edn. Oxford University Press, 2003.

Faucett, Bill F. *George Whitefield Chadwick: The Life and Music of the Pride of New England*. Boston: Northeastern University Press, 2012.

Gaskill, Howard, ed. *The Reception of Ossian in Europe*. London: Thoemmes Continuum, 2004.

Grimley, Daniel M. *Grieg: Music, Landscape and Norwegian Identity*. Woodbridge: Boydell Press, 2006.

Loya, Shay. *Liszt's Transcultural Modernism and the Hungarian-Gypsy Tradition*. University of Rochester Press, 2011.

MacDonald, Hugh. "Narrative in Janáček's Symphonic Poems." In *Janáček Studies*, ed. Paul Wingfield, 36–55. Cambridge University Press, 1999.

Macura, Vladimír. "Problems and Paradoxes of the National Revival." In *Bohemia in History*, ed. Mikuláš Teich, 182–197. Cambridge University Press, 1998.

Mikusi, Balasz. "Mendelssohn's 'Scottish' Tonality?" *19th-Century Music* 29, 3 (2006): 240–260.

Pisani, Michael. *Imagining Native America in Music*. New Haven: Yale University Press, 2005.

Tawaststjerna, Erik. *Sibelius*, trans. Robert Layton. 3 vols. Berkeley and Los Angeles: University of California Press, 1976.

Tick, Judith, ed. *Music in the USA: A Documentary Companion*. Oxford University Press, 2008.

Zychowicz, James. "Mieczysław Karłowicz, the New Symphony, and His Innovative Symphonic Style." In *European Fin-de-siècle and Polish Modernism: The Music of Mieczysław Karłowicz*, ed. Luca Sala, 289–308. Bologna: Ut Orpheus Edizioni, 2010.

## Chapter 9

Abbate, Carolyn. *Unsung Voices: Opera and Musical Narrative in the Nineteenth Century*. Princeton University Press, 1996.

Bellman, Jonathan. *Chopin's Polish Ballade: Op. 38 as Narrative of National Martyrdom*. Oxford University Press, 2009.

Deruchie, Andrew. *The French Symphony at the Fin de Siècle: Style, Culture, and the Symphonic Tradition*. University of Rochester Press, 2013.

Gelbart, Matthew. "Layers of Representation in Nineteenth-Century Genres: The Case of One Brahms Ballade." In *Representation in Western Music*, ed. Joshua S. Walden, 13–32. Cambridge University Press, 2013.

Kaminsky, Peter. "Ravel's Approach to Formal Processes: Comparisons and Contexts." In *Ravel Unmasked: New Perspectives on the Music*, ed. Kaminsky, 85–110. University of Rochester Press, 2011.

Pasler, Jann. *Composing the Citizen: Music as Public Utility in Third Republic France*. Berkeley and Los Angeles: University of California Press, 2009.

Stove, R. J. *César Franck: His Life and Times*. Lanham, MD: Scarecrow Press, 2012.

Whitesell, Lloyd. "Erotic Ambiguity in Ravel's Music." In *Ravel Studies*, ed. Deborah Mawer, 74–91. Cambridge University Press, 2010.

# Index

## Cambridge Introductions to Music

"Cambridge University Press is to be congratulated for formulating the idea of an 'Introductions to Music' series." *Nicholas Jones, The Musical Times*

Each book in this series focuses on a topic fundamental to the study of music at undergraduate and graduate level. The introductions will also appeal to readers who want to broaden their understanding of the music they enjoy.

- Contain textboxes which highlight and summarize key information
- Provide helpful guidance on specialized musical terminology
- Thorough guides to further reading assist the reader in investigating the topic in more depth

*Books in the series*

*Music Sketches*　Friedemann Sallis

*Program Music*　Jonathan Kregor

*Electronic Music*　Nicholas Collins, Margaret Schedel, and Scott Wilson

*Gregorian Chant*　David Hiley

*Music Technology*　Julio D'Escrivan

*Opera*　Robert Cannon

*Postmodernism in Music*　Kenneth Gloag

*Serialism*　Arnold Whittall

*The Sonata*　Thomas Schmidt-Beste

*The Song Cycle*　Laura Tunbridge